D0146685

SUSTAINABLE DEVELOPMENT: NATIONAL ASPIRATIONS, LOCAL IMPLEMENTATION

For my father
whose love made all things possible

Sustainable Development: National Aspirations, Local Implementation

Edited by

JENNIFER HILL, ALAN TERRY and WENDY WOODLAND
University of the West of England, Bristol, UK

ASHGATE

Published by
Ashgate Publishing Limited
Gower House
Croft Road
Aldershot
Hampshire GU11 3HR
England

Ashgate Publishing Company
Suite 420
101 Cherry Street
Burlington, VT 05401-4405
USA

Ashgate website: http://www.ashgate.com

British Library Cataloguing in Publication Data
Sustainable development: national aspirations, local
   implementation
   1.Sustainable development – Developing countries
   2.Sustainable development – Government policy – Developing
   countries
   I. Hill, Jennifer II. Terry, Alan III. Woodland, Wendy
   338.9'27'091724

Library of Congress Control Number: 2006926065

   ISBN-10: 0 7546 4605 X
   ISBN-13: 978-0-7546-4605-1

Printed and bound in Great Britain by TJ International Ltd, Padstow, Cornwall.

Contents

List of Figures

List of Tables

List of Boxes

List of Contributors

Nicola Ansell is a Senior Lecturer in the Department of Geography and Earth Sciences at Brunel University. Her research interests focus on the geographies of young people in southern Africa, and in particular their responses to education and to the AIDS pandemic. She is the author of *Children, Youth and Development* (Routledge 2005).

Giles Atkinson is Lecturer in Environmental Policy in the Department of Geography and Environment at London School of Economics and Political Science. An environmental economist by training, his research and teaching interests cover wide aspects of environmental policy. Much of his published research, however, has focused on the measurement of sustainable development and green accounting. This has included investigations of the link between international trade and sustainability, green national accounting and deforestation and the relationship between savings, growth and the resource curse hypothesis. He is author of *Measuring Sustainable Development: Macroeconomics and the Environment* (Edward Elgar Publishing, 1997).

Christian Brannstrom is Assistant Professor of Geography at Texas A&M University specializing in human impacts on the environment. His work focuses on decentralization policies for environmental management, impacts of agriculture on Brazil's savanna ecoregion and environmental history. He has edited a book on Latin American environmental history, *Territories, Commodities and Knowledges* (Institute for the Study of the Americas, 2004) and has published on environmental policy in *Geoforum, Environment and Planning C, Singapore Journal of Tropical Geography, European Journal of Development Research* and *World Development.*

Andrew Dougill is Head of Environment in the School of Earth & Environment at the University of Leeds. His research focuses on assessments of land degradation processes and their links to the underlying socio-economic root causes of environmental suffering. His most extensive experience focuses on the links between environmental change, farmer decision-making and livelihoods in the Kalahari of Southern Africa, though he is now applying the lessons learnt from integrated studies to research in West Africa, Asia and the UK. He has published over 20 articles on sustainable development issues over the past 10 years.

Jennifer A. Elliott is Principal Lecturer in Geography in the School of the Environment at the University of Brighton. She has a long-standing research interest in issues of rural resource management in Zimbabwe and is the author of *An Introduction to Sustainable Development* published by Routledge.

Therese Ferguson is a Research Fellow in the Department of Geography and Geology at the University of the West Indies. Her doctoral research concerns discourses of environmentalism in Jamaica, with an emphasis on the methods used for operationalizing environmental management priorities through education.

Anthony M. Filippi is Assistant Professor of Geography at Texas A&M University. He specializes in remote sensing and Geographic Information System (GIS)-based modelling applications, encompassing coastal ocean, wetlands and terrestrial vegetation/agricultural. He has published recently in *Remote Sensing of Environment*.

Jennifer Hill is a Senior Lecturer in the School of Geography and Environmental Management at the University of the West of England, Bristol. Her research interests include environment-society inter-relationships and issues of water management in semi-arid areas. She is a joint author of research articles examining sustainable water management, sustainable communities and impacts of globalization on culture in Tunisia.

Nick James is affiliated to the Open University and the University of the West of England, Bristol. He has undertaken research concerning Zambia, Mozambique, Southern Africa and Zimbabwe. He is working on synthesizing understandings from scientific research in agro-ecological settings and their social settings and he aims to pursue research into indigenous and local food production. Linked areas for research include agrarian and environmental change in rural Africa; livelihoods and household food security; regional and place geography; and development and local studies. He has published research articles and book chapters from his findings.

Bill Kinsey holds a number of research posts internationally, at the Free University Amsterdam, the University of Oxford and the University of Zimbabwe. His major research interests centre on the long-term impacts of technical and economic change in African agriculture, land reform programmes in southern Africa and the welfare effects of adjustment on rural households. He has served as a policy advisor and consultant in these areas and has published extensively since 1980. He was the Guest Editor for the recent special issue of World Development on land reform and conflict in southern Africa.

Dominik Kwesha has post-graduate qualifications and substantial experience in the areas of Geographic Information Systems. He has worked in the Research and Development Division at the Forestry Commission in Zimbabwe since 1986 and is a specialist in forest inventory and remote sensing image interpretation.

Susan Marriott is a Reader in Earth Sciences at the University of the West of England, Bristol. Recent research projects include bank accretion and habitat studies on the River Parrett, UK; a study of cadmium distribution pathways in the Severn

Estuary, UK; studies on floodplain management and river rehabilitation in KwaZulu-Natal, South Africa; environmental change on the Mkuze and Pongolo floodplains in KwaZulu-Natal, South Africa; and models for development of channels and floodplains in dryland areas. She is author of numerous research articles and book chapters and she has edited a number of research collections, particularly concerning fluvial sedimentology.

Janet Momsen is Professor of Geography at the University of California, Davis. She works on gender and development, particularly in rural areas. She has carried out fieldwork in the Caribbean, Brazil, Central America, Mexico, Hungary, China and Bangladesh. She has published *Gender and Development* (Routledge, 2004), *Gender at the Border: Entrepreneurship in Rural Post-socialist Hungary* with I. Szorenyi and J. Timar (Ashgate, 2005) and *Environmental Planning in the Caribbean* with J. Pugh (Ashgate, 2006). She also produced a *Gender Atlas of Bangladesh* with S. Hussain and A. Khan in 2006. She is currently editing the *Encyclopedia of Women and Development* for Routledge.

Julie Newton is a research officer currently working for the Wellbeing in Developing Countries (WeD) ESRC Research Group based at the University of Bath. She is responsible for locating the social and cultural construction of wellbeing in households and communities within Bangladesh, Ethiopia, Peru and Thailand within the broader regional, national and global structures. Her research interests cover sustainable livelihoods, wellbeing, gender mainstreaming, natural resource management and agricultural extension, and bridging the policy/research divide.

Nevil Quinn is a Senior Lecturer in Hydrology in the School of Geography and Environmental Management at the University of the West of England, Bristol. His research interests lie in the areas of catchment and water resources management. He has a special interest in environmental hydrology and the law and policy of water management. He has published numerous research articles, book chapters and reports for external bodies concerning his research.

Mark Reed is a lecturer in participatory conservation in the Sustainability Research Institute at the School of Earth & Environment, University of Leeds. His expertise in participatory conservation focuses on land degradation, sustainability indicators and participatory processes. He has applied these skills in a range of interdisciplinary projects in the UK and Africa. His work has been published in peer-reviewed articles for international journals, book chapters, magazine articles and other publications, in addition to receiving extensive media coverage. He has been involved in international consultancy and, over the last 10 years, he has led research proposals that have secured over £0.8M from organizations such as the Global Environment Facility, the Royal Society, the Royal Geographical Society and the UK Government's Research Councils.

Samantha Shepherd has recently finished writing her PhD at the University of the West of England, Bristol. Her thesis was concerned with evaluating the use of Quality of Life Indicators in UK local authorities. Prior to this, she studied Geography and Environmental Management at UWE, Bristol and as part of her course examined the Bajau community in the Wakatobi National Park, Indonesia. Her undergraduate dissertation won the Royal Geographical Society (with the Institute of British Geographers) Developing Areas Research Group undergraduate prize in 2001. She has recently begun working as a Community Support Officer in South Oxford Council.

Alan Terry is a Senior Lecturer in the School of Geography and Environmental Management at the University of the West of England, Bristol. His research interests include rural development issues and community led development. He has authored research articles examining agricultural development in Swaziland, the use of community developed indicators for local development initiatives, and the production of a toolkit for users of quality of life indicators. Alan has published in *Singapore Journal of Tropical Geography*, the *South African Geographical Journal* and *Geography*.

Elizabeth Thomas-Hope is Professor of Environmental Management in the Department of Geography and Geology at the University of the West Indies. Her research interests include agro-biodiversity and land management in the Caribbean, poverty and urban environmental management, environment and health, environmental perception and its implications for environmental management, and international migration policy in regard to the Caribbean. She has published extensively in the form of peer-reviewed articles for international journals, academic books, book chapters and external reports.

Erik Van Waveren has worked for over twenty years in rural development programmes in various countries in southern and eastern Africa and the near East. He is currently employed as a senior advisor in natural resource management with an international NGO in northern Ghana. He holds a PhD in land management under customary tenure arrangements from the University of the West of England, Bristol. His professional interests focus strongly on natural resource management in relation to rural poverty and customary tenure systems.

Wendy Woodland is a Senior Lecturer in the School of Geography and Environmental Management at the University of the West of England, Bristol. Her research interests include environmental change and water management in semi-desert areas. She is a joint author of research articles examining sustainable water management, sustainable communities and impacts of globalization on culture in Tunisia.

Chapter 1

Uniting National Aspirations and Local Implementation in Sustainable Development: An Introduction

Alan Terry, Jennifer Hill and Wendy Woodland

Background

In 1992, the United Nations Conference on Environment and Development (UNCED), the 'Earth Summit', was held at Rio de Janeiro. The primary output was the Agenda 21 document which delineated a global programme of action for sustainable development into the twenty-first century (UNCED, 1992). It resulted in governments making commitments to adopt national strategies for sustainable development. These National Environmental Action Plans (NEAPs) were envisaged as a way to integrate environmental considerations into a nation's overall economic and social development; to '… harmonize the various sectoral, economic, social and environmental policies and plans that are operating in the country' (UNCED, 1992: Chapter 8, paragraph 8.7). The key to successful implementation was believed to be that each country would choose its own solutions to the problems that needed to be overcome in order to move successfully to a more sustainable path of development. There was an acknowledgment that '… strategies which have departed from the original model and express true national identity have tended to be the most successful' (Carew-Reid *et al.*, 1994: 42). The ability to be flexible was further emphasized by Dalal-Clayton & Bass (2002: 30) who stressed the need for '… a continuing participatory approach, with monitoring, learning and continuous improvement'.

The Millennium Development Goals, emanating from the Millenium Summit of 2000, emphasized the integration of sustainable development into country policies and the need to reverse the loss of environmental resources. Similarly, the 2002 World Summit for Sustainable Development (WSSD) in Johannesburg urged, in its Plan of Implementation, that states should take immediate steps to progress with the elaboration of their national strategies for sustainable development and to begin their implementation by 2005. Despite this rhetoric, there have been few examples that demonstrate real improvements in sustainable outputs that arise from the plans. Middleton & O'Keefe (2003) set out the post-Rio situation clearly and they show

how the dominant neo-liberal political climate has succeeded in diluting progress towards sustainability, a situation that still exists in the post-Johannesburg era.

In the period since the Earth Summit, a body of research has emerged which challenges many of the simple neo-Malthusian assumptions that lay behind early development strategies, whether they be multi- or single-sector. With reference to the quality of environmental data, Ives & Messerli (1989), Leach & Mearns (1996), Fairhead & Leach (1996) and Tiffen *et al.* (1994) have all illustrated the extent to which deeply entrenched received wisdoms invoke neo-Malthusian crisis narratives that emphasize the negative impact of indigenous groups on the environment in the developing world. These views are particularly prevalent amongst the institutions and individuals who have been at the forefront of developing sustainable development strategies. Common mistakes include: a misreading of recent environmental history; false assumptions or black-boxing of uncertainties; the failure to engage with local voices; the failure to use locally available archives, such as early records of travellers and photographic evidence; the misinterpretation of evidence such as air photographs; errors in data sets; extrapolating information from one scale to another inappropriately and dependence upon measurements that distort natural processes. The extent to which such views have influenced environmental policy-making in Africa has been discussed by Keely & Scoones (2003) and in the Himalaya region by Blaikie & Muldavin (2004). The institutionalization of supposedly objectively gathered scientific evidence on which policies are made is therefore shown to be heavily compromised. The whole process has been deeply politicized, itself a long-term legacy of European colonial impacts on their former colonies and spheres of influence. Because of a lack of political representation of the majority of the population in the colonies, it was relatively easy for colonial administrators to perpetuate many environmental 'myths'. No effective opposition existed that could advocate for indigenous knowledge and environmental management practices.

Whilst many of the chapters in this book provide evidence that supports the need to engage proactively with indigenous groups, others are more circumspect, particularly in outlining the contradictions that exist between the goals of sustainability for the many within communities and the tendency for the few to retain power over key resources. Thus, unless questions of power are addressed, it would appear that the goal of attaining a more sustainable development path as measured, for example, by the reduction in poverty amongst the most marginalized, will be unsuccessful (Carney & Watts, 1990; Rocheleau *et al.*, 1996). Centralized power tends to favour the *status quo* and this, in turn, represents a significant challenge for the role of education in sustainable development. In most cases, the education system is dependent upon state finances and it thereby follows the will of its paymasters.

A further challenge to those charged with plotting sustainable development strategies has been the reappraisal of fundamental concepts that underpin the established understanding of how natural systems function. Ecological sustainability is tied closely to the concepts of equilibrium and balance and there is little evidence that theories and empirical data which challenge these core ideas have been incorporated into sustainable development strategies. Non-equilibrium or 'new ecology' (Botkin, 1990) developed from a growing realization by some ecologists that empirical evidence failed to support equilibrium models of ecosystems (Schaffer, 1985; Holling, 1986). This led to questions regarding what was a 'normal' state for ecosystems (Sprugel, 1991). The new ecology replaced assumptions of equilibrium, predictability and permanence with instability, disequilibria, flexibility and dynamism (Sullivan, 1996; Sullivan & Rohde, 2002; Neumann, 2005). This necessitated a new metalanguage for ecologists, which was more accepting of change (Stott, 1998). There are serious implications for those whose job it is to attempt to maintain some ideal state of the environment. Many of the assumptions on which they base their management strategies are undermined by these new models and the task of achieving sustainable development of any given part of the biosphere is infinitely more difficult if there is uncertainty as to what that state should be. However, although Stott (1997) argues that the concept of equilibrium in nature should be abandoned, it has not been so entirely, even by those who initially drew attention to the problems of environmental equilibrium (Holling, 1986). Whittaker (2000) argues that a variety of states of nature prevail, from dynamic equilibrium to static non-equilibrium.

Aim of the book

This book examines the discontinuities that exist between national aspirations and local implementation of sustainable development strategies. It compares what is happening on the ground with formal national environmental action plans, sectoral plans or less formalized policies that are supposed to steer individual countries onto a more sustainable path. It examines whether local knowledge, aspirations and actions are undermining national aspirations or whether they are being ignored at the national level with detrimental consequences to sustainable development. A range of case studies provides opportunities to compare progress, or lack of progress, between different sectors, cultures, regions and resources within the developing world. The book attempts to situate the case studies within a global context, but it is concerned more with a national and sub-national scale of analysis than was the case for Middleton & O'Keefe (2003). The overall aim is to draw lessons from those cases which appear to be experiencing positive moves towards sustainability and then to see whether common frameworks exist which point to the possibility that good practice may be transferable from one milieu to another.

Structure of the book

Although the case studies are eclectic in terms of subject matter and location, three themes can be identified. Issues surrounding the measurement of sustainable development are considered in Chapters 2 to 5; the role of formal and informal education in sustainable development is considered in Chapters 6 to 8, whilst

Chapters 9 to 14 deal with the significance of diverse voices in the practice of sustainable development.

Measuring sustainable development

Any debate concerning environmental response to human impact, whether it follows a more or less sustainable path, requires some ability to measure and understand past, present and future states of that environment. In Chapter 2, Elliot *et al.* consider such issues within the contested topic of land resettlement in Zimbabwe. The land reform and resettlement programme in this country has experienced a dramatic and controversial expansion in recent years, characterized by relatively haphazard and rapid invasion of former commercial farmlands. In contrast, the first twenty years of land resettlement in the country was based on the controlled movement of settlers according to a small number of planned resettlement models. From the outset of the programme in 1980, issues of sustainability were highlighted within both political and popular debate. In short, concern centred on the resource-plentiful conditions of the scheme areas and the possible replication of communal area conditions through the sub-division and transfer of large-scale commercial farms to small-scale indigenous farmers. These debates were revitalized in 2000 with the move to the so-called 'fast track' approach to land reform. Elliot *et al.* present data based on sequential air photo analysis covering five resettlement scheme areas in three agro-ecological zones over a period in excess of twenty years. Key patterns of land cover change are explored and the difficulties of assessing and/or asserting sustainability of resettlement are illustrated through an examination of the multi-directional and spatially complex patterns of woodland change. Additionally, the authors effect a critical analysis of some of the predominant 'received narratives' on environmental change (Leach & Mearns, 1996) within the small-scale farming sector. The chapter highlights how evaluation of the impact of resettlement has been impeded by a lack of good environmental baseline data and a lack of funds to enable continuous monitoring of resettled areas. Thus, government officials have to work in an environment where the data received are distorted by short or medium term variability in the physical and politico-regional environment, as well as being incomplete in temporal and spatial terms. The chapter also demonstrates how questions of sustainability, and of who defines it, are closely tied to politics.

In Chapter 3, Dougill and Reed examine how development of community-based rangeland sustainability indicators is an attempt to democratize the environmental debate in Botswana. The chapter provides a critical analysis of 'bottom-up' sustainability as envisaged by Agenda 21 and, more pertinently for this chapter, the United Nations Convention to Combat Desertification (UNCCD). The authors present a methodological framework being developed in collaboration with the Botswanan Ministry of Agriculture which focuses on participatory identification of rangeland degradation indicators for three contrasting physical and socio-economic environments in the Kalahari rangelands. Using a Sustainable Livelihoods Approach, the attempt is to identify how long-term rangeland degradation and short term events such as drought undermine livelihoods of pastoralists and to identify key natural indicators used by these groups which can be used to monitor the degree and direction of the quality of grazing. The methodology is therefore grounded in the belief that indigenous knowledge has a crucial role to play in understanding the dynamics that underpin the relationship between local management systems and the physical systems on which they depend. Dougill and Reed discuss the practical problems and opportunities that working at the local scale presents to researchers and national policy makers. Of crucial importance is the training of extension workers to be able to work in a participatory framework, requiring them to recognize that the transfer of knowledge is not one way, namely from top to bottom, but often requires a fundamental re-education of such workers to be able to recognize the merits of locally developed knowledge in the form of indicators. As such, emphasis in the chapter is placed on moving from the local to the regional and national, in a case study where the process is supported by global and national agreements and policy statements. The process of scaling up requires transparent aggregation of indicators that would provide a rapid summary of the state of the environment. These could become the basis of a more scientific analysis using a complementary range of technologies and methods.

In contrast to Dougill and Reed's analysis of community-led indicators, Atkinson (Chapter 4) is concerned with an economic analysis of sustainability indicators that have been identified by outside experts. This chapter investigates how Peru and India might green their national accounts in order to reflect the sustainability of activities that (permanently) clear land of tropical forest. Typically, past studies have focused upon the value of timber lost when land is deforested. However, forested land provides a great many additional benefits and these must be taken into account in order to obtain a clearer picture of the sustainability of forest land clearance, acknowledging the full social costs and benefits of such changes. The examples illustrate the complexities involved in identifying and applying a financial cost to the loss of tropical forest. This is further complicated by the impact of population growth. The chapter raises the issues of the scale at which such accounts are best used, whether regional, national or global, and, perhaps of greater importance for those charged with managing such resources in a sustainable manner, the notion of critical thresholds (Ekins *et al.,* 2003) below which forest resources may fail to deliver all their social benefits.

The final chapter which addresses the measurement of sustainability (Chapter 5) is concerned with an evaluation of South Africa's 1998 National Water Act. Water is acknowledged as a scarce and development-limiting resource in South Africa and it follows that achieving sustainable development requires appropriate strategies for this resource. Over the last decade, South Africa has transformed its approach to water management, tabling far-reaching policies and legislation to international acclaim. It is consequently opportune to examine whether these initiatives are achieving their stated objectives. Quinn and Marriott adopt two seminal works by Gleick (1998) and Dowdeswell (1998) to construct an eight point framework by which to measure the legislators' ambitious social and ecological targets that are set out in the Act. The significance of this example is that, following the installation of the first democratic government in 1994, there has been a marked shift from a centralized, exclusive system of water management to one that places social equity and environmental sustainability at the heart of the management of this key resource. In many respects, therefore, South Africa can be considered as a model of how to develop a sustainable water management system and it is one of the few countries in the world where the right to water is enshrined with the concept of ecosystem rights within legislation. Encouragingly, Quinn and Marriott's conclusions are optimistic for the majority of the eight criteria measured, although they acknowledge that evaluating the long-term impact of such a change in the law is still problematic. They also caution about the slow pace of change in terms of, for example, implementing new catchment management plans which require much greater coordination and agreement between multiple actors, many of whom have had little, if any, experience of engaging with such institutions in the past. Implicit in this analysis is the problem of scaling up from local to regional and national scales such that decisions taken at one location do not impact negatively in other locations.

The role of education in sustainable development

Chapters 6, 7, and 8 are concerned with the role of education in the move to a more sustainable future. As the concept of sustainable development is rooted in the idea of inter-generational equity, it is unsurprising that the international community has emphasized the role of children in relation to achieving sustainability. Environmental education has been recognized as a critical means of bringing about the attitudinal and behavioural changes necessary to foster respect for nature, to reduce the environmental destruction and degradation threatening nature and to ensure the survival of humans who depend upon its resources. The first two chapters in this section deal with the formal school systems in Jamaica and Lesotho, whilst the last chapter considers the role of the agricultural extension system in Namibia.

In Chapter 6, Ferguson and Thomas-Hope raise the issue of formal environmental education in Jamaica to ask two main questions. The first is whether national constructions of sustainable development in Jamaica and the global construction of sustainable development are competing or complementing narratives as they are articulated in current environmental education curricula. The second, based on this, is whether environmental education for sustainable development is fulfilling its intended role and can thus be viewed as an agent of change or, if it is not, then how it should be viewed as a subject of change. They conclude that, to be an effective vehicle for sustainable development, environmental education in Jamaica needs to undergo a critical shift in order to move beyond its lingering role as a reproducer of hegemonic environmental values. Local and individual knowledges need to be acknowledged and pedagogic practices need to be changed such that students become active thinkers and not passive recipients of other people's knowledge. This will align more closely with the aims of sustainable development.

In Chapter 7, Ansell examines efforts to incorporate education for sustainable development into the curriculum in Lesotho, beginning with the adoption of 'development studies' as a curriculum subject, and moving on to explore how sustainability is being 'mainstreamed' across the curriculum. She demonstrates that the move from existing passive models of education to one where children become more active participants in learning, combined with a need for inter-disciplinarity between teachers in different specialist subjects, are key pedagogic aims of the Lesotho Environmental Education Support Project. They are both, however, difficult strategies to implement. This is due to the long-established top-down, compartmentalized western model of teaching that was transposed onto the country by the British. The ability of teachers and pupils to produce new knowledge has not been easy, whilst the incorporation of indigenous knowledge into the formal curriculum also presents a major challenge. However, the degree to which new ideas are incorporated differs greatly between schools, varying from encouraging pupils to help rewrite the school environmental plan to teaching them not to drop litter. Progress has been hampered by civil unrest and changes to curricula, which demonstrates that the positive role that education could make depends upon the political context in which it operates. As in many southern African countries, progress is also likely to have been delayed by the impact of HIV/AIDS on the teaching population and pupils. Ansell demonstrates that, although proposals for education for sustainable development as set out in Agenda 21 recognize that learners should play a participatory role, implementation of these proposals in formal education systems has been fraught with difficulties.

In contrast to examining the role of the formal education sector, Newton's analysis (Chapter 8) on the attempt to make Namibia's agricultural extension service more gender-aware highlights the role of a less formal education system in promoting more sustainable skills and attitudes. The chapter examines attempts within the Namibian Ministry of Agriculture, Water and Rural Development to integrate a gender responsive approach within its recent National Agricultural Policy. Specific attention is given to the interrelationships at the local, regional and national scale involved in the implementation of this policy through agricultural extension at the micro level. It asks why and how attempts to introduce a more participatory, gender-responsive agricultural extension service have encountered problems. The research demonstrates that institutional weaknesses preclude effective communication between extension workers and women farmers and it uncovers the importance of informal social capital through links with family, friends and neighbours, which official channels have tended to ignore. Even if such links were established, however, Newton concludes that women may not gain access to and control over key resources, one of the most critical factors that would improve the security of their livelihoods. Therefore, although the inclusion of marginalized groups such as women in development programmes have been seen as intrinsic to the ultimate goal of sustainable development and the eradication of poverty, unless fundamental socio-economic relationships within communities are challenged, then the goal of attaining a more sustainable development path via a more equitable gender-neutral policy is likely to remain thwarted.

The significance of diverse voices in the practice of sustainable development

There has been increasing criticism of a simplistic understanding of communities in sustainable development literature. Communities are socially differentiated in a number of ways, including gender, ethnicity, religion, economic status and political persuasion (Leach *et al.,* 1997; Agrawal & Gibson, 1999). Participation of relevant and empowered stakeholders is thereby crucial to sustainable development (Craig & Mayo, 1995) and this is the focus of the final section of the book. Chapters 9 to 14 concentrate on a variety of issues surrounding the ability of the 'other' to participate effectively in the move to a more sustainable use of the natural resources upon which they depend.

It must be stated, however, that many chapters highlight the importance of diverse voices within the development process. Dougill and Reed (Chapter 3), for example, demonstrated that a multiplicity of stakeholders should identify range degradation indicators if a successful community-based natural resource management project was to be established in Botswana. Newton's research of agricultural extension services in Namibia (Chapter 8), in addition to examining the role of women in informal education, also showed that the creation of committee structures responsible for disseminating agricultural knowledge across communities gave limited recognition to existing networks of social interaction, many of which were gendered. These structures should be inclusive of the wider community if they are to become more sustainable in the long term.

In Chapter 9, Momsen examines recent changes in relation to gender, agriculture and tourism in the Caribbean. In this case study, the farmers are commercial rather than subsistence and they operate in an international rather than a local economic system. In theory, efforts to increase the output of produce free of chemical residues through greater use of Integrated Pest Management (IPM) strategies will improve the quality of local food and encourage the expansion of small-scale agriculture as their products become more acceptable to the local Caribbean hotel and restaurant trade, the main clients of which are from North America and Europe. This initiative takes place in an environment where small-scale farmers are turning to the local tourist markets as their traditional export markets decline. Within this group, women appear to be more responsive than men to the possibilities of these new markets. The chapter provides an insight into the complex ways in which sustainable ideas, practices and policies can be influenced by outside pressures, in this case flowing from the developed to the developing world. Whether or not the concept of long-range tourism can ever be considered sustainable is, however, an issue that is not dealt with in this book.

In Chapter 10, James analyses the relative sustainability of cotton as a crop that communal smallholder farmers in Zimbabwe depend upon for their livelihoods. The chapter analyses the development of environmental policies and how these have been implemented in the North West region of the country and Gokwe North District in particular. Recent shifts to participatory approaches to rural development have emerged from long-term conservation policies. Analysis at the household level provides an insight into the agro-ecological and socio-economic advantages in this region for growing cotton. However, household food insecurity and other forms of poverty in the region can be traced back to the political-economic relations between the state and the study area since the 1960s. Cotton cropping among households and the agro-ecological dynamics in the area of Nembudziya are analysed and an assessment is made of the changing decisions by householders in their cropping strategies. This demonstrates a range of efforts by householders to protect and sustain soil fertility under cotton. There is support, therefore, for different 'pathways' of change based on particular stakeholders and their circumstances in different rural areas (Scoones & Wolmer, 2002). Overall, despite national and institutional ambitions to increase productivity, yields within the communal areas have remained low and, moreover, environmental degradation has become increasingly evident. No appropriate sustainable development policies have been implemented and so people are taking the initiative to seek alternatives and to avoid being impoverished by cotton production. James argues that the neglect of soil fertility reflects the focus that has been placed on other sectors including wildlife, forests and mechanical soil conservation.

James's somewhat pessimistic assessment of the future of communal land is echoed by Van Waveren's detailed analysis of the system of land allocation on Customary Tenured Land in Swaziland (Chapter 11). Subsequent to the Earth Summit of 1992, Swaziland set up the Swaziland Environment Authority whose brief was to promote sustainable development within the Kingdom. However, rapid population growth, industrialization, urbanization, increasing agricultural demands and a declining economy are among factors which are fast degrading the natural resource base and this, in turn, is posing a threat to sustainable development. In 1997, the Cabinet approved the Swaziland Environment Action Plan (SEAP). Amongst the six objectives of the SEAP, of particular relevance to this chapter, is that which seeks to propose solutions to environmental problems in the form of programmes and institutional reforms, together with details of their human resource/capacity-building needs. The chapter outlines the practical limitations to ensuring a more sustainable use of customary tenured land, upon which powers of allocation rest with the chiefs. It examines the consequence of this system for the rational allocation of land for agricultural purposes and questions the extent to which chiefs take into account the agro-environmental potential of land when allocating it for small-scale farms. The chapter reports that significant misallocation of land has occurred, with many farmers subsisting on land with low agro-ecological potential, whilst in close proximity to them, good quality land lies idle. Although individual farmers are seen to rationalize the use of the land which has been allocated to them, the question arises as to whether Swaziland can afford to maintain such a seemingly irrational system of land allocation in the face of significant land hunger and rural poverty. Although institutional reform has been identified as a key aim of the SEAP, to what extent does the power of traditional authority, at the apex of which is the King, undermine the aims of sustainable agricultural development as set out in that document?

In contrast to the downbeat messages in Chapters 10 and 11, Woodland and Hill (Chapter 12) demonstrate how, after a long period of marginalization, indigenous skills and knowledge are being re-integrated with modern methods in the sustainable management of water resources in Tunisia. A number of distinctive methods of water management for agriculture are visible across the country. The central region supports modern dam irrigation, whilst traditional rainwater harvesting is practiced in the south. These contrasting techniques are described, and evaluated in terms of sustainability, using empirical field data and secondary literature for two study sites. Research focuses primarily on the physical environment, but socio-cultural and economic viability are also identified. Analysis indicates that traditional water management advantageously partitions the continuum dividing hazards and resources through subtle manipulation of the environment. A potentially hazardous environment is rendered secure by resourceful water management based on community action and cumulative knowledge. This practice minimizes community dependency and local economic imbalance. With dam irrigation, carrying capacity is established more forcibly by centralized control in order to place society within world markets. An almost total break from environmental variability is made in the short term, but this can lead to disequilibrium over longer durations. Additionally, the spatial and social distributions of development are uneven. In Tunisia, maintenance of traditional methods can reduce the negative impacts caused by modern programmes and support their positive characteristics. A mix of both methods seems to offer a foundation to a more sustainable management of water resources in the new millennium.

In response to over-exploitation of communal marine resources, many national governments have sought to introduce new management regimes to replace pre-existing indigenous systems. However, with the increasing popularity of community-led, participative development projects amongst mainstream development agencies, the direction is now to reintegrate such systems into 'modern' management solutions. This may be appropriate under certain circumstances, but it tends to oversimplify and overlook the contradictory motivations of subgroups within any single community. In Chapter 13, Terry and Shepherd present a case study of the fishing practices and management of marine resources by the Bajau community of the Tukangbesi Archipelago off the south-east corner of the island of Sulawesi in Indonesia. The chapter provides an insight into the practical problems of implementing national plans at the local level. It questions the extent to which the Bajau carry out sustainable management of their local marine resources and to what extent, therefore, the community represents a model of small-scale, community-based, indigenous communal resource management which can be harnessed in the promotion of sustainable development. The conclusion is an ambivalent message about the ability of national aspirations to be translated into local action. To rely upon local management systems appears to be naïve, but conflicting power bases within national and regional organizations make it difficult to create rational sustainable planning from the top down.

To conclude this section, Brannstrom and Filippi (Chapter 14) examine the difficulties in reconciling the goals of sustainable development with the encouragement of export-oriented commercial farming in Bahia state, Brazil. The authors examine the development of environmental policies for modern agriculture in the north-eastern region, where dryland and irrigated crops have been established. The key actor in environmental planning is not the federal or state government; rather, it is a private organization representing large-scale commercial farmers (AIBA) based in the western region of Bahia state. The chapter indicates that, in response to criticisms, government pressure and a possible backlash from European export markets, AIBA has developed environmental initiatives including recycling of agro-chemical containers, participating in water-resources governance and conservation of Cerrado vegetation. In fact, AIBA's leadership in environmental policies places the organization ahead of the state in several ways, which creates difficulties for state agencies: to support AIBA's potentially effective policies, or to implement command-control policies in a potentially hostile setting. In addition, an analysis of remotely sensed imagery indicates the potential shortcomings of AIBA's conservation program as Cerrado vegetation has dramatically declined. It is not yet clear whether the policies of AIBA amount to 'greening' or 'greenwashing', but the case study makes clear that local private interests have captured the national 'sustainability' discourse. The private sector is an unexpected actor, omitted from Agenda 21 concerns in Brazil, but it is also both a powerful ally and formidable opponent in sustainability policymaking.

Whilst the following chapters unlock the rich detail of these varying case studies, the final chapter attempts to draw out the lessons learnt and possible ways forward in uniting the global and the local in order to encourage progress towards sustainable development.

References

Agrawal, A. & Gibson, C.C. (1999) Enchantment and disenchantment: the role of community in natural resource conservation. *World Development,* 27, 629-649.

Blaikie, P.M. & Muldavin, J.S.S. (2004) Upstream, downstream, China, India: The politics of the environment in the Himalayan region. *Annals of the Association of American Geographers*, 94, 520-548.

Botkin, D. (1990) *Discordant Harmonies: A New Ecology for the Twenty-First Century.* Oxford University Press, Oxford.

Carew-Reid, J., Prescott-Allen, R., Bass, S. & Dalal-Clayton, B. (1994) *Strategies for National Sustainable Development: A Handbook for their Planning and Implementation*. Earthscan, London.

Carney, J. & Watts, M. (1990) Manufacturing dissent: work, gender and the politics of meaning in peasant societies. *Africa,* 60, 207-241.

Craig, G. & Mayo, M. (eds) (1995) *Community Empowerment: A Reader in Participation and Development*. Zed Books, London.

Dalal-Clayton, B. & Bass, S. (2002) *Sustainable Development Strategies: A Resource Book*. OECD, Paris and UNDP, New York, Earthscan, London.

Dowdeswell, E. (1998) Where peaceful waters flow. *Water International*, 23, 13-16.

Ekins, P., Folke, C., Groot, R., de Simon, S., Deutsch, L., Perk, J. van der, Chiesura, A., Vliet, A., van Skanberg, K., Douguet, J.M. & O'Connor, M. (2003) Identifying critical natural capital. *Ecological Economics*, 44, 159-292.

Fairhead, J. & Leach, M. (1996) *Misreading the African Landscape: Society and Ecology in a Forest-Savanna Mosaic*. Cambridge University Press, Cambridge.

Gleick, P.H. (1998) Water in crisis: Paths to sustainable water use. *Ecological Applications*, 8, 571-579.

Holling, C. (1986) The resilience of terrestrial ecosystems: local surprise or global change. In Clarke, W.C. & Munn, R.G. (eds) *Sustainable Development of the Biosphere*. Cambridge University Press, Cambridge, pp. 292-317.

Ives, J.D. & Messerli, B. (1989) *The Himalaya Dilemma: Reconciling Development and Conservation*. John Wiley and Sons, London.

Keely, J. & Scoones, I. (2003) *Understanding Environmental Policy Processes: Cases from Africa*. Earthscan, London.

Leach, M. & Mearns, R. (eds) (1996) *The Lie of the Land: Challenging Received Wisdom on the African Environment*. The International African Institute, James Currey, Oxford.

Leach, M., Mearns, R. & Scoones, I. (1997) *Environmental Entitlements: A Framework for Understanding the Institutional Dynamics of Environmental Change*. IDS Working Paper 359, Brighton.

Middleton, N. & O'Keefe, P. (2003) *Rio Plus Ten: Politics, Poverty and the Environment*. Pluto Press, London.

Neumann, R. (2005) *Making Political Ecology*. Hodder Arnold, London.

Rocheleau, D, Thomas-Slayter, B. & Wangari, E. (eds) (1996) *Feminist Political Ecology: Global Issues and Local Experiences*. Routledge, New York.

Schaffer, W. (1985) Order and chaos in ecological systems. *Ecology*, 66, 93-106.

Scoones, I. & Wolmer, W. (eds) (2002) *Pathways of Change in Africa. Crops, Livestock and Livelihoods in Mali, Ethiopia and Zimbabwe*. James Currey, Oxford.

Sprugel, D. (1991) Disturbance, equilibrium and environmental variability: what is 'natural' vegetation in a changing environment? *Biological Conservation*, 58, 1-18.

Stott, P. (1997) Dynamic forestry in an unstable world. *Commonwealth Forestry Review*, 76, 207-209.

Stott, P. (1998) Biogeography and ecology in crisis: the urgent need for a new metalanguage. *Journal of Biogeography*, 25, 1-2.

Sullivan, S. (1996) Towards a non-equilibrium ecology: perspectives from an arid land. *Journal of Biogeography*, 23, 1-5.

Sullivan, S. & Rohde, R. (2002) On non-equilibrium in arid and semi-arid grazing systems: A critical comment on A. Illius & T.G. O'Connor (1999) On the relevance of nonequilibrium concepts to arid and semiarid grazing systems. *Ecological Applications*, 9, 798-813. *Journal of Biogeography*, 29, 1595-1618.

Tiffen, M., Mortimore, M., & Gichuki, F. (2004) *More People, Less Erosion: Environmental Recovery in Kenya*. Wiley, Chichester.

UNCED (1992) *Agenda 21*. United Nations, New York.

Whittaker, R.J. (2000) Scale, succession and complexity in island biogeography: are we asking the right questions? *Global Ecology and Biogeography*, 9, 75-85.

Chapter 2

Gathering Evidence: The Challenge of Assessing Sustainability after a Resettlement Programme in Zimbabwe

Jennifer Elliott, Bill Kinsey and Dominik Kwesha

Introduction

Zimbabwe's land reform and resettlement programme has experienced a dramatic and controversial expansion in recent years. The widespread seizure and invasion of white-owned commercial farmlands starting in 2000 became the focus of substantial national and international visibility. The subsequent 'Fast Track' approach to resettlement announced by the Government in that year led to a rapid escalation of farm designation and resettlement and new targets to redistribute as much as 80 per cent of land in the commercial farming sector to African households and farmers. The disorder and chaos of the farm invasions (Chaumba *et al.*, 2003), the regime-sanctioned, confiscatory nature of land acquisition (Bernstein, 2004) and cronyism in the allocation of lands (Chaumba *et al.*, 2003) are all features of the considered 'land crisis' in Zimbabwe that have come to symbolize the country (Kinsey, 2004a) and are central to external perceptions of the wider region (Lahiff, 2003). For many Zimbabwean people within and beyond resettlement areas, meeting immediate needs of food and shelter have become extremely difficult and issues of sustainable development have become less visible in Zimbabwean national planning.

There is little doubt that 'by any measure, Zimbabwe is in crisis' (Hammer *et al.*, 2003: 3), economically, socially and politically. These various crises are acknowledged to have provided the conditions for a 'dramatic departure from the constitutionally based resettlement policies of the past' (Lahiff, 2003: 57) with potentially detrimental implications for environmental resources. But there is much debate over what constitutes and has caused these multi-layered crises, what the consequences are and for whom (Hammer *et al.*, 2003). Furthermore, there is a need to avoid narrow understandings of a 'land crisis' in contemporary Zimbabwe. By the time of the land invasions of 2000, for example, the country was already experiencing declines in agricultural output, severe drought and problems of food supply and distribution (Bernstein, 2004). There were also many other conflicts surrounding land and natural resources outside of the commercial farming sector (Marongwe, 2002), the origin of which may be complex and long-standing. In short, the interests in land in Zimbabwe need to be considered as complex and contested, with many questions pertaining to land rather than a particular question or crisis.

The outcomes of the Fast Track approach to land resettlement occurring currently in Zimbabwe have yet to be researched. As Bernstein (2004) identifies, key questions for the future will include who got what land, what are they doing with it and what will they do with it. But it is not only in Zimbabwe that land and land policy are being rethought. In southern Africa more widely, these issues are back on policy agendas after a gap of several decades (Toulmin & Quan, 2000; Lahiff, 2003; Bernstein, 2004). The last few years have seen a reassessment of many of the 'conventional wisdoms' (Toulmin & Quan, 2000) on behalf of international institutions, donors, national governments and civil society organizations. For example, the necessity of individual titling is being rethought and there is a greater openness to the potential of communal systems and more decentralized control in natural resource management (Toulmin & Quan, 2000; Elliott & Campbell, 2002). In general, there is greater adherence to market-orientation (Lahiff, 2003) and donor investments being made in land-related activities rather than land reform *per se* (Toulmin & Quan, 2000). However, moving forward on these issues rests on substantial reappraisal of past approaches and interventions in land reform and resettlement. Whilst Zimbabwe can be regarded as something of an exception in the region in terms of its continued commitment to a radical land reform agenda, private property ownership and capitalist models of settlement and production continue to be the basics of Fast Track resettlement as was the case in earlier phases of the programme. Chaumba *et al.* (2003) also identify the continued salience and operation of long-established mechanisms of planning and allocation within this current approach. Evidently, there is a continued need to understand in detail the outcomes and benefits of the resettlement programme in Zimbabwe as conceived and implemented over the first twenty years.

This chapter focuses on the mapping from sequential aerial photography of land cover outcomes for two resettlement scheme areas that are amongst the oldest in the country. The data presented form part of the findings of a wider research project that took shape in the late 1990s (Elliott & Kinsey, 2003), designed to look back on a programme that was clearly heading for substantial change and to contribute to future policy development and practice in resettlement in the region. This wider research encompassed five scheme areas and has produced a data set that remains unique in the monitoring of the resettlement programme in Zimbabwe, as discussed in sections below. The research combined the interest of the authors concerning the environmental outcomes of resettlement in Zimbabwe (Elliott, 1996, 2000; Elliott & Campbell, 2002), the substantial monitoring of poverty and welfare outcomes undertaken since 1983 under the umbrella of the Zimbabwe Rural Household Dynamics Study (Kinsey *et al.*, 1998; Kinsey 1999; Kinsey 2000), and with emerging work at the Zimbabwean Forestry Commission particularly in the area of woodland resource mapping. The project aims are shown in Box 2.1. The chapter effects a critical analysis of some of the predominant 'received narratives' on environmental change (Leach & Mearns, 1996) within the small scale farming sector and raises a number of questions concerning the prospects of assessing the sustainability of resettlement as illustrated through an examination of the spatially complex patterns of woodland change specifically.

Box 2.1   The aims of the wider research project

- To document objective patterns of land feature change across five resettlement scheme areas that encompass the principal argo-ecological zones of the country and taking advantage, in particular, of the last set of blanket air photography available for the country, flown by the RAF in 1995–97
- To investigate the linkages between welfare outcomes and resource entitlements in resettlement areas towards identifying people and environments with particular needs.
- To investigate the challenges and opportunities of linking remote sensing and social methodologies.

Source: Elliot & Kinsey (2003)

At the time of the research design, there was widespread acceptance on behalf of all the major stakeholders involved (including the Commercial Farmers' Union, the Government of Zimbabwe and amongst donors) of the need to speed further land reform and an understanding that the continued impasse in policy was neither politically nor economically sustainable. In the event, however, the period of the research encompassed a turbulent time in Zimbabwe, and in continuity with all parts of the country, the pressures on resources and livelihoods within resettlement scheme areas were quickly understood as unprecedented. Many new questions of sustainability were therefore raised during the course of the project and they led to modifications in its implementation.

Assessing the sustainability of resettlement in Zimbabwe

For twenty years land acquisition, redistribution and settlement in Zimbabwe occurred through an orderly and constitutionally based programme encompassing market transactions, voluntary movements and a small number of planned resettlement models. In an evaluation of resettlement over the period of British aid involvement from 1980 to 1987, the programme was referred to as a 'considerable success' and a 'most worthwhile investment' (Cusworth & Walker, 1988:11). On independence in 1980, the Government of Zimbabwe had committed itself to a programme of land reform designed to overcome the inequities of a colonial system of land apportionment and development that had left 6,000 white farmers with access to 42 per cent of the land area of the country and an estimated 700,000 indigenous farmers occupying a similar proportion, but often in regions much less well suited to agricultural production. Political objectives were clearly to the fore at this time, focused on ensuring a more equitable racial distribution of land and extending the livelihood opportunities for the poorest groups, including the landless and those who had been displaced during the war of liberation (Zimbabwe, 1980). The objectives of the resettlement programme also included the alleviation of population pressure in the communal lands. Those early years of the programme can be considered the 'Golden Years' (Kinsey, 2004a) within which the Government of Zimbabwe displayed a conviction regarding the central role of land redistribution in alleviating poverty. These varied objectives remained relatively consistent through two revisions to the Policies and Procedures for Resettlement in 1985 and 1992 (Zimbabwe, 1985, 1992a).

Of three 'models' initially designed for resettlement, only one received British financing and it encompassed the majority of resettlement. This model was based on individual family farming and the allocation of three permits to beneficiaries; to cultivate a standard plot of a maximum of 5 hectares (applied uniformly throughout the country irrespective of agricultural potential), communal grazing rights for a specified number of livestock units (modified according to the suitability of cropping and carrying capacities in the region) and a permit to reside in a resettlement 'village'. Permits were issued (but could be revoked at any time by the responsible Minister) that required settlers to 'permanently and personally reside' on the residential stand allocated to them (i.e. to be engaged in full-time farming) and to renounce all rights to cultivate land or depasture stock in the communal areas. The technical, economic and financial viability of each scheme was appraised on the basis of existing technical information on the farms purchased, target incomes to be achieved from a combination of crops and livestock within different agro-ecological regions, and accepted methodologies for project appraisal in use by international funding agencies (Cusworth & Walker, 1998).

Early in the programme, a preoccupation for evaluations in terms of the quantity of land being redistributed, rather than with the performance of the land reform program or the impact on the beneficiaries, could be identified (Cusworth & Walker, 1988; Deininger *et al.*, 2004). In 1982, for example, the Government of Zimbabwe raised the target for resettlement to 162,000 households on 10 million hectares of land through an 'accelerated' resettlement programme within which purchased land was settled with only the minimum amount of planning, with no provision for infrastructural development and 'without any indication of where the resources for this were to come from' (Cusworth & Walker, 1988: 4). Increasing tensions started to be evident between the Government of Zimbabwe, which was determined to speed up the programme, and the British Government's insistence (on the basis of their experience in Kenya) that there was more to resettlement than land transfers. Whilst the British Government was influencing the implementation of resettlement through its financial control over land purchases, it was quickly proven to be less effective in its intended support for monitoring of the programme. For example, it was identified early on (amongst all parties) that the creation of a Monitoring and Evaluation Unit with the Ministry of Lands, Resettlement and Rural Development was desirable (and the finances from the British Government were in place), yet the establishment of the Unit took a long time to be enacted. Furthermore, although systems for monitoring of the programme (designed to be annual) were subsequently launched, in practice these have appeared as *ad hoc* reviews of the status of implementation in a sample of schemes rather than continuous or consistent reports. The first assessment of the status of settler households, for example, was only published in 1986 (Zimbabwe, 1986) and the second took a further six years to emerge (Zimbabwe, 1992b).

The lack of evidence of what was happening on the ground did not stop a 'flood of criticisms and negative evaluations' (Kinsey, 2004a: 1672) concerning the resettlement programme during these first decades. For example, long-held fears relating to the negative impact of resettlement on agricultural productivity, which were evident prior to the programme, rose again in the 1990s in the course of the Economic and Structural Adjustment Programme (ESAP) (Moyo, 2000). Whilst ESAP itself said nothing specifically on land reform, the policy framework for land policy changed significantly but failed to stimulate any overarching performance review of land reform. Similarly, with the ending of the period of the Lancaster House Constitution and a new Land Apportionment Act of 1992 that enabled the compulsory acquisition of land for state purposes, new Policies and Procedures for Resettlement were published (Zimbabwe, 1992a). These now explicitly linked resettlement to the concurrent reorganisation and development of the communal areas, but again policy changes were undertaken 'in the face of inadequate evidence on what was happening at the level of the resettled household' (Kinsey, 2004a: 1672) within existing schemes.

Questions of environmental sustainability of resettlement, both in terms of the outcomes and processes of the policy, have also regularly been invoked particularly in arguments against the expansion of the programme (Elliott, 1995). In short, environmental debates contrast the resource use and management contexts of the African farming areas (the predominant source of settlers) with the European farmed lands to which households were moved. Whilst the former are framed as degraded, overcrowded and problematic, the destination areas are conceived as productive and resource-plentiful (Cliffe, 1988; Bradley & Dewees, 1993). Fears over the suggested replication of communal area conditions with resettlement were evident prior to the programme and have been highlighted during the course of implementation. Instances of cattle being held in excess of permits allocated (Jinya, 1991) and the failure of resettled farmers to give up land formerly held in the communal areas (Cusworth & Walker, 1988) are given as evidence of these processes of conceived degradation. Questions are also raised concerning the incentives for conservation and the prospects of sustainable management in the context of the suggested 'plentiful' resource conditions in the destination areas and the uncertainties of administrative control in the dynamic institutional context of scheme areas (Nhira & Fortmann, 1993; Kinsey, 2004a). At times, these debates have come together and invoked

Hardin's (1968) 'Tragedy of the Commons' scenario whereby the land tenure models adopted within the programme are framed as the problem. In particular, public tenure of grazing lands, combined with the absence of mechanisms to ensure that cattle owners do not exceed herd sizes and stocking rates, underpin an expectation that the environments of resettlement areas would soon deteriorate to the 'situation of the communal areas' (Tawonezi, cited in Kinsey, 2004a: 1686). Whilst Cusworth & Walker (1988) acknowledged that in many resettlement schemes, households at that time were holding less than their stocking permits allowed (and indeed, were not able to cultivate the full extent of their arable units), their prediction for the environments of resettlement areas was similarly deterministic:

> The ecological time bomb of overgrazing is almost certain to occur if settlers with cattle are not restricted in their size of their livestock holding ... since the lack of authority or control over the public grazing on the communal lands has led directly to environmental degradation, the reproduction of this model within the programme ... will face exactly the same problems in time (Cusworth & Walker, 1988:32/3, emphases added).

In short, evaluations of the sustainability of the resettlement programme in Zimbabwe to date have been limited in a number of ways. Firstly, there is a general lack of objective evidence *per se* and at all scales to underpin these arguments concerning the impacts of resettlement. In the case of environmental outcomes, there has been no systematic monitoring nor comprehensive identification of the spatial patterns of resource use within resettlement schemes, or any comparative studies of local ecological or land feature variation. In addition, many evaluations have been based on snap-shots taken at particular times that miss seasonal variations or the impacts of external factors such as drought or economic restructuring. Fundamentally, many pronouncements can be considered to have been premature in that they have been asserted over very short time horizons, when it is widely acknowledged that the benefits of programmes involving large scale population movement may take at least a generation to become apparent (Kinsey, 2000).

Case study areas and research findings

The Tokwe I resettlement scheme covers an area of approximately 68,000 hectares, the northern boundary of which is located 45 km east of Gweru (Figure 2.1). It lies in 'Natural Region' III and IV with rainfall levels decreasing from around 750 mm per annum in the north to less than 600 mm in the south. Crop production consequently becomes more marginal towards the south of the scheme area. The Wenimbi-Macheke resettlement scheme encompasses an area of just under 36,000 hectares, located 90 km southeast of Harare in Natural Region IIb. It has a mean annual rainfall in excess of 850 mm and is relatively well suited to both intensive crop and livestock production. Both scheme areas are based on sandy soils and support vegetation dominated by miombo woodland (comprising largely Brachystegia and Julbernardia genera). Both scheme areas were amongst the earliest to be settled after independence and comprise villages of a similar size (of around 30 families). The village areas are larger in Tokwe to take account of the lower carrying capacities of the region. The research identified a random 25 per cent sample of village areas (defined by old farm boundaries) within the scheme areas.

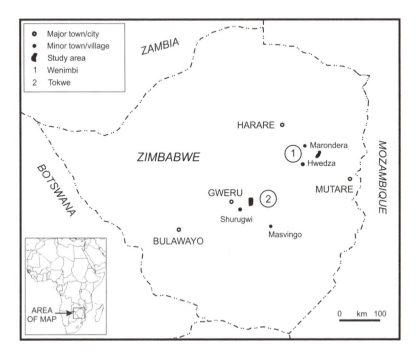

Figure 2.1   The location of study areas

Three sets of 1:25,000 black and white air photography were secured for each scheme area; the latest available (1996-97); a set for the mid-1980s (1985-87) and an earlier set prior to designation within the land reform programme (1972 in Tokwe and 1981 in Wenimbi). Evidently, whilst the precise dates for the two scheme areas are different, two time periods can be identified for the analysis; 'T1-T2' encompassing the first five years of resettlement and 'T2-T3' encompassing the subsequent 10-12 years of resettlement. All air photos were scanned, geo-referenced and interpreted by a team at the Forestry Commission in Harare using land feature classes that are well-rehearsed within previous work at the Commission and are shown in Box 2.2. These processes led to the production of three data sets for each of the sampled villages across the two scheme areas.

Box 2.2   Land feature classes used to analyse environmental change in this study

> **Woodland**:   >20% canopy; trees >5 m height
> **Bushland**:   >20% canopy; smaller trees and few scattered big trees
> **Grassland**:   <20% trees/bush
> **Cultivation**: Areas showing evidence of present or past cultivation

In the space of a generation resettlement in Zimbabwe, as evidenced in the two research areas, has been associated with quite dramatic environmental changes. Table 2.1 shows the overall land feature change within villages encompassing the time of designation through to 1997. Across the two scheme areas, resettlement has been associated with an expansion in cultivation and bushland and a loss of woodland and grassland area over the period. However, whilst there has been a certain uniformity of outcome in the aggregate, Table 2.1 also shows that there were significant differences between the scheme areas in terms of the extent of these overall land cover changes.

Table 2.1   Percentage land feature change, T1-T3 (scheme averages) for Wenimbi and Tokwe

Land Feature	Total Percentage Change	Wenimbi	Tokwe
Cultivation	17	21	12
Grassland	-15	-22	-7
Bushland	12	13	11
Woodland	-15	-13	-17

Whilst such linear expressions of environmental change can be (and regularly are) used to support images of resource degradation (such as the loss of woodland area or the conversion of woodland to more open bushland and/or wider grassland/ savanna vegetation), the analysis of a third set of air photography within the period of resettlement gives important insights into these transformations and, indeed, the drivers of the differences identified between scheme areas. For example, Table 2.2 shows that in Tokwe, despite the large percentage loss of woodland over the total period of resettlement, there was no overall loss of woodland between T1 and T2; such loss came later (and also more extensively than in Wenimbi). However, the expansion of cultivation in Tokwe was less in the later period (and was lower in comparison to Wenimbi). In Wenimbi, it is the loss of grassland area that is the most significant landscape feature change across both time periods.

Table 2.2   Percentage land feature change, T1-T2 and T2-T3 compared, for Wenimbi and Tokwe

Land Feature	T1-T2		T2-T3	
	Wenimbi	Tokwe	Wenimbi	Tokwe
Cultivation	9	7	12	5
Grassland	-11	-8	-11	1
Bushland	6	-0.1	7	11
Woodland	-5	0	-8	-17

The limitations of all such linear expressions of environmental transformations, however, are exposed very quickly and simply in a GIS analysis. Using the cross-tabulation function of ArcView it is possible to consider every pixel, how it is classified at a particular point in time and what its status is at a subsequent date. This kind of spatial analysis shows that, although there was no overall loss of woodland area in Tokwe between T1 and T2, a very dynamic situation underpins this outcome on the ground (Table 2.3a). For example, only 79 per cent of woodland areas so defined in 1972 remained woodland in Tokwe in 1985; 6 per cent had converted to cultivation, 10 per cent to grassland and 5 per cent to bushland. This means that the overall 'static' situation at a scheme level (shown in Table 2.1) masks diverse transformations over space, which include woodland losses and gains at the pixel scale. Substantial areas of both bushland and grassland in 1972 hosted woodland by 1985 (Table 2.3a). A similar analysis for the subsequent period (Table 2.3b) confirms that only 36 per cent of woodland in 1985 remained so defined in 1997; 5 per cent had converted to cultivation, 22 per cent to grassland and 36 per cent to bushland. Six per cent of the area formerly under grassland and 4 per cent of bushland evidenced 'reforestation' in that they were classified as woodland by 1997.

In contrast to the Tokwe situation, the most significant landscape feature transformation in the Wenimbi scheme as revealed by the gross analysis in Table 2.1, was the conversion of grassland areas. Similar cross-tabulation analyses (Tables 2.4a and b) suggest that, in the period encompassing the first five years of resettlement (T1-T2), 66 per cent of grassland identified in 1981 remained in 1986-87; but the most important transformation (see Table 2.4a) had been to cultivation, with significant conversions also occurring to bushland (7 per cent) and woodland (6 per cent). These principal spatial patterns were consolidated in the later time period as seen in Table 2.4b.

Table 2.3   Landscape feature transitions Tokwe scheme area

(a) T1-T2 (percentage)

Landscape features (1972)	Woodland	Cultivation	Grassland	Settlement	Bushland	Total (1972)
Woodland	79	6	10	0	5	38
Cultivation	5	52	39	1	3	5
Grassland	14	16	63	0	6	46
Settlement	0	0	0	0	100	0.03
Bushland	35	15	17	1	33	10
Total (1985)	41	14	37	0.6	8	

(b) T2-T3 (percentage)

Landscape features (1985)	Woodland	Cultivation	Grassland	Settlement	Bushland	Total (1985)
Woodland	36	5	22	0	36	34
Cultivation	1	80	16	1	3	14
Grassland	6	12	67	1	14	41
Settlement	1	7	13	74	6	0.6
Bushland	4	5	47	3	42	10
Total (1997)	15	19	42	1	23	

In short, this kind of analysis is starting to reveal the substantial multi-directional changes that underpin the gross patterns of land feature change and the varied experience by scheme and time period. It is evident in this analysis of the longer term impacts of resettlement, that the outcomes are complex and less unidirectional than is generally framed within conventional wisdoms considered above, or as suggested by tabulations of aggregated changes (Table 2.1) that typify most analyses to date. Rather, transitions between the major land cover categories are identified here as occurring in all directions simultaneously. Most significantly, it is evident that if the analysis is left at the level of coarse changes, it is very easy to assume a dominant image of resource degradation, when quite simple GIS analysis enables exposure of processes of reforestation, for example, in particular places as well as deforestation.

Table 2.4 **Landscape feature transitions Wenimbi scheme area**

(a) T1-T2 (percentage)

Landscape features (1981)	Woodland	Cultivation	Grassland	Settlement	Bushland	Total (1981)
Woodland	72	4	9	0.3	11	30
Cultivation	2	82	10	3	3	10
Grassland	6	19	66	1	7	48
Settlement	0	7	23	25	29	0.2
Bushland	10	5	24	1	53	6
Total (1986/7)	25	19	37	1	10	

(b) T2-T3 (percentage)

Landscape features (1986/7)	Woodland	Cultivation	Grassland	Settlement	Bushland	Total (1981)
Woodland	46	9	10	0.3	34	25
Cultivation	0	83	12	1	3	19
Grassland	6	24	59	1	10	37
Settlement	1	7	4	81	6	1
Bushland	11	14	27	1	47	10
Total (1995/7)	15	29	29	2	19	

A further illustration of the potential of this kind of analysis, to critically investigate images of resource degradation under resettlement and for understanding the principal drivers of these transformations, comes through preliminary analysis of the spatial patterning of woodland 'losses'. Within GIS, it is relatively simple to quantify the number and average area of 'patches' of land so classified. Under dominant narratives of environmental change under small scale, rain-fed farming livelihoods, woodland areas are framed as becoming more diffuse through foraging and cutting for fuelwood, for example, and cultivation activities expand haphazardly at the expense of other resources. Table 2.5 quantifies the number and area of woodland patches identified within the sampled villages in the two resettlement schemes under study. It also considers the intra-scheme variation and temporal change that is enabled through the interpretation of sequential aerial photography and the use of ArcView software.

Table 2.5   The spatial patterning of woodland patches over time within and between the two study areas

	T1		T3		T1-T3 change	
	Tokwe	Wenimbi	Tokwe	Wenimbi	Tokwe	Wenimbi
Number	38	17	11	5	-27	-12
Range	37	9	28	7	-9	-2
Mean Area (ha)	27	11	46	20	19	9
Range (ha)	62	29	123	52	61	23

It is apparent that the number of woodland 'patches' has declined in both scheme areas across the time period and the average area of those patches has increased. This could suggest that woodland resources available to resettled households have become more confined to a smaller number of increasingly defined 'woodland areas' and this is apparently more pronounced in Tokwe. In Tokwe at T1, prior to designation within the resettlement programme, there is a much larger number and area of woodland patches than in Wenimbi, but also greater diversity within the scheme at the village level (as indicated by the higher range value). This suggests that there were very contrasting opportunities for resource management in different villages at the outset that were not considered as part of the planning or management processes within the land reform programme as it initially existed.

If the analysis is extended to consider the spatial pattern of cultivation across time in the two scheme areas (Table 2.6), the data confirm and further reveal not only the importance of contextual factors, such as the local ecology, but also the historical regional political economy in understanding environmental transformations. Table 2.6 indicates that across the period T1-T3, for both scheme areas, there has been a small increase in the number of cultivation patches and an increase in the average size of these patches over time. This is as expected under a resettlement programme where settlers are allocated designated plots for cultivation and move to extend their arable entitlements to the five hectares over time. However, there are important differences between the scheme areas; it is evident that the average area of cultivation patches in the Wenimbi villages is larger and is achieved earlier within the programme than is the case in Tokwe. In addition, the range of experience across villages within the Wenimbi scheme is wider. The drivers of these patterns in Wenimbi may include the ecology of the area that is better suited to intensive maize production and also to tobacco cultivation than in Tokwe. But this region was also an area of substantial land invasion and squatting in the years up to independence and designation within the land reform programme. In contrast, in the more southern Tokwe region, many European farms were abandoned in the late 1970s and resettled households have been slower to take up their maximum allocated plots in a physical environment that is less suited to intensive crop production. However, the greater range of this pattern across the villages within the Tokwe scheme suggests that other important drivers may be operating such as restricted access to draught power at the household level (that is known from farmer narratives within the wider research, for example).

Table 2.6   The spatial patterning of cultivation over time in Wenimbi and Tokwe villages

	T1		T3		T1-T3 change	
	Tokwe	Wenimbi	Tokwe	Wenimbi	Tokwe	Wenimbi
Number	8	4	10	9	2	5
Range	20	8	9	20	-11	12
Mean Area (ha)	11	38	43	63	32	25
Range (ha)	13	78	58	220	45	142

Summary

There is no doubt that there are substantial challenges in assessing the sustainability of resettlement in Zimbabwe. Since 1980 and the establishment of the programme, theoretical and practical questions regarding both the concept and assessment of sustainability have become increasingly common-place but no less complex or contested (see Elliott, 2005; Bell & Morse, 1999). Over the course of twenty five years, there have been many factors external to the resettlement policy (such as drought and economic restructuring) that have shaped the context of land and livelihoods in Zimbabwe and will have influenced environmental and social outcomes in resettlement schemes. In 2005, it is unclear whether any evaluation of a resettlement programme in Zimbabwe, as originally conceived and implemented in a substantially consistent form for twenty years, will turn out to be an assessment of an 'historical artefact' (Kinsey, 2004b) or whether it may be part of advancing land reform in that country in a more inclusive and locally grounded manner.

This chapter has, however, confirmed that issues of sustainability were at least implicit at the outset of the programme of resettlement in Zimbabwe; in the varied and integrated objectives, as stated in 1980, that included poverty alleviation, a focus on the most needy sectors of society and on relieving identified resource pressures in the existing communal areas. Furthermore, the major financier of the programme, the British Government, was also concerned explicitly with the sustainability of land reform; as confirmed in their intentions, for example, to retain a 'hands off' approach to policy formulation and implementation of resettlement (Cusworth & Walker,

1988) in recognition of the capacity and potential within Government of Zimbabwe bureaucratic, planning and technical structures. The chapter has also identified that problems in achieving these ends became quickly apparent in the course of implementation of resettlement. There were no environmental or social baselines established for monitoring the programme, for example, and critical concern regarding the appropriateness of standardized crop-livestock models, particularly in the drier regions, soon emerged. In addition, whilst the Overseas Development Administration recognized that the establishment of new systems for monitoring the programme as a whole were needed, these took a long time to effect and what was realized in practice were largely limited and *ad hoc* assessments rather than comprehensive or systematic reviews.

The chapter has given a very brief insight into the substantial data set that is available concerning landscape feature outcomes and changes associated with the period of resettlement in Zimbabwe. It has also demonstrated the utility of simple methodological tools for revealing landscape level changes (such as in woodland extent) and distribution of longer-term drivers of change (such as cultivation activities). However, the chapter has also shown the difficulties of both establishing and understanding patterns of environmental change. The brief analyses have revealed substantial spatial and temporal variation across and within two resettlement scheme areas and two time periods. The complex, dynamic and multi-directional transformations identified have certainly contested the narratives of linear patterns of resource degradation that continue to shape sustainability debates in Zimbabwe and the wider region. Insight has been given into quite different drivers of change operating at the landscape level, to the significance of local ecologies and to factors of the regional political economy that underpin particular outcomes.

Through the course of the wider research, the primary intention has been to deliver to policy makers data that have not been available in Zimbabwe at a time when many component pieces of land policy within development agendas are 'up in the air' (Toulmin & Quan, 2000) and when Zimbabwe specifically is searching for new models of land redistribution and settlement. It is hoped that the data can be used to make environmental issues more visible in future resettlement planning and, indeed, to integrate issues of sustainable development into mainstream policy making in a way that they have not been to date. If sustainability is conceived as the ability to recover from (as well as cope with) stresses and shocks (be they natural or structural), it is evident that the people of existing resettlement schemes in Zimbabwe have substantial challenges ahead.

References

Bell, S. & Morse, S. (1999) *Sustainability Indicators: Measuring the Immeasurable?* Earthscan Publications Limited, London.

Bernstein, H. (2004) 'Changing before our very eyes': agrarian questions and the politics of land in capitalism today. *Journal of Agrarian Change*, 4, 190-225.

Bradley, P.N. & Dewees, P. (1993) Indigenous woodlands, agricultural production and household economy in the communal areas. In Bradley, P.N. & McNamara, K. (eds) *Living with Trees: Policies for Forestry Management in Zimbabwe.* World Bank Technical Paper, Washington, No. 210, pp. 63-138.

Chaumba, J., Scoones, I. & Wolmer, W. (2003) *From Jambanja to Planning: the reassertion of technocracy in land reform in South-eastern Zimbabwe.* Sustainable Livelihoods in Southern Africa Research Paper 2, IDS, Brighton.

Cliffe, L. (1988) The conservation issue in Zimbabwe. *Review of African Political Economy*, 42, 48-57.

Cusworth, J. & Walker, J. (1988) *Land Resettlement in Zimbabwe: A Preliminary Evaluation.* Evaluation Report no. EV434, ODA, London.

Deininger, K., Hoogeveen, H. & Kinsey, B.H. (2004) Economic benefits and costs of land redistribution in Zimbabwe in the early 1980s. *World Development*, 32, 1697-1709.

Elliott, J.A. (1995) Processes of interaction across resettlement/communal areas boundaries in Zimbabwe. *Geographical Journal of Zimbabwe*, 26, 1-17.

Elliott, J.A. (1996) Resettlement and the Management of Environmental Degradation in the African Farming Areas of Zimbabwe. In Eden, M. and Parry, T. (eds) *Degrading Environments and Management Policies in the Tropics.* Pinter, London, pp. 115-125.

Elliott, J.A. (2000) Resource implications of land resettlement. In Bowyer-Bower, T. & Stoneman, C. (eds) *Land Reform's Constraints and Prospects: Policies, Perspectives and Ideologies in Zimbabwe Today.* Ashgate Publishing Ltd, London, pp. 145-158.

Elliott, J.A. (2005) *An Introduction to Sustainable Development.* Routledge, London, 3rd edition.

Elliott, J.A. & Campbell, M. (2002) The environmental imprints and complexes of social dynamics in rural Africa: cases from Zimbabwe and Ghana. *Geoforum*, 33, 221-237.

Elliott, J.A. & Kinsey, B.H. (2003) *Long-term changes in land-use and resource entitlements with resettlement in Zimbabwe.* Research Report SSR R8004, DFID, London.

Government of Zimbabwe (1989) *National Land Policy, Draft Plan.* Ministry of Lands, Agriculture and Rural Resettlement. Harare.

Hammer, A., Raftopoulos, B. & Jensen, S. (eds) (2003) *Zimbabwe's unfinished Business: Rethinking Land, State and Nation in the Context of Crisis.* Weaver Press, Harare.

Hardin, G. (1968) The tragedy of the commons. *Science*, 162, 1243-8.

Jinya, S.M. (1991) *Resettlement schemes permits administration and management: A diagnostic study of permit violations.* Resettlement Progress Report as at June 30 1991. Ministry of Local Government, Rural and Urban Development, Harare.

Kinsey, B.H., Byrger, K. & Gunning, J.W. (1998) Coping with drought in Zimbabwe: survey evidence on responses of rural households to risk. *World Development*, 26, 89-110.

Kinsey, B.H. (1999) Land reform, growth and equity: emerging evidence from Zimbabwe's resettlement programme. *Journal of Southern African Studies*, 25, 173-196.

Kinsey, B.H. (2000) The implications of land reform for rural welfare. In Bowyer-Bower, T. & Stoneman, C. (eds) *Land Reform's Constraints and Prospects: Policies, Perspectives and Ideologies in Zimbabwe Today*. Ashgate Publishing Ltd, London, pp. 103-118.

Kinsey, B.H. (2004a) Zimbabwe's land reform program: underinvestment in post-conflict Zimbabwe. *World Development*, 32, 1669-1696.

Kinsey, B.H. (2004b) Guest Editor's introduction. *World Development*, 32, 1663-1667.

Lahiff, E. (2003) Land and livelihoods: the politics of land reform in Southern Africa. *IDS Bulletin*, 34, 3, 54-63.

Leach, M. & Mearns, R. (eds) (1996) *The Lie of the Land: Challenging Received Wisdom on the African Environment*. James Currey, London.

Marongwe, N. (2002) *Conflicts over Land and other Natural Resources in Zimbabwe*. ZERO Regional Environment Organisation, Harare.

Moyo, S. (2000) *Land reform under Structural Adjustment in Zimbabwe: Land Use Change in the Mashonaland Provinces*. Nordiska Afrikainstitutet, Stockholm.

Nhira, C. & Fortmann, L. (1993) Local woodland management: realities at the grass roots. In Bradley, P.N. & McNamara, K. (eds) *Living with Trees: Policies for Forestry Management in Zimbabwe*. World Bank Technical Paper No. 210, Washington, pp. 139-156.

Toulmin, C. & Quan, J. (eds) (2000) *Evolving Land Rights: Policy and Tenure in Africa*. IIED, London.

Zimbabwe (1980) *Resettlement Policies and Procedures*. Ministry of Lands, Resettlement and Rural Development, Harare.

Zimbabwe (1985) *Intensive Resettlement: Policies and Procedures*. Ministry of Local Government Rural and Urban Development, Harare.

Zimbabwe (1986) *A Sample Survey of Settler Households in Normal Intensive Model A Resettlement Schemes*. Ministry of Lands, Agriculture and Rural Resettlement Monitoring and Evaluation Unit, Harare.

Zimbabwe (1992a) *Policies and procedures: resettlement and the reorganisation and development of communal lands*. Ministry of Local Government, Rural and Urban Development, Department of Rural Development, Harare.

Zimbabwe (1992b) *Second report of Settler Households in Normal Intensive Model A Resettlement Schemes*. Ministry of Lands, Agriculture and Rural Resettlement, Monitoring and Evaluation Unit, Harare.

Chapter 3

Frameworks for Community-based Rangeland Sustainability Assessment: Lessons from the Kalahari, Botswana

Andrew Dougill and Mark Reed

Introduction

Methods for choosing 'sustainability indicators' to measure progress towards (or away from) social and environmental goals abound in both the academic and practitioner literature (see Bell & Morse, 1999, 2003). These range from situations where development experts and environmental managers simply choose what they see as the most relevant indicators, to participatory processes to help communities identify their own indicators. The academic and policy literature on sustainability indicators is now so prolific that King *et al.* (2000: 631) refer to it as 'an industry on its own'. However, it is increasingly claimed that indicators provide few benefits to users (for example, Carruthers & Tinning, 2003), and that, 'millions of dollars and much time … has been wasted on preparing national, state and local indicator reports that remain on the shelf gathering dust' (Innes & Booher, 1999: 2). This is partly a problem of scale, since the majority of existing indicators are based on a top-down definition of sustainability that is fed by national-level data (Morse & Fraser, 2005). This may miss critical sustainable development issues at the local level and may fail to measure what is important to local communities or to policy makers.

The formalization of the use of community-based sustainability indicators is part of the wider adoption of 'bottom-up' community involvement in environmental management projects, as supported in various United Nations (UN) Conventions, including the UN Convention to Combat Desertification (UNCCD). This shift to 'bottom-up' approaches has been driven by recognition of the past failings of 'top-down' interventions that have been widely criticized in the development literature (for example, Chambers, 1997). A number of important texts (Hilhorst & Muchena, 2000; Stocking & Murnaghan, 2001; Reij & Waters-Bayer, 2001; Pound *et al.*, 2003) have recently initiated discussions on how community participation in natural resource management initiatives can be extended to include monitoring and evaluation of environmental sustainability, or its converse, land degradation. The majority of this literature focuses on arable farming systems, either through development of indicator sheets for assessing visible soil degradation (Stocking &

Murnaghan, 2001), or through participatory nutrient budget approaches capable of identifying areas where nutrient depletion is a significant problem (Hilhorst & Muchena, 2000). Recently, however, this approach has been extended to examine the utility of such participatory approaches to dryland pastoralist systems (Heffernan *et al.*, 2004; Conroy, 2005). This shift in emphasis requires careful analysis using a range of case study environmental and socio-economic settings, to analyse the extra benefits provided to local communities and to the rangeland ecosystems upon which pastoralist livelihoods depend.

Botswana represents a relatively wealthy African nation that has engaged meaningfully in the global sustainability debate and produced a National Action Programme for the UNCCD based on formalising community involvement in land management initiatives (Republic of Botswana, 2004). In addition, it has produced a National Development Plan that advocates 'sustainable economic growth and development which takes into consideration efficient use of both renewable and non-renewable resources, equitable distribution of assets, community participation in natural resources management, poverty eradication, and minimum land, water and air pollution' (Republic of Botswana, 1997).

This chapter presents a methodological framework that has been used to identify, monitor and evaluate sustainability indicators for three study regions in the Kalahari rangelands of Botswana. Discussion focuses on the transferability of the approach and the practical issues identified as critical in scaling up from local-scale participatory development and indicator monitoring to national-scale support for community-based approaches. As such, our emphasis is on moving from the local to the regional and national, in a case study where the process is supported by global and national agreements and policy statements.

Case study region and study sites

The Kalahari, as demarcated by the 2.5 million km^2 of southern Africa covered by Kalahari sand deposits (Thomas & Shaw, 1991), represents a diverse dryland region that has been widely reported as suffering from extensive environmental degradation (for example, Cooke, 1985; Darkoh, 1999) and socio-economic problems in terms of livelihood security and sustainability (for example, Arntzen & Veenendaal, 1986; Sporton & Thomas, 2002). In particular, over 80 per cent of Botswana's land area is Kalahari rangeland, making it an essential precursor of national sustainable development that improved understanding and monitoring of rangeland degradation is provided to support national strategies to implement the United Nations Convention to Combat Desertification (Masilo *et al.*, 1999; Republic of Botswana, 2004).

There has been a wide range of attempts to assess rangeland degradation in the Kalahari. Approaches have used all the main methods for monitoring dryland degradation, including expert opinion (for example, Oldeman *et al.*, 1990), satellite remote sensing (for example, Ringrose *et al.*, 1999; Moleele *et al.*, 2002), plant ecology (for example, Perkins & Thomas, 1993; Moleele & Mainah, 2003), soil hydrochemical properties (for example, Dougill *et al.*, 1999), economic analysis (for example, Perrings & Stern, 2000) and participatory interviews (for example, Thomas *et al.*, 2000; Reed & Dougill, 2002). Results from these various approaches have been conflicting and have rarely been communicated to either communal or commercial pastoralists (as the key land managers). There is, therefore, a clear need for the implementation of approaches that can provide pastoralists (and their community groups) with the capacity to monitor rangeland degradation threats on a local scale with a view to enabling sustainable land use management. It is also essential that such community-led studies are viewed objectively and used in national policy decision-making on land rights and tenure policies. Government policies in this regard (Agricultural Policies of 1975, 1991 and 2001) have been widely criticized for their continued reference to 'Tragedy of the Commons' based solutions of fencing and private land ownership (Perkins, 1996; Adams *et al.*, 2002). Such rangeland privatization policy initiatives are now globally identified as a cause of worsening rangeland degradation and deepened social and economic inequalities (Scoones, 1995; Toulmin & Quan, 2000). Analysis of local case studies are likely to be more powerful in influencing national decision-making rather than this international academic debate that has failed to change Government policy due to the continued push for further privatization of land ownership (Sporton & Thomas, 2002).

As part of international efforts to implement greater community-based monitoring and management of communally-owned rangelands, the Global Environment Facility (instigated by the UN Environment Programme) is currently (2002–07) funding a pilot project in Botswana, Mali and Kenya on 'Management of Indigenous Vegetation for the Rehabilitation of Degraded Rangelands in the Arid Zone of Africa' (Indigenous Vegetation Project, or IVP, for short). The aim of this project is 'to empower local pastoral communities to monitor and manage their rangeland and to develop, adapt and apply traditional and innovative rangeland management strategies'. This involves the establishment of community rangeland committees in three study regions in the Kalahari of Botswana (South West Kgalagadi, mid-Boteti and Kweneng Districts) in a move to transfer community-based natural resource management initiatives from their usual focus on wildlife management zones (Twyman, 2000; Taylor, 2003) towards communal rangelands. The project is supported by (and based in) the Ministry of Agriculture, which has provided logistical field support throughout as an initiative of the National Action Programme on Desertification (Republic of Botswana, 2004).

A key first stage in establishing a successful community-based natural resource management project intervention is the inclusion of all stakeholders (especially local communities) in identifying the mechanisms, or indicators, for assessing problems of resource degradation and evaluating the impact of management decisions on environmental and livelihood sustainability (van Rooyen, 1998). Whilst many authors are reflecting on the problems of using participatory processes to try to gain a single community view on key development issues (Cooke & Kothari, 2001), others continue to highlight the empowering role that participatory research can have in the development arena (Williams, 2004; Chambers, 2005). To this end, preliminary research by the authors (Reed & Dougill, 2002; Dougill & Reed, 2005) in Southern Kgalagadi District was identified by IVP as a methodological tool capable of empowering communities to identify suitable indicators of rangeland degradation. In this context, IVP supported a participatory research process in two of their three study regions (South West Kgalagadi District and mid-Boteti in Central District). This chapter focuses on analysing the findings of participatory environmental research in these three communal rangeland regions (Figure 3.1), each of which has a distinctly different environmental and social setting (Table 3.1) that offers a useful framework for comparative analysis. Prior to this analysis it is essential that the methodological framework followed be detailed.

Table 3.1   Key differences between study areas used for participatory indicator development research in the Kalahari

Site Characteristics	Study Area 1 (Tsabong-Werda)	Study Area 2 (Bokspits)	Study Area 3 (Mid-Boteti)
Average annual rainfall (mm)	315	150–200	372
International rainfall variability (%)	45	>50	35
Soil type (FAO classification)	Arenosols	Arenosols	Arenosols and luvisols
Vegetation type	Southern Kalahari bush savanna	Arid bush savanna	*Colophospermum* mopane woodland and pan grassland
Ethnic composition	Batswana, Herero and Eurasian	Mixed race	Bakalanga,Bahurutse Bangwato, Banajwa Barotsi, Bayei Nyadzwbye
Community interest	Community leaders and local extension workers expressed a strong desire to collaborate during reconnaissance visit	Communities actively involved in IVP	Communities actively involved in Indigenous Vegetation Project
Logistic support provided by	South Kgalagadi Veterinary Services	IVP	IVP

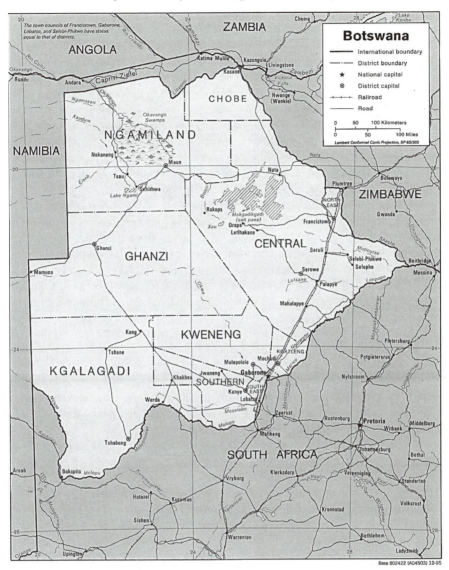

(Summarized from Reed, 2005)

Figure 3.1   **Study areas within Botswana (Study area 1 is Southern Kgalagadi District; Study Area 2 is South West Kgalagadi District; Study Area 3 is Mid–Boteti District)**

Methodological framework: Participatory indicator development

The literature on sustainability indicators falls into two broad methodological paradigms (Bell & Morse, 2001): one that is expert-led and top-down and one that is community-based and bottom-up. The first finds its epistemological roots in scientific reductionism and uses explicitly quantitative indicators. This reductionist approach is common in many fields, including landscape ecology, conservation biology, soil science, as well as economics. Expert-led approaches acknowledge the need for indicators to quantify the complexities of dynamic systems, but do not necessarily emphasize the complex variety of resource user perspectives. The second paradigm is based on a bottom-up, participatory philosophy. It draws on the social sciences, including cultural anthropology, social activism, adult education, development studies and social psychology. Research in this tradition emphasizes the importance of understanding local context to set goals and establish priorities and it acknowledges that sustainability monitoring should be an on-going learning process for both communities and researchers (Freebairn & King, 2003). Proponents of this approach argue that to gain relevant and meaningful perspectives on local problems, it is necessary to actively involve social actors in the research process to stimulate social action or change (Pretty, 1995) and to enable discussions to span a range of spatial scales (Williams, 2004). Whilst it is simple to view these two approaches as fundamentally different, there is increasing awareness and academic debate on the need to develop innovative hybrid methodologies to capture both knowledge repertoires (Batterbury *et al.*, 1997; Nygren, 1999; Thomas & Twyman, 2004) and that can then go further by applying this integrated knowledge to inform land managers and policy-makers (Kiker *et al.*, 2001; Folke *et al.*, 2002). As yet, there remains no consensus on how this integration of methods can be best achieved (Abelson *et al.*, 2003) and our analysis is designed to inform these ongoing debates.

The process used to harness community participation in this study is summarized in Figure 3.2. It uses semi-structured interviews with members of each community to develop a series of indicators that identify environmental degradation so that communities can then monitor environmental change with the use of a rangeland condition assessment guide developed for each of the study areas. The framework outlined in Figure 3.2 was developed over an 18-month timeframe of collaborative research between the researchers and Ministry of Agriculture extension staff on a 100 km transect from Tsabong to Bray in South Kgalagadi (Study Area 1 in Figure 3.1). It was then applied in streamlined form during three-week study visits at two of the IVP study sites (South West Kgalagadi and mid-Boteti) where logistical interview support was available from both IVP and Ministry of Agriculture staff who were trained in the participatory research methods needed for such a community-led indicator development approach. This support of such bottom-up initiatives displays the Botswana Government's engagement with supporting community-based natural resource management initiatives as part of its Sustainable Development Plans (Republic of Botswana, 1997, 2004).

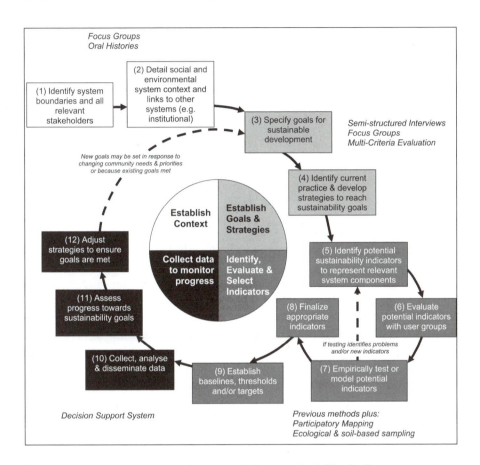

Figure 3.2   Methodological framework for sustainability indicator development and application used in all three Study Areas

The methodological approach starts with household-scale livelihood analyses in which livelihood constraints and opportunities are identified and discussed. Changes in natural capital (or environmental resources) form a key part of such discussions and respondents in all areas identified threats caused by both long-term rangeland ecological change and recent drought events. The approach was based on a 'sustainable livelihoods analysis' (SLA) that involved semi-structured interviews to examine social, financial, physical, human and natural capital assets used by households to ensure livelihood security (Scoones, 1998). SLA analyses have been used widely throughout Southern Africa to examine the links between land use decisions and ecological changes (see Scoones & Wolmer, 2003, for a recent review). The SLA approach provides a mechanism to facilitate an extended discussion between researchers and community members of rangeland degradation indicators and how these indicators have changed through time, specifically in association with rainfall variations, policy changes and market shocks. These iterative discussions between researchers (who have both ecological and social science training) and local pastoralists provide a range of sustainability indicators and management strategies that are then discussed further in community focus groups and with agricultural extension workers from across a District. The iterative nature of the community-science dialogue is central to establishing a more diversified understanding that combines scientific and local knowledge. The framework outlined in Figure 3.2 builds on the view that community empowerment can be enabled by using local knowledge as the starting point in research and then using scientific tools as a means of extending the local findings to wider areas for environmental management.

Table 3.2   Breakdown of types indicators identified by community in initial semi-structured interviews in three Botswana study cites

Category/ Dimension	% of indicators in Study Area 1	% of indicators in Study Area 2	% of indicators in Study Area 3	Selected Examples
Vegetation	54	58	39	Decreased grass cover; Increased *Acacia mellifera* cover; increased weed/ creeper cover
Soil	16	9	19	Increased soil 'looseness' increased incidence of dust storms
Livestock	21	11	19	Declining livestock weight; increased rates of Aphosphorosis (Stiff Sickness)
Wild animal and insects	5	14	17	Decreased abundance of small antelope species; decreased abundance of harvester termites
Socio-economic	4	9	7	Increased household expenditure on food; increased out-migration

Research findings

The initial semi-structured interview stage of the research (67, 40 and 53 respondents in Study Areas 1, 2 and 3 respectively) produced long lists of indicators based on local knowledge in each of the three study sites (83, 57 and 75 indicators provided in Study Areas 1, 2 and 3 respectively). This displays the wealth of information available in pastoral communities, and also the breadth of this information, with indicators covering vegetation changes, soil attributes, livestock condition, wild animal and insect communities and socio-economic conditions (Table 3.2). Evaluations of the utility of each of the different indicators was then conducted in two stages (right hand side of Figure 3.2): (1) with communities in focus group meetings (three village meetings in each area with typically over 20 people present); and (2) in scientifically led appraisals based on field monitoring at sites of different degradation status and in discussions between ecological researchers, key informants and agricultural extension workers. This two-stage process qualitatively evaluated the 'accuracy' and 'ease of use' of each indicator proposed before testing them empirically. Focus group meetings were held in three communities at each site and ranked indicators against accuracy and ease of use criteria. Group discussions were also initiated in these meetings on what communities perceived as 'early warning indicators' that were defined as 'the first signs that land is going to lose its productive potential due to human use'. Discussion on these early warning indicators proved valuable in linking environmental monitoring to the management decision-making process. This process produced significantly shorter lists of agreed early warning indicators (9, 12 and 14 indicators agreed as useful by at least two of the focus group meetings in Study Areas 1, 2 and 3 respectively – see Table 3.3).

Early warning indicators were evaluated using appropriate scientific sampling at sites of different degradation status assigned using a grazing gradient sampling approach with degraded sites sampled close to boreholes and with degradation viewed as declining exponentially with distance from borehole (as per Perkins & Thomas, 1993). The involvement of key informants from communities and extension workers in the ecological sampling process enabled a greater depth of management information to be obtained from land users in terms of their use of different ecological habitats at different times of a year, and between years, through discussion whilst actually in the rangelands rather than the usual interview setting of a homestead.

There was considerable overlap between local knowledge of indicators and scientific literature. In addition, the majority of indicators suggested by community members were validated through soil-based and ecological sampling (Reed, 2005). Indicators were measured along degradation gradients to determine their capacity to represent degraded land states i.e. accurate degradation indicators should be present in degraded land and absent from non-degraded land, evidenced by a decreasing frequency of indicator measurements along degradation gradients. Although it was not possible to test all suggested indicators, the majority were tested in the field. Evidence was found to support 67 per cent, 35 per cent and 80 per cent of indicators in Study Areas 1, 2 and 3 respectively. The lower figure at Study Area 2 is most likely related to spatial patterns of degradation being associated with complex linear dune patterns in the area (Thomas & Shaw, 1991) rather than simply a gradient away from a waterpoint. Some key indicators, for example reduced grass cover and increased bare ground, were identified by community members and supported by field observations at all study areas (Table 3.4 presents a summary of these indicators).

Table 3.3   Early warning degradation indicators prioritized by community focus groups in the three study areas

Study Area 1 – South Kgalagadi	Study Area 2 – South West Kgalagadi	Study Area 3 – Mid-Boteti
	Vegetation Indicators	
Decreased grass cover	Decreased grass cover	Decreased grass cover
Increased proportion of trees dropping leaves	Trees and bushes stunted	Trees and bushes stunted
Decreased abundance of trees	Decreased abundance of trees	Decreased abundance of trees
Increased abundance of unpalatable grasses	Decreased abundance of palatable creepers	Increased quantity of dead treees
Decreased abundance of palatable grasses	Decreased abundance of veld fruits	Decreased rain use efficiency of vegetation
Increased abundance of unpalatable forbs	Increased abundance of *Rhigozum Trichotomum* bush species cover	Increased ability to see through vegetation stands
		Decreased availability of thatching grass
		Decreased grass height
	Soil Indicators	
Increased soil looseness	Active unvegetated dunes	Softer, more powdery, appearance
	Increased soil looseness	Increased incidence of dust storms
	Reduced soil moisture retention (soil dries out faster)	Reduced soil moisture retention (soil dries out faster)
		Increased water infiltration rate
	Livestock Indicators	
Reduced livestock weight	Livestock walk further from water	Decreased abundance of game and predators
Increased incidence of botulism		
	Wild animal and Insect indicators	
	Decreased abundance of game and predators	
	Decreased abundance of grasshoppers	
	Increased abundanceof harvester termites	
	Increased abundance of 'mqalelekatou' ants	

Table 3.4   Indicators considered accurate and easy to use by stakeholders in all three study areas

Indicator
Agricultural
Declining livestock condition/loss of weight
Decreased calving rate
Increased livestock mortality/declining herd size
Decreased milk production
Livestock walk further from water/spend longer between drinking
Increased incidence of Aphosphorosis (Stiff Sickness) due to consumption of poor grasses
Vegetation
Decreased grass cover
Decreased vegetation cover/increased bare ground
Decreased abundance of wild fruits
Decreased abundance of trees
Increased abundance of dead trees
Decreased abundance of *Grewia flava* bushes
Decreased rain use efficiency
Trees and bushes are increasingly stunted
Decreased plant diversity
Decreased abundance of medicinal plants
Soil
Increased soil looseness
Decreased soil organic matter content
Increased density of cattle tracks
Wild animals and insects
Decreased abundance of birds
Decreased abundance of game (grass-eating antelope disappear first) and predators
Socio-Economic
Increased polarisation of rich and poor
Increased household expenditure on products formerly obtained from rangeland and decreased income from range products
Out-migration of farmers

By evaluating and disseminating local indicator suggestions, the research was able to build upon and share valuable local knowledge as well as to facilitate some interesting discussions in areas where disagreements were apparent between community members. The indicators developed through this research are therefore highly familiar to land managers who have the capacity to apply them without any need for specialist training or equipment. Land managers also had the opportunity to reject or adapt indicators (from other study areas or literature) that were not considered to be relevant locally.

This research, in a similar vein to previous studies elsewhere in the Kalahari displays that communities have spatial and temporal awareness of the environmental variability that typifies dryland environments. It also supports the conclusion that conventional expert-led indicators of degradation (for example, percentage cover of palatable perennial grasses) over-simplify degradation assessment by leading to polarized views of either 'good or bad' rangeland (Thomas & Twyman, 2004), rather than focusing on the management adaptations to ecological changes that retain overall pastoral system productivity. Our findings show the need to integrate studies on local knowledge, ecological monitoring approaches and policy discussions from the start of any project involvement. This is vital for grazed rangelands as traditional scientific views on using individual grass species fodder assessments (for example, van Oudsthoorn, 1999) provide only single species views rather than considering the fodder heterogeneity of a landscape that is vital to livestock health and thus pastoralist decision-making (Scoones, 1995). Our findings also demonstrate that the process of involving all key stakeholders in the provision of a list of scientifically 'accurate', locally 'easy to use' and policy 'relevant' indicators can achieve the hybrid knowledge that is conceptualized in academic debates. In our studies, the scientific evaluation stage successfully tied each of the agreed early warning indicators to management suggestions for the specific region and guided the production of rangeland assessment guides that will facilitate community monitoring of rangeland condition (Reed, 2005). The rangeland assessment guides produced in the communities in each region will be distributed more widely by the Ministry of Agriculture to attempt District-scale adoption of participatory rangeland monitoring and management.

The participatory methodological framework developed (Figure 3.2) has successfully engaged a wide range of stakeholders (communal and commercial pastoralists, rich and poor, extension workers and policy-makers) in the identification and evaluation of degradation indicators, resulting in the production of three sub-District level rangeland assessment guides. The differences in the lists of key 'early warning degradation indicators' between the three sub-District regions (Table 3.3), and between conventional scientific indicators (Field, 1978; van Oudtshoorn, 1999), displays that the bottom-up indicator development process can be usefully integrated with participatory, expert and scientific evaluation to provide shorter, sub-District specific lists of indicators that can then guide wider community-based rangeland monitoring and management. The impact of assessment guides on longer-term livelihood and environmental sustainability remains to be seen. However, preliminary indications suggest that the process has aided community empowerment and provided a formal framework that the Ministry of Agriculture could use to move to the participatory methods of environmental monitoring and management advice recommended by international environmental conventions. Indeed through IVP, the Ministry of Agriculture is now looking at establishing a methodology that can be applied at a national scale based on the lessons learnt in this research and mirroring much of what is displayed in Figure 3.2.

Discussion: Scaling up from the local

Whilst the local-scale studies outlined here, for Study Areas of up to 100 km by 100 km, (in Districts with total populations of less than 10,000 people and *c.* 100,000 livestock) have significant benefits for community capacity-building and empowerment, the ability to upscale from such local-scale studies to national implementation has been questioned (Fraser *et al.*, 2006). Our findings have successfully scaled up from the three Study Areas to enable production of sub-District level rangeland assessment guides (and lists of degradation indicators) that have gained acceptance by a range of key stakeholders and other communities across the sub-District scale (100 km x 100 km). However, there remains a very significant challenge to assess the ability to upscale beyond the sub-District scale, such that improved District or National monitoring of degradation problems can be initiated based on community-led approaches, as recommended in global environmental agreements and national sustainable development policy statements. One mechanism to achieve this is the shared evaluation of lists of indicators from a range of different study areas through community focus groups. We have recently used such a participatory (multi-criteria) approach for our three Study Areas and this has produced a shorter list of agreed 'degradation indicators' (Table 3.4) that could be used as a starting template of indicators that are both accurate and easy to use across the wider scale of Kalahari rangelands (i.e. a single agro-ecological zone). However, we would stress that this list hides important differences between the study regions (Table 3.3) and it is not a list that could be used for the whole of Botswana due to the very different agro-ecological conditions found outside the Kalahari (notably in the Eastern Hardveld, but also in dry sub-humid Northern regions). As such, any truly national study would need to be founded on integrated (community-led and scientifically evaluated) approaches in each agro-ecological zone found within a country. Thus, participatory research should only offer a methodological template for use on a local-scale and it should not claim to provide widely applicable lists of degradation indicators or management practices.

We argue that the feasibility of moving to adoption of national approaches developed from local community-led studies rests not in further methodological developments. This view is based on our wider experience of adapting and applying the research framework proposed here (Figure 3.2) into other agro-ecological zones globally. Most notably, we have used this framework as the methodological guide in applied land use scenario studies in identifying and assessing multiple land use options in an upland UK based study (Dougill *et al.*, in press). Instead, we argue that what is needed is the institutional support (from Government and UN agencies) required to move extension services from being top-down dissemination and education-driven, to being bottom-up and facilitative of implementing community-led monitoring and management planning. Achievement of such a fundamental and radical move needs to start by training agricultural staff in the participatory approaches needed to identify relevant and innovative local knowledge on agricultural management practices (Chambers, 2005). This process has been initiated through the Indigenous

Vegetation Project (IVP) with extension staff trained in the use of participatory methodologies in each of their three study areas. Further training is now needed for all extension staff on the use of such methods, together with their inclusion in agricultural extension staff training programmes, such as at the Botswana College of Agriculture. Ultimately, such initiatives require local institutional support for community-based natural resource (rangeland in our case) management institutions where all community members (and extension staff) can discuss and implement management options in a manner that will enable collaborative learning by all involved. Ideally, such bodies will also then be able to monitor the effectiveness of different management strategies by using the lists of degradation (or sustainability) indicators deemed relevant for their study region. More conventional environmental degradation monitoring approaches (ecological survey, satellite remote sensing and economic analyses of agricultural outputs) will retain a role in evaluating the relevance of such community-based assessments of land degradation problems. These conventional approaches should not be seen as the methods that can justify the need for continued large-scale desertification funding due to the limitations in these broader-scale analyses.

In conclusion, we have outlined a methodological framework capable of use by communities to select and choose relevant rangeland degradation indicators to monitor and guide planning towards sustainable development. We stress, however, that these community-led methods must be more directly and quickly fed back into the formal planning process and that new community-based institutions must have formal Government support, especially through reform of Extension Services. This remains a significant challenge for the UN funded IVP and the Government of Botswana's Ministry of Agriculture, where this project is based, as it will require a fundamental change in the training programmes of range ecology staff. The incorporation of such approaches into Government agricultural policy or extension services practices outside of the IVP study areas has been minimal, suggesting that much greater efforts are required to institutionalize such participatory land degradation assessment methodologies. Counter to this are powerful, often neo-Malthusian narratives of degradation and desertification, which continue to dominate policy discourse and limit the extent to which hybrid combined local and scientific knowledges have provided improved land degradation assessment in southern Africa (Stringer & Reed, in press). We argue that for such community-led approaches to be relevant, degradation indicators need to be collected at as local a level as possible and then scaled up using relatively simple and transparent aggregation processes. If achieved, this would allow information to be both summarized quickly for policy makers, and unpacked for more careful (and larger-scale) monitoring and follow-up in terms of community-scale management decisions.

Our approach has shown that local participation in indicator development can create assessment guides that enhance the accuracy and relevance of land degradation assessment. This work needs to be extended by evaluation of the impact that this improved assessment, and the collaborative learning between and within communities, can have in enabling sustainable land management that provides greater livelihood security for pastoralist communities. Equally, without valuing the inclusion of local and integrated forms of degradation assessment within national policy, the extent to which communities can be empowered and their knowledges applied over larger areas, remains limited. While the importance of degradation in hindering sustainability has been recognized in the UNCCD, as yet national level policy interventions in Botswana fail to address the land degradation issues that matter to rural people and their livelihoods. Despite research providing information on both local and scientific indicators of degradation, policies remain focused on traditionally powerful degradation narratives. The result of this is that the broader structures within which land users operate remain unchanged as the root causes of the problem are ignored. Therefore, if participatory methodologies (such as those developed in this research) are to be incorporated into policy, greater attention must be paid to these broader systems of policy-making and governance. Without this sort of reflection, the broad applicability of participatory degradation indicator development could remain elusive.

References

Abelson, J., Forest, P.G., Eyles, J., Smith, P., Martin, E. & Gauvin, F.P. (2003) Deliberations about deliberative methods: issues in the design and evaluation of public participation processes. *Social Science and Medicine,* 57, 239-251.

Adams, M., White, R., Raditloaneng, N., Aliber, M., Stracey, G., McVey, C., Kalabamu, F., McAuslan, P., Kgengwenyane, N., Sharp, C. & Egner, B (2002) *National Land Policy: Issues Report.* Republic of Botswana Ministry of Lands, Housing and Environment, Department of Lands, Natural Resource Services (Pty) Ltd, Gaborone.

Arntzen, J. & Veenendaal, E.M. (1986) *A Profile of Environment and Development in Botswana.* National Institute of Research, Gaborone.

Batterbury, S., Forsyth, T. & Thomson, K. (1997) Environmental transformations in developing countries: hybrid research and democratic policy. *The Geographical Journal,* 163,126-132.

Bell, S. & Morse, S. (1999) *Sustainability Indicators: Measuring the Immeasurable.* Earthscan, London.

Bell, S. & Morse, S. (2001) Breaking through the Glass Ceiling: who really cares about sustainability indicators? *Local Environment,* 6, 291-309.

Bell, S. & Morse, S. (2003) *Measuring Sustainability: Learning from Doing.* Earthscan, London.

Carruthers, G. & Tinning, G. (2003) Where, and how, do monitoring and sustainability indicators fit into environmental management systems? *Australian Journal of Experimental Agriculture,* 43, 307-323.

Chambers, R. (1997) *Whose reality counts? Putting the first last.* Intermediate Technology Publications, London.

Chambers, R. (2005) *Ideas for Development.* Earthscan, London.

Chanda, R., Totolo, O., Moleele, N.M., Setshogo & M., Mosweu, S. (2003) Prospects for subsistence livelihood and environmental sustainability along the Kalahari Transect: The case of Matsheng in Botswana's Kalahari rangelands. *Journal of Arid Environments*, 54, 425-445.

Conroy, C. (2005) *Participatory Livestock Research: A guide*. ITDG Publications.

Cooke, H.J. (1985) The Kalahari today: a case of conflict over resource use. *The Geographical Journal*, 151, 75-85.

Cooke, B. & Kothari, U. (2001) The case for participation as tyranny. In Cooke, B. & Kothari, U. (eds) *Participation: The New Tyranny?* Zed Books, London, pp. 1-15.

Darkoh, M.B.K. (1999) Desertification in Botswana. In Arnalds, O. & Archer, S. (eds) *Case studies of Rangeland Desertification*. Agricultural Research Institute, Rekjavik, pp. 61-74.

Dougill, A.J., Thomas, D.S.G. & Heathwaite, A.L. (1999) Environmental change in the Kalahari: Integrated land degradation studies for nonequilibrium dryland environments. *Annals of the Association of American Geographers*, 89, 420-442.

Dougill, A.J. & Reed, M.S. (2005) Participatory Indicator Development for Sustainable Natural Resource Management: Kalahari, Botswana. In Holland, J.D. and Campbell, J. (eds) *Methods in Development Research: Combining Qualitative and Quantitative Approaches*. ITDG Publications, London, pp.163-176.

Dougill, A.J., Fraser, E.D.G., Holden, J., Hubacek, K., Prell, C.S., Reed, M.S., Stagl, S. & Stringer, L.C. (in press) Learning from doing participatory rural research: Lessons from the Peak District National Park. *Journal of Agricultural Economics*.

Field, D.I. (1978) *A Handbook of Basic Ecology for Range Management in Botswana*. Ministry of Agriculture, Government of Botswana, Gaborone.

Folke, C., Carpenter, S., Elmqvist, T., Gunderson, L., Holling, C.S. & Walker, B.H. (2002) Resilience and sustainable development: Building adaptive capacity in a world of transformations. *Ambio*, 31, 437-440.

Fraser, E.D.G., Dougill, A.J., Mabee, W., Reed, M.S. & McAlpine, P. (2006) Bottom up and top down: Analysis of participatory processes for sustainability indicator identification as a pathway to community empowerment and sustainable environmental management. *Journal of Environmental Management*, 78, 114-127.

Freebairn, D.M. & King, C.A. (2003) Reflections on collectively working toward sustainability: indicators for indicators! *Australian Journal of Experimental Agriculture*, 43, 223-238.

Heffernan, C., Nielsen, L. & Misturelli, F. (2004) *Restocking Pastoralists: A manual of best practice and decision support tools*. ITDG Publications, London.

Hilhorst, T. & Muchena, F. (2000) *Nutrients on the move: Soil fertility dynamics in African farming systems*. IIED, London.

Innes, J.E. & Booher, D.E. (1999) Indicators for sustainable communities: a strategy building on complexity theory and distributed intelligence. *Working Paper 99-04, Institute of Urban and Regional Development.* University of California, Berkeley.

Kiker, C.F., Milon, J.W. & Hodges, A.W. (2001) Adaptive learning for science-based policy: the Everglades restoration. *Ecological Economics*, 37, 403-416.

King, C., Gunton, J., Freebairn, D., Coutts, J., Webb, I. (2000) The sustainability indicator industry: where to from here? A focus group study to explore the potential of farmer participation in the development of indicators. *Australian Journal of Experimental Agriculture,* 40, 631-642.

Masilo, B. Lesolame, B. Gabaitse, H.M., Segonetso, M. & Sekoto, M. (1999) *Botswana national report on the implementation of the United Nations Convention to Combat Desertification Report.* <http://www.unccd.int/cop/reports/africa/national/1999/botswana-eng.pdf>

Moleele, N.M., Ringrose, S., Matheson, W. & Vanderpost, C. (2002) More woody plants? The status of bush encroachment in Botswana's grazing areas. *Journal of Environmental Management,* 64, 3-11.

Moleele, N.M. & Mainah, J. (2003) Resource use conflicts: the future of the Kalahari ecosystem. *Journal of Arid Environments,* 54, 405-423.

Morse, S. & Fraser, E.D.G. (2005) Making 'dirty' nations look clean? The nation state and the problem of selecting and weighting indices as tools for measuring progress towards sustainability. *Geoforum*, 36, 625-640.

Nygren, A. (1999) Local knowledge in the environment-development - Discourse from dichotomies to situated knowledges. *Critique of Anthropology*, 19, 267-288.

Oldeman, L.R., Hakkeling, R.T.A. & Sombroek, W.G. (1990) *World Map of the Status of Human-induced Soil Degradation: An Explanatory Note.* 2nd Edition, ISRIC & UNEP, Wageningen & Nairobi.

Perkins, J.S. (1996) Botswana: fencing out the equity issue. Cattleposts and cattle ranching in the Kalahari Desert. *Journal of Arid Environments,* 33, 503–517.

Perkins, J.S. & Thomas, D.S.G. (1993) Spreading deserts or spatially confined environmental impacts - land degradation and cattle ranching in the Kalahari desert of Botswana. *Land Degradation and Rehabilitation*, 4, 179-194.

Perrings, C. & Stern, D.L. (2000) Modelling loss of resilience in agro ecosystems: Rangelands in Botswana. *Environmental and Resource Economics,* 15, 243-256.

Pound, B., Snapp, S., McDougall, C. & Braun, A. (2003) *Managing natural resources for sustainable livelihoods: Uniting Science and Participation.* Earthscan, London.

Pretty, J.N. (1995) Participatory learning for sustainable agriculture. *World Development*, 23, 1247-1263.

Reed, M.S. & Dougill, A.J. (2002) Participatory selection process for indicators of rangeland condition in the Kalahari. *The Geographical Journal*, 168, 224-234.

Reed, M.S. (2005) *Participatory Rangeland Monitoring and Management in the Kalahari, Botswana.* University of Leeds unpublished PhD Thesis.

Republic of Botswana (1997) *Vision 2016: A Framework for a Long Term Vision for Botswana.* Government Printer, Gaborone.

Republic of Botswana (2004) *Botswana National Report on the Implementation of the United Nations Convention to Combat Desertification.* Available from - http://www.unccd.int/cop/reports/africa/national/2004/botswana-eng.pdf.

Reij, C. & Waters-Bayer, A. (2001) *Farmer Innovation in Africa: A source of inspiration for agricultural development.* Earthscan, London.

Ringrose, S., Musisi-Nkambwe, S., Coleman, T., Nellis, D. & Bussing, C. (1999) Use of Landsat Thematic Mapper data to assess seasonal rangeland changes in the southeast Kalahari, Botswana. *Journal of Environmental Management,* 23, 125-138.

Scoones, I. (1995) *Living with Uncertainty: New Directions in Pastoral Development in Africa.* Intermediate Technology Publications, London.

Scoones, I. (1998) *Sustainable Rural Livelihoods: A Framework for Analysis.* Vol. 72. Institute of Development Studies, Brighton.

Scoones, I. & Wolmer, W. (2003) Introduction: Livelihoods in crisis: Challenges for rural development in southern Africa. *IDS Bulletin-Institute of Development Studies,* 34, 1-14.

Stringer, L.C. & Reed, M.S. (in press) Land degradation assessment in Southern Africa: integrating local and scientific knowledge bases. To be submitted to *Land Degradation & Development.*

Sporton, D. & Thomas, D.S.G. (2002) *Sustainable Livelihoods in Kalahari Environments.* Oxford University Press, Oxford.

Stocking, M.A. & Murnaghan, N. (2001) *Handbook for the Field Assessment of Land Degradation.* Earthscan, London.

Taylor, M. (2003) Trajectories in Community Based Natural Resource Management in southern Africa. *Proceedings of the Arid Climate Adaptation and Cultural Innovation in Africa Conference.* University of Cologne, 1-3 October.

Thomas, D.S.G. & Shaw, P.A. (1991) *The Kalahari Environment.* Cambridge University Press, Cambridge.

Thomas, D.S.G., Sporton, D. & Perkins, J. (2000) The environmental impact of livestock ranches in the Kalahari, Botswana: Natural resource use, ecological change and human response in a dynamic dryland system. *Land Degradation & Development,* 11, 327-341.

Thomas, D.S.G., & Twyman, C. (2004) Good or bad rangeland? Hybrid knowledge, science and local understandings of vegetation dynamics in the Kalahari. *Land Degradation & Development,* 15, 215-231.

Toulmin, C. & Quan, J. (2000) *Evolving land rights, policy and tenure in Africa.* DFID/IIED/NRI Publications, London.

Twyman, C. (2000) Participatory Conservation? Community-based natural resource management in Botswana. *The Geographical Journal,* 166, 323-335.

Twyman, C., Dougill, A.J., Sporton, D. & Thomas, D.S.G. (2002) Community fencing in open rangelands: a case study of community self-empowerment in Eastern Namibia. *Review of African Political Economy,* 28, 9-26.

van Oudtshoorn, F. (1999) *Guide to Grasses of Southern Africa*. Briza Publications, Pretoria.

van Rooyen, A.F. (1998) Combating desertification in the southern Kalahari: connecting science with community action in South Africa. *Journal of Arid Environments,* 39, 285-297.

Williams, G. (2004) Evaluating participatory development: tyranny, power and (re)politicisation. *Third World Quarterly*, 25, 557-578.

Chapter 4

Sustainability Indicators and Forest Wealth in the Developing World

Giles Atkinson

Introduction

Efforts to improve the treatment of forest resources in green accounts offer a number of policy-useful benefits. Firstly, an accounting approach provides a consistent and coherent framework for analysing detailed and diverse data describing the net welfare cost when forests, essentially multiple-use resources, are being depleted. Secondly, given one particular focus of these accounts on the better measurement of income and wealth, they are ideally suited to measuring those losses in wealth that occur when, for example, land-use is switched from forest to other uses. In this way, the depletion of forests in the developing world (and elsewhere) is inextricably linked to current concerns about the measurement of sustainable development. Pezzey (1989) offers a widely cited definition that a development path is sustainable if welfare per capita does not decline along that path. Achieving sustainability, in turn, has been equated with propositions regarding how an economy should manage its wealth over time. For example, key propositions in this respect include that of *weak sustainability*, which emphasizes changes in the real value of wealth in the aggregate and *strong sustainability,* which (typically) also emphasizes the conservation of critical natural capital (for which there are essentially no substitutes).

In this chapter, empirical efforts to account for tropical forest resources are linked to the on-going discussion of green accounting and sustainable development and, in particular, current proposals to measure sustainability with reference to savings rules based either on assessing (net) changes in total wealth or changes in per capita wealth. In so doing, the chapter provides illustrations from case studies in Peru and India. It then turns to the concerns of those who argue that tropical forests are critical resources. For example, a number of contributions such as Ekins *et al.* (2003) have sought to construct indicators of changes in critical natural capital: that is, where forest services and climate functions are maintained by holding relevant stocks and liabilities at target physical levels. Lastly, the chapter offers some concluding remarks and comments on the feasibility of implementing such accounting at the national, as well as local, levels.

Concepts of green national accounting

While the latter parts of this chapter are concerned with the estimation of an 'adjusted' account for forest wealth, it is important to place this empirical work in the relevant theoretical context. The literature on green national accounts arises from a concern that economic indicators, such as Gross National Product (*GNP*), do not reflect the depletion and degradation of the environment and so may lead to incorrect development decisions, in much the same way that cost-benefit analyses, that do not include the values people place on the environment, may yield poor investment decisions. This literature builds on important contributions by Weitzman (1976), Hartwick (1990) and Mäler (1991). The framework in most contributions is 'extended Hicksian' as the focus typically is on accounting for the value of changes in total wealth in national income. This work has focused on a diverse range of candidate adjustments to conventional measures of national income (for example, Atkinson *et al.*, 1997). Broadly speaking, this has included guidelines for accounting for natural assets used in production and environmental liabilities that negatively affect wellbeing. An expression for an adjusted or green (net) national income aggregate, which allows for the breadth of these contributions, is:

green Net National Product = *Consumption + net change in total assets*
= *Consumption + genuine saving*

Hence, green Net National Product (*gNNP*) is equivalent to the (dollar) value of consumption plus the sum of net changes in *all* assets, each valued at its shadow price.[1] Alternatively, this can be written as consumption plus adjusted net or genuine saving. This expression is simply an extension of conventional *NNP* which is measured, in existing national accounts, as consumption plus net saving. The difference is that 'net saving' in the conventional accounts is measured rather narrowly as gross saving[2] minus the depreciation of produced capital (for example, machines and infrastructure). The greener measure of national income, *gNNP*, reflects net changes in a broader range of stocks that comprises the wealth of a given country. For example, it might reflect the fact that development in part rests on the liquidation of a sub-soil asset (such as copper), the clearing of land which was previously standing forest, or by degrading an environmental resource such as a wetland. In principle, the measure of genuine saving should reflect all of these changes in (net) wealth.

In fact, it is this measure of genuine saving that provides important signals to policy-makers about whether development, in a given country, is sustainable or not. The reason for this is the following. Broadly speaking, sustainability is inherently about future (development) prospects and gaining some indication of these prospects now is likely to hinge on an assessment of how much (net) wealth is passed on to future generations (as this, in large part, will determine how much wellbeing future

---

1   A shadow price refers to the social value of a unit of a good or bad received.

2   Defined as: (i) investment plus exports minus imports or (ii) Gross National Product minus consumption.

generations are able to enjoy). More specifically, the contribution of some of those exploring the theory of green accounting has been to develop rather more precise propositions about exactly what information measuring genuine saving rates provides about prospects for sustaining development and the future path of wellbeing across generations. For example, the change in net wealth is zero if genuine saving is zero (Dasgupta & Mäler, 2000). Given an interpretation of sustainability, that the change in the value of *total* wealth should not be negative in the aggregate, this suggests that sustainability could be secured by simply avoiding *negative* genuine saving. Indeed, the key finding in this literature is that a point measure of negative genuine saving means that a development path is unsustainable (Hamilton & Clemens, 1999).[3] That is, negative genuine saving implies that the level of wellbeing over some interval of time in the future must be less than current wellbeing.

What about positive genuine saving, where development is sustainable if the rate of genuine saving is above zero? Unfortunately, the answer to this important question is less straightforward. However, if genuine saving is *persistently* greater, then it can be asserted that not only will more wealth be passed onto the future, but development in certain circumstances is sustained in the sense of wellbeing also growing over time (Hamilton & Hartwick, 2004; Hamilton & Withagen, 2005).[4]

The key conclusion, then, is that (persistent) *negative* genuine savings is a sure sign of unsustainability, in terms of declining aggregate wealth. This is consistent with more popular notions of 'not eating into one's capital' or 'not selling the family silver'. Persistent *positive* genuine savings is fairly indicative of sustainability, although the conclusion in this respect is less certain than for negative genuine savings.

Pearce & Atkinson (1993) provided one of the earliest suggestions for a practical indicator, which Hamilton (1994) later termed 'genuine' saving, based on the notion that negative net saving should be avoided. Estimated rates of genuine saving for a broad range of countries are now published annually by The World Bank (for example, World Bank, 2003). These data make it clear that *persistently* negative genuine saving rates characterize a number of countries at various periods over the past three decades.

An important contribution is offered by Hamilton (2003) in response to the question as to how sustainability should be measured when population is growing. That is, genuine saving measures only the change in total wealth whereas, in much of the developing world, the reality is that population is growing at relatively rapid rates. This means that total wealth must be shared amongst even more people. In

---

3   The finding that negative genuine saving is unsustainable holds for (characterisations of) non-optimal development paths (Dasgupta & Mäler, 2000).

4   The exact circumstances under which this is the case are important to note, but rather convoluted. Positive genuine saving results in development being sustained so long as the rate of change in genuine saving is no greater than the interest rate. That is, for example, an outcome which can be achieved by a policy rule of constant (positive) net saving.

such circumstances, the net change in total wealth per capita is a better measure of sustainability. This can be written as follows:

Change in wealth per capita = Genuine saving per capita – (wealth per capita × population growth rate)

Ferreira *et al.* (2003) refer to the latter component (right-hand side) of the above expression as a 'wealth-dilution' term. Put another way, it represents the sharing of total wealth with the extra people implied by a country's growth in population. Clearly, for a population growth rate that is strongly positive then the change in wealth per capita could provide a very different signal to policy-makers about sustainability prospects than the 'traditional' genuine savings rate. The case studies discussed later in this chapter make use of both of these indicators.

Forestry and green national accounting

A large number of empirical studies have focused on accounting for the net accumulation of timber that arises when forest is cleared or harvested (for a review, see Vincent & Hartwick, 1997). These resources grow, can be harvested and are used commercially in production. Indeed, the basic model underlying many of these calculations views the exploitation of (primary) forest as akin to a 'timber mine' where 'reserves' can be augmented via natural growth (Nordhaus & Kokkelenberg, 1999). A sophisticated treatment of this problem is offered by Vincent (1999a), which takes account of the age class of timber on a unit of land as well as the volume of resource harvested. Specifically, it is proposed that the harvest of mature trees and the growing stock of immature trees should be valued differentially. Hassan (2000) provides an empirical application of this approach to calculate the timber value of forest wealth in South Africa. That study additionally valued net changes in the stock of carbon embodied in the forests. A number of other studies have attempted to account for the value of net carbon accumulation or sequestration, with Anielski (1992) for Canada providing one of the first (physical) accounts of this type. Depending on the shadow price of a unit of carbon used, Nordhaus & Kokkelenberg (1999) speculate that carbon stored in trees has a social value 'comparable' in terms of its empirical importance to commercial values (such as timber).

A number of studies have constructed accounts that encompass a wider notion of land value across a range of developed and developing countries. Thus, forestry accounts exist for non-timber forest products (NTFP) (for example, Hultkrantz, 1992), environmental services such as watershed services and soil conservation functions (for example, Hassan, 2000), and fuelwood (for example, Peskin, 1989). Fewer studies have estimated the value of biodiversity, although Hultkrantz (1992) proposes an estimate for Sweden, based on the opportunity costs of conserving land. A particularly novel treatment is reported by Vincent *et al.* (1993) for Malaysia, which seeks to account for the value of species extinctions. More recently, Haripriya (2000) accounted for the pharmaceutical benefits of forests in India based on an estimate of option value. There have been fewer attempts to account comprehensively for the value of tropical forests, although see Torres (2000) and Atkinson *et al.* (2004). The latter of these studies concludes that, given current knowledge about local and global willingness to pay for the benefits of standing forest, a comprehensive measure of net accumulation in the forest sector is dominated by changes in net timber and carbon accumulation rather than the (net) loss of other values. This suggests that, from an empirical perspective, there is a stronger rationale for focusing forest accounting efforts on timber and carbon. This is the approach taken, for example, in Atkinson & Gundimeda (2004).

Case studies

Deforestation in Peru

The previous section introduced the idea that for many forest resources, such as tropical forests, the valuation of depletion raises an interesting challenge. The issue is essentially one of land use, with standing forest being one use among many for a particular land area. This suggests, as in Hartwick (1993), that the correct way to value deforestation is to measure the change in land value (which should represent the present value of the net returns under the chosen land use). For example, Vincent (1999b) and Atkinson *et al.* (2004) show that this term reflects the difference between the present value of the economic activity that displaces standing forest on a unit of land and the present value of a range of forest services that are lost in perpetuity when forest is permanently cleared. If deforestation was optimal then we would expect these two terms to be equivalent.[5] However, in a world of policy distortions and market imperfections, there are good reasons to argue that deforestation is non-optimal. This could lead to *excess* deforestation where 'excess' can be interpreted as deforestation yielding a decline in the *social* value of the land. Put another way, where distortions prevail, the value of the activity on the alternative (non-forest) land use could well be less than the value of the standing forest it displaces (because of forest-related externalities).

A recent paper by Atkinson *et al.* (2004) has provided an empirical application of this notion to deforestation in the Peruvian Amazon. While this study focuses on the better measurement of income and wealth in a green national accounting framework, it is also suited to evaluating whether the switch of land-use from forest to agriculture is actually wealth-increasing (or 'sustainable'). While Atkinson *et al.* (2004) investigate how Peru might green its national accounts for current 'excess' deforestation, arising from slash-and-burn farming, this is in essence also a cost-benefit exercise. Focusing on a broad range of costs and benefits of deforestation, the net cost of 'excess' deforestation is defined as the sum of the (present) values of sustainable timber harvest and the value of the carbon sequestered by that natural growth and local and global willingness to pay (WTP) for conservation, minus

---

5   When land clearance is costly there is some additional term reflecting investment in land-use change that must be taken account of.

agricultural returns on deforested land. Using a range of market and non-market data, reflecting these changes, the authors' results are summarized in Table 4.1. These data assume that slash-and-burn farming is replaced by pasture, a social discount rate[6] of 5 per cent and a 20 year period for the calculation of present values. This indicates that excess deforestation is $1286 per hectare (ha) in the year 1995. Regarding the components of excess deforestation, it is evident that the sum of (present values of) local and global WTP (where the latter is made up of non-use value), that is $1015 per ha, is only a little in excess of the (present) value of agricultural returns. In other words, the estimated value of excess deforestation in the table is sensitive to the estimate of the timber and carbon value of the (foregone) sustainable harvest in that it is these values that 'tip' the balance such that the switch from forest to slash-and-burn agriculture can be characterized as, other things being equal, wealth-decreasing.

Table 4.1   Value of excess deforestation in Peru in 1995

	Components of Excess Deforestation (US$ current)
Local willingness to pay for conservation	$868
+ Global willingness to pay for conservation	$147
+ Value of sustainable timber harvest	$858
+ Value of carbon stored in sustainable timber harvest	$310
− Agricultural returns	$897
= Value of excess deforestation	$1286

Notes: *Data refer to present values (PV); assumed social discount rate equals 5%; lifetime for PV calculation is 20 years*

Regarding the bigger picture, the authors show that the effect of accounting for (net) changes in wealth that arise when forest land is cleared for slash-and-burn farming is to reduce the estimated genuine savings rate for Peru. Despite this, however, this adjusted saving rate remains strongly positive in the study year. Of course, the genuine saving calculation is an estimate of *total* saving effort, whereas the Peruvian population is growing at a rate of 1.7 per cent per year (World Bank,

---

6   Discounting refers to the process of assigning a lower weight to a unit of benefit or cost in the future than to that unit now. One interpretation of the social discount rate is that it should reflect society's preferences for the trade-off between present and future consumption. While some form of discounting is standard economic practice, rightly or wrongly, it remains controversial in, for example, the context of environmental policy (for a review of these issues, see Pearce *et al.*, 2005).

2003). Performing the savings analysis in per capita terms requires, first, calculating genuine saving per capita, roughly $58 (for a population of 25.6 million). Then a 'wealth-diluting' term, representing the sharing of total wealth with this extra 1.7 per cent of the population in 1995, must be subtracted. This can be calculated to be about $131 in 1999. Atkinson *et al.* (2004) argue that this indicates that genuine saving per person in Peru is probably not robust, at $58, and that the change in wealth per capita is quite likely to be negative.

India's forest wealth

Atkinson & Gundimeda (2004) have sought to account for India's forest wealth and, in so doing, to illustrate the importance of including population growth in this analysis. Changes in forest land and volume in India derive from a number of sources, such as logging (both legal and illegal) and agriculture (shifting cultivation and grazing), as well as losses arising from forest fires and exposure to disease and pathogens. Forest resources are also augmented by such means as natural growth and managed regeneration. Atkinson & Gundimeda's (2004) study quantifies all of these changes in terms of the volume and value of the timber and carbon that is lost or gained. Clearly, timber is valuable in the sense of providing a commercially valuable resource. Carbon is valuable in the sense of mitigating or contributing to climate change (in the case of storing/sequestering carbon and releasing carbon respectively).

With regards to net timber accumulation, the magnitude of these changes in relation to India's *GNP* is the following. Depletion arising from logging is equivalent to -2.5 per cent of *GNP*. This is offset to a large extent by the timber value of natural growth (1.8 per cent of *GNP*) and regeneration of previously cleared land (0.6 per cent of *GNP*). However, other losses of timber (due to forest fires, for example) mean that net accumulation of timber is, overall, 0.7 per cent of *GNP*. Accounting for timber resources is relatively straightforward given that there is a market price for harvested timber. Deriving estimates for net accumulation of (forest) carbon raises the additional challenge of quantifying the value of carbon. This, in itself, has generated a large literature as well as a notable degree of controversy (for a review, see Pearce, 2003). However, a widely cited estimate of the social cost of carbon is about $20 per tonne (for example, World Bank, 2003). This refers to the money value of the global (future) damage that emitting a tonne of carbon today will cause (which in turn reflects a range of commercial and non-commercial impacts). Using this 'best guess', Atkinson & Gundimeda (2004) estimate that net carbon accumulation is, overall, equivalent to 0.2 per cent of *GNP*, with its largest negative and positive components being logging (-0.5 per cent) and natural growth (0.3 per cent) respectively. On balance, net timber and carbon accumulation in India's forests is -0.9 per cent of *GNP*. This magnitude gives an indication of the additional savings effort required in order to avoid negative genuine savings as a result of activities in the forestry sector.

This measure of total asset change does not tell the whole story. Population growth in India was about 1.8 per cent over the period 1993-94. As reviewed earlier in this chapter, this gives rise to a 'wealth dilution' effect. Positive growth rates of population imply that an additional savings effort is required in order to keep the real value of per capita (net) wealth constant. A better indicator is the change in *forest* wealth per capita. In this calculation, the forest 'wealth dilution' effect is equal to 2.1 per cent of *GNP* per capita and the *total* change in forest wealth per capita is equivalent to about 3.0 per cent of *GNP* per capita. This is an empirically more significant magnitude than is the case when the wealth diluting effects of population growth are ignored. Put another way, an additional savings effort of some 3.0 per cent of per capita income is needed to sustain forest wealth in per capita terms.

Table 4.2   Change in wealth per capita in India over 1993-94

	Changes in Total Wealth (Rupees per capita)
Genuine saving per capita (G/N)	796.7
Wealth dilution (gW/N)	−2480.6
Of which:	
Produced assets	*747.6*
Sub-soil assets	*81.9*
Agricultural land	*1425.9*
Forest assets: Timber	*188.7*
Forest assets: Carbon	*36.5*
Change in wealth per capita	−1684.0

Source: Forest depletion – Atkinson & Gundimeda (2004); World Bank (1997)

Performing this analysis in per capita terms requires that we have an estimate of total wealth in India (Table 4.2). As well as accounting for (per capita) changes in forest wealth, this also takes stock of changes in produced capital (machines and physical infrastructure), sub-soil assets (minerals and energy resources) and agricultural land. The table shows that the change in total wealth per capita was negative (−1,684 Rupees). That is, the superficially robust positive rate of genuine savings is not enough to sustain development when the savings analysis is conducted in per capita terms. Table 4.2 also indicates the components of this wealth dilution term. It can be seen that the timber and carbon value of forests accounts for just below 10 per cent of this term (which is otherwise mostly determined by the value of agricultural land and produced assets).

Forests and strong sustainability

For many of those contributing to the on-going debate about sustainable development, accounting for India's forest wealth within the typical terms of reference of green national accounting falls foul of the imperative to view forests as an explicitly strong sustainability problem. That is, in the context of forests, a guiding principle should be the protection of absolute levels of ecological goods that are provided by standing forest. The rationale for this management rule is that the diminished capacity of these complex systems to provide (irreplaceable) environmental functions is likely to place highly undesirable burdens on human wellbeing, or even survivability (for example, Norton & Toman, 1997; Ekins *et al.*, 2003). Clearly, it is important to consider this perspective and its implications for the accounting approach that has, thus far, been adopted in this chapter.

On the one hand, it is overly simplistic to claim that so-called 'weaker' approaches to accounting mean that forest wealth can be liquidated almost with impunity. Studies such as Torres (2000) demonstrate that incorporating available estimates of the market and non-market value of forests can provide a powerful rationale for a significant increase in forest conservation. More ambitious studies such as Costanza *et al.* (1997) have similarly sought to demonstrate the value of conservation more generally. With regard to the case of forestry, to the extent that a proportion of deforestation occurs because of what can be broadly termed 'policy failures', then correcting these failures, such as removing distorting public subsidies to forest clearance, is a recommendation regardless of whether proponents are of a weak or a strong (sustainability) persuasion.

Conversely, while a variety of forest-related ecological phenomena (such as natural growth) underpin our summary accounts in Tables 4.1 and 4.2, it remains true that these data neither capture the idea of critical thresholds nor, more specifically, examine to what extent thresholds are being reached or perhaps even breached. If, however, India's forest wealth is a natural asset characterized by important limits on exploitation, then a genuine concern is that, if exceeded, this might lead to large-scale and irreversible ecological losses with possibly dramatic implications for negative impacts on human wellbeing. In such a case, it would be a misguidedly daring, and not to say foolhardy, decision to exploit a critical asset such that its stock is driven below its threshold or critical level. Assuming that policy-makers wish to avoid such recklessness, the key issues then are the identification of critical assets, their threshold levels and indications regarding how serious for human wellbeing a breach of a relevant threshold is likely to be. Just as pertinent is sensible guidance regarding decision-making when there is uncertainty about any (or all) of these parameters.

Even accepting the view that forests are critical natural capital, this leaves open the question of how this insight is interpreted either as a condition for sustainable development or, by implication, its inference for constructing indicators of forest wealth. A simple rule of thumb would be to say that India's forests should be left intact at the current level, in which case a casual glance at either of Tables 4.1 and 4.2 might indicate that this condition is plainly not being met (at least at the aggregate level). Of course, in reality, even an apparently simplistic approach can quickly descend into relatively complicated discussion about whether this constraint to preserve the current stock refers to the global (that is India's tropical forests as one component of global forests), national (India) or regional (India's individual states or some other geographical emphasis) level.

Numerous candidate indicators of strong sustainability exist which might be relevant for the problem of accounting for forest wealth. For example, Chambers *et al.* (2000) estimate ecological footprints which compare required forested area implied by a country's economic activity and actual forest land available to that country. Another notion is that of a critical or minimum area of forest that must be preserved intact. For example, Kramer & Mercer (1997) cite an 'expert consensus' that maintaining the integrity of the global rain forest ecosystem would require protection of at least a given proportion of remaining forest. However, in assessing the quantity of land either to be protected or the area actually protected, matters are complicated in that there are a range of sustainable forestry options between the extremes of 'fence-and-forget' conservation and liquidating the forest asset. Indeed, many of these options balance, in varying combinations, market (tangible) and non-market (intangible) values. As an example, agroforestry (mixing trees with farming) offers one means of achieving a greater balance between commercial production with carbon storage and biodiversity protection relative to 'fence and forget' or (certain) modern agricultural practices. Indeed, it has been argued by forestry experts that agroforestry not only provides ecological benefits but also protects such functions supplied by nearby protected forest areas. Moreover, these activities allow farmers to capture at least some of the benefits of forest conservation, thus helping to ensure that there are incentives for these ecological services to continue to be provided (Schroth *et al.*, 2004; Pearce *et al.*, 2002). In practice, therefore, sustainability indicators should also be linked to this wider set of policy options.

Can the notion of strong sustainability be reconciled with the accounting approach that has been drawn upon in this chapter? There are two positive responses to this question although, at present, it is only the second of these that constitutes a workable approach.

One way of capturing the strong sustainability notion of a critical amount of a resource or natural asset is by assuming that as the stock or size of the forest is reduced towards its critical level, its 'shadow price' increases dramatically. This simply reflects the fact that the resource provides extremely important services and there is now less of it providing these vital functions. Indeed, at some point, the resource might reach dangerously low levels. Thus, as the forest resource declines to this critical amount, arbitrarily large losses in welfare are associated with depletion of a marginal unit. In principle, the resulting adjustment to NNP and G would show up as a correspondingly large loss in value of the critical natural asset (that is as its stock level reaches the critical amount). If preferences for critical resources are taken into account, then the most socially desirable policy is to be strongly sustainable (that is set limits on resource depletion so as to avoid the prospect of rapidly increasing losses in welfare). In practice, however, this approach runs into questions about the sufficiency of available scientific and economic information for preferences to be relied upon to reflect the appropriate trade-offs that would underpin this willingness to pay estimate.

Another related approach, of focusing on the essential idea that a given physical amount of the forest resource must be preserved intact, does not mean that the standard green national accounting approach can be altogether discarded. To see this, an analogy can be drawn with the implications of the concept of a safe minimum standard (SMS) in such terms whereby policy-makers follow standard cost-benefit rules unless there is a compelling reason not to; for example, to conserve a critical natural asset (Farmer & Randall, 1998).[7] In terms of indicators of sustainable development, Pearce *et al.* (1996) provide an illustration of how this two-tier approach might operate in the case of a given area of forest. In this example, preserving some quantity of the forest is considered to be critical for the long-term wellbeing of humanity; rapid deterioration in forest quality occurs once a critical threshold has been breached. The effect of this preservation is to reduce the amount of forest that can be considered to be an economic resource (that is it reduces the quantity of harvest that can be carried out from the non-conserved stock). The key indicators for a forested country operating under this regime are twofold: are stocks of this critical natural asset declining and are genuine savings rates (savings net or the change in the non-conserved resource stock), or change in per capita wealth, negative? A positive answer to either of these questions would be an indication of unsustainability. This illustrates that, in general, it is not credible to think that there is a single indicator that can describe all relevant aspects of the development path. A better picture of whether countries are developing sustainably will ultimately require a judicious mix of distinct but complementary indicators.

Discussion and conclusions

Accounting for forest wealth has a number of policy-useful benefits including the provision of a framework for analysing detailed and diverse data. These accounts can be presented in terms of land area (under forest), physical volume (of forest biomass) and, finally, monetary values. All of these accounts are useful extensions of standard approaches. However, it is the final 'type' of account and its concern for the better measurement of forest income and wealth and, in turn, its link to the measurement of sustainable development, that has been the primary focus of this chapter.

This focus has given rise to a number of issues. For example, if such accounts are to extend beyond timber values, there are important challenges that need to be confronted as regards valuing multiple-uses of forests. Indeed, the situation is more complicated than this in that non-users of, for example, tropical forests might also have preferences for forest conservation. All of these values must be accounted for

---

7   However, this conservation rule can itself be overridden if its costs are 'intolerable'.

if a 'complete' picture of the social cost of deforestation is to be sought. This, in turn, is crucial for determining how much wealth, on balance, is altered when forest land is permanently cleared to make way for some other land-use such as farming. In this chapter, these efforts have been placed within the broader conceptual debate about evaluating prospects for sustaining development as well as providing two case studies of forest accounts for Peru and India.

The accounting concepts and practices that have been discussed in this chapter are of far more than just academic interest. Many governments around the world are currently implementing green accounting frameworks as one response to the need to monitor progress towards (or otherwise) sustainable development. A recent review by the United Nations (2003) notes that this includes Botswana, Mexico, the Philippines and Namibia, with a further number of countries, such as South Africa, making more occasional 'official' forays into this accounting terrain. Given growing experience of these accounts and their usefulness in providing a coherent and consistent framework for organising disparate environmental and resource data, more countries can be expected to begin their own programmes in the future.

However, a notable feature of much of this work is that its focus has not primarily been on monetising changes in natural wealth. That is, apart from (commercial) resources for which market prices are available, it is physical accounts that have been the focus of these green accounting activities. There are notable exceptions, such as the work of The World Bank, discussed earlier in this chapter. Nevertheless, in the latest version of UNSTAT's[8] Satellite Environmental and Economic Accounting (SEEA) (United Nations, 2003), land accounting is largely conceived in physical terms where 'land' covers a diverse range of categories including agricultural land, forest or wooded land and other land (which itself includes, for example, types of grassland). This accounting framework includes land cover and land use by area and an array of matrices describing, for instance, land cover according to use and land use by economic activity. These accounts describe a 'snap-shot' of current land-use as well as changes in the composition of land-use between periods. This framework constitutes a very useful means of organizing heterogeneous data about land in a manner that is amenable to policy analysis. However, constructing green accounts is not a costless activity. Care must be taken in scrutinizing properly whether this policy usefulness will be enjoyed in practice.

In common with the theme of this chapter, the SEEA (United Nations, 2003) discussion of land makes explicit reference to the multiple goods and services provided by this asset (in different uses). However, there is less explicit guidance within this framework with regards to how to arrive at a monetary counterpart to physical land accounts. Thus, while the SEEA devotes an entire chapter to non-market valuation, the context for that discussion is largely the consideration of valuation methods and their application to the impacts of air and water pollution rather than to valuing non-produced services provided by forest land.

---

8   UNSTAT is the United Nations Statistical Office.

There are many reasons that might explain, more generally, the lack of emphasis on accounting in monetary terms. Some of these reasons are technical and based on the problems of valuing the quantity and quality of tropical forest wealth for the *whole* nation (rather than for a particular 'marginal' project for which there are now an increasing number of studies). There remains an enormous challenge also in understanding the social value of biodiversity conservation, which is clearly a key function of tropical forests. It is also important to note that there is more than a suspicion that tropical forests provide unique and important functions which cannot be replaced once thresholds (with regards to forest extent and so on) have been breached. These concerns have traditionally been articulated, in rather abstract terms, under the heading of 'strong sustainability'. There is, clearly, a need for greater effort to link that debate with more specific efforts to understand the workings of forest ecosystems.

What about the prospects for implementing green accounts at the local level? Green accounts were primarily conceived as adjuncts to *national* accounts rather than as tools for use at the local or regional level. It may be that more simple indicators are of use at the local level. This has certainly been the experience in Europe, particularly when the goal is to engage the wider population using sustainability indicators. However, an interesting project in India, Green Accounting for Indian States & Union Territories Project (GAISP), has sought to construct regional accounts in monetary terms of India's wealth. This includes a forest land account for 26 regions of the country. While this disaggregated and regional focus is rare, it is to be welcomed. Lastly, it is worth noting that there is also a global element to interest in green accounting. Many of the values provided by forests in the developing world are actually enjoyed by citizens in other (possibly richer) countries. Relaying this message in accounting terms reinforces the call for conservation efforts that can be captured by those making land-use decisions in developing countries.

References

Anielski, M. (1992) *Accounting for Carbon Fixation by Alberta's Forests and Peatlands*. Paper presented at the Second Meeting of the International Society of Ecological Economists, Stockholm, August 3-6, 1992.

Atkinson, G. & Gundimeda, H. (2004) *Accounting for India's Forest Wealth*. Madras School of Economics, mimeo.

Atkinson, G., Hamilton, K. & Nalvarte, W. (2004) *Sustainability, Green National Accounting and Deforestation*. London School of Economics and Political Science, mimeo.

Atkinson, G., Dubourg, W.R., Hamilton, K., Munasinghe, M., Pearce, D.W. & Young, C.E.F. (1997) *Measuring Sustainable Development: Macroeconomics and Environment*. Edward Elgar, Cheltenham.

Costanza, R., d'Arge, R., de Groot, R., Farber, S., Grasso, M., Hannon, B., Limburg, S., Naeem, S., O'Neill, R., Paruelo, J., Raskin, R., Sutton, P. & van den Belt, M.

(1997) The value of the world's ecosystems services and natural capital. *Nature*, 387, 253-260.

Chambers, N., Simmons, C. & Wackemagel, M. (2000) *Sharing Nature's Interest*. Earthscan Publications Ltd, London.

Dasgupta, P. & Mäler, K.-G. (2000) Net national product, wealth and social well-being. *Environment and Development Economics*, 5, 69-93.

Ekins, P., Folke, C., Groot, R., de Simon, S., Deutsch, L., van der Perk, J., Chiesura, A., Vliet, A., van, Skanberg, K., Douguet, J.M. & O'Connor, M. (2003) Identifying critical natural capital. *Ecological Economics*, 44, 159-292.

Farmer, M.C. & Randall, A. (1998) The rationality of a safe minimum standard. *Land Economics*, 74, 287-302.

Ferreira, S., Hamilton, K. & Vincent, J.R. (2003) *Comprehensive Wealth and Future Consumption*. The World Bank, mimeo.

Hamilton, K. (1994) Green adjustments to GDP. *Resources Policy*, 20, 155-168.

Hamilton, K. (2003) Sustaining economic welfare: Estimating changes in total and per capita wealth. *Environment, Development and Sustainability*, 5, 419-436.

Hamilton, K. & Clemens, M. (1999) Genuine savings rates in developing countries. *World Bank Economic Review*, 13, 333-356.

Hamilton, K. & Hartwick, J.M. (2004) Investing exhaustible resource rents and the path of consumption. *Canadian Journal of Economics*, 38, 615-621.

Hamilton, K. & Withagen, C. (2005) *Savings, Welfare and Rules for Sustainability*. Environment Department, World Bank, Washington, D.C.

Haripriya, G.S. (2000) Integrating forest resources into the system of National Accounts in Maharashtra. *Environment and Development Economics*, 5, 143-156.

Hartwick, J.M. (1990) Natural resources, National accounting and economic depreciation. *Journal of Public Economics*, 43, 291-304.

Hartwick, J.M. (1993) Forestry Economics, Deforestation and National Accounting. In Lutz, E. (ed.) *Toward Improved Accounting for the Environment*. World Bank, Washington D.C. pp. 289-314.

Hassan, R.M. (2000) Improved measure of the contribution of cultivated forests to national income and wealth in South Africa. *Environment and Development Economics*, 5, 157-176.

Hultkrantz, L. (1992) National account of timber and forest environmental resources in Sweden. *Environmental and Resource Economics*, 2, 283-305.

Kramer, R.A. & Mercer, D.E. (1997) Valuing a global environmental good: US residents' willingness to pay to protect tropical rain forests. *Land Economics*, 73, 196-210.

Mäler, K.-G. (1991) National accounts and environmental resources. *Environmental and Resource Economics*, 1, 1-15.

Nordhaus, W.D. & Kokkelenberg, E.C. (eds) (1999) *Nature's Numbers: Expanding the National Economic Accounts to Include the Environment*. National Academy Press, Washington, D.C.

Norton, B.G. & Toman, M.A. (1997) Sustainability: Economic and ecological perspectives. *Land Economics*, 73, 663-568.

Pearce, D.W., (2003) The social cost of carbon and its policy implications. *Oxford Review of Economic Policy*, 19, 362-384.

Pearce, D.W. & Atkinson, G. (1993) Capital theory and the measurement of sustainable development: An indicator of weak sustainability. *Ecological Economics*, 8, 103-108.

Pearce, D.W., Hamilton, K. & Atkinson, G. (1996) Measuring sustainable development: Progress on indicators. *Environment and Development Economics*, 1, 85-101.

Pearce, D.W. Putz, F. & Vanclay, J.K. (2002) Is Sustainable Forestry Economically Possible? In Pearce, D.W. Pearce, C. & Palmer, C. (eds) *Valuing the Environment in Developing Countries: Case Studies*. Edward Elgar, Cheltenham, pp. 447-500.

Pearce, D.W., Atkinson, G. & Mourato, S. (2005) *Cost-Benefit Analysis and the Environment: Recent Developments*. Organisation for Economic Co-operation and Development (OECD), Paris.

Peskin, H.M. (1989) *Accounting for Natural Resource Depletion and Degradation in Developing Countries*. Environment Department Working Paper No. 13, World Bank, Washington D.C.

Pezzey, J. (1989) *Economic Analysis of Sustainable Growth and Sustainable Development*. Environment Department Working Paper No. 15, World Bank, Washington D.C.

Schroth, G., da Fonseca, G.A.B., Harvey, C.A., Gascon, C., Vasconcelos, H.L. & Izac, A.-M.N. (eds) (2004) *Agroforestry and Biodiversity Conservation in Tropical Landscapes*. Island Press, Washington, D.C.

Torres, M. (2000) The total economic value of Amazonian deforestation, 1978-1993. *Ecological Economics*, 33, 283-297.

United Nations (2003) *Integrated Environmental and Economic Accounting*. United Nations, New York.

Vincent, J.R. (1999a) Net accumulation of timber resources. *Review of Income and Wealth*, 45, 251-262.

Vincent, J.R. (1999b) A framework for forest accounting. *Forest Science*, 45, 1-10.

Vincent, J.R. & Hartwick, J.M. (1997) *Accounting for the Benefits of Forest Resources: Concepts and Experience*. FAO Forestry Department, Food and Agriculture Organisation, Rome.

Vincent, J.R.,Wan, L.F., Chang, Y.T. ,Noriha, M. & Davison, G.W.H. (1993) *Malaysian National Conservation Strategy. Volume 4: Natural Resource Accounting*. Economic Planning Unit, Prime Minister's Department, Kuala Lumpur.

Weitzman, M.L. (1976) On the welfare significance of national product in a dynamic economy. *Quarterly Journal of Economics*, 90, 156-162.

World Bank (2003) *World Development Indicators 2003*. CD-ROM, World Bank, Washington D.C.

Chapter 5

Sustainable Water Resource Management in South Africa: A Decade of Progress?

Nevil Quinn and Susan Marriott

Introduction

The transformation of South Africa into a democracy in 1994, just two years after the World Summit, created the opportunity to redefine the basis of natural resource management consistent with the principles of the Rio Declaration and Agenda 21. Shortly after coming to power, the Government of National Unity started a process of policy dialogue which resulted in a range of new statutes dealing with natural resources. Perhaps foremost among these were those dealing with water, not only because they dealt with such a regionally important scarce resource, but also because of the extent to which they reflected a radical departure from the prevailing paradigm of entrenched riparian rights and centralized water resource management. The new water law was to be based on principles of sustainability and equity, best expressed in the Department of Water Affairs and Forestry slogan 'some for all, for ever'. For leading this initiative, Professor Kader Asmal, Minister of Water Affairs and Forestry, was awarded the 2000 Stockholm Water Prize. It is nearly ten years on from the start of this process and therefore timely that we examine the extent to which the South African water law and policy environment provides a framework for achieving its stated principles of equity and sustainability in water management. It is also timely given the hosting of the World Summit on Sustainable Development by South Africa in 2002, the principal purpose of which was to reflect on progress in the ten years subsequent to the Rio Declaration.

This chapter will provide a brief overview of the water policy and law reform process in South Africa before considering the difficulties in defining and assessing sustainability in water resource management. A framework based principally on the criteria of Gleick (1998) and Dowdeswell (1998) will be presented and the current approach to water resource management in South Africa will be reviewed in light of these criteria. The focus of the review is an evaluation of firstly, the extent to which the policy and legal framework conforms to the criteria, and secondly, the extent of implementation of the mechanisms identified in law and policy. The source of information with respect to the latter has been the Department of Water Affairs and Forestry annual reports (up to 2003/4), together with information from the Department's website.

Overview of the policy and law development process

One of the first actions of the newly-elected Government of National Unity with respect to water resource management was the formal commissioning of a water policy review in May 1994, followed shortly after by the publication of a White Paper on Water Supply and Sanitation in November 1994 (de Coning & Sherwill, 2004). The transformation of South Africa into a democracy was centred on the finalization of a Constitution in 1996 which incorporated a Bill of Rights. The Bill of Rights established a far-reaching set of human rights and required that government develop legislation to safeguard these rights. What followed was a continuation of the comprehensive public debate to establish the vision that should underpin water law reform, resulting in the publication and revision of a set of key principles and objectives for a new Water Law (DWAF, 1996). These principles were integrated into a White Paper on National Water Policy in April 1997, in preparation for the formulation of legislation. In 1997 the Water Services Act (Act No 108 of 1997) was promulgated, followed by the 1998 National Water Act (Act No 36 of 1998). The new legislation removed private ownership of water and placed all water resources in public trust, with the Minister having the ultimate responsibility of 'ensuring that water is allocated equitably and used beneficially in the public interest, while promoting environmental values'.[1]

Defining sustainability in water resource management

The debate around sustainability is contentious; Mitcham (1995) has argued that some of the value of the concept lies in its 'creative ambiguity' whilst others see the 'ambiguously conceptualized' central objectives of the paradigm as a major weakness (Lele, 1991). Castro (2004: 195) has recently defined it as 'one of the most ubiquitous, contested and indispensable concepts of our time'.

The difficulty in firstly defining sustainability, and secondly in defining indicators that can be used to measure progress has meant that many view it as a 'lame' concept. Tortajada (2003: 9) for instance, has argued that 'global paradigms such as sustainable development and integrated water resources management are conceptually attractive, but their actual implementation in operational terms has much to be desired'. Similar views are expressed by Biswas (1996: 90) with respect to water resources; 'there is now too much rhetoric on the importance of sustainability all over the world, but not enough serious thinking and research on what it really means in operational terms'. The view that 'operational definitions and indicators are a prerequisite for implementing sustainability in practical terms' (Rennings & Wiggering, 1997: 25) has led to considerable effort being directed towards the characterization and measurement of sustainable development (OECD, 2001; Parris & Krates, 2003).

Within the area of water resources management some progress has been made and there are emerging frameworks that have some value in assessing progress in

---

1   Section 3(2).

the often-stated goal of achieving sustainability. Gleick (1998: 574) has proposed a working definition of sustainable water use as 'the use of water that supports the ability of human society to endure and flourish into the indefinite future without undermining the integrity of the hydrological cycle or the ecological systems that depend on it.' Further to this, Gleick (1998) has proposed a set of seven explicit criteria which provide a means of evaluating sustainability (Table 5.1).

Similarly, in her address to the Tenth World Water Congress, the then Director General of the United Nations Environment Programme, Elizabeth Dowdeswell called for a 'fair share' approach to a water policy that is needed as 'a crucial and integral part of the new agenda for sustainable development' (Dowdeswell, 1998: 14). Her vision for a new water ethic based on equity comprises seven elements (Table 5.1). This contribution is based on the premise that, within the context of water resource management, sustainability can be defined and assessed. We have, therefore, combined these sets of criteria to form a framework for evaluating progress in working towards sustainability.

Table 5.1   The eight sustainability criteria in water resource management used in this assessment, based on those defined by Gleick (1998) and Dowdeswell (1998)

Gleick (1998)	Dowdeswell (1998)	Criteria for Assessment
• A basic water requirement will be guaranteed to all humans to maintain human health	• The top priority for resources management everywhere must be the provision of drinking water and sanitation for the poor majority of people • There must be a fair share of safe water and water-based services for the poor majority • There must be a fair share for women and children since the costs of too little or unsafe water are borne disproportionately by women and children who spend long hours collecting water, get less for drinking and personal hygiene, and suffer most from poor water quality and water related diseases	1. Basic water rights

Gleick (1998)	Dowdeswell (1998)	Criteria for Assessment
• A basic water requirement will be guaranteed to restore and maintain the health of ecosystems	• There must be a fair share for the environment since human self-interest demands that aquatic species, habitats and ecosystems also get their fair share of water	2. Ecosystem water rights
• Water quality will be maintained to meet certain minimum standards. These standards will vary depending on location and how the water is to be used		3. Water quality management
• Data on water resources availability, use and quality will be collected and made accessible to all parties		4. Access to information
• Institutional mechanisms will be set up to prevent and resolve conflicts over water •	There must be a fair share among competing users	5. Institutional structures for preventing and resolving conflicts
• Water planning and decision-making will be democratic, ensuring representation of all affected parties and fostering direct participation of affected interests		6. Participative decision-making
	• There must be a fair share among riparian countries	7. Sharing international waters
• Human action will not impair the long-term renewability of freshwater stocks and flows	• There must be a fair share for future generations	8. Ensuring renewability

Review of progress towards sustainability

Basic water rights

Policy and legal framework

Gleick (1999) has argued strongly that access to a basic water allocation is a fundamental human right. This was recognized explicitly at one of the first international water conferences (Mar del Plata in 1977) and is reiterated in Chapter 18 of Agenda 21; 'all peoples, whatever their stage of development and their social and economic conditions, have the right to have access to drinking water in quantities and of a quality equal to their basic needs'. Provision of a basic water requirement is therefore seen as a cornerstone of sustainable water management. Gleick (1998, 1999) suggests a basic water requirement of 50 litres per person per day.

South Africa is one of the few nations that explicitly recognize a human right to water. Section 27(1)(b) of the Bill of Rights in the 1994 Constitution of South Africa states that 'everyone has the right to have access to sufficient food and water'. This constitutional right is given effect in the National Water Act (Act No 36 of 1998) (hereafter referred to as the NWA) which defines the concept of the 'Reserve' to include the quantity and quality of water required to satisfy basic human needs – called the 'basic needs' Reserve. This volume of water must be determined on a catchment basis and enjoys priority of use. In terms of the Water Services Act (Act No 108 of 1997), all water service institutions must take reasonable measures to realize the right of access to a basic water supply, which must be outlined in a water services plan. The National Water Act sets a clear intention for the future in the statement of purpose; resources must be managed in such a way as to:

1. Meet basic human needs of present and future generations
2. Promote equitable access to water
3. Redress the consequences of past racial and gender discrimination
4. Promote the efficient, sustainable and beneficial use of water in the public interest
5. Facilitate social and economic development
6. Provide for growing demand for water use.[2]

The implementation of a Constitutional right to water and the emphasis on equity in access and supply would suggest that, from the perspective of an enabling legislative framework, the first criterion articulated by Gleick (1998) and Dowdeswell (1998) is largely met.

---

2   Section 2 (a to f).

Implementation

Since 1994, provision of water and sanitation has been one of the top priorities for the government. At the transition to democracy, 14 million citizens did not have access to clean, safe water. The early Reconstruction and Development Programme aimed to provide all households with a safe water supply of 20 litres to 30 litres per capita per day, and subsequent policy initiatives set higher targets, with the ultimate goal of providing safe drinking water to all South Africans by 2008. This rate of delivery was given international recognition when the Community Water Supply and Sanitation Programme was selected as the best programme at the 'Globe Awards' for Sustainable Development in Water (DWAF, 2002). After a decade of effort, in November 2004 the 10 millionth household to be served with water was marked by a celebration (Sonjica, 2004).

Current Government policy recognizes a basic water right of 25 litres per person per day which is to be provided free of charge to poor households (Palmer Development Group, 2001). This is in recognition of the premise that economic principles should only be applied to water services once access to basic need has been guaranteed (Muller, 2004). Although the current policy falls below Gleick's (1998) recommendation of 50 litres per person per day, the effort and achievement of the Department of Water Affairs and Forestry in striving towards and meeting these targets is commendable. As of the end of June 2005, fractionally short of 70 per cent of South Africa's population had been served with clean drinking water (DWAF, 2005).

Ecosystem water rights

Policy and legal framework

Protecting ecosystems and ensuring their integrity through sustainable water resource management was recognized as one of seven key challenges in the Ministerial Declaration of The Hague on Water Security in the twenty-first century, and Chapter 18 of Agenda 21 identifies protection of aquatic ecosystems as an important programme area. Gleick (1998) and Dowdeswell (1998) take this further by arguing that a volume of water to meet the need of aquatic ecosystems must be guaranteed.

Protection of aquatic and associated ecosystems and their biological diversity is an explicit purpose of the NWA, as is reducing and preventing pollution and degradation of water resources.[3] Several methods for achieving this will be noted in subsequent sections, while the principal mechanism for ensuring water for the environment is the ecological Reserve. The concept of the Reserve referred to above includes not only the basic human needs element but also a component of sufficient quantity and quality 'to protect aquatic ecosystems in order to secure ecologically sustainable development'. As mentioned above, the Reserve enjoys priority of use and before any water can be allocated for industry, agriculture or any other use, the Reserve for a particular resource must be determined and gazetted. In this context

---

3   Section 2(g and h).

'resource' is interpreted broadly and includes rivers, groundwater, wetlands and lakes and would be assessed on a quaternary catchment basis. This volume is then reserved and the balance of the water resource is then available for allocation through a licensing system. The Reserve is determined according to the classification[4] of the water resource and, if this has not occurred, the Minister is permitted to make a preliminary determination of the Reserve which would then be superseded by a subsequent full determination.[5]

Thus, within the South African water law framework there is the clear commitment and mechanism to guarantee a basic water allocation for the environment (Criterion 2). Indeed, South Africa is one of the few countries in the world to make legal provision for a water allocation to the environment.

Implementation

Since the early 1990s aquatic scientists in South Africa had been developing techniques for estimating the freshwater requirements of rivers and estuaries (Adams & Bate, 1994; King & Tharme, 1994). The water law reform process provided further impetus to this research endeavour resulting in a range of innovative approaches to determining ecological flows for rivers (Tharme & King, 1998) and estuaries (Quinn, 1998; Morant & Quinn, 1999). By 1999 the first departmental manual documenting techniques for estimating the reserve for rivers, wetlands, estuaries and groundwater was published (DWAF, 1999). Four levels of Reserve determination were outlined; desktop, rapid, intermediate and comprehensive. As the Reserve would have to be legally defensible, only the highest level – comprehensive – would be suitable for a full determination. The other levels could however be used in providing a preliminary Reserve.

Whilst there has been considerable investment in developing the techniques for determining the freshwater requirements of aquatic ecosystems, and a high number of preliminary assessments have been undertaken (Table 5.2), not a single Reserve has been gazetted. All licenses for water use issued under the NWA are thus in terms of preliminary Reserve determinations (Table 5.3).

---

4   The classification is based on the quality of the resource and is associated with a set of resource quality objectives (Sections 12 and 13).

5   Section 17.

Table 5.2   Annual reported progress in ecological Reserve determinations for river systems across South Africa

Year	Progress	Source
2000/1	• Preliminary determinations of the Reserve for about 200 catchments and water resources • Major studies initiated on the Elands and Crocodile Rivers	DWAF (2001)
2001/2	• Preliminary determinations of the Reserve for approximately 400 catchments and water resources • Major studies initiated on Thukela and Olifants rivers • Reserve studies complete for Mhlathuze and Amatole • Voëlvlei Reserve study in advanced stage	DWAF (2002)
2002/3	• Continuation of the Reserve determination for the Thukela • Lower Berg Reserve completed	DWAF (2003)
2003/4	• Preliminary Reserve determinations done for 201 water resources	DWAF (2004)

Table 5.3   Status of ecological Reserve determination for river systems across South Africa as at November 2003 (Bodurtha *et al.*, 2006)

Component	Number
License applications requiring a Reserve determination	1100
Formally approved preliminary Reserve determinations	480
Fully completed medium to high confidence Reserve determinations	12
Catchments in the process of a high confidence Reserve determination	4

Water quality management

Policy and legal framework
In the South African legislative framework, water quality management is considered under the aegis of 'protection of water resources', the first step of which is the classification of the resource. The NWA requires that a classification system be developed and thereafter the class of all water resources must be established on a catchment basis. For each water resource, specific resource quality objectives must be set. These objectives are defined for particular locations and for specific time periods. They extend beyond the traditional dimension of the presence or absence of particular substances in the water to include, for example, instream flow; water level; instream and riparian habitat; and the characteristics and distribution of biota. As indicated above, determination of the Reserve for a resource is dependent on a classification system having been established by the Minister and resource quality objectives set for the resource.

Chapter 14 of the Act deals with monitoring, assessment and information and requires the establishment of a national monitoring information system. Again, resource quality is defined broadly and, in addition to water quality, the following elements must also be monitored; quantity, use, rehabilitation, and ecosystem health. The information system must include water use authorizations and must be generally accessible to water users and the general public.

Pollution management is supported through the implementation of the 'polluter pays' principle via a waste discharge charge system. Thus a discharge to a water resource may only be made under licence and provided that specific conditions are met. Such use of a resource would furthermore attract a charge. A further important development in the legislation was the introduction of a wide and retrospective liability for pollution to a resource.

As the South African system for water quality management includes the specification of objectives, accounts for regional variability and includes a use element, we consider the third criterion to have been met.

Implementation

The initial emphasis for setting up a framework for water quality management has focused on establishing the information system to support it and the extension of monitoring in accordance with a set of strategies, for example around groundwater or eutrophication (Table 5.4). In some areas new infrastructure has been required and there has been considerable work required to rehabilitate the monitoring network damaged in the floods in January and February 2000. Of particular note, is the piloting of approaches for more integrated measures of river system health. However, there has been little progress with respect to the establishment of a classification system and, consequently, the determination of resource quality objectives for individual resources. Development of a draft classification was a specific objective in the 2003/4 reporting year with the indicator being that the draft system would be gazetted for public comment. The 2003/4 report indicates that only a draft framework has been developed. Similarly, a specific target was the preparation of a guideline document for resource quality objective determination. The annual report indicates that, in this case, the project was delayed due to resource constraints.

Table 5.4   Progress in meeting national water quality management objectives

Year	Progress	Source
2000/1	• Pilot implementation of river health monitoring in all provinces by March 2001 • State of the Rivers reports completed for 3 catchments • Groundwater quality monitoring network design complete and groundwater quality monitoring implemented in 3 regions • Policy and strategy for groundwater quality management published • National salinity monitoring programme in place • Implementation plan for national microbiological programme completed • Development of a waste discharge system (framework documents and project reports)	DWAF (2001)
2001/2	• Further State of the Rivers report completed • National eutrophication programme in place	DWAF (2002)
2002/3	• Groundwater quality system fully operational • National Water Quality Management Framework Policy completed • Several key water quality assessment reports completed	DWAF (2003)
2003/4	• Revision and development of various water quality guidelines • Draft Resource Directed Water Quality Management Policy and draft Prototype Protocol produced • Guidelines for water quality assessment for catchment management strategies produced • Draft 5 year plan for resource quality monitoring developed • 222 polution incidents dealt with	DWAF (2004)

Access to information

Policy and legal framework

Access to information is a Constitutional right in South Africa and is given effect in the Promotion of Access to Information Act (Act No 2 of 2000). This legislation sets out the general principles as well as the process for obtaining access to any information which might be material to the protection of any of the rights set out in the Bill of Rights. The National Water Act reinforces this general right to information in specific areas. For example, as indicated above, information in the national information system must be available to the general public. Secondly, the NWA imposes a specific duty on water management institutions to make the following information available to the public at its own expense:

1. Potential and past flood events
2. Potential and past drought events
3. Waterworks failure that may threaten life
4. Dam risks
5. Flood levels
6. Risks arising from poor water quality.

As access to information is a Constitutional right and further, that there are specific obligations with respect to access to water-related information, we would argue that criterion 4 is met.

Implementation
Considerable effort has been focused on developing and extending the system for monitoring a range of aspects of water quality and quantity (Table 5.5). This has involved gauging station infrastructure development and upgrading as well as extension of the monitoring system to groundwater resources and the implementation of a new information management system (Hydstra). Commitment to responding to the information needs of the public is evidenced in the appointment of 40 information officers for this purpose in 2001. Since the 2002/3 reporting year the annual report has included a 'State of Water Resources' report covering water availability and use, as well as a 'State of Water Services' report covering access to basic services and water tariffs. A weekly bulletin on the state of reservoirs is produced (DWAF, 2003).

Institutional structures for preventing and resolving conflicts

Policy and legal framework
Gleick (1998) regards the existence of institutional mechanisms to prevent and resolve conflicts over water as an essential condition for sustainability. We argue that this condition is also met. Chapter 15 of the NWA sets out procedures for appeals and dispute resolution, including the establishment of a Water Tribunal. The function of the Water Tribunal is to hear appeals regarding decisions made by water management institutions including the Minister and the Department of Water Affairs and Forestry. Under certain conditions decisions of the Water Tribunal may be reviewed by the High Court. In addition to the defined appeal process, there are also specific provisions for mediation.[6]

---

6 Section 150.

Table 5.5   Progress with respect to the provision of access to information regarding water resources availability, use and quality

Year	Progress	Source
2000/1	• Near real-time flow in the Limpopo and Inkomati systems provided on website for access by international users • Extension of flow network to former Transkei (50% of planned complete) • 167 gauging stations repaired and 5 new stations constructed • Flow data collected at 1,706 gauging stations and 1,774 datasets processed • 1,219 groundwater and river sites monitored for water quality	DWAF (2001)
2001/2	• Extension to flow network in Transkei (80%) • Groundwater storage measured for 30% of the country • 23 Gauging stations repaired and 3 new stations constructed • Flow data collected at 1,304 gauging stations and 3,228 datasets processed • 1,517 groundwater and river sites monitored for water quality • 40 deputy information officers appointed to deal with requests in terms of the promotion of Access to the Information Act • 5 formal requests for information handled • Groundwater storage measured for 55% of the country • 39 gauging stations repaired and 9 new stations constructed • Implemented new server-based information system (Hydstra) January 2003, 85% functional	DWAF (2002)
2002/3	• 2,153 groundwater and river sites monitored for water quality • Flow data collected at 1,555 gauging stations and 2,246 datasets processed • 951 requests for data	DWAF (2003)
2003/4	• 13 new gauging stations constructed and 2 repaired • 23 gauging stations equipped with real-time data capturing devices in Limpopo for flood management • 3,346 groundwater and river sites monitored for water quality • Flow data collected at 1,792 gauging stations and 2,193 datasets processed • Information requests not included in annual report	DWAF (2004)

Although the Act provides for dispute resolution, the focus of the legislation is management by consensus, and at a local level. To this effect, a Catchment Management Agency (CMA) is to be established for each of the 14 Water Management Areas (WMAs), which are defined on a catchment or grouping of catchments basis. Each Catchment Management Agency will be controlled by a Governing Board, whose responsibility it will be to ensure that water resources are managed in accordance with a Catchment Management Strategy (CMS). The CMA is under a legal obligation to 'strive towards achieving co-operation and consensus in managing the water resources under its control'[7]. A further institutional structure provided for in the Act is the Water User Association (WUA). These are localized groups of water users usually, but not necessarily, organized around an economic use of a particular water resource. As the purpose of both these structures is to implement local-level, participative decision making, we will consider their role further below.

Implementation
The Water Tribunal was established in 1998. Several appeals have been brought before it and over 20 cases have already been decided, with a number of lodged appeals subsequently withdrawn.

Table 5.6   Progress with respect to the establishment and operation of institutional mechanisms to prevent and resolve conflicts over water

Year	Progress	Source
2000/1	• Water Tribunal became operational	DWAF (2001)
2001/2	• 13 appeals lodged and 3 withdrawn • Legal officer and secretary appointed • First case decided	DWAF (2002) DWAF (2005wt)
2002/3	• 10 appeals lodged and 2 withdrawn • 8 cases decided	DWAF (2005wt)
2003/4	• 3 appeals lodged and 5 withdrawn • 11 cases decided	DWAF (2005wt)

---

7   Section 79(4)(b).

Participative decision making

Policy and legal framework

Gleick (1998) regards participative decision making as a fundamental tenet of sustainable water resource management. This is consistent with the first principle of the 2002 Stockholm Statement; 'water users must be involved in the governance of water resources' and the second principle of the 2000 Dublin Statement; 'water development and management should be based on a participatory approach, involving users, planners and policy-makers at all levels'. A recurring theme of Chapter 18 of Agenda 21 is the participation of local people, and especially women, in the management of water resources.

Participative decision making was acknowledged as an essential principle that should inform the water law development process in South Africa, and characterized the consultative process which led to the NWA (de Coning & Sherwill, 2004). The purpose of establishing CMAs is defined in the preamble of Chapter 7 as 'to delegate water resource management to the regional or catchment level and to involve local communities'. Furthermore, a key purpose of a catchment management strategy (see below) is to 'enable the public to participate in managing the water resources within its water management area',[8] whilst 'taking into account the needs and expectations of existing/potential water users'.[9] Additionally, the composition of the water management institutions referred to above must be such that there is 'appropriate community, racial and gender representation'[10] and consequently members of a CMA Governing Board must reflect 'a balance among the interests of water users, potential water users, local and provincial government and environmental interest groups'.[11] Once established, a Catchment Management Agency is duty-bound to:

1. strive toward achieving consensus in managing the water resources,[12]
2. promote community participation in the protection, use, development, conservation, management and control of the water resources within its water management area, and
3. seek cooperation and agreement from various stakeholders and interested persons.

It is clear that participative decision making is a mandatory requirement in the vision of water resource management that is set out in the Act.

---

8   Section 9(g).
9   Section 9(h).
10 Section 2.
11 Section 81(1).
12 Section 79(4)(b).

Implementation

Implementing participative decision making remains one of the greatest challenges to implementing sustainable water resource management. While progress with respect to WUAs has been good, only one CMA has been established (Table 5.7). Effort has been directed at developing guidelines for effective public participation and building capacity amongst stakeholders. Publication of the National Water Resources Strategy and the subsequent public consultation is evidence of a continued commitment to participative decision making. Nevertheless it would be true to say that the pace of reform and transformation to localized water management has been slower than hoped.

Table 5.7   Progress with respect to the implementation of participative and democratic decision making through the establishment of Water Management Institutions (WMIs)

Year	Progress	Source
2000/1	• Regional plans for the development of WMIs in the 19 WMAs developed • Guidelines for the establishment of WMIs prepared • Establishment of forums and committees in WMAs • Pamphlets on capacity building in stakeholders distributed • Proposal for the establishment of the first CMA submitted (Inkomati)	DWAF (2001)
2001/2	• Facilitation of public participation in 4 new DWAF projects • Implementation of women empowerment programme in the Luvuvhu Government Water Scheme • Generic public participation guidelines prepared and distributed • 154 catchment liaison forums active • 33 Water User Associations created (30 Irrigation Boards were transformed into Water User Associations)	DWAF (2002)
2002/3	• Proposed National Water Resource Strategy published for comment in August 2002 – 36 sectoral and public meetings held and 1,800 formal comments received • 3 CMA proposals evaluated internally, Inkomati CMA proposal published for comment • 50 Irrigation Boards transformed • 8 new WUAs established	DWAF (2003)
2003/4	• Establishment of the first CMA (Inkomati) in March 2004 • Operation and maintenance of assets delegated to 3 WUAs (Vaalharts, Boegoeberg and Kakamas) • 1 Irrigation Board transformed into a WUA and 5 further proposals under consideration • 85 catchment management forums in place with good stakeholder participation	DWAF (2004)

Sharing international waters

Policy and legal framework
Although Gleick (1998) does not mention international waters explicitly, it is implicit in the principle of decision-making regarding water being participative and democratic. Dowdeswell (1998) raises this as a specific objective, calling for a 'fair share' among riparian countries. In Southern Africa, this is recognized as a critical issue as many of the larger basins are shared across three or more international boundaries (Kidd & Quinn, 2005). Meeting international obligations with respect to water is recognized as an express purpose of the National Water Act,[13] and Chapter 11 addresses international water management. The NWA provides for the establishment and funding of bodies formed to implement any international agreement entered into between South Africa and a foreign government. Whilst such measures do not in themselves guarantee a fair share to riparian states, there is at least a tacit acknowledgement of the need to honour international obligations.

Implementation
South Africa participated in the revision of the Southern African Development Community (SADC) Protocol on Shared Watercourses, which was signed in August 2000 and ratified in 2003 (Table 5.8). A further international agreement was signed by South Africa, Swaziland and Mozambique at the WSSD in August 2002, and there appears to have been significant progress with respect to the establishment of institutions for the purpose of managing transboundary water resources (Table 5.8).

Ensuring renewability

Policy and legal framework
As is evident from the preceding discussion, Dowdeswell's notion of a 'fair share' for future generations is a primary purpose of the NWA and a number of specific mechanisms have been devised to help ensure this. Indeed, many of the foregoing mechanisms (for example, the Reserve; resource quality objectives; waste discharge charge system) are part of a broad suite of approaches aimed at ensuring renewability. Although a comprehensive review of all these mechanisms is beyond the scope of this paper, a few additional elements will be discussed further.

---

13 Section 2(i).

Table 5.8   Progress with respect to the sharing of international waters

Year	Progress	Source
2000/1	• Inco-Maputo international agreement signed • Formation of the Orange-Senqu Basin Commission (March 2001) • SADC Revised Protocol on Shared Watercourses signed (August 2000) • Initiation of negotiations with Mozambique on water sharing in the Inkomati and Maputo rivers • Negotiations for establishment of Limpopo River Commission made good progress • Joint water commissions with Swaziland, Mozambique and Namibia and technical water committee with Botswana • Tripartite technical committee with Mozambique and Swaziland functioned well	DWAF (2001)
2001/2	• Many bi-national commission/committee meetings were held to discuss issues of mutual interest • Negotiations with Mozambique on water sharing in the Inkomati and Maputo rivers and with Botswana, Zimbabwe and Mozambique on the establishment of a Limpopo River Commission	DWAF (2002)
2002/3	• Agreement between South Africa, Swaziland and Mozambique: Co-operation on the protection and sustainable utilisation of the water resources of the Inkomati and Maputo watercourses signed at the WSSD in August 2002	DWAF (2003)
2003/4	• Agreement to establish the Limpopo River Commission signed by South Africa and Mozambique in November 2003 (Botswana and Zimbabwe still to sign) • Revised SADC Protocol ratified in 2003	DWAF (2004)

Although water resources are to be managed and allocated at a local level, such management must be consistent with the National Water Resource Strategy (NWRS). This strategy sets out the national objectives and plans for water management, including the requirements of the Reserve, international obligations, water use of strategic importance and the actions to be taken to meet projected future needs and other macro-scale planning issues.[14] There is a legal obligation to review the national strategy every five years or less. At a more localized level, CMAs are required to prepare a Catchment Management Strategy (CMS) which must be consistent with the NWRS. A CMS must take into account the resource quality objectives and the Reserve and set out the objectives, plans, guidelines and procedures for the 'protection, use, development, conservation, management and control of water

---

14 Sections 5 to 7.

resources'[15] within its area of jurisdiction. Central to this process is the authorization and licensing of all forms of water use. A licence for a particular water use is granted by the CMA after due consideration of the Reserve requirements, the National Water Resources Strategy and the local Catchment Management Strategy. The Act has provisions for water use charges, which are not only intended to fund the direct and indirect costs of water management, but also to achieve an equitable allocation of water and to encourage effective and efficient water use.[16] Water conservation is thereby supported through the introduction of water pricing and, importantly, this is not limited to direct abstraction. The concept of streamflow reduction activities is introduced in the NWA, whereby land uses such as forestry are deemed to be users of water and therefore fall within the programme of licensing and charges.[17]

The range of measures for ensuring sustainability of resource use in the Act is impressive and perhaps not unsurprising given the somewhat dire predictions for water supply in the region in the future (Ashton, 2002, 2004). Although this is a particularly difficult criterion to assess, we are of the opinion that a relatively comprehensive framework for ensuring renewability is outlined and the last criterion is therefore met.

Implementation

A key element of the strategy for ensuring renewability has been firstly the registration of all water use (including streamflow reduction activities) and secondly the licensing of this use and subsequent recovery of the water management charge. This has required the development of administrative procedures, as well as the need for legal action against illegal water use and defaulters (Table 5.9).

A second component has been the development of the National Water Resources Strategy (NWRS). This proceeded more slowly than planned with the intended publication of the draft strategy being successively postponed from September 2000 to August 2003. However, the first draft has now been published and has been subject to an intensive round of public consultation.

A further innovative aspect of the Department's work has been the internationally acknowledged 'Working for Water' programme. This initiative aims to improve water resources and biodiversity through the removal of alien invasive species from water courses and land. This has provided employment and an opportunity to develop skills for 20,000 previously disadvantaged individuals.

---

15 Section 9(c).
16 Chapter 5.
17 Section 36.

Table 5.9   Progress with respect to measures aimed at ensuring renewability

Year	Progress	Source
2000/1	• Work initiated on the National Water Resources Strategy • Formulation of regulations governing the use and protection of water in mining and related sectors • Development of a system to manage water use authorizations and registrations implemented March 2001 • Registration of water users on the National Register of Water Use begun • 404 licences assessed and 1,140 unlawful water users identified • 97,411 ha of alien invasives cleared and follow-up on 124,720 ha	DWAF (2001)
2001/2	• Data on 4,600 water users in 9 regions captured, representing an estimated 80% of the country's water use making SA one of the first countries in the world to achieve information regarding water use at property level • 21 licences assessed and 1,079 unlawful water users identified • Initial clearing of 227,400 ha and follow-up on 285,000 ha	DWAF (2002)
2002/3	• Launch of the draft National Water Resources Strategy in August 2002 • Policy and strategy for raw water pricing developed • Water resource management charges formalized • 534 licences assessed and 563 unlawful water users identified • 466,279 ha of alien invasives cleared and follow-up on 523,618 ha	DWAF (2003)
2003/4	• National Register of Water Use extends to 63,987 users • 710 licences assessed and 325 unlawful water users identified • A number of directives were issued against illegal water users • Above 70% of revenue from water resource management charge collected with follow-up action taken against defaulters • 161,250 ha of alien invasives cleared and follow-up on 557,945 ha	DWAF (2004)

Discussion

One of the most successful elements of the water reform process has been the significant improvement in water supply to previously disadvantaged households and the provision of free basic water. Although somewhat short of Gleick's (1998) recommendation of 50 litres per capita per day, there is a clear commitment and demonstrated trajectory towards the goal of a guaranteed basic human water right.

The situation is not as clear, however, for ecosystem water rights. Whilst mechanisms and techniques for determining the Reserve are in place, progress in formally gazetting Reserve amounts has been slow. In part, this may be due to slow progress in developing the classification system for water resources, as a draft framework was only developed in 2003/4. As formal determination of the Reserve is dependent upon, firstly, there being a classification system in place and, secondly, that the class of the particular resource has been determined, until such time as this happens only preliminary Reserves can be determined. There may also be concerns that one of the consequences of declaring a Reserve for a particular resource will be the mounting of legal challenges, particularly if the Reserve means a reduction in existing water allocations. Whatever the reasons for the low level of implementation, the concept of the Reserve is a centrepiece of the National Water Act and there is an urgent need to move forward in this respect.

Water quality management has been the focus of a number of developments, including the extension of monitoring activities and the development of additional policies, protocols and standards. Monitoring is not limited to traditional measurement of water quality parameters, but rather a more holistic assessment of river system health as evidenced by the work of the River Health Programme. The opportunity for protection and enforcement of water quality standards is improved through the introduction of a wide and retrospective liability for pollution, and the polluter pays principle has been formalized by the introduction of a waste discharge charge system. Whether Gleick's (1998) criterion of water quality being maintained will be met in the long term will largely depend on whether the monitoring system is responsive enough to detect deterioration and its causes and whether there is sufficiently rapid prosecution of offenders. There have been encouraging developments in this regard (Pole, 2002) and the legal services within the Department have acknowledged the need to have protocols in place to deal with this situation.

As is the case in other parts of the world, access to information has come to be seen as a democratic right. The Promotion of Access to Information Act (Act 2 of 2000) provides a means of acquiring information even if this was not provided for in the NWA. The National Water Act has specific information provision requirements and the Department has appointed a significant number of staff to deal expressly with this objective. Annual reports deal explicitly with both the state of service delivery and the state of water resources, and the Departmental website provides further monthly, weekly or in some cases, live updates. It would seem that Gleick's criterion of access to information is being well-implemented.

The fifth criterion is that institutional mechanisms will be set up to prevent and resolve conflicts over water. The various water management institutions established by the NWA have a statutory obligation to work towards consensus and to seek agreement and cooperation between stakeholders. Nevertheless, disputes are likely to arise and it is for this reason that a Water Tribunal has been established. Several cases have already been decided while, in at least eight cases the appeal has been withdrawn or the dispute was settled between parties, suggesting the institution is fulfilling the intended role in dispute resolution.

Participative decision-making in water resources is now widely recognized as good practice and it has received special attention in revision of the water law.

Representation of all users and their participation in managing water resources at a local level is essential under the new Act. Ironically this may be the reason why progress in the establishment of CMAs has been so slow. It has taken time, and not insubstantial resources, to start the process of enabling participation in a society wholly unaccustomed to such participation. At least one proposal for the establishment of a CMA has been returned for further development on account of insufficient public participation, and it is clear from the level of advertising, consultation and expenditure that the Department has every intention of ensuring that the transformation is true to the intended outcome of participative decision making.

With respect to the sharing of international waters, there has been clear progress with several international agreements signed as well as the establishment of several transboundary institutions. Real progress, however, in this area can only be measured by the extent to which riparian States believe they have an equitable share of the resources. This has not been the case in the past and, furthermore, until relatively recently, relations between neighbours on the subcontinent have been characterized by conflict rather than co-operation. Developing a relationship of trust and co-operation will take time, and measures other than the number of institutions established or agreements signed will have to be developed to measure progress in relation to this criterion. Nevertheless, the outward signs of cooperation are there and this is an encouraging sign.

The final criterion is that 'human action will not impair the long-term renewability of freshwater stocks and flows' (Gleick, 1998). This is possibly the most difficult criterion to evaluate, particularly since the success of this endeavour will only be known many years from now. Incremental improvement is perhaps the best indicator of a long-term trajectory, but this implies that we need to evaluate improvements against goals and targets set out in a plan. The purpose of the National Water Resource Strategy and the individual Catchment Management Strategies is to ensure that plans are tabled, reviewed and revised in light of progress. The establishment of the Reserve is an obvious step in securing the continuing functioning of aquatic ecosystems. So too is the stricter regulation of all forms of water use, direct and indirect. Establishing a water pricing system, whereby charges are re-invested in catchment management, must also be a step in the right direction. Water conservation strategies such as the removal of alien vegetation are equally important. With water scarcity predicted to increase in the region and the cost and impacts of further dam development limiting solutions through increased storage, it is clear that ensuring renewability of stock and flows must be a major focus of water management efforts.

Conclusion

This chapter has documented the significant progress made in the transformation of South Africa's water sector to a management milieu aimed at sustainability and equity. Assessment against the criteria suggested by Gleick (1998) and Dowdeswell (1998) indicates that in all cases, the legal and policy framework supports sustainability through a range of innovative mechanisms. Efforts to improve the delivery of basic services have been commended internationally. However, implementation of some of these measures has proceeded more slowly than perhaps hoped for. At the time of writing, only one Catchment Management Agency had been established and not a single Reserve had been gazetted. This is perhaps not surprising given the extent of the transformation that has been required. In the case of the former, it has meant significant capacity building; entirely new water management institutions are being established where there were none before. In the case of the latter, it has meant developing a range of techniques and procedures for determining the Reserve that are likely to withstand legal challenge. However, there is a danger that if key mechanisms such as the Reserve are not implemented soon, perceptions of the National Water Act not living up to its promise will be created.

References

Adams, J.B. & Bate, G.C. (1994) *The freshwater requirements of estuarine plants incorporating the development of an estuarine decision support system.* Water Research Commission Report, 292/2/94. Water Research Commission, Pretoria.

Ashton, P. (2002) Avoiding conflicts over Africa's water resources. *Ambio*, 31, 236-242.

Ashton, P. (2004) Water and Development: A Southern African Perspective. In Trottier, J. & Slack, P. (eds) *Managing Water Resources: Past and Present.* Oxford University Press, Oxford, pp. 149-174.

Biswas, A.K. (1996) Sustainable Water Development from the Perspective of the South: Issues and Constraints. In Abu-Zeid, M. & Biswas, A.K. (eds) *River Basin Planning and Management.* Oxford University Press, Calcutta, pp. 87-100.

Bodurtha, A., Schendel, K. & Quinn, N.W. (2006) South Africa's reserve: Challenges and recommendations for implementing sustainable development policies. *Journal of Environmental Assessment Policy and Management*, 8, 1-23.

Castro, C.J. (2004) Sustainable development: Mainstream and critical perspectives. *Organisation & Environment*, 17, 195-225.

De Coning, C. & Sherwill, T. (2004) *An Assessment of the Water Policy Process in South Africa (1994 to 2003).* WRC Report No TT232/04. Water Research Commission, Pretoria.

Dowdeswell, E. (1998) Where peaceful waters flow. *Water International*, 23, 13-16.

DWAF (1996) *Water Law Principles.* Department of Water Affairs and Forestry, Pretoria.

DWAF (1999) *Resource Directed Measures for Protection of Water Resources.* Volumes 1-6, Version 1. Department of Water Affairs and Forestry, Pretoria.

DWAF (2001) *Annual Report 2000/1.* Department of Water Affairs and Forestry, Pretoria.

DWAF (2002) *Annual Report 2001/2.* Department of Water Affairs and Forestry, Pretoria.

DWAF (2003) *Annual Report 2002/3*. Department of Water Affairs and Forestry, Pretoria.

DWAF (2004) *Annual Report 2003/4*. Department of Water Affairs and Forestry, Pretoria.

DWAF (2005) *Free Basic Water Implementation Status*. http://www.dwaf.gov.za/ FreeBasicWater/Defaulthome.asp. Accessed 26/6/05.

Gleick, P.H. (1998) Water in Crisis: Paths to Sustainable Water Use. *Ecological Applications*, 8, 571-579.

Gleick, P.H. (1999) The Human Right to Water. *Water Policy*, 1, 487-503.

Kidd, M. & Quinn, N.W. (2005) Public participation in southern African watercourses. In Bruch, C., Jansky, L., Nakayama, M. & Salewicz, K.A. (eds) *Public Participation and Governance in International Watercourse Management*. United Nations University Press, Tokyo, pp. 156-168.

King, J.M. & Tharme, R.E. (1994) *Assessment of the Instream Flow Incremental Methodology and initial development of alternative instream flow methodologies for South Africa*. Water Research Commission Report, 295/1/94. Water Research Commission, Pretoria.

Lele, S.M. (1991) Sustainable development: A critical review. *World Development*, 19, 607-621.

Mitcham, C. (1995) The concept of sustainable development: Its origins and ambivalence. *Technology in Society*, 17, 311-326.

Morant, P. & Quinn, N.W. (1999) Influence of man and management of South African estuaries. In Allanson, B. & Baird, D. (eds) *Estuaries of South Africa*. Cambridge University Press, Cambridge, pp. 289-320.

Muller, M. (2004) *Introduction to the 2003/2004 Report of the Department of Water Affairs and Forestry*. http://www.dwaf.gov.za/Documents/AnnualReports/2004/ AnnualReport04Part1.pdf. Accessed 29/6/05.

OECD (2001) *Sustainable Development: Critical Issues*. Organisation for Economic Cooperation and Development, Paris.

Palmer Development Group (2001) *Free Basic Water: Implementation Strategy Document*. Prepared for the Directorate: Interventions and Operations Support, Department of Water Affairs and Forestry, South Africa. Department of Water Affairs and Forestry, Pretoria.

Parris, T.M. & Krates, R.W. (2003) Characterising and measuring sustainable development. *Annual Review of Environment and Resources*, 28, 1-13.28.

Pole, A.L. (2002) *Factors Preventing the Successful Implementation of the Polluter Pays Principle: A Case Study of the Bayne's Spruit*. Unpublished MEnvDev dissertation, Centre for Environment and Development, University of Natal.

Quinn, N.W. (1998) *An integrated modelling approach to the management of freshwater inflow to South African estuaries*. Unpublished PhD thesis, University of Natal, South Africa.

Rennings, K. & Wiggering, H. (1997) Steps towards indicators of sustainable development: Linking economic and ecological concepts. *Ecological Economics*, 20, 25-36.

Sonjica, B.P. (2004) *Celebration of the 10 millionth South African Household to receive water*. Address by the Minister of Water Affairs and Forestry Ms BP Sonjica at Soverby, Northern Cape, 12 November. http://www.dwaf.gov.za/Communications/MinisterSpeeches/2004/10million12Nov04. doc. Accessed 29/6/05.

Tharme, R.E. & King, J.M. (1998) Development of the building block methodology for instream flow assessments and supporting research on the effects of different magnitude flows on riverine ecosystems. *Water Research Commission Report*, 576/1/98. Water Research Commission, Pretoria.

Tortajada, C. (2003) Rethinking development paradigms for the water sector. In Figueres, C., Rockstrom, J & Tortajada, C (eds) *Rethinking Water Management: Innovative Approaches to Contemporary Issues*. Earthscan, London, pp. 8-24.

Chapter 6

Environmental Education and Constructions of Sustainable Development in Jamaica

Therese Ferguson and Elizabeth Thomas-Hope

Introduction

Environmentalism in the 1960s was regarded as a movement reflecting the concern of Western European and North American middle classes. Countries of the developing world had not yet become engaged in discussion relating to the environment, largely because they were preoccupied with trying to keep development programmes 'afloat' in an effort to deal with poverty. Since the late 1970s, concern about links between the environment and development at the global level, and then also in the developing world, became a central feature of rhetoric and thinking. Whatever the complexities, the interdependence of environment and development was recognized internationally.

The Bruntland Commission, an independent group established by the United Nations (UN) with the mandate to prepare environmental strategies at the global level, identified sustainable development as an overall strategy, linking development initiatives with environmental concerns. The growth of sustainable development as a paradigm for conceptualising nature and the environment has evolved within the framework of global institutions such as the UN, the World Bank and donor agencies in developed countries. Consequently, Jamaica, like most other developing countries party to Agenda 21 and receiving assistance, has subscribed to sustainable development ideas and programmes as part of the provision of development financing.

The international agenda gave rise to discourses on nature, the environment and sustainable development. These environmental discourses have comprised views concerning ways of acting out 'ideal' relationships with the environment, chiefly so that environmental resources may be available to generations in perpetuity. The discourses also included ideas about social constructs and representations of nature and of the environment. Indeed, the idea of a social construction of nature is an important preface to understanding the concept of environmental discourses because environmental discourses are themselves based on the idea of a 'social construction' of and ideas about nature. People verbalize their views and perceptions through language and action. From this perspective, nature has never been an objective reality; rather, humans have 'constructed' nature in two primary ways. Firstly, they 'create' nature in a literal sense; physically shaping it. Secondly, humans perceive and interact with nature and give it meaning (Greider & Garkovich, 1994; Blaikie, 1995; Escobar, 1996; Castree & Braun, 1998; Peterson, 1999).

As specific series of representations, practices and performances through which meanings are produced, discourses are legitimized. As they relate to the environment, they provide explanations of the world around us and, as stated by Benton & Short (1999: 2), 'they are deep structures which pattern thought, belief and practices, and allow us to understand why human-environmental relationships take the forms that they do'. Discourses thus represent particular constructions and viewpoints, they are characterized by both language and action; and they are related to knowledge and, by extension, power. They can take hold and become universal, and can influence relationships towards persons and entities. All of these aspects have implications for the environment.

Since the formulation of a global agenda in the 1970s, environmental education has been recognized as a critical means of bringing about the attitudinal and behavioural changes necessary to foster respect for nature, slow down and/or halt the environmental destruction and degradation threatening nature and to ensure the survival of humans who depend upon its resources.

Notwithstanding the importance of environmental education for sustainable development, two basic problems, often either unnoticed or dismissed, remain and need to be explored. Jickling (1994) points out that the notion of education for sustainable development makes two assumptions. The first is that sustainable development is an uncontested concept, meaning that it has just one common meaning for all, and the second is that education should be used for the advancement of this pre-determined goal. In terms of his second point, this could be likened to the first by saying that the notion assumes that everyone agrees on the purpose of education. Sauvé (1996) takes Jickling's (1994) position further, pointing out that environmental education for sustainable development is actually predicated on three concepts that have multiple and varying meanings for different societies and, moreover, for different individuals. These three concepts are the 'environment,' 'sustainable development,' and 'education' and variation in how they are conceived results in different practices of environmental education for sustainable development. This study isolates a fourth concept; that of 'nature'. Although it is recognized that nature is a component of the 'environment', it is seen as so crucial that it has been added to Sauvé's list of the problematic and contested concepts upon which environmental education for sustainable development is based. This chapter acknowledges and supports Sauvé's viewpoint and puts the varying conceptualizations of three of these concepts: 'nature,' the 'environment' and 'sustainable development' under direct scrutiny, and also takes into account the differing concepts of 'education'.

While such realization engendered interest in this investigation, this chapter delves even further into an exploration of whether, and how, the global and hegemonic sustainable development discourse can be institutionalized within a nation's formal education system. Sustainable development can be viewed as a global environmental discourse, that is, an articulation of knowledge and power that serves to legitimize dominant ideas and beliefs about how the environment should be conceptualized, viewed, and utilized. If this is in fact the case, then environmental education for sustainable development, and the education system in which it works, actually become an institutionalized means of transmitting and ingraining these dominant ideas and beliefs in local and global societies. There are two critical problems with this. Firstly, albeit the globally dominant and accepted paradigm, sustainable development is only one way of viewing the environment, only one way in which human-environment relationships can be conceived and practiced. What then happens to the other ways in which nature and the environment can be 'constructed' and conceptualized, which are neglected in or marginalized by the sustainable development narrative? Secondly, sustainable development is also a highly problematic paradigm in practice; this will be elaborated upon later.

A formal system of environmental education for sustainable development then, if based on the problematically conceptualized economic and political systems to which sustainable development adheres, simply works to reproduce these values, beliefs and systems in the wider populace. A formal system of environmental education for sustainable development, if focused on only one way of viewing nature and the environment at the neglect of other conceptualisations, is inadequate and possibly counter to the national and local needs of a country. Therein lies the essential paradox: while education is indeed critical for sustainable development, it simultaneously could be educating people for unsustainability (Sterling, 1996). Thus, within the context of formal environmental education in Jamaica, two main questions will be raised in this chapter. The first is whether national and individual constructions of sustainable development in Jamaica, and the global construction of sustainable development, are competing or complementing narratives as they are articulated in current environmental education curricula. The second, based on this, is whether environmental education for sustainable development is fulfilling its intended role, and thus can be viewed as an agent of change, as the global mindset suggests or, should it itself be the subject of change?

Global and national discourses on sustainable development

The global environmental discourse

In global discourses, there are many different conceptualisations and definitions of sustainability, but a few main 'entities' are generally recognized. Firstly, nature is viewed primarily as a provider of natural resources; aspects of the natural environment that are critical to satisfying human needs and wants. This view of nature as resource is implicit in the World Commission on Environment and Development (WCED) definition of sustainable development (WCED, 1987), which focuses on the present and future needs of humankind. In conjunction with this, nature is also viewed as a 'fragile' natural resource that can be overexploited and degraded, jeopardising human existence. The other main entities which are recognized are interconnected ecological, social, economic and political systems, all of which influence each other. According to the proponents of sustainability, these systems can exist in harmony.

The discourse also spotlights some main relationships. Specifically, there is an implicit hierarchy of humans above nature, with humankind's survival and development being given priority over the 'rights' of nature. As an adjunct to this, human control and management of nature, and thus its subordination, is also recognized.

Discourse reflects the understanding that a cooperative effort among all nations and individuals is necessary in order for sustainable development to be achieved; global problems are caused by all and affect all. A participatory effort is needed to address these problems and other sustainability issues. The discourse posits that nested systems can co-exist in harmony, mutually reinforcing each other. In terms of the agents within the discourse, there are many actors or stakeholders, operating at all levels, for the global, national and individual good. The conservation of resources for humankind is the main goal and this results in common good for humankind.

Finally, in terms of the key metaphors and rhetorical devices used, the main ones are those of 'progress,' 'organic growth' and 'reassurance', viewing sustainable development as a process that can be achieved over time, step by step, with everyone's cooperation.

The dominant elements of discourse on sustainable development that are represented in the literature can be summarized using Dryzek's (1997) framework for the construction of discourses (Table 6.1). These elements are the basic entities that are recognized, assumptions about natural relationships, agents and motives, and metaphors and other rhetorical devices.

Table 6.1   **Summary analysis of global discourse on sustainable development**

Basic Entities Recognized or Constructed	Assumptions About Natural Relationships	Agents and Motives	Key Metaphors and Rhetorical Devices
▪ Fragile natural resources ▪ Inner nature ▪ Nested ecological, economic, political, and social systems	▪ Hierarchy ▪ Control ▪ Cooperation ▪ Co-existence of nested systems	▪ Many agents at all levels ▪ Global or public interest ▪ Preservation of nature ▪ Conservation of natural resources	▪ Progress ▪ Organic growth ▪ Concern and reassurance

The Jamaican national discourse on sustainable development

Faced with increasing awareness of the deepening environmental crisis in the Caribbean; reflected in high levels of pollution and deforestation, sustainable development discourses were taken up by a number of Caribbean governmental and non-governmental agencies during the 1980s and 1990s after the World Summit held in Rio de Janeiro (1992) and the Conference on Small Island Developing States (SIDS) held in Barbados (1994). In general, theirs was a pragmatic approach to the linkages between over-exploitation of environmental resources and the negative impact on the economy. Tourism was paramount in the minds of government agencies, and so the discourses concerning constructions and representations of nature and the environment were not widely discussed.

In the pursuit of a solution to the crisis and, in particular, the quest of identifying where the behaviours and practices that were causing the crisis might lie, attention turned briefly to the idea that the perpetrators of environmentally negative activities should be made to pay. The difficulty encountered at various levels in bringing about, and successfully implementing, such a regulatory framework directed more attention towards education as the means of making the difference.

In Jamaica, environmental education has been encouraged through both informal means, geared to the general public, and formal means, such as its integration in the primary to tertiary level curricula. The National Environmental Education Committee (NEEC), a subdivision of the National Environment and Planning Agency (NEPA), was established in 1993 to promote environmental education activities in support of sustainable development. In 1998, the NEEC produced a National Environmental Education Action Plan for Sustainable Development (NEEAPSD), which is to be implemented over a 12 year period that began in 1998 and culminates in 2010. It is this Action Plan that guides national environmental education initiatives in both the formal and non-formal sectors.

As reflected in the title of its Action Plan, Jamaica's environmental education initiatives are set within the context of sustainable development, the origins of which can be traced to the global environmental 'discourse' that essentially began under the auspices of the UN in the mid 1980s. The Action Plan states that 'sustainable development is an overarching concept, relating to the harmonization of social, environmental and economic considerations in the cause of long-term human development' (NEEC, 1998: 106). This seems to mirror the global concept of sustainable development as promulgated by the Bruntland Commission.

The NEEAPSD is used as the main framework through which environmental education for sustainable development is conceptualized and institutionalized. Undoubtedly, sustainability is basically constructed in the same way as in the global discourse. The same key entities, relationships, agents and motives, and metaphors present in the global discourse are also present in the Action Plan, with only one main difference. In terms of the rhetorical devices that are employed, the key device that emerges in the Jamaican NEEAPSD is that of 'vision'. Reference to the vision of a sustainable society or a broadly shared vision is made. Overall, the Action Plan has a positive tone, implying that all will be well for the economic, social, political, and environmental progress of the country. Reassurance is also specifically given through the positive assertion that the vision of sustainable development can be achieved. Other differences in the global and national discourses can be observed in that 'inner nature', and the 'preservation of nature' for its own sake are absent from or subsumed in the representation of the national discourse in the NEEAPSD.

Jamaica's NEEAPSD was used to analyse the major aspects of national discourse that have direct relevance for environmental education in the country. Within the curriculum, the 'constructions' of nature, the environment and sustainable development are not as rigid or as clear-cut as in the Action Plan. In the primary education curriculum, in the humanities subjects, there is leeway for students to openly engage with and creatively construct nature and the environment in ways that they themselves choose. Where specific views of nature and the environment are inscribed within the curriculum, it is as a fragile resource, something upon which not only humans depend for their basic needs and wants, but upon which other elements within nature also depend.

At the secondary education level, nature is primarily inscribed (to a noticeable extent) within the social studies and science curricula, likewise as a fragile resource integral to human beings and Jamaica's economy, but also as something detached, to be observed and examined. There is no inclusion of the need for the relationship of humans with nature or environment.

Environmental education

Environmental education needs to not only challenge 'prevailing ways of living with nature', but should also challenge 'existing economic, political and cultural realities' (Bynoe, 1997: 115). The notion of environmental discourses allows for this because it alerts persons to the fact that these discourses are constructed for particular interests, and can therefore be deconstructed and reconstructed for alternate interests that coincide more closely with the realities of particular cultures and countries. Environmental education should not just blindly 'reproduce' the current realities of living with nature. Rather, it should alert persons to alternate realities, and enable them to critically evaluate these realities and make informed decisions as to what the appropriate interaction with nature should be in their local context. The notion of environmental discourses allows for this acceptance of alternate ways of interacting with nature.

In terms of the basis for formal environmental education, which is most often scientific knowledge, the notion of environmental discourses illustrates that science too can 'construct' nature, and shape environmental problems and their solutions. This paves the way for the acceptance of alternate knowledge systems, such as indigenous knowledge, to address environmental problems. This is important since education should be the primary means of bringing about attitudinal and/or behavioural change. Education becomes not only an 'agent of change' for improved people-nature interaction; it also becomes a 'subject of change'. Thus, education has to be critically reoriented to take into account the challenges of a post-modern world and its varying conceptualisations of nature.

In varied (and even contradictory) ways the formal curricula reflect the central tenets of this sustainability discourse. An important factor in the ways the curricula were modified to include this issue has been shaped in accordance with the ways in which the stakeholders have understood the national and local agendas of formal environmental education for sustainable development.

The effect of the National Education Action Plan for Sustainable Development in Jamaican schools

The Jamaican case study is based on a sample of 394 secondary school students from four schools (Ferguson, 2005). The criterion for the selection of the schools was their involvement in the Advanced Schools Programme (ASP), a programme that is specifically geared towards environmental education for sustainable development implemented by some Jamaican schools. Thus, two schools that had adopted the Advanced Schools Programme were selected, one urban and the other rural. As 'control' schools, one urban and one rural school were also selected that had not introduced the Advanced School Programme into their curricula. Of the total of 394 students included in the study, 70 were selected from School A, 83 from School B, 126 from School C, and 115 from School D.

The students were selected from Grades 7, 8 and 9 and were between the ages of 11 and 16. Two main reasons formed the rationale for this selection. Firstly, a preliminary review of the curriculum revealed that students in Grades 7 to 9 should have learned about sustainable development. Secondly, students at this level theoretically should have semi- or fully-formed views on environmental issues that still show some independence of thought.

Concepts of nature

Students were asked what the concept 'nature' meant to them. More than one in five students (23.9 per cent of the sample), were unable to offer their ideas at all, or voiced ideas that were either unclear or ambiguous. Of the remaining students, the conceptions offered were categorized under four broad headings (Figure 6.1).

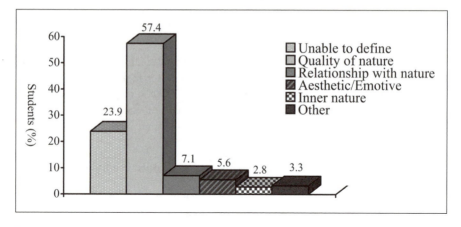

Figure 6.1   Concepts of nature expressed by the children in the study

The majority of students (57.4 per cent) gave definitions of nature which fell under a broad category in which the focus was on its creation. This included, for example, who is or who is not responsible for the creation of nature; of what it is comprised; and its quality (such as whether it is natural). In this first set of views, children were focusing on different characteristics pertaining to nature. They focused on the types of things one finds in nature, or the types of organisms that inhabit nature, for instance 'the living and non-living things around us'. In many cases, students listed specific examples of aspects of nature. One student said that 'sun, trees, flowers, sky, rocks, mountains' were part of the natural world. Some students described nature in terms of 'things that man doesn't make like trees, seas, rivers, lakes, rainfall, mountains, valleys and fishes and rocks'. Several of these students then went further than regarding nature as not a man-made entity to acknowledging all of nature as a creation of God: 'Everything around that God created, the oceans, sea, land, forests, flowers and more'. Chi-square tests were carried out to check for any significant associations between child age and types of definitions given of nature, but no significant associations were found (at $p=0.05$).

A small number of students (5.6 per cent) focused on emotive or aesthetic aspects of nature. Although these definitions could also have fit into the 'characteristics of nature' category, they were isolated and placed into a separate category as they pointed to intrinsic emotive or aesthetic aspects, inherent qualities that are crucial to environmental ethics. Examples of ideas voiced included: 'Like going outside and seeing nature or going to the forest and seeing the trees, the birds, a little stream that looks so beautiful' and 'the beautification of the island due to the fact that there is green in grass and yellow in the sunset'.

While the preceding examples pointed to the beauty of nature, the following illustrations pointed to other intangible qualities, such as its freshness, its wildness and its peacefulness; nature as a place where people could go to relax and find solitude. Views included nature as a 'natural environment, fresh and wild' and as 'peace and quiet, nice and breezy, where people enjoy themselves'.

Only 7.1 per cent of the views expressed focused on the relationship between humans and nature and these were mixed among children of different ages. Some highlighted a relational view between nature and humans, emphasising that nature was 'a resource which is created by God' and 'natural things that God made; things that are useful'. Thus, nature was conceptualized as a useful resource to humans; something needed for the sustaining of human life. One student moved a step further, indicating that nature was something that humans should care for and live with, alluding to a harmonious existence. This student said 'nature is all about what we do to care for it and how we live with it. Nature is a free place'. A mutually enhancing relationship between nature and humans was portrayed by some students. For instance, the following portrayed a picture of the human-nature relationship by characterising nature as 'the physical things that were put on the earth for our use, our enjoyment, something not to destroy'. A second view was that nature was 'something around you and it gives the environment beauty' and that 'I think people must take care of nature because it is very important to human beings'. This suggests the view that humans should take care of nature and/or should not do anything to destroy it because it provides human beings with aesthetic and recreational pleasure.

A minority (2.8 per cent of the sample) viewed nature as inner nature, a person's mind, body, and/or spirit, as in the following depictions: 'The way human beings express themselves'. A second view was expressed as 'I think nature means ... to have feelings, not for someone or something directly, but just to have feelings'.

A comparison of the definitions of nature given by students in different types of schools reflected the enhanced awareness of those children in schools engaged in the Advanced Environmental Education Schools Programme. In the schools not engaged in the ASP there were a larger number who were unable to offer definitions of nature than was the case in the schools engaged in the programme. Whether or not the schools were engaged in the ASP, the High Schools and the rural schools were those in which there was greater emphasis placed by students on concepts of nature that involved a relational view of humans and nature and that drew attention to an emotive or aesthetic quality of nature. The relative strength of high school status or rural location in explaining these views could not be determined in this study. Additionally, the Advanced Schools Programme does seem to have a significant association (at $p=0.05$) with the fact that more students in this programme were able to offer definitions of nature, as well as definitions that emphasized a relational view with nature and an emotive or aesthetic aspect of nature, both of which are important in terms of environmental ethics.

Of interest is the fact that the majority of students did not hold views of nature that emphasized a human-nature relationship or the aesthetic or emotive character of nature. While this could be problematic in terms of fostering an environmental ethic and stewardship of nature, this does match the concept of nature espoused in sustainable development; that is nature as resource, as being of instrumental use to humans and as being subject to man.

Concepts of the environment

As with the term nature, students were asked what the 'environment' meant to them. Of the 343 students who offered their ideas, their conceptions were categorized in two main ways; either object focused, seeing the environment merely as an object, or relation focused, seeing some sort of relationship between the environment and people. On the basis of their study in Australia, Loughland *et al.* (2002) identified six sub-categories into which the various views fell (Table 6.2). These categories moved from representing simple to more complex or broad conceptions.

Table 6.2   Concepts of the environment

Object Focus	Relational Focus
1. The environment is a place 2. The environment is a place that contains living things 3. The environment is a place that contains living things and people	1. The environment does something for people 2. People are part of the environment and are responsible for it 3. People and the environment are in a mutually sustaining relationship

The majority of the students surveyed (54.1 per cent) saw the environment in its most limited sense, simply as a place. Examples of the notions that were given included students describing the environment as 'the place around you', 'our surroundings', 'an area or surroundings you live within' and 'your habitat, community and everything in it'.

A very small number of students (6.1 per cent) referred to the environment as 'a place' containing living things, adding a new dimension by highlighting the life or life forms dwelling within this 'place'. This thought was encapsulated in the following expressions of the environment as 'all the things around us, the air we breathe, the water we drink, seas, rivers, forests, wetlands, etc.' and 'our surroundings, air, animals, plants, land, water, etc'.

Other students (8.1 per cent) saw the environment as a place that contains both living things and people. With the addition of the presence of humans, this conception is the broadest expression of the 'object' focus typology. Thus, the environment now has various life forms dwelling within it, including humans. Examples of ideas voiced included: 'The Environment means a clean place full of people, animals, insects and nature's things' and 'your surroundings; a place that has trees, animals, people and also the forest'. These three conceptions, the environment as a place, the environment as a place that contains living things, and the environment as a place that contains living things and people, all converge under an object focus view of the environment.

In terms of a relational view of people and the environment, only three students (0.8 per cent) regarded the environment as something that does something for people or that has some function for humans. One simply stated that the environment is comprised of 'our resources', while the other, with a similar sentiment, elaborated upon it by stating that it is 'the surroundings in which we live. We use some of these things as resources, whether human, man-made or animal resources'. These two students thus saw a relationship between people and the environment in which the environment provides people with the resources with which to live and survive. The third student voiced that 'the environment means a clean place where people enjoy themselves', highlighting the environment as a place that provides people with recreational support.

A larger proportion of students (17.3 per cent) viewed people as part of the environment with a responsibility to care for it or protect it. In this case, the emphasis was not on what the environment does for people but on what people should do for the environment. The emphasis was on action associated with caring for the environment, for example, the environment means 'keeping your surroundings clean' and 'not littering the place. Not throwing garbage in the river. Not throwing garbage in the gully. Not throwing garbage on the floor'. In the preceding instances, even though the presence of human beings in the environment was not clearly stated, it was implied through the suggestion that the environment had to be kept clean and not be polluted, since it is people who contributed to environmental degradation and who shared the responsibility of keeping it unpolluted. One student stated that it was simply 'a place where people live and take care of the environment', underscoring care for the environment, whatever action that might entail. This student also explicitly mentioned that people live in the environment.

Only three students (0.8 per cent) saw people and the environment as being in a mutually sustaining relationship, even though this is the principal idea behind the sustainable development concept. One student's notion of the 'environment' was that it involved 'keeping the surroundings clean so that we can have a good lifestyle', showing recognition of the relationship between keeping the environment clean and a good quality of life for humans. Another student stated 'we should clear up the place and it can stop us from getting disease and other infections', acknowledging a relationship between environment and health, that is, that a clean environment results in improved human health. Finally, the third student felt that an 'environment' was 'a group of people and organisms living in a place and sharing things'. Thus, a harmonious relationship was implied in which people and the natural world coexisted, sharing assets.

In summary, the majority of students surveyed (68.3 per cent) had an object focus in their perspectives on the environment while 18.8 per cent offered relation-focused ideas (Figure 6.2). The remaining students (approximately 13 per cent) were either unable to conceptualize the environment or put their views into words.

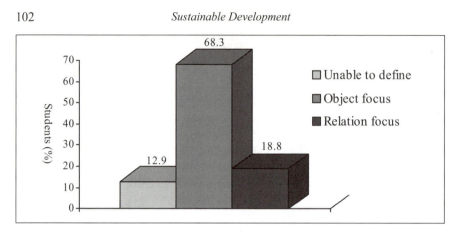

Figure 6.2   Concepts of environment expressed by the children in the study

Unlike the term nature, the majority of students were able to offer their perspectives on the 'environment'. Most students conceived of the environment in object-focused ways, with the majority of them conceiving of it in its narrowest sense, as a place. Again, although more students engaged in the Advanced Schools Programme gave relation-focused definitions of the environment, it is a matter of concern that only three students regarded people and the environment as being in a mutually sustaining relationship, a concept that is theoretically at the heart of sustainable development. As Loughland *et al.* (2002) indicated in relation to their study, the fact that most students hold an object view of the environment is troubling since students will act towards the environment based on the views that they hold. They question whether environmental education then could be alienating children from the environment by propounding an objectified, non-relational view.

Concepts of sustainable development

A higher number of those students in schools that were part of the Advanced Schools Programme (24.5 per cent) had heard the term sustainable development mentioned in some context, compared with 13.6 per cent of those who attended schools that were not a part of the ASP (Figure 6.3). A chi-square test showed that this was a significant difference (at p=0.05). Of the students in the Advanced Schools who claimed that they had heard mention of the term sustainable development, only 3.6 per cent offered ideas that in some way matched the concept. Of the 48 students in the schools that were not a part of the ASP who said that they had heard mention of the term sustainable development, nine of these voiced their views (Figure 6.4).

The idea of caring for the environment and nature was implicit in some notions of sustainable development. Some students said that it was about 'a clean environment with fresh air', as well as other variations, such as 'developing a clean environment and keeping it clean' and 'taking care of our environment and nature'.

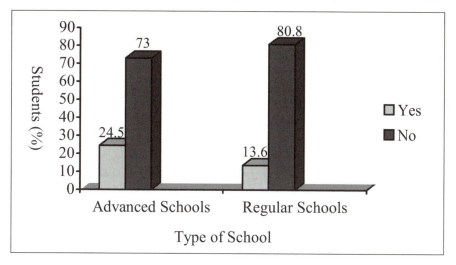

Figure 6.3   **Students who have heard of sustainable development by type of school**

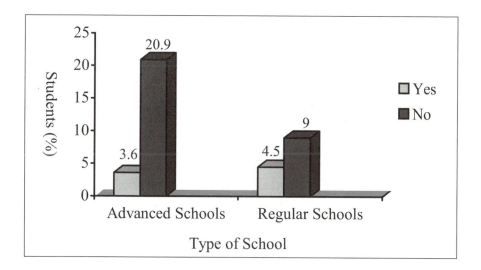

Figure 6.4   **Students who could define sustainable development by type of school**

A few students also highlighted notions of progress, growth, and harmonious relationships, for instance, those who stated that sustainable development involved 'developing something that can last a very long time' and 'protecting nature and humans while there is growth'. One student said that sustainable development meant 'to gradually keep and develop in the world and to take something to a higher level'. For another young person, sustainability referred to 'an environment in which we can all live healthily'.

The emphasis of those involved in setting and implementing the formal environmental education agenda was upon sustainable development as a pragmatic outcome of environmental education. Less emphasis was placed upon ideas of constructed notions of nature, the environment and sustainable development.

The students' lack of knowledge of sustainable development, despite the fact that elements are included in the curriculum, is problematic since environmental education for sustainable development is predicated on a) persons having some view of what sustainable development is about and b) a consensus of persons agreeing on what sustainable development is. Moreover, it might also signal the existence of a gap between the curricula content and the dissemination or transfer of knowledge within the classroom. Moreover, the formal education system itself is important as the framework within which environmental education for sustainable development is set. The majority of teachers surveyed (212 or 76.3 per cent) had attained Ordinary (O) Levels, Advanced (A) Levels, Caribbean Advanced Proficiency Examination (CAPE) or other equivalent examinations. Only thirteen trained and pre-service teachers (4.7 per cent) had obtained some type of associate degree or other equivalent diploma and five trained/pre-service teachers (1.8 per cent) had received a University degree (Figure 6.5). Consequently, issues such as literacy levels, equity, enrolment and attendance figures, and the quality of education (the qualitative aspects of the educational system) are crucial.

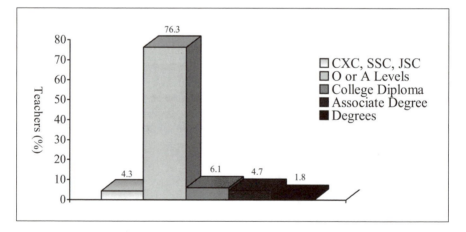

Figure 6.5   Highest educational status obtained by teachers in the study

The working environments of the schools were also important in terms of the context of teaching about sustainable development. The conditions in the schools included in the study varied considerably. For instance, at one of the schools, an environment prevailed which was typified by respectful relations, for instance between teachers and students, and one in which students had access to learning facilities such as, computers and a large library. At another school, by contrast, resources were lacking and a sense of social unease prevailed in which corporal punishment was carried out and verbal abuse and disrespect of teachers by students, and vice versa, were observed. These students also exhibited generally low literacy levels and behavioural problems. Thus, issues of equity (both between schools and within schools), literacy, basic infrastructure, overcrowding, corporal punishment and violence in schools, and respect/disrespect, for instance, were observed. Although relationships between such contextual variables and the types of views given by children were not tested statistically, the school demonstrating the least knowledge was also the one suffering from the most problems, whilst the school demonstrating the most knowledge did not experience such problems. Until fundamental issues such as these are addressed, they continue to undermine the education system in which environmental education for sustainable development can be effective and, by extension, through which the very notion of sustainable development can be a realistic objective.

The findings of the Jamaican case study reinforce the need to consider a reformulation of environmental education for sustainable development to better address the critical issues that lie at the heart of sustainable development.

Environmental education for sustainable development as an 'agent' of change versus a 'subject of change'

Environmental education is recognized globally as critical for the successful pursuit of sustainable development initiatives (WCED, 1987; Martin, 1990; UNESCO, 1997, 2002). Notwithstanding the crucial role of education in the transfer of knowledge, the inculcation of values and attitudes, and the moulding and practice of environmentally 'appropriate' behaviour, it is being questioned by theorists internationally and in this study as it pertains to Jamaica, as to whether environmental education for sustainable development is indeed the agent of change that the world sees and accepts, or whether it actually needs to be a subject of change.

Although education is widely recognized as essential for promoting sustainable development, nevertheless one finds that in many situations worldwide children are being trained to live in a world that cannot be sustained. This is the fundamental paradox of environmental education. As Sterling (1996: 18) states, 'Education is proclaimed at high level as the key to a more sustainable society, and yet it daily plays a part in reproducing an unsustainable society'.

At the core of liberal approaches to education is the idea of knowledge as a social construction, in which meanings are produced and negotiated. Thus, education and schooling in general have often been explored in terms of their roles in the transmission and reproduction of hegemonic values, whether economic, cultural, social or otherwise. This idea can be extended to environmental education as critical thinkers are now recognising that there can be, and oftentimes are, fundamental contradictions in the purpose and practice of environmental education within formal education.

Stevenson (1987) finds that the historical role of schools, and education systems in general, contradicts the actual rhetoric of environmental education. He writes that from a historical perspective, schools worldwide 'were not intended to develop critical thinkers, social inquirers and problem solvers, or active participants in environmental and political (or even educational) decision making' (Stevenson, 1987: 73). Thus, while environmental education is based on the view of schools as an agent of change, traditionally, schools were never actually seen as these agents of change that they were purported to be.

Thus, 'in environmental education rhetoric students are active thinkers and generators of knowledge, but in schools students are usually in the passive position of spectators and recipients of other people's knowledge and thinking' (Stevenson, 1987: 76). Indeed, as Jickling (1994) points out, the very notion of environmental education for sustainable development presupposes that sustainable development is the end goal of this education. He argues 'I would rather have my children educated than conditioned to believe that sustainable development constitutes a constellation of correct environmental views or that hidden beneath its current obscurity lies an environmental panacea' (Jickling, 1994: 6).

Gough (1987, 1989) also differentiates between an epistemological and ecological or ecopolitical (environmental) education, arguing that education and, by extension, environmental education, is characterized by an epistemological world-view and argues for the move towards an ecological or ecopolitical world-view. His distinctions between the two are expressed in his statement that:

> A paradigm shift involves changes in our total worldview, and it may be very difficult for most educators – even for environmental educators who are confident of the depth of their own ecological understanding – to accept that the education system in which they practice, and of which they are themselves products, provides a structured misrepresentation of reality, nature and human nature. (Gough, 1987: 53)

In other words, an epistemological worldview is very much characterized by factors that constrain individual and local knowledges, factors such as 'rote' learning activities; standardized laboratory exercises or activities; knowledge transfer; socially structured knowledge and a controlled learning environment in which students depend upon teachers for a one-way transfer of knowledge. An ecological or ecopolitical worldview, however, would be characterized by factors such as reality-centred projects; individually structured knowledge; perception and discovery of knowledge; and mutual and cooperative learning. Thus, in general, and in Jamaica specifically, more local and individual knowledges need to be acknowledged and pedagogical practices need to be changed.

These contradictions between traditional education or schooling and environmental education (for sustainable development) are closely intertwined with the notions of the social construction of nature and environmental discourses. Environmental education (for sustainable development) is underpinned by various ideologies pertaining to epistemologies, teaching styles, resources, views of place and community, sustainability, and so on (Payne, 1999). This is problematic in itself. Furthermore, if hegemonic constructions of nature and the environment are inscribed in the sustainable development discourse, then the education system becomes an institutionalized way to reproduce these dominant values and 'knowledges' within the general population, albeit in covert ways.

Based on the research carried out, several recommendations for the practice of environmental education for sustainable development (EESD) within the formal education sector in Jamaica can be made. Before doing this, however, acknowledgement is made that many varied steps have already been taken towards the institutionalization and practice of EESD in Jamaica. There is, therefore, no doubt that EESD is being emphasized on a national and individual level both in rhetoric and in practice.

The question then is how, based on the results of the research, can EESD in Jamaica be improved in practice? Firstly, taking into account this research and possibly utilising the results of follow-up research on environmental discourses used by students and teachers, the notion of environmental education for sustainable development should be re-examined. EESD presupposes sustainable development as the goal of environmental education, as Jickling (1994) points out. After further investigation, however, it might be discovered that this discourse is not the only one, or the main one, that individuals subscribe to as the one that defines the 'perfect' human-nature-environment dynamic. In other words, environmental education might have to be re-conceptualized in a manner that not only takes into account the sustainable development global environmental discourse, but other environmental discourses as well. There is nothing wrong with learning about sustainable development, but children should be taught that there are interests that lie underneath this discourse and that there are criticisms of this discourse (Jickling, 1994). They should also be allowed to explore alternative environmental discourses.

Secondly, in terms of curriculum development and implementation, curricula can be developed that take into consideration the multiple views held by students and teachers in this research and the multiple views that are possibly (and probably) held by those who have not participated in this research. 'Curricula can be developed or modified with teachers and can include the perspectives of children and parents' (Bartlett *et al.*, 1999: 172). Curricula modification is obviously a long-term process that will no doubt be protracted to some extent within a participatory process such as this. This process, though, can be made easier using the existing Jamaican curriculum, which has quite an extensive infusion of nature, environment and sustainable development themes within it, making only modifications necessary.

Thirdly, in terms of the practice of EESD, there are some pedagogical implications of the study that warrant further research and consideration. Although nature, environment and sustainable development themes are found within the primary and secondary curriculum, the seeming lack of knowledge on the part of students about these concepts did emerge in the research. This could point to several problems, such as the inability of students to convey their knowledge of, and perspectives on, these concepts because of low or sub-standard literacy levels; a gap in teachers' knowledge of these concepts and consequent ability to teach them; a gap in the material contained in the curriculum and what is taught and the need to produce innovative and dynamic ways of exploring these concepts on the parts of both students and teachers. This would mean research into the kind of educational tradition that Jamaican schooling falls within (for example, traditional, progressive or liberal) and the kinds of processes that take place within the classrooms with respect to knowledge creation and transfer. It would also mean that teachers and others in the education sector would need to play a vital role in evaluating the various scenarios and educational methodologies for exploring nature and environment themes.

Fourthly, the practice of EESD is not only in terms of the creation, dissemination and/or transfer of knowledge. It also encompasses action. As Bartlett *et al.* (1999: 172) point out 'schools should bear in mind that environmental education is pointless if the school itself engages in wasteful or destructive practices'. This was noticeable in at least one of the schools that was part of the ASP. Although engaged in this programme with many diverse environmental activities as a part of the school and high knowledge levels (compared with its 'control' school), the students, teachers and/or staff of this school threw garbage into a gully adjacent to the school. Thus, knowledge that results from EESD is being detached from action. This cannot be the case for any successful attempt at practicing EESD.

Additionally, as pointed out earlier, issues noticed in the schools during fieldwork, such as inequity, illiteracy and a lack of mutual respect, to name a few, undercut the notion of sustainable development, rendering it an unrealisable goal until such times as they are addressed.

The teacher education institutions also need to play a part. The student teacher environmental education programme is excellent because it has brought these institutions into the conceptualization and practice of EESD in the six aforementioned areas: environmental stewardship; capacity development; curriculum development and implementation; research and evaluation; monitoring and influencing policy; and networking and partnerships. This means that these institutions can play a significant role in how EESD is viewed and practiced. Hopkins & McKeown (2001) highlight the crucial role that these institutions can play. They write:

> Institutions of teacher education have the potential to bring about significant change because they manage the teacher education curriculum, train new teachers, provide professional development for practising teachers, consult with local schools, and often provide expert opinion to regional and national ministries of education. (Hopkins & McKeown, 2001: 8)

Taking into account all factors relating to environmental education, it is important to acknowledge the very real constraints and limitations within which the Jamaican education system and its educators operate. These include infrastructural constraints such as overcrowding, inadequate furniture, inadequate resources and materials and undesirable student-teacher ratios; social constraints such as violence, illiteracy, and teacher migration; structural features of the education system, such as streaming and the shift system and the financial constraints within which all sectors of a developing country operate.

Conclusion

Research presented in this chapter focused on a discursive examination of the sustainable development discourse globally and nationally within Jamaica; it is this discourse that is at the centre of environmental education for sustainable development (EESD). Future research needs to take the findings further on a number of levels. Conceptions of nature, the environment and sustainable development were demonstrated among individuals, but possible alternative discourses were not explored as this was outside the scope of study.

Exploration of possible alternative discourses mobilized by students and teachers could be an interesting next step for future research endeavours. For instance, in her research with twenty-five children in a Catholic primary school in Australia, Barron (1995) takes a gendered approach to the analysis of how children take up environmental discourses and the implications of these possibly contradictory discourses for environmental education. She uses different environmental narratives and has discussions with the students to find out their reactions and opinions, categorizing their views according to technocentric, consumerist, conservationist and any other discourses. The investigation of alternative discourses employed by students and teachers is a necessary and relevant next step.

While this research has uncovered some of the views held by individuals, it has not explored the 'how' behind these views. In other words, how do students, teachers, and other individuals come to conceptualize their views of nature, the environment and environmental discourses? What are the influences on and processes behind the varying constructions? For example, in speaking of children's relationships with the environment, Thomas-Hope (1996: 11) points out that their attitudes towards nature and the environment are influenced at two levels: 'the perceptual level' and 'the level of thought and imagination'. From an early age, how a child perceives nature and/or the environment will subconsciously influence their interactions with nature and/or the environment, even as (and after) their conscious knowledge takes over (Thomas-Hope, 1996). No doubt other factors will contribute to how people view nature and the environment; factors such as their exposure to it, the memories associated with it, social constructs such as race, class and gender and superstitions and myths related to it. Finding out how children and other individuals come to conceptualize nature and the environment is a necessary and crucial next step in research that could be carried out in conjunction with an investigation of the possible alternative discourses employed, possibly in a longitudinal study, as these processes would take shape over time.

The research limited itself to verbal conceptions of nature, the environment and sustainable development, due primarily to the time-constraints imposed by the schools. A discursive approach, however, looks not only at verbalized statements, but also looks at actions within the discourse or which result from the discourse. This, however, is not a flaw in the research, since examination of actions are connected with discourses, and, as already stated, the children's understanding of the sustainability discourse was extremely limited. Thus, examination of discursive actions should be carried out in conjunction with a more in-depth investigation of alternative discourses (including a re-examination of the sustainable development discourse) already called for.

It was pointed out that differing and possibly contested views of 'education' are one of the problematic notions lying beneath EESD. To a limited extent, this was investigated in the discussion of how EE, ESD, EESD and other formulations have emerged over the years. It was also explored to some extent in discussion with the interviewees, the people who contributed to the development of the NEEAPSD, as they voiced their own conceptions of EE and EESD. This was only probed to a limited extent in this study because it was felt that the differing conceptions of 'education' could truly be seen in action, that is how schooling and education were actually carried out within the schools. This would involve looking at interactions in the classrooms: for example, which students receive which kinds of knowledge (Apple, 1979). It would also involve a broadening of the notion of 'curriculum' to include the courses offered, course topics, textbooks used and their content, teaching materials, tests, information that is emphasized by teachers, and more (Evans, 2001). Again, how this curriculum is translated into action within the classrooms becomes critical.

Finally, further research should be done on how the notion of environmental education for sustainable development has been discursively formed internationally and nationally. In other words, in the same way that the construction of the sustainable development discourse was formed globally, an examination of a similar kind would have to be carried out for the construction of EESD worldwide and in the Jamaican context. For instance, Kelsey (2003) takes a look at how environmental education is discursively formed in international environmental agreements and the implications of this for knowledge forms used in education and public participation. Taking this further, an examination could and should be carried out as to how EESD is discursively formed in global agreements, and the implications of this for Jamaica's EESD policy.

There is no doubt that education must play a crucial role in sustainable development, particularly because education is itself a key aspect of sustainable development. The question concerns what type of education is needed, especially in specific national contexts, and how to go about delivering it. This idea links with the question of whether environmental education for sustainable development is the agent of change that organizations, governments and individuals claim it to be, or whether it needs to be the subject of change. As Sterling puts it, the question is raised as to 'how far education (particularly formal education which is typically less free to innovate than non-formal) can contribute to radical social change, or whether it is necessarily constrained by an encompassing culture' (Sterling, 1996: 21).

Sterling also contrasts two differing approaches in strategizing about education for sustainability. In the first approach, an instructive approach or education about sustainability, education is seen as important to the implementation of environmental policy, alongside other instruments. The public and other target groups receive knowledge and information generated and disseminated by professionals, with power and control being maintained at the centre.

Fien (1993, 2000) argues that environmental education that is truly transformative needs to integrate the liberal, progressive tradition with the social justice emphasis of the socially-critical tradition. Further, education needs to take a view of knowledge as socially constructed, having also an emphasis upon learning in the community and democratic forms of decision making within the school itself (Fien, 1999). Vargas (2000) considers ways of improving what she terms sustainable development education to make it more culturally relevant and sensitive; that is, taking into account cultural values and traditions. Environmental education should also aim to promote political and social literacy, so that people are able to cope with various views and interests concerning nature (Lijmbach *et al.*, 2002). This is consistent with the UNESCO statement suggesting that 'Education for sustainable development must explore the economic, political and social implications of sustainability by encouraging learners to reflect critically on their own areas of the world, to identify non-viable elements in their own lives and to explore the tensions among conflicting aims' (UNESCO, 2002: 11).

Despite the many weaknesses in the ways in which environmental education is conducted, the common view of nations, individuals, and organisations is one of education playing a major role as an agent of social change rather than as an agent of social reproduction. To be an effective vehicle for sustainable development, environmental education for sustainable development might very well need to undergo a critical shift in order to move beyond its lingering role as a reproducer of hegemonic environmental values. Although this means that environmental education for sustainable development needs to be the subject of change in order to be an effectual and valuable agent of change, a position does not need to be taken for one or the other. On the contrary, environmental education for sustainable development needs to be both.

References

Apple, M.W. (1979) *Ideology and the Curriculum*. Routledge and Kegan Paul, London.

Barron, D. (1995) Gendering environmental education reform: Identifying the constitutive power of environmental discourses. *Australian Journal of Environmental Education*, 11, 107-120.

Bartlett, S., Hart, R., Satterthwaite, D., De La Barra, X. & Missair, A. (1999) *Cities for Children: Children's Rights, Poverty and Urban Management*. Earthscan Publications Ltd, London.

Benton, L.M. & Short, R. (1999) *Environmental Discourse and Practice*. Blackwell Publishers Ltd, Oxford.

Blaikie, P. (1995) Changing environments or changing views? A political ecology for developing countries. *Geography*, 80, 203-214.

Bynoe, P. (1997) Education: A priority for the sustainable development of Guyana. *Transition*, 26, 112-118.

Castree, N. & Braun, B. (1998) The construction of nature and the nature of construction: Analytical and political tools for building survivable futures. In Castree, N. & Braun, B. (eds) *Remaking Reality: Nature at the End of the Millennium*. Routledge, London, pp. 3-42.

Dryzek, J.S. (1997) *The Politics of the Earth: Environmental Discourses*. Oxford University Press, Oxford.

Escobar, A. (1996) Poststructural political ecology. In Peet, R. & Watts, M. (eds) *Liberation Ecologies*. Routledge, London, pp. 46-68.

Evans, H. (2001) *Inside Jamaican Schools*. University of the West Indies Press, Kingston, Jamaica.

Fien, J. (1993) *Education for the Environment: Critical Curriculum Theorising and Environmental Education*. Deakin University, Geelong.

Fien, J. (1999) Towards a map of commitment: A socially critical approach to geographical education. *International Research in Geographical and Environmental Education*, 8, 140-158.

Fien, J. (2000) 'Education for the environment: A critique' – an analysis. *Environmental Education Research,* 6, 179-192.

Ferguson, T. (2005) *A Discursive Approach to Environmental Education for Sustainable Development in Jamaica.* University of the West Indies, Unpublished PhD thesis.

Gough, N. (1987) Learning with environments: Towards an ecological paradigm for education. In Robottom, I. (ed.) *Environmental Education: Practice and Possibility*. Deakin University Press, Victoria, pp. 49-67.

Gough, N. (1989) From epistemology to ecopolitics: Renewing a paradigm for curriculum. *Journal of Curriculum Studies*, 21, 225-241.

Greider, T. & Garkovich, L. (1994) Landscapes: The social construction of nature and the environment. *Rural Sociology*, 59, 1-24.

Hopkins, C. & McKeown, R. (2001) Reorienting teacher education to address sustainability. *Environmental Education*, 66: 8-9.

Jickling, B. (1994) Why I don't want my children to be educated for sustainable development. *The Trumpeter*, 11, 1-8. Available online at http://trumpeter. athabascau.ca/content/v11.3/jickling.pdf.

Kelsey, E. (2003) Constructing the public: Implications of the discourse of international environmental agreements on conceptions of education and public participation. *Environmental Education Research*, 9, 403-427.

Lijmbach, S., Margadant-Van Arcken, M., Kris Van Koppen, C.S.A. & Wals, A.E.J. (2002) 'Your view of nature is not mine'! Learning about pluralism in the classroom. *Environmental Education Research*, 8, 121-135.

Loughland, T., Reid, A. & Petocz, P. (2002) Young people's conceptions of environment: A phenomenographic analysis. *Environmental Education Research*, 8, 187-197.

Martin, P. (1990) *First Steps to Sustainability: The School Curriculum and the Environment*. World Wide Fund for Nature, Surrey, UK.

National Environmental Education Committee (NEEC) (1998) *The National Environmental Education Action Plan for Sustainable Development*. NEEC Secretariat, Kingston, Jamaica.

Payne, P. (1999) Postmodern challenges and modern horizons: Education 'for being for the environment'. *Environmental Education Research*, 5, 5-34.

Peterson, A. (1999) Environmental ethics and the social construction of nature. *Environmental Ethics*, 21, 339-357.

Pratt, V., Howarth, J. & Brady, E. (2000) *Environment and Philosophy*. Routledge, London and New York.

Sauvé, L. (1996) Environmental education and sustainable development: A further appraisal. *Canadian Journal of Environmental Education*, 1, 7-33. Available online at http://eduweb.brandonu.ca/~science/ee/sau96.htm.

Sterling, S. (1996) Education in change. In Huckle, J. & Sterling, S. (eds) *Education for Sustainability*. Earthscan Publications Ltd, London, pp. 18-39.

Stevenson, R.B. (1987) Schooling and environmental education: Contradictions in purpose and practice. In Robottom, I. (ed.) *Environmental Education: Practice and Possibility*. Deakin University Press, Victoria, pp. 69-82.

Thomas-Hope, E. (1996) *The Environmental Dilemma in Caribbean Context*. Grace Kennedy Foundation, Kingston, Jamaica.

United Nations Educational, Scientific and Cultural Organization (UNESCO) (1997) *Educating for a Sustainable Future: A Transdisciplinary Vision for Concerted Action*. UNESCO, Paris.

United Nations Educational, Scientific and Cultural Organization (UNESCO) (2002) *Education for Sustainability: From Rio to Johannesburg – Lessons From a Decade of Commitment*. UNESCO, Paris.

Vargas, C.M. (2000) Sustainable development education: Averting or mitigating cultural collision. *International Journal of Educational Development*, 20, 377-396.

World Commission on Environment and Development (WCED) (1987) *Our Common Future*. Oxford University Press, Oxford.

Chapter 7

Children, Education and Sustainable Development in Lesotho

Nicola Ansell

Introduction

Given that the concept of sustainable development is rooted in the idea of inter-generational equity, it is unsurprising that the international community has emphasized the role of children and youth in relation to achieving sustainability. Agenda 21, the programme of action which emerged from the Rio Earth Summit in 1992, contains a chapter on 'Children and Youth in Sustainable Development' (Chapter 25). This recognizes that 'children in both developing and industrialized countries are highly vulnerable to the effects of environmental degradation. They are also highly aware supporters of environmental thinking' (United Nations, 1992: paragraph 12). The chapter therefore calls for children's concerns to be incorporated into all policies for environment and development at local, regional and national levels and, in particular, for the involvement of children and youth in decision-making processes.

The education sector is generally seen as the most appropriate forum for involving children and youth in sustainable development, and initiatives to this end have been adopted in many countries. This chapter begins by examining the relationship between children and their environments, and the relevance of 'sustainable development' to children's lives. It goes on to explore the roots of Environmental Education (EE) and its transformation, in response to Agenda 21, into Education for Sustainable Development (ESD). The chapter then proceeds to an examination of the implementation of education for sustainable development into the curriculum in Lesotho, beginning with the adoption of 'development studies' as a curriculum subject and moving on to explore how sustainability is being 'mainstreamed' across the curriculum today.

Context

Children and environment

Environmental degradation has both physical and social consequences for children that differ from the effects on adults. Children have been described as 'canaries in the mines' because their bodies are more sensitive than those of adults to deteriorating environmental conditions (Stephens, 1994: 4). While it is important not to subscribe to the romanticized notion that children are closer to nature than adults (Jenks, 1996), children are both physiologically more sensitive to environmental change and also interact with their environments in ways that can put them at greater risk. Young children, for instance, explore their environments by putting things in their mouths, and older children often venture into areas that adults would choose not to frequent (Stephens, 1994). Children may thus not be protected by environmental guidelines and legislation based on the assumed 'normality' of adult experience and behaviour.

For many children in the Third World local environments are deteriorating, a situation linked to global processes of uneven development (Stephens, 1994). It is the immediate impacts on children's health that are the most prominent concerns for international agencies. Numerous diseases are spread through contaminants, to which children may be exposed due to factors over which their families have no control. Globally 1.7 billion people lack safe water and 3.3 billion lack access to adequate sanitation (Mehrotra *et al.*, 2000). Some households are located in areas affected by domestic or industrial contamination or exposed to animal waste. It is often the poor who are compelled to live in the least healthy environments. Each year, 1.8 million children under the age of five die from diarrhoeal diseases (Bryce *et al.,* 2005), most of which are acquired from contaminated food or water. The incidence of diarrhoea is, however, reduced where, as among more affluent households in northern Pakistan, there is sufficient income to afford less crowded living space, separate rooms for food preparation, houses with cement floors and screened windows, separate accommodation for animals and, in some cases, flush toilets (Halvorson, 2003). Standing water also contributes to the spread of malaria, another major childhood killer disease (Bryce *et al.,* 2005).

Contaminants in food and water actually kill fewer children annually than contaminants in the air. More than two million children under five die each year from acute respiratory infections such as pneumonia (Bryce *et al.,* 2005). Exposure to indoor air pollution (through the burning of coal, wood, dung or fibre residues for cooking and heating), combined with poor ventilation, is particularly hazardous, but outdoor pollution also poses a very significant threat. In Sao Paulo, Brazil, strong air pollution control programmes for fixed sources of particulate matter and sulphur dioxide, and emission controls on cars, have been partly neutralized by an almost trebling of the number of cars on the roads (Ribeiro & Cardoso, 2003). There remains a correlation between levels of pollution due to sulphur dioxide and particulates and respiratory symptoms in 11 to 13 year old children (Ribeiro & Cardoso, 2003). In Mexico City schools are closed during January because the pollution levels at that time of year are sufficient to cause children to faint in the playgrounds at break times (Stephens, 1994).

Environmental changes affect not only children's health but also other aspects of their everyday lives. Although 'there is a sense among some researchers that it is almost a luxury to worry about the sorts of 'subjective' children/environment issues foregrounded in the North' (Stephens, 1994: 7), and an inclination to focus instead on serious environmental risks to health, '[c]hildren in the South also, of course, experience more personal and subjective aspects of environmental change' (Stephens, 1994: 7). Conventional psychological models conceive of children's interactions with their physical environments as crucial to their development. While this approach neglects both the importance of children's social environments and other (non-developmental) aspects of children's environmental experiences, it exemplifies how the environment is, in many respects, central to young people's lives. Children's play, for instance, often puts them in particular and close relationships with their environments (Stephens, 1994). Satterthwaite *et al.* (1996) suggest that four aspects of children's environmental context are particularly significant: the indoor environment; immediate outdoor environment; infrastructure and service provision in the residential area and controls over air, water, food, soil and noise pollution. It is important for children's social identities that they have adequate access to space within and outside the home, and also that such areas are as free as possible from environmental hazards (Bartlett *et al.*, 1999). Environmental conditions impact not only on children's immediate welfare, but also their future lives. Katz (1993, 1994, 1998) suggests that the level of spatial autonomy young people have traditionally exercised in rural Sudan has allowed them to develop particularly sophisticated environmental knowledges. Increasingly, however, the environment is being commodified through the encroachment of agricultural development projects. Intensively farmed land is deteriorating in quality and young people's time is occupied in travelling longer distances to procure fuelwood and water, for sale or domestic use, as well as engaging in labour on household farms. There are few prospects of young people being able to employ their environmental knowledges in adulthood, as the environment deteriorates further, particularly given the slim likelihood of obtaining land of their own.

Children and sustainable development

Agenda 21 recognizes not only young people's particular needs with respect to the environment, but also considers them well equipped to contribute to sustainable development. Children's vulnerability is exacerbated by the fact that, in general, they have less power than adults to argue for improvements to the environmental conditions that affect them. However, through participation in environmental projects and decision-making, young people may not only contribute to improving the immediate conditions of their lives, but also acquire a long-term interest in the environment. An example is the Growing Up in Cities project (GUIC). Funded by UNESCO, GUIC was first undertaken in the 1970s and revived in the 1990s. Ten to 15 year olds in poor urban neighbourhoods around the world engage in research, action and dissemination of their ideas. GUIC has five objectives:

• gaining an understanding of children's environmental interests and needs through participatory research

- applying this information to the design of programmes and activities to improve life quality for children and their communities
- pressing for effective urban policies for children
- organizing public events to draw attention to urban children's rights and needs; and
- increasing the capacity for participatory research and action among academic researchers and the staff of community-based organizations. (Griesel *et al.*, 2002: 84)

Through the use of a range of children-centred methods, including drawings, stickers on maps to show good and bad places, and transect walks to identify problems (Swart Kruger & Chawla, 2002), children have demonstrated their capabilities as commentators on their environments, the ways they use them and the ways they are affected by them.

The ideas about children and sustainable development contained in Agenda 21 have been taken on board in the wider international policy environment. The WHO has recently launched a 'Healthy Environments for Children Alliance' that has identified thirteen environmental risk factors for children. It hopes to reduce disease by focusing on six priority issues: household water security, hygiene and sanitation, air pollution, disease vectors, chemical hazards, and injuries and accidents (WHO, 2002). The United Nations Conference on Human Settlements (Habitat II) in Istanbul in 1996, launched 'Child Rights and Habitat' (UNHCS/Habitat, 1996) which, alongside UNICEF's 'Child-friendly Cities' initiative, confirms the need to recognize children's particular needs in urban development and planning, as well as the contributions they might make towards human settlement development. The United Nations' 'World Programme of Action for Youth to the Year 2000 and Beyond' also incorporates environment as one of its fifteen priority areas (United Nations, 1996).

While the involvement of children and their needs in sustainable development has been taken on board in many sectors, it is generally the education sector that is seen as the most appropriate forum for involving children and youth.

Environmental Education (EE)

Environmental education has a long history, with its roots in Europe in the nineteenth century. It was in the 1970s that EE caught the imagination at an international level. The IUCN International Conference on Environmental Education in 1970 was followed by the UNESCO initiated UN Environmental Education Programme in 1975. Most influential, however, was the 1977 UNESCO/UNEP Inter-governmental Conference on Environmental Education. The outcome of this conference, the Tbilisi Declaration (UNESCO/UNEP, 1977), enshrines twelve guiding principles which have informed most subsequent EE initiatives. The Declaration states that environmental education should:

1. consider the environment in its totality
2. be a continuous life-long process
3. be interdisciplinary
4. examine major environmental issues at scales from the local to the international
5. focus on current and potential environmental situations
6. promote the value of local, national and international cooperation in preventing and solving environmental problems
7. explicitly consider environmental aspects in plans for development and growth
8. enable learners to have a role in planning their learning experiences and provide an opportunity for making decisions and accepting their consequences
9. focus particularly on learners' own communities in early years
10. help learners discover the symptoms and real causes of environmental problems
11. emphasize the complexity of environmental problems and thus the need to develop critical thinking and problem-solving skills
12. utilize diverse environments and a broad array of educational approaches to teaching, and learning about and from the environment with due stress on practical activities and first-hand experience.

The Tbilisi Declaration thus breaks with conventional educational traditions in its emphasis on holistic, interdisciplinary understandings of the environment; real world relevance; diversity of modes of learning, including through participatory learning processes; an emphasis on values, attitudes, decision-making skills and on action as the intended outcome (Gough, 2002; UNESCO/UNEP, 1977).

Historically, the 'aims of environmental education were often concerned with stimulating a sense of individual responsibility for the physical and aesthetic quality of the total environment' (Gough, 2002: 1201). The idea was that this could be achieved by providing accurate scientific information which would inevitably prompt change in values, attitudes and behaviour (Gough, 2002). Although most school-based environmental education still adopts this approach, many scholars now argue that emotional responses to the environment guide actions and opinions more than detached scientific knowledge can. Hence, one outcome of the Tbilisi Declaration's emphasis on attitudes, values and actions is the view that rather than focusing exclusively on scientific or cognitive knowledges, environmental education should assist children to develop forms of environmental knowledge rooted in the affective domain (involving emotion and sensation).

Encouraging the development of affective knowledge is far from straightforward. Affective knowledge is not generally associated with formal environmental education and it is arguably more likely to develop from persistent contact with a relatively pristine environment alone or with a few others from an early age, than from formal planned engagement (Hsu & Roth in Gurevitz, 2000). Furthermore, assumptions are made about the types of experience and forms of emotional attachment that arise out of engagement with environments (Gurevitz, 2000). Gurevitz suggests that these assumptions may be rooted in nostalgia. Adults concerned about the environment today often recall childhood experiences in natural environments and attribute much greater formative significance to these than to knowledge imparted through formal education. Their retrospective views may depend, however, on romanticized recollections of an idealized childhood, made to conform to the associations of children and nature that prevail in Western culture (Gurevitz, 2000). Little research has been undertaken to see how today's children value and experience environments (Gurevitz, 2000).

Agenda 21 and Education for Sustainable Development (ESD)

It was the 1992 United Nations Conference on Environment and Development that took existing ideas about environmental education, modified them and promoted them to a new audience. Chapter 36 of Agenda 21 declares:

> Education is critical for promoting sustainable development and improving the capacity of the people to address environment and development issues … Both formal and non-formal education are indispensable to changing people's attitudes so that they have the capacity to assess and address their sustainable development concerns. It is also critical for achieving environmental and ethical awareness, values and attitudes, skills and behaviour consistent with sustainable development and for effective public participation in decision-making. To be effective, environment and development education should deal with the dynamics of both the physical/biological and socio-economic environment and human (which may include spiritual) development, should be integrated' in all disciplines, and should employ formal and non-formal methods and effective means of communication. (United Nations, 1992: paragraph 36.3)

While upholding the principles of the Tbilisi conference, Agenda 21 sets out proposals to 'reorientate' educational systems of signatory states towards Education for Sustainable Development. The key distinctions between ESD and earlier environmental education are the emphasis on the needs and rights of human beings, and the global perspective (Sauvé, 1996). ESD emphasizes that environmental problems are fundamentally social and are related to deep-seated values, social systems and practices. Understanding of the social, economic and political character of environmental issues is thus deemed necessary in relation to identifying appropriate action for the environment (LEESP[1], 2000; Summers & Kruger, 2003).

Agenda 21 makes clear its recommendations as to how ESD should be delivered. Environment and development concepts are expected to be integrated into all educational programmes, focusing particularly on major issues in local contexts and 'drawing on the best available scientific evidence and other appropriate sources of knowledge' (para 36.4 d). It should be integrated as a cross-cutting issue, taking a multidisciplinary approach examining socio-cultural aspects and giving respect

---

1   Lesotho Environmental Education Support Project.

to 'community-defined needs and diverse knowledge systems, including science, cultural and social sensitivities' (para 36.5 b). ESD, as envisaged by Agenda 21, is also participatory: 'Relevant authorities should ensure that every school is assisted in designing environmental activity work plans, with the participation of students and staff' (para 36.5 e). Moreover, it is expected that innovative teaching methods should be developed, while recognising 'appropriate traditional education systems in local communities' (para 36.5 f).

ESD is now an established part of the curriculum in most European and many Third World countries (Bonnett, 2003). In reorientating their education systems, these countries have inevitably faced a number of issues. Some of these are at a rather abstract or definitional level. Since sustainable development is itself a contested concept, so too is education for sustainable development (Summers & Kruger, 2003). Paradoxically, however, the fact that sustainable development can be understood in such diverse ways has not only enabled it to speak to many constituencies, but it also fuels 'critical reflection, discussion, contestation and evolution' (Sauéve, 1996: 29). Hence, rather than seeking universal consensus, the concept is employed to promote debate (Sauvé, 1996). Echoing earlier debates about Environmental Education, Bonnett (2003: 680) asks: 'just what *kind* of knowledge will best illuminate, and equip us to deal with, issues of sustainability?' He calls for a critical approach: 'If we are to enable pupils to address the issues raised by sustainable development rather than to preoccupy them with what are essentially symptoms masquerading as causes ... we must engage them in those kinds of enquiry that reveal the underlying dominant motives that are in play in society' (Bonnett, 2003: 690). Effective education for sustainability is said to require education *about* the environment (information); education *in* the environment (time spent out of doors); and education *for* the environment (learning how to act effectively on issues of concern) (Chawla, 2002).

While there has been plenty of polemical writing on ESD, there has been less analysis of its implementation (Summers & Kruger, 2003). A few studies have examined the implementation of ESD in UK schools where it was introduced into the revised National Curriculum in 1999. Here, the fact that ESD has not been made to conform to the 'attainment target' driven structure of conventional subjects, combined with absence (until recently) of guidelines and limited preparation of teachers, have seriously hampered progress (Chatzifotiou, 2002; Summers & Kruger, 2003).

In a follow-up report on Agenda 21 coinciding with the Johannesburg World Summit for Sustainable Development (WSSD) in 2002, the UN Secretary-General reiterated the importance of ESD but declared: 'Few successful working models of education programmes for sustainable development currently exist' (cited in Ministry of Education and Science, 2004: 9). The realization that education systems have not been 'reoriented' to deliver ESD has inspired renewed attention. An international conference in Sweden in 2004 identified the obstacles to ESD as (principally) the organization of knowledge into closely maintained disciplines; but also lack of leadership, lack of economic resources, attitudes, culture, institutions and the short-term focus of decision-makers (Ministry of Education and Science,

2004: 57). Building on the WSSD, the United Nations proclaimed 2005-2014 the UN Decade of Education for Sustainable Development, with UNESCO as the lead agency (UNESCO, 2003). Once again, a holistic, interdisciplinary approach is called for, developing 'knowledge and skills needed for a sustainable future as well as changes in values, behaviour, and lifestyles' (UNESCO, 2003: 4). There is an emphasis on cultural appropriateness and local relevance, critical thinking, communication, collaboration, conflict management, problem solving and practical citizenship. Key themes are identified which emphasize the social, economic and political above the purely biophysical: overcoming poverty, gender equality, health promotion, environmental conservation and protection, rural transformation, human rights, intercultural understanding and peace, sustainable production and consumption, cultural diversity and information and communication technologies (UNESCO, 2003).

Lesotho case study

The remainder of this chapter examines the implementation of ESD in Lesotho. Lesotho is a small country, about the size of Belgium, entirely surrounded by South Africa. About a third of its two million inhabitants dwell in the mountainous three quarters of the country, the remaining two thirds in the foothills and lowlands (see Figure 7.1). Since long before the notion of sustainable development gained currency, concern has been expressed about environmental degradation in Lesotho and the declining capacity of the land to sustain its population.

Environmental degradation and sustainable livelihoods

Soil erosion, in the form of widespread sheet and gully erosion, is commonly identified as the country's most significant environmental problem (Gay *et al.*, 1995; LEESP, 2000). It is generally attributed to removal of vegetation (deforestation); continuous single cropping; overgrazing; lack of maintenance; poorly designed roads and tracks and poor tillage practices (Schmitz & Rooyani, 1987). About a quarter of the cultivated land is said to be so eroded that it should not be cultivated; up to 0.25 per cent of the cultivated land is lost to erosion each year, and an average of 40 tonnes of topsoil is removed annually from each hectare of farmland, amounting to a depth of 25 cm over 100 years (Schmitz & Rooyani, 1987). This is a problem for both cultivation (only 9 per cent of the country's land is arable (LEESP, 2000)) and grazing, as the biodiversity and quality of rangeland is in decline. Food production in Lesotho has been falling for 30 years (LEESP, 2000). Furthermore, Lesotho's climate inhibits successful farming: rainfall tends to be inadequate and droughts are frequent, although rainfall can be so intense that more than a tenth of the year's rain falls in one hour. Hail, too, destroys crops, and while intense heat is not uncommon in summer, frost can occur at any time of year (Gay *et al.*, 1995).

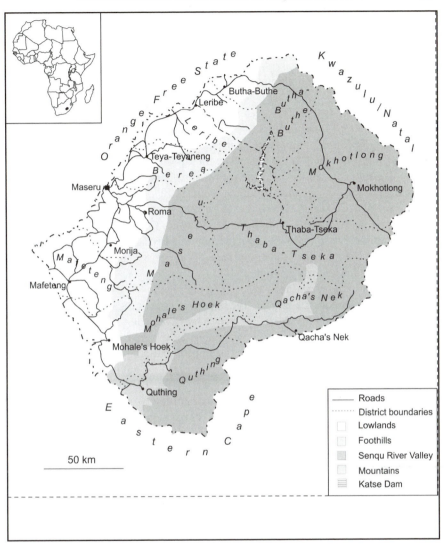

Figure 7.1   Map of Lesotho

The impact of environmental degradation is felt today, as well as carrying problematic implications for future generations. In 1993 women spent an average of 90 minutes a day collecting fuel (wood, dung and crop residues) (Gill, 1994). In the mountains, where the land is less productive, the average was three hours. It is not only women who collect fuel, however, but also children, for both domestic and school use (Gill, 1994). As population grows, land itself becomes scarce, and few households are now allocated the traditional three fields that are deemed appropriate for household sustenance. Children are not only affected by environmental degradation, they also play a role in its maintenance. Roughly 10 per cent of primary school-aged boys are full-time herdboys. If the quality of the rangeland diminishes they have to move further afield to graze their livestock. They also play a crucial role in monitoring environmental quality and abiding by, or disregarding, measures taken to restrict grazing of vulnerable land.

Environmental degradation needs to be seen in a wider historico-political-economic context. Environmental decline began when the Basotho first ventured into the fragile Maluti Mountains in the nineteenth century, as colonial settlers encroached on their land to the West (Gay *et al.*, 1995). Since the late nineteenth century Lesotho has served as a labour reserve, dependent economically on the remittances of labour migrants working in South Africa's mines. It was not in South Africa's (or wider colonial) interests that Lesotho should be self-sustaining, hence it has been a net importer of foodstuffs for 70 years (LEESP, 2000). Furthermore, access to alternative livelihoods through mine employment has meant that people have felt little need to invest in conservation, as they have not been very dependent on scarce natural resources (Turner, 2001).

This points to the importance of focusing on livelihoods and their sustainability, rather than the maintenance of objective biophysical qualities. Although livelihoods in Lesotho depend less directly on the natural environment than in some countries, the land remains important for the poor. Moreover, the environment provides other livelihood resources including energy supplies, building materials, water and medicines (Turner, 2001). These assets are accessed through systems of common property ownership and management (Turner, 2001). Land tenure is particularly significant. Customary tenure (allocation to families by a village chief or land allocation committee) is frequently criticized for being insecure and hence inhibiting conservation practices such as tree planting or fencing of land, although it is quite effective in securing the livelihoods of the rural poor (Gill, 1994).

Another practice that is subject to frequent criticism is the loss of arable land to housing. However, most peri-urban areas are intensively cultivated, and are more productive than rural land. Urban dwellers grow vegetables and fruit, keep chickens and livestock, and cultivate the land around their homes in a way that makes the land less vulnerable to erosion (Gay *et al.*, 1995). Even deforestation is exaggerated. While few indigenous trees remain, through a range of tree-planting initiatives of varying success, Lesotho probably has more trees now than a century ago (Gill, 1994).

Other environmental problems receive less attention. Only 45 per cent of rural people have access to safe drinking water, and smoke from cooking fires causes respiratory diseases and eye complaints (LEESP, 2000). In urban areas aerial pollution arises from vehicles and domestic fires (LEESP, 2000). In some rapidly expanding suburbs sanitation and refuse disposal are inadequate. Furthermore, although many men still work as miners, Lesotho's largest employment sector is now an export-oriented garment industry. This brings environmental problems, notably watercourse pollution.

A number of other environmental resources play significant economic roles. Water is now exported to South Africa through the Lesotho Highlands Water Project, a major engineering venture. Lesotho has also attempted to mine diamonds, although this proved uneconomical due to the low-yield and logistical difficulties (Gay *et al.*, 1995).

Environmental policies in Lesotho

Lesotho's 1993 constitution expresses a commitment to the environment: 'Lesotho shall adopt policies designed to protect and enhance the natural and cultural environment of Lesotho for the benefit of both present and future generations and shall endeavour to assure to all citizens a sound and safe environment adequate for their health and well-being' (Kingdom of Lesotho, 1993: section 36). This commitment has been addressed through a decade of initiatives. In 1994 a National Environment Secretariat was established under the Prime Minister's office, charged with coordinating a National Action Plan to implement Agenda 21. In 1996 a National Environmental Policy was introduced, with a goal 'to achieve sustainable livelihoods and development for Lesotho' (Government of Lesotho, 1996: section 2.1).

The Environment Act of 2001 has similar goals but carries considerably greater legal force, guaranteeing individuals the right to a clean and healthy environment; imposing on all citizens a duty to protect, maintain and enhance the environment and giving citizens the right to take legal action against anyone damaging the environment (Sekhamane, 2002). It also replaces the National Environment Secretariat with the semi-autonomous Lesotho Environment Authority, vested with the responsibility to implement and administer the Environment Act (Sekhamane, 2002). Most recently, the government reaffirmed its commitment to a healthy environment in a national vision statement: Vision 2020. Most of these environment-focused initiatives have envisaged a role for education.

Lesotho's education system

Lesotho's education system was established under British colonial influence in the late nineteenth century and, it is argued, subsequent reforms have been 'characterized more by continuities rather than discontinuities' (Muzvidziwa & Seotsanyana, 2002: unpaged; see also Ansell, 2002a). The majority of schools are owned by churches: the Basotho represent their education system as a 'three-legged stool' wherein control is shared between government, churches and communities. In practice, the role of the churches is declining, the influence of communities remains slight, and many aspects of the education system are highly centralized. School curricula at primary and junior secondary levels are determined by the National Curriculum Development Centre (NCDC), although the Examinations Council of Lesotho (ECOL) assesses a narrower area of the curriculum, in practice determining what is taught in schools. The whole system remains closely constrained by the demands of High School examinations, which are still developed and administered in the UK (Ansell, 2002b). These examinations skew the content and ethos of schooling such that, beyond the basic level, it does little to address the needs of the majority of the population, especially in rural areas, and among girls in particular (Ansell, 2000; Ansell, 2002b; Ansell, 2004).

Lesotho's education system is currently undergoing review to take into account international concerns, notably Education for All, the UN Convention on the Rights of the Child, and the Millennium Development Goals, as well as Lesotho's constitutional commitment to free and compulsory education and Vision 2020 which aims to eradicate poverty through provision of basic education for all (Ministry of Education and Training, 2004). A Free Primary Education programme, introduced in 2000, is being phased in one year at a time. This has reversed declining primary attendance such that 85 per cent of six to 12 year olds attend school[2] (Ministry of Education and Training, 2004). Drop out and repetition rates remain high, however, and only 70 per cent of students completing primary education progress to secondary.

The Education Sector Strategic Plan (Ministry of Education, 2002), beyond increasing access to education, proposes changes to content and assessment. Three key 'emerging issues' are identified: mitigating the impact of HIV and AIDS (currently a major challenge for the sector), developing a 'gender responsive curriculum', and environmental education for sustainable development (Ministry of Education and Training, 2004: 8). This reflects the commitment of the National Environmental Policy: 'To impart knowledge and skills, both indigenous and non-indigenous, of how to manage environment in sustainable ways [and to] increase public awareness and understanding of the imperative of sustainable economic growth through sustained environmental protection, conservation and management': goals which were to be achieved by, among other things, 'Develop[ing] a national plan of action for carrying out environmental awareness through formal and non-formal education programmes' (Government of Lesotho, 1996: section 4.26). Further, the Education Sector Strategic Plan included provision of specialist training to teachers on EE by 2003 and a longer term intention to roll out an information campaign to school communities on environmental education (Ministry of Education, 2002). It is noteworthy that the focus of these proposals is on skills, awareness and understanding, rather than attitudes, values and action. Furthermore, the goals are future-oriented and say little about the role of young people today. Indeed, the National Environmental Policy conceptualizes children as a vulnerable group, rather than as actors in the environment, and even the 1994 National Plan of Action for Children, which includes a section on prevention of degradation of the environment, says little about children's roles as participants (Ministry of Education, 2002).

An emphasis on development is not new to education in Lesotho. Development studies entered the secondary curriculum in the 1980s, although it is not taught in all

---

2   The fact that many children begin school late is responsible for many of the 'missing' 15 per cent.

schools and it is perceived as an alternative to history or geography. Development studies is interesting to examine as a forerunner of ESD as, in many ways, it echoes the approach to ESC promulgated in Agenda 21. Based partly on the ideas of Patrick van Rensburg (who established the Foundation for Education with Production in 1980), the development studies syllabus stresses combining academic and practical work: 'They should not only learn about development but also participate in development' (Examinations Council Of Lesotho, 1996: unpaged). Proposed activities include school maintenance and improvement (repairs, building, tree-planting), food production (vegetable growing, pig or poultry projects) and community development work (in areas such as conservation, public health and literacy). Practical projects are intended 'to foster a spirit of self-reliance, to make students more productive, to develop problem-solving and decision-making skills, and to illustrate social and economic concepts' (Examinations Council Of Lesotho, 1996: unpaged).

Development studies has achieved a high profile, arguably because it was introduced as a fully-fledged curriculum subject, with examinations and specialist teachers. By fitting the subject to the conventional model, however, concern with problem-solving and integrating the academic and practical is diminished. I once observed a development studies lesson in which problem-solving skills were practised in relation to the environment. Students were asked to work in groups to decide how they would deal with overgrazing, grass burning and tree felling (all common local causes of soil erosion) and to report back in the next lesson. It was emphasized that their own opinions were required. For once they were asked to engage in knowledge production. Most development studies lessons, however, involve rote learning of facts.

Lesotho Environmental Education Support Project (LEESP)

The Lesotho Environmental Education Support Project began as a 3 year project running from August 2001 to July 2004. It was set up in relation to the National Environmental Policy with a remit 'to strengthen and support the introduction and development of Environmental Education within the formal school system in Lesotho' (LEESP, 2000: 5). Focusing on curriculum development, teacher development and material development (LEESP, 2000), there were four elements to the project:

1. capacity development of those involved in curriculum development and support to issuing immediate amendments to current curriculum to enhance its EE content
2. capacity development at institutional level for training teachers to implement EE
3. capacity development in curriculum performance monitoring, specifically monitoring EE as a cross-cutting theme
4. establishment of Model Schools to create a resource of practising and experienced teachers for diffusion of EE to other schools.

LEESP was initiated and funded by the Danish Cooperation for Environment and Development (DANCED) to the tune of 13 million DKK (R10 million, further funding was provided by the Government of Lesotho). Its rationale was that 'Lesotho lacks sufficient human and material resources to design and implement Environmental Education based on a comprehensive and complete anthropocentric approach' (LEESP, 2000: 12), and no significant assistance was available from elsewhere. In particular, in existing curricula, the 'elements of environmental education are mainly based on isolated considerations of environmental degradation' (LEESP, 2000: 13) and could usefully include more social, economic and political aspects. Drawing on Denmark's experience of integrating EE into curricula, seven Danish consultants would be employed to work with subject specialists at the National Curriculum Development Centre (LEESP, 2000). There was concern, however, that the project would not simply seek to impose a Danish approach. 'Lesotho is keen to arrive at a design of Environmental Education that will be relevant, appropriate and effective for the local circumstances rather than simply taken over in complete form programmes developed for other environments' (LEESP, 2000: 13). Thus the National Environment Secretariat was given a monitoring, guiding and advisory function, while the day-to-day implementation of LEESP was allocated to the Ministry of Education.

Despite the project's name, LEESP is inspired by the view of ESD enshrined in Agenda 21, particularly in its long-term perspective:

> The central problem focuses on increase of environmental awareness in order to improve the population's environmental behaviour and encourage local initiatives for protecting the environment. The project as such is, therefore, not directed towards solving any of Lesotho's immediate environmental problems, but the effect on the environment will be seen in the long term. (LEESP, 2000: 12)

The emphasis is on finding appropriate strategies for the context and 'incorporating initiatives close to school level which usually constitute the major bottleneck for success of environmental education projects' (LEESP, 2000: 12). The project's pedagogical aim is to ensure that each learner develops the necessary 'action competencies' to manage environmental issues and support sustainable development:

> Action competency aims at building up a sustainable citizenship in each learner. Action is associated with behaviour, activities, traditions, life skills, etc. An action must be conscious, reflective and aimed. Competency is associated with a capability and willingness to a [sic] responsible participation in society, its necessary decision making and problem solving. (Rohde, 2002: 7)

In practical terms, the project included capacity building with NCDC personnel, which took the form of short courses combined with long-term on-the-job coaching (LEESP, 2000). Workshops were held for District Resource Teachers (DRTs – advisory teachers working in Lesotho's 10 districts) and for staff at the Model Schools. The project adopted a whole school approach through Model Schools, rather than the more usual cascade model (training one teacher to pass training on to other teachers in the school). At the 20 Model Schools (a primary and a secondary in each district), teachers were trained in action reflection/research in order to achieve self-learning competence (LEESP, 2000). The project also involved the development of teachers' guides (LEESP, 2003) and support for the development of learners' textbooks. The Examinations Council of Lesotho (ECOL) was to be trained in ways to monitor and evaluate EE outcomes (LEESP, 2000) and, in 2004, the project was extended to cover teacher education institutions. A policy document was also released (LEESP, 2004) requiring, among other things, that all schools develop their own EE policies. Finally, regional cooperation with similar initiatives in South Africa and Namibia is being promoted through the Southern Africa Development Community regional environmental education programme (SADC-REEP, 2005).

Problems encountered in implementing LEESP

LEESP has not yet been fully implemented in Lesotho schools, but the initial stages are complete: NCDC officials have received training, workshops have been held with District Resource Teachers and 10 staff development workshops have been conducted at each Model School. Built into the project was a research and monitoring exercise undertaken by a team of four researchers: two from the university, one from the teacher training college and one from NCDC. Members of this team attended a number of the DRT and school-based workshops. The analysis that follows draws largely on their report (Mokuku *et al.*, 2004).

One of the key challenges in the implementation of environmental education in Lesotho schools is the fact that EE, as conceived in the Tbilisi Declaration and in Agenda 21, does not fit the educational paradigm that currently exists in Lesotho (Mokuku *et al.*, 2004). The role of the staff development workshops was thus not simply to introduce new material, but to effect a paradigm shift in the way in which teachers think about their role. At one level is the challenge of interdisciplinarity. In line with Tbilisi, LEESP intended that EE should not be taught as an isolated subject. A distinction was, however, made between *integration* and *infusion* into the curriculum. Teachers were presented with the idea that EE could be infused into non-biophysical subjects such as languages and maths, but integrated into carrier subjects. At primary level, carrier subjects would be agriculture, health and physical education, home economics, science and social studies; at secondary level, agriculture, health and physical education, home economics, sciences (physical and biological) and social sciences (geography and development studies) (LEESP, 2000). This was complicated by the fact that non-biophysical aspects such as the concept of 'democracy' would be infused into the biophysical carrier subject. Mokuku *et al.* (2004) argue that this distinction is problematic because it draws an unhelpful dualistic distinction between biophysical and non-biophysical aspects of sustainable development. Disciplinary boundaries posed considerable difficulties for teachers in secondary schools, where these are closely guarded. 'Embarking on cross-curricular or thematic teaching and learning, where subjects are used to analyse issues and provide multi-faceted understanding, requires a drastic change of the teachers' mind set' (Mokuku *et al.*, 2004: 51). EE requires teachers to work together to construct complex ideas that transcend disciplinary boundaries – one history resource teacher, for instance, had difficulty imagining how to incorporate the concept of 'biodiversity' into her subject. At primary level, where multidisciplinary teaching is more common, these difficulties were much less pronounced (Mokuku *et al.*, 2004).

A second epistemological difficulty relates to the fact that Lesotho's education system has historically focused on the transfer of imported (Western) knowledges, with teachers serving as conduits and students as passive recipients (Ansell, 2002a; Ansell, 2002b; Mokuku *et al.*, 2004; Muzvidziwa & Seotsanyana, 2002). The Tbilisi Declaration, and LEESP, envisage roles for both teachers and students as producers of new knowledge (LEESP, 2000). Lesotho's government has stressed the importance of indigenous knowledges in relation to the environment, and LEESP recommends that attention be given (particularly in the Sesotho curriculum) to proverbs, idioms, songs, stories, games, riddles and totems that transmit beliefs and values concerning the environment, as well as taboos and customary laws that contribute to the conservation of resources and of biodiversity (LEESP, 2003). Storytelling and oral traditions are also viewed as ways of encouraging free expression of thoughts (Mokuku *et al.*, 2004), for instance through 'storylines' that emulate traditional bed-time story-telling, and the collection of oral histories from community members (LEESP, 2003).

Both the workshops and teachers' handbooks were somewhat contradictory in the extent to which they encourage creativity. The handbooks (LEESP, 2003) repeatedly stress the role of teachers in deciding exactly what to teach and how to teach it, but the largest of three sections is devoted to 'Environmental concepts and issues in the curriculum'. This presents environmental issues in a rather didactic way, which, while emphasising that they often reflect conflicting interests, does not acknowledge that environmental knowledges are themselves contested, without unequivocally 'correct' answers. The school workshops were intended to be an empowering process, enabling teachers to create knowledge. Some teachers, however, were uncomfortable that they were not 'given information on what EE really is' (Mokuku *et al.*, 2004: 17). By contrast, other teachers felt that the workshop organizers started with fixed views of what they wanted the teachers to arrive at, and that the creative role of the participants was illusory. Beyond transforming the way teachers think about knowledge production, collaboration involving teachers is essential 'to avoid creating new alienating orthodoxies' (Mokuku *et al.*, 2004: 31).

A related difficulty lies in the way EE conceptualizes children. The workshops introduced to teachers the idea that there are four levels of knowledge – action knowledge, judgement knowledge, explanation knowledge and data knowledge. The emphasis of environmental education, they were told, was on students developing action knowledge (Mokuku *et al.*, 2004). The teachers initially found it difficult to recognize the different epistemologies underlying different teaching methods, but they began to recognize that different types of questions called for different types of knowledge, and, on this basis, became critical of examinations which failed to go beyond 'explanation knowledge' to value 'judgement knowledge' or 'action knowledge' (Mokuku *et al.*, 2004). Nonetheless, 'the teachers struggled to perceive and define learners' roles as planners but [instead saw them] as implementers of pre-determined knowledge (e.g. plans and policies)' (Mokuku *et al.*, 2004: 39). It is common practice for teachers to instruct learners to clean up their surroundings, by removing litter. For some teachers, this was an appropriate example of teaching about, in and for the environment. By contrast, at one primary school, teachers reported having consulted students to revise the school's environmental education policy (Mokuku *et al.*, 2004).

A further problematic area was the conceptualisation of EE. On the whole, the workshops with District Resource Teachers were successful in getting them to engage with 'a broad view of environmental issues as concerned with competing interests, and not as merely biophysical phenomena' (Mokuku *et al.*, 2004: 22), although some retained reductionist views, or an understanding that it was simply about 'keeping the environment clean' (Mokuku *et al.*, 2004: 23). Although the notion of 'sustainable development' is highly prominent as the key concept underlying EE in all LEESP documents, in the school-based workshops, it was only introduced in the last session. Only then was emphasis placed on the interaction of biophysical, social, political and economic phenomena, and of "conflicting interests' between people as the underlying causes of environmental problems' (Mokuku *et al.*, 2004: 67).

Another problem identified by the monitoring and research team was over-optimism about EE. One resource teacher described it as 'the messiah who has come to save' (Mokuku *et al.*, 2004: 16), suggesting undue emphasis on what it can achieve. There remains a need to recognize the 'complex socio-political and structurally rooted nature of many EE problems, whose solutions lie beyond the realms of the school contexts' (Mokuku *et al.*, 2004: 17). In some workshops the potential role of EE in relation to poverty was addressed, poverty being viewed as both cause and outcome of many environmental problems in Lesotho. Participants 'grappled with what it meant to treat 'poverty' in the context of classroom teaching, and contested the possibilities and limits of learners' 'action competence' to address environmental issues' (Mokuku *et al.*, 2004: 52). If expectations are unattainable, the result might be apathy rather than 'action competence'.

Beyond the difficulty of achieving a school level paradigm shift, LEESP has been beset by other problems. It was designed in 1997, but administrative delays and civil unrest intervened in 1998. When the project eventually began in 2001, the educational context had changed. Implementation of new primary and secondary curricula was well underway. The new curricula included elements of environmental education, and 'it was decided that initiating a new curriculum reform supported by the project, in order to fully integrate environmental education, would disturb the current curriculum implementation and waste considerable work already done on school level' (LEESP, 2000: 1).

Change is also seriously constrained by current assessment practices. Some teachers refused to put some of the ideas into practice because they feared they would not finish their examination syllabuses (Mokuku *et al.*, 2004).[3] Although the Education Sector Strategic Plan suggests a reconsideration of assessment methods, the new report books for the Free Primary Programme were introduced with quarterly test columns, conveying the assumption that schools will test their students in every subject on a quarterly basis (Mokuku *et al.*, 2004). Continuous assessment is considered more appropriate to the objectives of ESD, but ECOL is resisting its implementation in schools[4] (Mokuku *et al.*, 2004).

In part, the education system continues to be examination-driven because of the perception of teachers that change should be initiated from above. Teachers dislike the current assessment practices and can see good reasons for change, but they view this as requiring change at the centre rather than local resistance. 'The present centralized education system is a driving force in the implementation of curriculum initiatives and tends to undermine school-based curriculum initiatives and associated school visions' (Mokuku *et al.*, 2004: 63). By contrast, there have been problems in disseminating from the Model Schools where neighbouring schools refuse to participate, even though they were aware that LEESP is a government initiative. The difficulty is sometimes rooted in conflicts between the churches that own schools (Mokuku *et al.*, 2004).

Conclusions

Across the world, young people grow up in very varied environments: from dry deserts to lush forests; high mountains to coastal plains; high rise urban estates to refugee camps. They interact with their environments at a range of scales, and through different activities: at home, in the local neighbourhood, at school and (for many) at work. The proposals for ESD set out in Agenda 21 recognize that learners are actors in their environments and it expects them to play a participatory role. Implementation of these proposals in formal education systems has been fraught with difficulties, not least due to the poor fit between conceptions of education set out in Agenda 21 and the nature of currently existing education systems. One consequence of these difficulties is a tendency to focus on ESD as education for the (long term) *future* needs of society. The notion of inter-generational equity that underpins sustainable development should, however, be interpreted to incorporate concern for the immediate needs of children. If children are affected by environmental degradation today, this will have long-term consequences – and children have the longest future of any group in society (Chawla, 2002).

Education for sustainable development is geared not only to achieving a positive long-term impact on the biophysical environment; it also envisages significant

---

3   Negotiations are taking place with ECOL to develop examination protocols that ensure that the Model Schools are not disadvantaged relative to others in relation to the impacts on learning in other subjects (LEESP, 2000).

4   Development Studies teachers have, in the past, sought unsuccessfully to have this assessed as a practical subject (Mokuku *et al.*, 2004).

changes to education itself. LEESP (2000: 29) argues that 'environmental education is an excellent carrier of efforts to achieve improved learning practice in developing countries as it cuts across all traditional subjects and hence provides the fuel for integrating more holistic and systems thinking in the curriculum'. If successful, it could have implications far beyond what is conventionally understood to be the arena of environmental concern, contributing also to social and economic justice as envisaged in the concept of sustainable development.

References

Ansell, N. (2000) Sustainability: life chances and education in southern Africa. In Redclift, M. (ed.) *Sustainability: Life Chances and Livelihoods*. Routledge, London, pp. 144-157.

Ansell, N. (2002a) 'Of course we must be equal, but ...': imagining gendered futures in two rural southern African secondary schools. *Geoforum*, 33, 179-194.

Ansell, N. (2002b) Secondary education reform in Lesotho and Zimbabwe and the needs of rural girls: pronouncements, policy and practice. *Comparative Education*, 38, 91-112.

Ansell, N. (2004) Secondary schooling and rural youth transitions in Lesotho and Zimbabwe. *Youth and Society*, 36, 186-202.

Bartlett, S., Hart, R., Satterthwaite, D., de la Barra, X. & Missair, A. (1999) *Cities for Children: Children's Rights, Poverty and Urban Management*. Earthscan, London.

Bonnett, M. (2003) Education for sustainable development: sustainability as a frame of mind. *Journal of Philosophy of Education*, 37, 675-690.

Bryce, J., Boschi-Pinto, C., Shibuya, K., & Black, R.E. (2005) WHO estimates of the causes of death in children. *The Lancet,* 365, 1147-1152.

Chatzifotiou, A. (2002) An imperfect match? The structure of the National Curriculum and education for sustainable development. *The Curriculum Journal*, 13, 289-301.

Chawla, L. (2002) 'Insight, creativity and thoughts on the environment': integrating children and youth into human settlement development. *Environment and Urbanization*, 14, 11-21.

Examinations Council of Lesotho (1996) *Regulations and syllabuses for the Junior Certificate Examination*. ECOL, Maseru, Lesotho.

Gay, J., Gill, D. & Hall, D. (1995) *Lesotho's Long Journey: Hard Choices at the Crossroads: A Comprehensive Overview of Lesotho's Historical, Social, Economic and Political Development with a View to the Future*. Sechaba Consultants, Maseru, Lesotho.

Gill, D. (ed.) (1994) *The Situation of Children and Women in Lesotho*. Sechaba Consultants for the Ministry of Planning, Economics and Manpower Development, financed by UNICEF, Maseru, Lesotho.

Gough, A. (2002) Mutualism: a different agenda for environmental education. *International Journal of Science Education*, 24, 1201-1215.

Government of Lesotho (1996) *Lesotho National Environmental Policy.* http://www. ecs.co.sz/env_leg_lesothoenvpolicy.htm. Accessed 30/01/05.

Griesel, R.D., Swart Kruger, J. & Chawla, L. (2002) 'Children in South Africa can make a difference': an assessment of 'Growing Up in Cities' in Johannesburg. *Childhood*, 9, 83-100.

Gurevitz, R. (2000) Affective approaches to environmental education: going beyond the imagined worlds of chihldhood? *Ethics, Place and Environment*, 3, 253-268.

Halvorson, S.J. (2003) A geography of children's vulnerability: gender, household resources, and water-related disease hazard in northern Pakistan. *The Professional Geographer*, 55, 120-133.

Jenks, C. (1996) *Childhood.* Routledge, London.

Katz, C. (1993) Growing girls/closing circles: limits on the spaces of knowing in rural Sudan and United States cities. In Katz, C. & Monk, J. (eds) *Full Circles: Geographies of Women over the Life Course.* Routledge, London, pp. 88-106.

Katz, C. (1994) Textures of global changes: eroding ecologies of childhood in New York and Sudan. *Childhood*, 2, 103-110.

Katz, C. (1998) Disintegrating developments: global economic restructuring and the eroding of ecologies of youth. In Skelton, T. & Valentine, G. (eds) *Cool Places: Geographies of Youth Cultures.* Routledge, London, pp.130-144.

Kingdom of Lesotho (1993) The constitution of Lesotho. *Lesotho Government Gazette Extraordinary* 38. http://www.lesotho.gov.ls/constitute/gconstitute.htm. Accessed 8/7/05.

LEESP (2000) *Lesotho Environmental Education Support Project.* LEESP, Maseru. http://www.lea.org.ls/pdfdocs/LEES/lees.PDF. Accessed 8/7/05.

LEESP (2003) *Environmental Education: A Teacher's Handbook for Primary and Secondary Schools in Lesotho.* Lesotho Environmental Education Support Project, Morija, Lesotho.

LEESP (2004) *Reference note or policy document for environmental education in Lesotho.* Workshop, 22 March 2004, Maseru.

Mehrotra, S., Vandemoortele, J. & Delamonica, E. (2000) *Basic Services for All?* UNICEF Innocenti Research Centre, Florence.

Ministry of Education (2002) *Education Sector Strategic Plan.* MOET, Maseru, Lesotho.

Ministry of Education and Science (2004) *Learning to Change our World.* International consultation on education for sustainable development: learning to change our world Secretariat, Ministry for Education and Science, Sweden, Stockholm, Sweden.

Ministry of Education and Training (2004) *National Report on the Development of Education: Kingdom of Lesotho.* International Conference on Education, Geneva.

Mokuku, T., Jobo, M.E., Raselimo, M. & Mathafeng, T. (2004) *Lesotho Environmental Education Support Project: Research and Monitoring Repor*t. Maseru, Lesotho.

Muzvidziwa, V.N. & Seotsanyana, M. (2002) Continuity, change and growth: Lesotho's education system *Radical Pedagogy,* 4. http://radicalpedagogy.icaap. org. Accessed 8/7/05.

Ribeiro, H. & Cardoso, M.R.A. (2003) Air pollution and children's health in Sao Paulo (1986-1998). *Social Science and Medicine*, 57, 2013-22.

Rohde, K. (2002) Lesotho Environmental Education Support Project. *Our Environment*, 2, 6-7.

SADC-REEP (2005) SADC Regional Environmental Education Programme. http://www.sadc-reep.org.za/net_support.htm. Accessed 01/02/05.

Satterthwaite, D., Hart, R., Levy, C., Mitlin, D., Ross, D., Smit, J, & Stephens, C.(1996) *The Environment for Children: Understanding and Acting on the Environmental Hazards that Threaten Children and their Parents*. Earthscan, London.

Sauvé, L. (1996) Environmental education and sustainable development: a further appraisal. *Canadian Journal of Environmental Education*, 1, 7-35.

Schmitz, G. & Rooyani, F. (1987) *Lesotho: Geology, Geomorphology, Soils*. National University of Lesotho, Roma.

Sekhamane, L. (2002) Environment law: a dream come true. *Our Environment*, 2, 1-4.

Stephens, S. (1994) Children and environment: local worlds and global connections. *Childhood*, 2, 1-21.

Summers, M. & Kruger, C. (2003) Teaching sustainable development in primary schools: theory into practice. *The Curriculum Journal*, 14, 157-180.

Swart Kruger, J. & Chawla, L. (2002) 'We know something someone doesn't know': children speak out on local conditions in Johannesburg. *Environment and Urbanization*, 14, 85-96.

Turner, S. (2001) *Livelihoods in Lesotho*. CARE, Maseru, Lesotho.

UNESCO (2003) *United Nations Decade of Education for Sustainable Development (January 2005 - December 2014): Framework for a Draft International Implementation Scheme*. UNESCO, July 2003.

UNESCO/UNEP (1977) Tbilisi Declaration. http://www.gdrc.org/uem/ee/tbilisi.html. Accessed 8/7/05.

UNHCS/Habitat (1996) *Children's Rights and Habitat: Working Towards Child-Friendly Cities*. UNHCS/Habitat, New York.

United Nations (1992) *Agenda 21, Rio Declaration and Statement of Forest Principles*. United Nations, New York.

United Nations (1996) *Resolution adopted by the General Assembly: World Programme of Action for Youth to the Year 2000 and Beyond*. United Nations General Assembly, New York.

WHO (2002) *Strategic Directions for improving the Health and Development of Children and Adolescents*. WHO/FCH/CAH/02.21 Department of Child and Adolescent Health and Development, World Health Organization, Geneva.

Chapter 8

Gender Responsive Approaches to Sustainable Agricultural Extension: The Case of Namibia

Julie Newton

Introduction

Gender blindness has disguised the significant contributions of women to agricultural production in developing countries. The last ten years have been characterized by an increase in research on the 'feminisation of agriculture', accompanied by an emphasis on the inclusion of marginalized groups such as women as intrinsic to the ultimate goal of sustainable development and eradication of poverty. These debates have come to the forefront of the international development agenda through large international forums such as the United Nations Conference on Environment and Development (UNCED) in 1992 and the recent Millennium Summit in 2000, with specific millennium development goals targeted at gender equality and sustainable development[1]. This has resulted in an increasing number of developing countries including policies and plans to raise the participation of women within programmes for sustainable development. However, many have experienced implementation difficulties because of their neglect of the complexities of livelihoods and gender relations at the local level.

This chapter uses case study material from Namibia to examine attempts within the Namibian Ministry of Agriculture, Water and Rural Development (MAWRD) to integrate gender within its agricultural extension services through the Farming Systems Research and Extension (FSRE) approach[2]. Specific attention will be given to the mismatch between the rhetoric of policy at the national level and the implementation of gender responsive agricultural extension on the ground. It uses an actor oriented approach to investigate how gender responsive agricultural extension is internalized through existing networks of social interaction with a focus on the implications for women.

---

1   See http://www.un.org/millenniumgoals/.
2   The author would like to thank Professor Ian Gough for his comments.

Researching gender responsive approaches to agricultural extension

This chapter is based on doctoral research conducted in Namibia in 2001 and 2002, which explored the significance of gender relations to natural resource-based livelihoods in the communal lands of Namibia and the responsiveness of development policy to these dynamic relations. An integrated multi-methodological approach, drawing on a variety of different techniques from diverse disciplines, was used to facilitate an analysis across multiple scales. This was essential for understanding the complexity of gendered agricultural livelihoods within Namibia and the internalisation of gender responsive policy at multiple levels. The research involved policy reviews and discourse analysis and combined participatory methodologies with more in-depth ethnographic techniques, case studies and interviews.

The research took place within four settlements in Oshana region of North Central Namibia, formally known as 'Ovamboland'. Two remote, rural settlements (site 1) were compared with two settlements closer to the main urban centre of Oshakati (site 2) of North Central (Figure 8.1). North Central is the most populated area of Namibia with approximately 42.6 per cent of the total population including a large percentage of rural inhabitants (predominantly female) and high dependency on subsistence farming as a main source of income (Central Statistics Office, 2003). Currently, it is also subject to much intervention (particularly within the agricultural sector) due to its position as a SWAPO (South West African People's Organisation)[3] stronghold during the liberation struggle.

The research uses an actor oriented approach (Long, 1990, 1992) to understand *why* and *how* attempts to implement participatory gender responsive agricultural extension intervention, through the adoption of the FSRE approach, has encountered difficulties. Mainstream attempts to implement participatory development intervention have met criticism because of their tendency to treat the 'community' uncritically as a singular homogeneous entity at the expense of ignoring the diversity, heterogeneity and power structures within it (Guijt & Shah, 1998; Kothari, 2001; Cornwall, 2002; Williams, 2004). Critics argue that the treatment of 'the local' as an unproblematic site for intervention risks disguising the wider repressive power relations that are inherently gendered (Fine, 1999; Mohan & Stokke, 2000; Williams, 2004). The latter is a key reason why development interventions designed at the macro level may be interpreted by people at the meso and micro level in ways that contradict the main intentions of policy makers (Nustad, 2001). Within the Namibian context, attempts to make agricultural extension more participatory resulted in the creation of committee structures (Farmer Extension Development groups) responsible for disseminating agricultural knowledge across their respective communities with limited recognition of the existing networks of social interaction within communities, many of which are gendered.

---

3   SWAPO went on to become the ruling political party following independence in 1990.

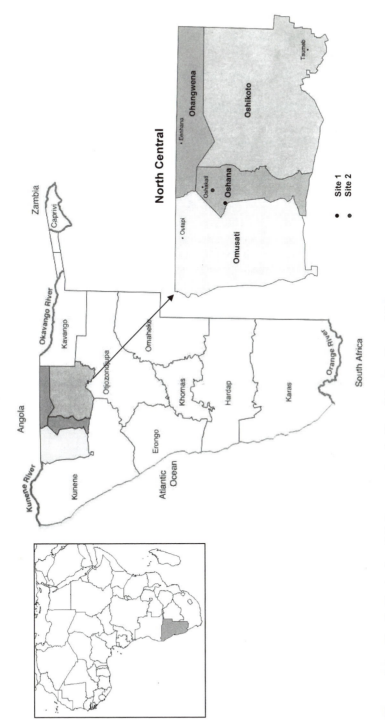

Figure 8.1   North Central and Oshana region in Namibia, Southern Africa

The actor oriented approach can offer a more dynamic understanding of social change, and the impact of development intervention on men and women, by reconceptualising the relationship between structure and agency and by reasserting the strength of human (re)action and consciousness (Long, 1992; Edwards, 1994; Arce *et al.*, 1994). Social actors are regarded as 'active participants who process information and strategize in their dealings with various local actors ... outside institutions and personnel' rather than 'disembodied social categories or passive recipients of intervention' (Long & van der Ploeg, 1994: 64). Schaffers's (1984) 'room for manoeuvre' concept expands these debates with its focus on the macro-meso-micro interaction: the middle ground between policy and the forms of negotiation adopted by different actors involved in the development process. This shares similarities with the term 'development interface' used to describe the dynamic interrelationship between agency and structure (Long, 1990; Edwards, 1994). It also parallels the call by Arce *et al.* (1994) for a wider framework of analysis taking into account how policies and interventions are 'internalized' or interpreted by different people at multiple scales and the power relations involved in these interactions.

The research draws on Woolcock's (1998) typology of social capital networks summarized in Box 8.1 to explain how different social interactions influence the internalisation of agricultural extension at the local level. Social capital has been well documented within the Western context throughout multiple disciplines. Within the development context, it has become increasingly recognized as a prerequisite for sustainable development and is used to refer to the ties, relationships, networks and social linkages between people that foster cooperation necessary for sustainable livelihoods (Pelling, 1998; Overseas Development Institute, 1999; Woolcock & Narayan, 2000; Fukuyama, 2001; Francis, 2002; Pretty, 2003).

Box 8.1   Typology of social capital

Bonding social capital	Connections between groups characterized by 'internal strength' and a strong sense of identity (e.g. family members) Useful for describing how people rely on remittances from extended family members at times of vulnerability (a key coping strategy at times of risk)
Bridging social capital	Weaker and more cross-cutting relationships between people within and outside a community (between neighbours and friends in the same village or in other localities) Useful for describing how information and assets are shared within communities
Linking social capital	Hierarchical relationships between people of different status of power Used in context of participatory development initiatives to describe the patron-client relationship between community based organisations and NGOs or governmental bodies

Adapted from: Woolcock (1998), Pelling (2003), Pretty (2003)

Gender and Development (GAD) debates expand this analysis by distinguishing how women and men have different capabilities for 'room for manoeuvre' that affect their ability to draw on different social capital networks and benefit from development intervention.

The research uses the 'gender planning'[4] terminology of practical and strategic gender interests (rather than needs[5]) to describe how agricultural extension assists women and men in different ways. Practical gender interests (PGI) are identified by women in their socially accepted roles in society (Molyneux, 1985; Moser, 1989, 1993). They frequently involve strategies in response to context-specific immediate perceived necessities for the survival of the whole family and they focus on a variety of basic needs such as water and health care provision. In contrast, strategic gender interests (SGI) are identified through women's unequal access to power and resources (Young, 1997). These advocate a more equal organisation of society requiring a change in the structure and nature of gender relations and they are consequently perceived as more 'empowering' because they directly challenge women's subordination through the sexual division of labour and they are central for tackling issues such as domestic violence, reproductive rights and equal wages (Moser, 1989, 1993). These concepts allow an investigation of how agricultural extension can constrain or enable the agency of women.

The rise of gender equality discourse in Namibia

The rise of the gender equality discourse in Namibia cannot be understood without situating it within the historical context of pre-colonial, colonial, liberation struggle and post-independence change. Current agricultural production systems within North Central originate from the early Ovambo migrants (an agropastoralist society of Bantu lineage) in the sixteenth century who remain the dominant ethnic group of the area. They were the first to introduce sedentary subsistence agriculture associated with specific agricultural practices and a distinct gendered division of labour (Williams, 1994). Women were responsible for reproductive roles within the household in addition to more labour-intensive tasks such as crop production and crop processing activities, whilst men were responsible for animal husbandry and heavy manual tasks such as ploughing and clearing. The performance of these roles

---

4 The theoretical transgression from Women in Development (WID) to Gender and Development (GAD) has been accompanied by recognition of the need to integrate gender into policy and practice (Byrne et al., 1996; Kanji, 2003). 'Gender planning' has become the tool for achieving this goal and can be considered as an approach to development planning based on the explicit recognition of unequal gender relations between women and men (Wieringa, 1994). Gender planning recognises that women and men have different roles in society and consequently have different needs (Moser, 1989, 1993; Wieringa, 1994).

5 For a more detailed discussion of why 'interests' have been used as opposed to 'need' see Kabeer (1994) and Wieringa (1994).

were (and still are) intrinsic to the performance of 'traditional' Ovambo agrarian feminine and masculine identity.

This unequal gendered division of labour was reinforced through colonial occupation by the Germans (early 1880s) and South Africans (1915 until 1990) to subsidize a system of cheap male migrant labour to support the colonial economy geared towards mining, fishing and farming industries in the South (Tapscott, 1993, 1995; Leys & Saul, 1995). This was sustained through a policy of limited infrastructural development and basic service provision (Pankhurst, 1996; Silvester *et al.*, 1998) and was particularly pronounced within the agricultural sector. While white commercial farmers had access to qualified extension staff, funding (cooperative and credit facilities) and a comprehensive research effort (Elkan *et al.*, 1992; Lau & Reiner, 1993), the majority of black communal farmers (who were predominantly women) were 'left to their own devices, with the expectation that they would produce enough food to feed their families, but not enough to earn an income to purchase consumer goods, which would have to be earned by men migrating to undertake contract work for minimal wages' (MAWRD, 1994: 1).

During the liberation movement commencing in the 1960s and lasting until the 1990s, North Central was described as a 'theatre of war' between South African paramilitary forces and Namibia's liberation movement led by SWAPO and the guerrillas of the People's Liberation Army of Namibia (Leys & Saul, 1995: 13). The struggle led to a growing climate of distrust amongst Ovambo communities because of the fear of secret informers working with the Apartheid regime. The liberation struggle had far wider repercussions for women in contemporary Namibia by laying the foundations for a new discourse of gender equality that rose up within the Namibian development agenda following independence in 1990 (Becker, 1993; FAO, 1995). This was partly the outcome of the efforts of women in exile, who were exposed to greater educational opportunities in refugee camps and universities abroad, which facilitated a 'rapid feminisation of a broad range of jobs and professions' following independence (Hishongwa, 1983; Becker, 2000: 187). This encouraged the desire to achieve greater levels of gender equality as they came into contact with women in greater political and professional positions (FAO, 1995; Girvan, 1995). Many of these women went on to take key positions in the new government and played an important role in mainstreaming gender at the national level.

Following independence in 1990, the new Namibian government focused on redressing the inequalities experienced by the majority of its rural population during the period of colonial rule. This involved extensive plans and policies to improve infrastructure within the former 'native reserves' including agricultural extension, improved water provision, road upgrades, and revitalized health and education systems (FAO, 1995). Specific attention was given to overcoming inequality caused by the legacy of racism and sexism enforced during Apartheid resulting in the implementation of the Namibian Constitution (the supreme law of Namibia) (Marcus & Baden, 1992; Cooper, 1997; Iipinge & LeBeau, 1997).

Gender equality came to the forefront of the international development arena and in Namibia after CEDAW (Convention on Elimination of all forms of Discrimination

Against Women) in 1981 and the Beijing Platform of Action in 1995 (UN, 2002). This legally bound Namibia to 'promote an active and visible policy of mainstreaming a gender perspective in all policies and programmes so that, before decisions are taken, an analysis is made of the effects on women and men, respectively' (UN, 1995, para 79). This resulted in the creation of a national women's machinery in the form of the Department of Women Affairs (DWA) under the Office of the President in 1991 which was later transformed into the Ministry of Women Affairs and Child Welfare in 2000 (Marcus & Baden, 1992).

These circumstances set the scene for the implementation of numerous key policy documents (for example, National Development Plan, National Gender Policy, National Agricultural Policy) focused on the institutionalisation of gender and participatory approaches to development. All shared the conviction that gender equality achieved through a process of gender mainstreaming was a prerequisite for sustainable development. The following section discusses the implications of this rhetoric for the Ministry of Agriculture, Water and Rural Development (MAWRD).

The policy context of gender responsive agricultural extension: The National Agricultural Policy and Farming Systems Research Extension (FSRE) approach

The momentum outlined above resulted in the publication of the National Agricultural Policy (NAP) in 1995. It was considered a 'unique' document at its time of publication because of its focus on the 'plight of the poor and vulnerable in both the communal and commercial set-up, obliging key stakeholders to adopt gender sensitive approaches' (Awases, 1997: 88). Although it was formulated with the overall aim of increasing levels of agricultural productivity, real farm incomes and national and household food security, it gave specific emphasis to recognising women as 'farmers in their own right' and the need to reorientate agricultural extension to 'take gender issues fully into account' in order to develop 'gender-specific strategies for increased household food security' (MAWRD, 1995: iii, para v, 46, 65). It was embedded within a Women in Development (WID)[6] discourse that linked sustainable development to the integration of women at the expense of ignoring the foundations of gender inequality. Nevertheless, the potential implications for women were significant considering the NAP was the 'guiding document' for the whole Ministry suggesting that theoretically all guidelines and interventions within the MAWRD had to meet the requirements of the Policy.

At the national level, the NAP, together with support from the Food and Agricultural Organisation (FAO), resulted in numerous programmes to train agricultural extension

---

6 WID emerged during the 1970s in response to the disillusionment with the 'development project' with an overriding goal to integrate women into development, increase their productive abilities and ensure they accrued benefits (Jackson & Pearson, 1998; Porter, 1999). Boserup (1970) was influential in highlighting that women were an untapped resource which could be used as rational economic agents to accelerate economic growth.

staff at multiple levels in the basics of gender responsive extension[7]. This was complemented by the creation of gender mainstreaming structures (Gender Unit and Association for Gender in Agricultural Development) at the national headquarters to facilitate gender mainstreaming throughout the MAWRD. Although these played a significant role in generating awareness of the importance of gender at the national level, their translation at the local level was hampered by structural and conceptual difficulties that cannot be discussed within the remit of this chapter. In spite of these difficulties, the NAP's most significant impact at the local level was through the adoption of a 'Farming System and Research Extension' (FSRE) approach. This involved a reorientation of agricultural services away from farmer support services such as ploughing, the sale of inputs (seeds and fertilizers) and the administration of non-extension activities including drought relief and credit schemes, towards advisory, information communications and farmer training services that recognized the importance of extension to productivity (MAWRD, 1994; Vigne, 1997).

The FSRE approach emerged within the development arena during the 1970s with the rise of populist approaches as a more 'sustainable' and 'participatory' alternative to the 'Transfer of Technology' approach adopted during the Green Revolution (Scoones & Thompson, 1994; Whiteside, 1998). The latter was characterized by limited interaction with farmers and focused on knowledge derived from research stations (Bembridge, 1997). In contrast, the FSRE approach was valued because it recognized the 'diversity and complexity of the small holder farming system' including appreciation of the agro-ecological context in which agriculture takes place (Whiteside, 1998: 19). It stressed the importance of designing research directly in line with the needs identified by the farmers themselves (Cornwall *et al.*, 1994). This changed the role of the extension technician from teacher, provider and adviser to facilitator (Horn *et al.*, 2000). Hence, it advocated research carried out by extension workers *with* farmers, as opposed to limited interaction with farmers and on-station based research (Vigne & Oates, 1992). This was similar to the 'Farmer First' approach that values the 'indigenous agricultural knowledge' of farmers who are the 'experts' on the complexity of farming systems and subsequently places farmers at the centre of strategies to develop 'sustainable agriculture' (Chambers, 1994a, b). In North Central, the FSRE approach has been implemented through two channels: the FSRE unit based at the North Central divisional headquarters, responsible for new *technology development*, and the Farming Systems and Extension Teams (FSE teams), spread throughout the four regions of North Central, responsible for *technology dissemination*.

The FSRE Unit was introduced after the second National Conference on Agricultural Extension (1997). It focuses on coordinating adaptive research and the development of new technology by working intensively with a small group of farmers in the form of eight 'focus communities' within North Central that are representative

---

7   'Training for the integration of women in agriculture and rural development' funded by the FAO and 'Improving information on women's contribution to agricultural production for gender sensitive planning' funded by the Norwegian government.

of various socio-economic and environmental situations (MAWRD, 2000). The unit brings specialist researchers from the Division of Agricultural Research and Training (DART) together with Agricultural Extension Officers (AEOs) with technical training from the Directorate of Extension and Engineering Services (DEES) under a 'Technology Development Coordination Group' to foster a multidisciplinary approach in order to make extension more responsive to farmers needs (MAWRD, 2000, 2002). These can include specialists in crops, pest management, livestock production, draft animal power, animal health, community-based organisations, range management, soil fertility and fencing using plants (MAWRD, 2002). The technologies developed with focus communities are then disseminated to the FSE teams in the form of extension messages and new agricultural inputs.

It is, however, the tripartite relationship between farmers, Agricultural Extension Technicians (AETS) and Farmer Extension Development (FED) groups under FSE teams that is the main form of extension because of the scale under which it operates, and it will be the focus of this discussion. Over fifty AETs[8] operate from Agricultural Rural Development Centres (ARDCs) dispersed throughout North Central and they are responsible for assisting the identification of farmers' objectives and needs, disseminating technical options regarding cultivation and livestock issues and monitoring the adoption of new technologies (MAWRD, 2000). AETs also organize exposure trips, disperse trial seeds and conduct demonstrations on new agricultural technologies such as drought-tolerant seeds or new ploughing technologies. Although information and new technologies are passed through a variety of means ranging from individual visits to homesteads to open meetings with communities, the main mechanism of information transfer is intended to be through the FED groups.

FED groups consist of groups of farmers (both women and men) selected by the community to work closely with the AET through demonstrations and trials and they are responsible for transmitting information to the rest of the community through open meetings. Approximately 300 FED groups[9] were in existence within North Central at the time of research (MAWRD, 2001). Working with groups is perceived to be more participatory and an effective way of fostering community based organisations to facilitate the 'delivery of extension and other supportive services, and ultimately contribute to broader empowerment objectives' (Vigne, 1997: 14). FED groups also alleviate the multiple tasks of the AETs by taking over some of the dissemination responsibilities. FED group members are intended to become key sources of agricultural information and advice for the rest of the community in

---

8   It was beyond the remit to investigate the training backgrounds of all AETs from North Central. However, from informal conversations with AETs and AEOs based at the regional headquarters, it was clear that they had diverse training backgrounds. Some had received formal technical training from Ogongo Agricultural College in Omusati region (the main agricultural college in North Central, whilst the other major college is located in the capital of Windhoek). This was largely the case of the newer recruits, whilst the older AETs received regular training in facilitating techniques when new technologies arose.

9   On average, each FED group comprises of approximately 5 to 8 people with a mixed gender composition.

order to take over the responsibilities of AETs and increase the overall efficiency of extension by reaching more farmers (increasing accessibility). AETs and FED groups are consequently key components of agricultural extension because they constitute the 'development interface' between agricultural policy at the national (macro) scale and people at the grassroots (micro) level (Long, 1990). It is through these channels that gender responsive agricultural extension is *intended* to benefit female and male farmers.

The internalization of gender responsive agricultural extension at the local level

While there was undeniably a strong rhetoric of participation and gender equality within agricultural policy at the national level, the research revealed the contrary at the micro level within the study areas due to the ways in which it was internalized. This section first focuses on the extent to which agricultural extension has 'recognized women in their own right' at the micro level and second, explains how the effectiveness of agricultural extension has been hindered by weak linking and bridging social capital networks.

'Recognizing women farmers in their own right': Fact or fallacy?

The Ministry of Agriculture, Water and Rural Development's (MAWRD) key mechanism of 'recognising women farmers in their own right' at the micro level was not through direct targeting. Rather, women and men were allegedly given the same opportunities to benefit from the availability of trial seeds, labour-saving technologies, and involvement with FED groups and exposure trips.

The research revealed that the most significant benefit of agricultural extension intervention, according to the majority of women, was 'on the food side' through the provision of advice and hybrid seeds and new varieties of crops, fruit and vegetables. Extension actively increased opportunities to invest in livelihood strategies relating to cropping and planting practices that increased production to be stored in the future for times of drought and enhance long term security of households. This consequently contributed to practical gender interests by enabling women to protect and enhance food security (Table 8.1). This was identified as a key dimension of livelihood security by women and it was also valued by men because of the role of agricultural products such as *mahangu* (millet: the staple grain of North Central) as symbols of Ovambo masculine identity and status.[10]

---

10 Large granary baskets filled with millet (*mahangu*) are displayed outside the homestead as a symbol of wealth and status. *Mahangu* has also been traditionally regarded as a male asset, as is the case today, in many male headed households and *de facto* female headed households.

Table 8.1   Impact of agricultural extension on women

Intervention	General Benefits	Benefits to women: practical (PGI) and strategic gender interests (SGI)
Hybrid seeds of millet and sorghum (okashana, macia, kangara)	Drought resistant, shorter growing season, ability to grow with poor rainfall; increases food security	Reduces vulnerability to drought, increases survival rates of crop production; increases ability to maintain food security (PGI)
New varieties of crops, vegetables and fruit (e.g. sweet potato, papaya etc.)	Diversification of production, consumption and income-generating activities	Diversifies consumption and increases nutritional benefits and contributes to food security which is a key element of livelihood security (PGI). Can also provide opportunities for income-generating activities (SGI) (e.g. women can sell vegetables and fruit)
Labour saving technologies	Decreases workload & increases chances of improving harvest with less effort	Decreases workload and frees up time for women to engage in alternative activities (PGI) Meets SGI by encouraging men to take on tasks 'tradionally' performed by women and consequently challenges the gender division of labour underpinning power dynamics within the space of the household
Tractor	Decreases workload involved in ploughing & threshing	Frees time for women and men to engage in alternative activities (PGI)
Cultivator	Decreases workload and time spent on weeding (most time consuming task during the growing season)	Decreases workload for women; gets men involved in female tasks (PGI).Challenges gender division of labour (SGI)
Mahangu crushing mill	Mechanism of pounding of *mahangu* which is only performed by women	Decreases workload for women; gets men involved in female tasks (PGI) even if this is just to transport the seed to the mill
Donkey cart	Transportation for people and acricultural products; decreases workload	or to pay for these services (PGI + SGI) Gets men involved in collection of water and fuelwood which are 'traditional' female tasks (SGI). Also saves women the time-consuming tasks of travelling long distances to collect water and fuelwood
Involvement in committee & exposure trips	Exposure to new technologies & knowledge which can be used to increase production and diversification	Challenges gender relations within the household as women are not 'traditionally' allowed to travel. Increases confidence in abilities and feelings of self-worth (SGI)

Source: fieldwork conducted by author (2001/2002)

Table 8.1 demonstrates, however, that the more 'empowering' interventions meeting strategic gender interests are those introducing new labour-saving technologies, involving individuals in exposure trips and membership to the FED group committee.

Labour-saving technologies such as the cultivator, tractor and *mahangu* milling machines have the potential to empower women and meet strategic gender interests by actively changing gender roles by 'getting men involved' in activities traditionally performed by women; thus enabling women to challenge existing gendered division of labour in a non-threatening manner. For example, several female respondents argued that women 'cannot go and tell' husbands to do particular tasks 'unless there is a machine' involved. This suggests that the gendered division of labour is not as rigid as initially implied since men are more willing to participate if a task becomes 'disembodied' through the use of machinery. Hence, the mechanisation of agricultural activities has the potential to transform social relations by changing the gender division of labour that underpins unequal power dynamics between women and men.

This supports Jackson's (1995) and Doss's (2001) argument that the use of technology can provide opportunities to 'bargain' or negotiate gender roles whereby women experience a reduction in time and work intensity in conjunction with the cooption of male labour, thus contributing to both women's practical and strategic gender interests. It also gives women more time to engage in alternative livelihood strategies that can be used to increase the long term security of the household. However, Bryceson (1995) and Doss (2001) warn that new technology can have negative effects by 'freeing up' women's time to engage in alternative tasks which can increase existing workloads. Many women cannot afford such equipment and are automatically excluded. Hence, it is important to interrogate *whose* labour is being saved and at what expense. Chant (1996) also warns against championing changes in gender roles unless they involve a change to gender relations (that is rights, agency, capability) that underpin gender inequality.

The research also revealed the importance of recognising women's own attitudes towards their gender roles and responsibilities. On numerous occasions, women were reluctant to change the *status quo* and took a particular pride in performing their agricultural tasks as these were intrinsic to the performance of 'traditional' Ovambo agrarian identity. Others argued that their 'culture cannot be changed' and likened change to an attack on cultural roots and heritage. As a result, the research concluded that the most effective means of meeting women's strategic gender interests is to increase the desire to change from within. Membership of the FED group committee was found to be one mechanism for beginning the process of changing attitudes amongst women. This guarantees first hand 'access to much information … concerning agriculture' and to an array of trainings taking women outside the realm of their household and agricultural field when 'in the past women were not allowed to leave the house'. Accessing new information and knowledge can be regarded as empowering on several counts. It increases women's capabilities to carry out activities *outside* their prescribed gender roles. Learning skills in animal draft power enables women to become more involved in livestock management when 'traditionally it is only men who can train animals and do the ploughing'. FED group membership also provides opportunities to leave the gendered space of the household on exposure trips to see new technologies, agricultural initiatives and meet women in similar circumstances undertaking a range of income-generating activities. This has an empowering effect by increasing enthusiasm, confidence and belief in one's own ability and it encourages demands for new knowledge. It also has the potential to 'kick start' a process of 'conscientization' whereby women are enabled to define and analyse their subordination and consequently construct and pursue a vision of the world that they would like to live in (Kabeer, 1994; Rowlands, 1997, 1999; Sharp *et al.*, 2003). These consequently have a more transformative potential to challenge the ways that both women and men think about their lives (Kabeer, 1994; Rowlands, 1999).

However, the research revealed that these more 'empowering' interventions (and the standard interventions to a certain extent) were not reaching the majority of the farming population, irrespective of female farmers. Contrary to the *intended* channels of agricultural extension implementation, Figure 8.2 illustrates how agricultural extension is hampered by weak linking and bridging social capital networks.

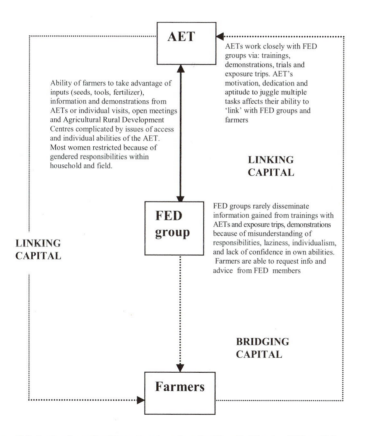

Figure 8.2 Actual agricultural extension in North Central Namibia

Source: fieldwork conducted by author (2001/2002)

Linking social capital: The AET's initial mobilisation of the community

Existing relationships of trust within the 'community', issues of access and the individual circumstances of the AETs were identified as key constraints to the successful implementation of agricultural extension via linking social capital networks (Figure 8.2). The legacy of Apartheid made it difficult for people to accept new ideas and technologies from governmental officials without a certain degree of suspicion. Access was a key factor behind the creation of FED groups where AETs were instructed to set up FED groups within 'accessible' communities defined as being 'within walking distance' (10 km) of the ARDC (Agricultural Rural Development Centre). This was necessary due to the poorly developed infrastructure within the areas and the initial lack of vehicles within the MAWRD. This automatically excluded many farmers within remote areas from benefiting from agricultural extension and was consequently a major restriction on AET ability to 'link' with communities (Figure 8.2).

While AETs were not given specific instructions of *who* to target for the FED group committee, the majority of committee members within the case study areas were female. Although both AETs claimed that the 'inclusion' of women was a reflection of their dominance at the first open meeting because of men's involvement in waged employment, the research revealed the situation to be more complex. In site 2, the FED group tended to 'include' well-connected and prominent individuals (or partners of these individuals) involved in other committees within the settlement (SWAPO, church, school committee, and so on). The situation was different in site 1, where people were asked to 'volunteer' at the first open meeting with the community. Since membership was conditional on attendance, only those who were both aware and able to attend had equal opportunities to join. Those who attended viewed the meeting as an opportunity to gain new knowledge to both increase and protect crop production and livestock maintenance.

A main channel for informing the community of meetings is through the church or at school through children. Information is also spread through more informal transfers between friends, neighbours and acquaintances at homesteads, *cuca*[11] shops, centre of the village, water points, and so on. Those who are unable to access these channels, such as individuals living in remote and peripheral settlements, physically constrained (elderly and disabled) and/or do not have time to participate because of other responsibilities, are automatically excluded. This was particularly the case for women in male headed households and *de facto* female headed households who were unable to benefit (unless they had hired labour) because of their reproductive roles within household and productive tasks within agricultural fields. Although *de jure* female headed households may have more flexibility because they do not have to negotiate responsibilities with a male partner, they may be restrained by

---

11 The local term used to describe any shop within North Central selling alcoholic and non-alcoholic beverages as well as cooked and canned foods and other basic necessities.

limited human capital to protect crops and/or livestock during their absence. This is particularly pertinent to widows who lack the financial capital to hire additional labour to perform these tasks because of discriminatory inheritance laws that deprive widows of their key capital assets upon their husband's death. In contrast, *de jure* female headed households who are supported by extended family members with well-paid employment may be able to hire labour to maintain fields and livestock whilst they attend such meetings. These factors, initially preventing people from being selected for the FED group, also apply to the linking social capital networks between farmers and the AET and restrict their ability to visit the AET at the ARDC, take advantage of trial seeds, volunteer for demonstrations and attend open meetings on a regular basis (see Figure 8.2). There is also a reluctance to seek assistance because of the uncertainty of whether the AET will be present. These findings demonstrate the importance of considering the circumstances of 'place' (remoteness or proximity to AET) in addition to the intricacies of social relations such as gender roles and responsibilities that can constrain the effectiveness of gender responsive agricultural extension. It also demonstrates the diversity amongst women, where different women, whether they live with husbands, are divorced, widowed or single, have different capabilities to benefit from agricultural extension.

The research also detected that many men and youths voluntarily chose to exclude themselves from opportunities to 'link' with agricultural extension. Several female respondents and key stakeholders attributed this to the increasing propensity of men to spend time at the *cuca* shops drinking alcoholic beverages. Others stated that their absence was a reflection of the subject material that tends to focus on crop production which is still regarded as a female domain, thus explaining why more men attend meetings on livestock issues. In comparison, the absence of youth was attributed to a growing disillusion and 'lack of interest' in agriculture. This raises questions concerning the role of agricultural extension services to livelihood security as the prioritization of agriculture is changing with younger generations. It also demonstrates the diversity and heterogeneity within communities and illustrates how different people have different opportunities to benefit from agricultural extension.

The AET's own motivation, dedication and individual aptitude to 'juggle' multiple tasks and responsibilities, in addition to the particular circumstances of 'place', also influenced their ability to 'link' with FED groups and farmers. Closer proximity to Oshakati and the regional extension services headquarters provides greater opportunities for the AET of site 2 to mobilize stakeholders involved in agricultural and rural development activities. The AET's personal involvement within the committee structures of institutions outside the MAWRD also provided ideas for new projects and trainings to share with FED groups and farmers. In contrast, the AET of site 1 was constrained by distance and fuel limitations that restricted the ability to make individual homestead visits and limited opportunities to interact with other stakeholders in Oshakati and develop ideas to share with farmers and FED groups.

Bridging social capital: Internal dynamics of FED groups

Weak 'bridging' social capital networks *within* the FED groups and the community also constrained the effectiveness of agricultural extension (Figure 8.2) and it illustrates how the introduction of 'participatory' structures may involve the creation of 'social' forms that do not conform to how people organize or perceive themselves (Cornwall, 2002). Misunderstanding concerning the FED group's designated role as the 'coordination between the office and the farmers' emerged as a significant problem in site 1. Whilst non-committee members blamed the FED group for being 'too lazy' to perform their designated functions, members believed it was their role to arrange open meetings for the AET rather than give feedback on their own trainings and exposure trips. In site 2, FED group members displayed individualistic tendencies that the benefits of the training and exposure trips were for their own use and not to be shared amongst fellow community members. Others justified their inactivity because of time constraints. This was particularly the case for members involved in other committees (for example, school and church committees) and women within male headed households and *de facto* female headed households whose reproductive roles restricted opportunities to engage in trainings and meetings.

Other committee members in both study sites attributed their reluctance to interact with the community to a crisis of confidence in their own knowledge and abilities gained through the AET. Members felt demoralized to go to the community with outdated or limited information[12] whilst others had the legitimacy of their knowledge challenged. FED group members within site 2 explained that the knowledge advocated by agricultural extension was regarded as superior to existing indigenous methods and was consequently only accepted (legitimized) by their community when disseminated by the AETs themselves. This was particularly felt amongst the female members of the FED groups in both sites, whose position as women within a traditionally patriarchal society, made it difficult for their knowledge and techniques (gained through training from the AET) to be accepted. This demonstrates how the legitimacy and authority of one form of knowledge through FED groups conflicts with the desire for the 'expert' knowledge of the AETs. Paradoxically, the dependency on 'expert knowledge' is the *very* problem that the FED groups are supposed to overcome as argued earlier. This proved frustrating for both the AETs in site 1 and 2 who are unable to be present at all FED group meetings because of transport difficulties and responsibilities for other FED groups. This supports Cornwall's (2002) claim that the biggest 'irony' of development agencies' attempts to foster

---

12 This was the case in site 1 where there was a change-over between AETs during the time of research and FED group committee members had not received any training for over 6 months. As a result, committee members did not feel confident in disseminating information until they had received further training.

autonomous spaces for local institutions and self-reliance is that their presence acts as an instigator of dependency.

One respondent claimed that the exchange of information through more informal gatherings with other women (for example, at church, *cuca* shops, informal visits) are more effective mechanisms of passing information as opposed to the formal crafted structure of the FED group. This is also the case for men who are more likely to exchange information when herding livestock, socialising at *cuca* shops, or at their place of employment. The research revealed that these ties of reciprocity in the form of strong bonding and bridging social capital networks were central to responses to stress. These same channels were relied upon to exchange agricultural inputs and information when linking social capital networks with agricultural extension are weak. Hence, 'effective agency' defined as the 'strategic generation/ manipulation of a network of social relations and the channelling of specific items (such as claims, orders, goods, instruments and information) through certain 'nodal points' of interaction' (Long, 1992: 23) plays an important role in negotiating one's 'exclusion' from agricultural extension. Those who cannot afford the cost of agricultural machinery or access benefits of agricultural extension can overcome their 'exclusion' by borrowing from neighbours, family and friends in exchange for similar assistance when they experience difficulties. The same is applicable to more vulnerable households who receive 'gifts' of seeds from neighbours, friends and relatives.

This demonstrates the complex and dynamic social interactions within communities. These findings support Cleaver's (2001a) observation that there is the danger that committees such as FED groups can become 'empty shells' as the more 'meaningful' participation takes place *outside* of these spaces. This supports the argument that future intervention should explore how existing intervention is internalized. A focus on these dynamics could strengthen the argument that the more partial and intermittent forms of daily interactions are arguably more effective mechanisms of information exchange (Cleaver, 2000, 2001a, b).

Discussion and conclusion

While the rhetoric of gender equality is strong within agricultural policy and practice at the national level, this chapter has demonstrated a mismatch with its implementation on the ground. Although the adoption of the Farming Systems Research and Extension (FSRE) approach provided considerable benefits for women in terms of meeting practical gender interests and improving access to a range of livelihood strategies, the majority remain excluded from more 'empowering' benefits that challenge the existing gender division of labour and the ways men and women think about these roles. While gendered responsibilities in the field and household were identified as a key factor behind women's inability to take advantage of these services, an actor oriented approach revealed that the implementation of gender responsive agricultural extension was more constrained by weak linking and bridging social capital networks between Agricultural Extension Technicians (AETs), Farmer Extension Development (FED) groups and farmers. For this reason, reliance on social capital networks (more informal networks through friends, neighbours and family) became a more effective channel for sharing ideas and information. In so doing, the chapter shows how attempts to implement gender responsive agricultural extension need to consider existing social capital networks and the diversity and heterogeneity within communities to enhance intervention effectiveness.

These findings suggest that policy makers should focus more on how development intervention is internalized at the development interface (that is which actors have room for manoeuvre) to allow more local and relevant strategies against vulnerability to evolve that are more inclusive to all the members of various communities and may be more sustainable in the long term. They have also contributed to wider debates on participatory development by demonstrating how the imposition of artificial committee structures such as the FED groups can fail to facilitate communication, whilst more informal mechanisms of interactions (local *cuca* shops and social gatherings) may be more effective. This demonstrates the importance of facilitating strong chains of communication prior to intervention in order to avoid conflict that can hinder the effectiveness of development intervention such as gender responsive agricultural extension. Once these are improved, agricultural extension has a greater potential to challenge the unequal gendered division of labour characterising Ovambo gendered agricultural livelihoods. However, it is important to note that such intervention may not explicitly improve women's control or authority over resources. A deeper attitudinal change amongst both men and women is required before the roots of gender equality can be tackled. This begs the question of whether agricultural extension is the most effective vehicle for empowering women.

References

Arce, A., Villarreal, M. & de Vries, P. (1994) The social construction of rural development: discourses, practices and power. In Booth, D. (ed.) *Rethinking Social Development: Theory, Research and Practice*. Longman, Harlow, pp. 152-171.

Awases, A. (1997) Consideration of gender issues towards the adaptation of the FSRE approach. MAWRD *Proceedings of the second national conference on agricultural extension in Namibia*. Safari Court, Windhoek, 23-25 September.

Becker, H. (1993) *From Anti-Colonial Resistance to Reconstruction: Namibian Women's Movement from 1980 to 1992*. Unpublished PhD thesis, University of Bremen.

Becker, H. (2000) A concise history of gender, 'tradition' and the state in Namibia. In Keulder, C. (ed.) (2000) *State, Society and Democracy: A Reader in Namibian Politics*. Gamsberg Macmillan, Windhoek, pp. 171-199.

Bembridge, T. (1997) The role of farming systems research extension in technology transfer. MAWRD *Proceedings of the second national conference on agricultural extension in Namibia*. Safari Court, Windhoek, 23-25 September.

Boserup, E. (1970) *Women's Role in Economic Development*. St Martin's Press, New York.

Bryceson, D. (1995) *Women Wielding the Hoe*. BERG, Oxford.

Byrne, B., Koch Laier, J., Baden, S. & Marcus, R. (1996) National machineries for women in development: experiences, lessons and strategies for institutionalising gender in development policy and planning. *BRIDGE Development-Gender*, Report 36. IDS, Brighton.

Central Statistics Office (2003) *2001 Population and Housing Census: Basic Analysis with Highlights*. National Planning Commission, Windhoek.

Chambers, R. (1994a) The origins and practice of Participatory Rural Appraisal. *World Development*, 22, 953-969.

Chambers, R. (1994b) Participatory Rural Appraisal (PRA): Analysis of experience. *World Development*, 22, 1253-1268.

Chant, S. (1996) Women's roles in recession and economic restructuring in Mexico and the Phillippines. *Geoforum,* 27, 297-327.

Cleaver, F. (2000) Moral Ecological Rationality, Institutions and the management of common property resources. *Development and Change*, 31, 361-383.

Cleaver, F. (2001a) Institutions, agency and the limitations of participatory approaches to development. In Cooke, B. & Kothari, U. (eds) *Participation: The New Tyranny?* Zed Books, London, pp. 36-55.

Cleaver, F. (2001b) Institutional Bricolage, conflict and cooperation in Usangu, Tanzania. *IDS Bulletin,* 32, 26-35.

Cooper, A. (1997) State sponsorship of women's rights and implications for patriarchism in Namibia. *The Journal of Modern African Studies,* 35, 469-483.

Cornwall, A. (2002) Making spaces, changing places: situating participation in development. *IDS Working Paper,* 170. IDS, Brighton.

Cornwall, A., Guijt, I. & Welbourn, A. (1994) Acknowledging process: challenges for agricultural research and extension methodology. In Scoones, I. & Thompson, J. (eds) *Beyond Farmer First: Rural People's Knowledge, Agricultural Research and Extension Practice*. Intermediate Technology Publications, London, pp. 98-116.

Doss, C. (2001) Designing agricultural technology for African women farmers: lessons from 25 years of experience. *World Development*, 29, 2075-2092.

Edwards, M. (1994) Rethinking social development: the search for 'relevance'. In Booth, D. (ed.) *Rethinking Social Development: Theory, Research and Practice*. Longman, Harlow, pp. 279-297.

Elkan, W., Amutenya, P., Andima, E., van der Linden, R. & Sherbourne, R. (1992) Namibian Agriculture: Policies and Prospects. *Namibian Economic Policy Research Unit (NEPRU) Research Report,* 5. NEPRU, Windhoek.

FAO (1995) *Women, Agriculture and Rural Development: National Sectoral Report for Namibia*. Prepared for the Fourth World Conference on Women, UN, Rome.

Fine, B. (1999) The developmental state is dead – long live social capital? *Development and Change,* 30, 1-19.

Francis, P. (2002) Social capital, civil society and social exclusion. In Kothari, U. & Minogue, M. (eds) *Development Theory and Practice: Critical Perspectives*. Palgrave, Basingstoke, pp. 71-91.

Fukuyama, F. (2001) Social capital, civil society and development. *Third World*

Quarterly, 22, 7-20.

Girvan, L. (1995) Namibia: National Report on Women, Agriculture and Rural Development for the Fourth World Conference for Women. *NEPRU Research Report*, 10. University of Namibia: Windhoek.

Guijt, I. & Shah, M. (1998) *The Myth of Community: Gender Relations and Participatory Development*. Intermediate Technology Publications, London.

Hishongwa, N. (1983) *Women of Namibia: The Changing Role of Namibian Women from Traditional Pre-Colonial Times to the Present*. IDAF Research and Information Centre, London.

Horn, P., Kambinda, M., Antindi, B. & Matanyaire, J. (2000) Annex 15: Options for operational organisation for FSRE approach implementation. MAWRD *Third Workshop on the Implementation of the Farming Systems Research and Extension Approach. MIDGARD 3*, Cresta Lodge, Ondangwa, 26-17 October, Windhoek.

Iipinge, E. & LeBeau, D. (1997) *Beyond Inequalities: Women in Namibia*. University of Namibia, Southern African Research and Documentation Centre (SARDC), Windhoek.

Jackson, C. (1995) From conjugal contracts to environmental relations: some thoughts on labour and technology. *IDS Bulletin*, 26, 33-39.

Jackson, C. & Pearson, R. (1998) *Feminist Visions of Development: Gender Analysis and Policy*. Routledge, London.

Kabeer, N. (1994) *Reversed Realities: Gender Hierarchies in Development Thought*. Verso, London.

Kanji, N. (2003) *Mind the Gap: Mainstreaming Gender and Participation in Development*. IIED/IDS, London.

Kothari, U. (2001) Power, knowledge and social control in participatory development. In Cooke, B. & Kothari, U. (eds) *Participation: The New Tyranny?* Zed Books, London, pp. 139-152.

Lau, B. & Reiner, P. (1993) 100 years of agricultural development in colonial Namibia: a historical overview of visions and experiments. *Archeia,* 17. The National Archives of Namibia, Windhoek.

Leys, C. & Saul, J. (1995) *Namibia's Liberation Struggle: The Two-Edged Sword*. James Currey, London.

Long, N. (1990) From paradigm lost to paradigm regained? The case for an actor-orientated sociology of development. *European Review of Latin American and Caribbean Studies*, 49, 3-24.

Long, N. (1992) From paradigm lost to paradigm regained? The case for an actor-oriented sociology of development. In Long, N. & Long, A. (eds) *Battlefields of Knowledge: Interlocking of Theory and Practice in Social Research and Development*. Routledge, London, pp. 16-46.

Long, N. & van der Ploeg, J.D. (1994) Heterogeneity, actor and structure: towards a reconstitution of the concept of structure. In Booth, D. (ed.) *Rethinking Social Development: Theory, Research and Practice*. Longman, Harlow, pp. 62-89.

Marcus, R. & Baden, S. (1992) Gender and development in Namibia: a country study. Report No.6 prepared for Directorate General of Development, Commission of

European Communities. *BRIDGE Development-Gender,* IDS, Brighton.

MAWRD (1994) *Towards an Extension Strategy for Namibia: A Discussion Paper.* DEES, MAWRD, Windhoek.

MAWRD (1995) *National Agricultural Policy.* MAWRD, Windhoek.

MAWRD (2000) *Third Workshop on the Implementation of the Farming Systems Research and Extension Approach. MIDGARD 3,* Cresta Lodge, Ondangwa, 26-17 October, Windhoek.

MAWRD (2001) *FSRE Task Force Presentation to the 4th National FSRE Workshop* Swakopmund, 10-14 September, Windhoek.

MAWRD (2002) *Northern Research Extension Epidemiology Support Project (NOREESP) Activity Report.* MAWRD, Windhoek.

Mohan, G. & Stokke, K. (2000) Participatory development and empowerment: The dangers of localism. *Third World Quarterly,* 21, 247-268.

Molyneux, M. (1985) Mobilisation without Emancipation: Women's Interests, State and Revolution in Nicaragua. *Feminist Studies,* 11, 227-254.

Moser, C. (1989) Gender planning in the Third World: Meeting practical and strategic gender needs. *World Development,* 17, 1799-1822.

Moser, C. (1993) *Gender Planning and Development: Theory, Practice & Training.* Routledge, London.

Nustad, K. (2001) Development: the devil we know? *Third World Quarterly,* 22, 479-489.

ODI (1999) *Social Capital: Policy Planning and Implementation (Key Sheets).* Overseas Development Institute, London. http://www.odi.org.uk/keysheets.

Pankhurst, D. (1996) Similar but different? Assessing the reserve economy legacy of Namibia. *Journal of Southern African Studies,* 22, 405-420.

Pelling, M. (1998) Participation, social capital and vulnerability to urban flooding in Guyana. *Journal of International Development,* 10, 469-486.

Pelling, M. (2003) Social capital, hazards and adaptation strategies for the vulnerable. *Justice in Adaptation to Climate Change: International seminar.* Tyndall Centre, IIED, Centre for Social and Economic Research on the Global Environment (CSERGE), University of East Anglia.

Porter, M. (1999) Caught in the web? Feminists doing development. In Porter, M. & Judd, E. (eds) *Feminists Doing Development.* London, Zed Books, pp. 1-15.

Pretty, J. (2003) Social capital and connectedness: Issues and implications for agriculture, rural development and natural resource management in ACP countries. Technical Centre for Agricultural and Rural Cooperation *(CTA), Working Document,* 8032. Technical Centre for Agricultural and Rural Cooperation, ACP-EU.

Rowlands, J. (1997) *Questioning Empowerment: Working with Women in Honduras.* Oxfam, London.

Rowlands, J. (1999) Empowerment examined. In Rowan-Campbell, D. (ed.) *Development with Women.* Oxfam Publication, Oxford, pp. 141-150.

Schaffer, B.B. (1984) Towards responsibility: public policy in concept and practice. In Clay, E.J. & Schaffer, B.B. (eds) *Room for Manoeuvre: An Exploration of*

Public Policy in Agriculture and Rural Development. Heinemann, London.

Scoones, I. & Thompson, J. (1994) *Beyond Farmer First: Rural People's Knowledge, Agricultural Research and Extension Practice*. Intermediate Technology Publications, London.

Sharp, J., Briggs, J., Yacoub, H. & Hamed, N. (2003) Doing gender and development: understanding empowerment and local gender relations. *Transactions of the Institute of British Geographers*, 28, 281-295.

Silvester, J., Hayes, P., Silvester, J., Wallace, M. & Hartmann, W. (eds) (1998) 'Trees Never Meet' Mobility & Containment: An Overview 1915-1946. In Hayes, P. *et al.* (eds) *Namibia under South African Rule: Mobility and Containment, 1915-1946*. James Currey, Oxford, pp. 3-50.

Tapscott, C. (1993) National reconciliation, social equity and class formation in independent Namibia. *Journal of Southern African Studies*, 19, 31-39.

Tapscott, C. (1995) War, peace and social classes. In Leys, C. & Saul, J.S. (eds) *Namibia's Liberation Struggle: The Two-Edged Sword*. James Currey, London, pp. 153-170.

UN (1995) *Beijing Platform for Action*. United Nations, New York.

UN (2002) *Gender Mainstreaming: An Overview*. Office of the Special Advisor on Gender Issues and Advancement of Women, United Nations, New York.

Vigne, P. (1997) Extension strategies in Northern Namibia: a review and recommendations. *Consultancy report for Northern Livestock Development Programme (NOLIDEP) (Internal document)*, Windhoek.

Vigne, P. & Oates, P. (1992) *Rural Development Priorities in Northern Namibia*. Namibian Economic Policy Research Unit (NEPRU) Research Report No. 2. NEPRU, Windhoek.

Whiteside, M. (1998) *Living Farms: Encouraging sustainable smallholders in Southern Africa*. Earthscan, London.

Wieringa, S. (1994) Women's Interests and Empowerment: Gender Planning Reconsidered. *Development and Change*, 25, 829-848.

Williams, F. (1994) *Precolonial Communities of Southwestern Africa: A history of Owambo Kingdoms, 1600-1920*. Arcaeia National Archives of Namibia, Windhoek.

Williams, G. (2004) Evaluating participatory development: tyranny, power and (re)politicisation. *Third World Quarterly*, 25, 557-578.

Woolcock, M. (1998) Social capital and economic development: toward a theoretical synthesis and policy framework. *Theory and Society*, 27, 151-208.

Woolcock, M. & Narayan, D. (2000) Social Capital: Implications for Development Theory, Research, and Policy. *Paper submitted to the World Bank Research Observer*.

Young, K., Visvanathan, N., Duggan, L., Nisonoff, L. & Wiegersma, N. (eds) (1997) Planning from a Gender Perspective: Making a World of Difference. In Visvanathan, N. *et al.* (eds) *The Women, Gender & Development Reader*. Zed Books, London, pp. 366-373.

Chapter 9

Sustainable Food for Sustainable Tourism in the Caribbean: Integrated Pest Management and Changes in the Participation of Women

Janet Momsen

Introduction

As new global food systems and World Trade Organization policies make it increasingly difficult for high cost Caribbean farmers to find export markets, they are turning to production for the local tourism market. Tourism is replacing agriculture as the main driving force of the economy in much of the region and both tourism and agriculture are increasingly focusing on sustainability. The inter-digitation of policies in the two dominant sectors of the economy raises issues of national sovereignty and of the role of outside agencies. It also questions the scale at which policies are designed and implemented and who benefits from sustainable practices. This chapter examines sustainability issues for small-scale farmers in the Caribbean and the links between agriculture and the new drive for sustainable tourism.

The Caribbean is the most tourism-dependent region in the world: '[B]y almost any economic indicator, the Caribbean is four times more dependent on the tourism industry than any other region of the world' (CTO, 1998: 5). Furthermore, this dependence grows daily as other economic sectors are marginalized by fast-moving global political and economic events (CTO, 1997: 8). For many Caribbean countries, tourism is the strongest and fastest growing sector of the economy. It attracts tourists with high disposable incomes, willing to pay for an up-market quality product and spending, on average, 31 per cent above the world average for tourists and second only to levels of visitor spending in North America (CTO, 1998). Such tourists are likely to be willing to pay for and even to demand organic and fresh local food while on holiday. Traditionally, the suppliers of these local foodstuffs, often produced organically, have been women small-scale farmers (Momsen, 1981). However, today it appears that these gender roles are changing as women farmers become more commercially oriented and male farmers lose their export markets. This chapter examines some of the recent changes in relation to gender, agriculture, tourism and sustainability.

The growth in international monitoring and management programmes in the tourism industry, such as the Green Globe 21 Standard scheme launched in 1994 by the World Travel and Tourism Council (WTTC), is indicative of a growing corporate interest in issues of sustainability (Pugh, 2001). Clearly, the adoption of sustainable practices can be both a rational business strategy that enhances efficiency and a 'green' marketing tool designed to compete for the rapidly growing numbers of alternative tourists. These practices became relevant to mass tourism with the certification of Sandals (Negril) in Jamaica, in 1998, as the first all-inclusive hotel in the world to attain the Green Globe 21 Standard for its environmental policies and management.

The Quality Tourism for the Caribbean project was set up in June 2002 by several regional tourism agencies: the Caribbean Tourism Organization (CTO), the Caribbean Alliance for Sustainable Tourism (CAST), which includes many hotel operators, and the Caribbean Epidemiology Centre (CAREC). It involves the Anglophone Caribbean countries of Barbados, Jamaica, Trinidad and Tobago, the Bahamas, and nine members of the Organization of East Caribbean States. The programme aims to strengthen the overall quality and competitiveness of the tourism industry in the Caribbean through the establishment and promotion of quality standards and systems, including the utilization of Integrated Pest Management (IPM) techniques, designed to ensure healthy, safe and environmentally friendly products and services. The project was, however, expedited by the decision of the European Union to allow European travel agencies to sue local hotels if their guests suffered from food-related illnesses. The result may consequently be sustainable tourism for foreign tourists as much as protecting the environment for Caribbean countries.

Benefits to the islands are increased if the tourism industry expands its use of local foodstuffs (Momsen, 1998; Ministry of Tourism, Barbados, 2003). Efforts to increase output of produce free from chemical residues, through greater use of IPM strategies, will improve the quality of local food, encourage the expansion of small-scale agriculture and reduce the loss of agricultural land and outflows of foreign exchange. Yet the trigger for the introduction of IPM was not safer food for locals and tourists, but the rejection of export crops, mainly by the United States, because of high pesticide residues. Thus, the move to both sustainable tourism and to sustainable food was strongly encouraged by the action of the two hegemonic powers traditionally seen as dominating the Caribbean region. Sustainability has become a postcolonial activity in terms of both tourists and funding agencies. Such top-down planning may lead to slower uptake at the grassroots levels because of poor implementation and lack of local understanding of the benefits of IPM (Momsen, forthcoming), but regional agencies can mitigate such problems.

Agenda 21 and Integrated Pest Management (IPM)

This chapter considers several objectives of Agenda 21 (Quarrie, 1992) in relation to IPM and how they have or have not been implemented in the Caribbean, with particular reference to tourism and gender roles. The use of agrochemicals, such as pesticides, insecticides, nematicides and herbicides, has been credited with increased crop yields and reduction of post-harvest losses but it has aggravated food safety, and environmental and public health concerns. Chapter 14 of Agenda 21 clearly highlighted the importance of agricultural policies that reduce pesticide use, decrease exposure to pesticides and enhance adoption of IPM and biological controls. Furthermore, 'Governments should develop and disseminate to farming households integrated farm management technologies, such as crop rotation, organic manuring, and other techniques involving reduced use of agricultural chemicals - taking particular note of the role of women' (Quarrie, 1992: Ch 14, C, Objective a). Conservative estimates put pre- and post-harvest losses caused by pests at 25 per cent to 50 per cent. Chemical control of pests has been the dominant method since the 1960s of reducing these losses and it is seen as an essential part of 'modern' agriculture. It was often encouraged by government subsidies for the import of agrochemicals. Farmers were taught that crops could not be successfully grown without the use of pesticides, especially in the case of commercial crops such as bananas (Grossman, 1998). But the overuse of these chemicals has detrimental effects on human health, farm budgets, the environment and international trade. In small islands, especially in a coralline island such as Barbados where the only source of drinking water is ground water, pesticide pollution would be a catastrophe. The Director of Research in the Ministry of Agriculture for Trinidad and Tobago has pointed out that the issue of pesticide use generally impacts more on and often has more serious implications for island states than on larger continental countries (Clarke-Harris, 2002). However, on the Caribbean coast of Costa Rica damage to the coral reef in Cahuita National Park was traced to pesticide residues from large banana plantations (Martin, forthcoming). Thus, it is not only in terms of drinking water that pesticides can affect tourism, but also in relation to marine pollution and the survival of living coral reefs.

In the Caribbean, the production of Non Traditional Agricultural Exports (NTAEs), such as flowers, herbs and specialist vegetables, is being encouraged as traditional plantation crops such as sugar and bananas lose their protected markets and subsidized prices following implementation of World Trade Organization policies. These NTAE crops are generally high value and require intensive production methods. This makes them very suitable for farmers on smallholdings, generally defined as less than 10 acres or under four hectares. Such farmers form the majority of agriculturalists in the Caribbean, but they occupy only a small proportion of farmland. Island governments see NTAEs, and production of the same crops for the domestic market, as a way of improving the value of rural life and improving the balance of payments in food crops by increasing both food exports and production for local consumption (BMARD, 2004). In Jamaica, between 1996 and 2001, the value of traditional export crops fell from US$89.2 million to US$57 million, while that of non-traditional agricultural exports increased from US$80.8 million to US$95 million (PIOJ, 2002).

In the commercial production of vegetables, Caribbean farmers have adopted systems of intensive pesticide applications using chemicals which pose high risks to human health and the environment (Clarke-Harris & Fleischer, 2003). Overuse and misuse of chemicals has allowed the development of resistant pests with the result that farmers feel they need to use more and more chemicals (Patterson, 1996). Since 1993, the United States Agency for International Development (USAID) has been funding IPM research in Jamaica, and in many other extra-Caribbean countries, aimed at decreasing use of toxic materials and demonstrating that the new biorational and less dangerous selective pesticides can produce comparable crop yields, improve farm worker safety and contribute towards resistance management (Clarke-Harris & Fleischer, 2003). This research has focused on high value NTAE crops exported to the USA such as hot peppers, vegetable amaranth (callaloo), cabbage and sweet potatoes, where high levels of pesticide residues have led to the rejection of shipments by the United States Department of Agriculture (USDA) inspectors at the port of entry. It appears that the USDA has more stringent limits for pesticide residues compared to the other main export markets of Canada and the United Kingdom.

IPM is a management intensive technology, requiring a dynamic decision-making process on the part of the grower. Rather than relying on predetermined prophylactic chemical applications with the goal of pest eradication, IPM emphasizes the importance of non-chemical preventative measures and the use of pesticides only when necessary and based on economic threshold levels. Active management on the part of farmers is required: they must constantly gather and evaluate information about pests, crops and weather conditions. This level of management is especially difficult for smallholder, part-time West Indian farmers who rarely keep records. In addition, the use of IPM practices frequently requires a greater reliance on contact with agricultural advisors and researchers. Such contact is least available to small-scale, semi-commercial farmers, especially women, as the few available advisors tend to concentrate on working with large scale export producers (Saito, 1991; Morgan, 2004). In Latin America and the Caribbean, in 1993, the proportion of women farmers receiving technical assistance from extension services was less than 10 per cent, and in most of these countries it was less than two per cent (Kleysen & Campillo, 1996). In Jamaica only 12 per cent of women farmers had received training in appropriate technology, despite expressing a great desire for such training (Kleysen & Campillo, 1996). In Trinidad an FAO study in 1995 showed that 43 per cent of female farmers had never been visited by an extension agent and only nine per cent used government extension as a source of information (Payson, 2005). In Barbados, of the 70 farmers surveyed who used chemical pesticides only eight, of which two were women farmers, got their information from government agricultural sources (Momsen, 2003).

Dissemination of IPM policies

Chapter 14 of Agenda 21 mentions the need 'to improve and implement programmes to put integrated pest management practices within the reach of farmers through farmer networks, extension services and research institutions - and not later than 1998, to establish operational and interactive networks among farmers, researchers and extension services to promote and develop integrated pest management' (Quarrie, 1992, Ch 14, I, Objective b). Our studies in the Caribbean revealed that many small farmers had heard of IPM but few were applying it. A few specialist exporters had benefited from working directly with researchers. Where dissemination of IPM was left to extension agents of the various Ministries of Agriculture, acceptance was less successful. In most Caribbean islands the extension service has been cut back as agriculture has become less important in the general economy. An understaffed service does not have time to explain to farmers why they should be using certain methods and so they are misapplied. In Jamaica we found that farmers had put pheromone traps in the middle of their fields, thinking that would protect the whole field, only to find that the insects attracted fell onto the ground where they hatched out as sweet potato weevils and infested the crop. Placement of these traps around the edges of fields, as recommended by researchers, would have had a beneficial effect. Some farmers had an original solution: they gave up growing sweet potatoes commercially and concentrated on marijuana, a more lucrative and less pesticide-dependent crop (Somerville, 2004).

The Caribbean Agriculture and Fisheries Programme (CAFP), a public regional programme for agricultural development, has also encouraged the spread of knowledge about IPM. This Programme has had no interaction with the USAID funded Integrated Pest Management Collaborative Research Support Program (IPM CRSP), although some of the same people are involved on the ground. CAFP has had success with Farmer Field Schools (CAFP, 2004) as has the IPM CRSP in Jamaica. These provide several days of intensive training to a few farmers and the knowledge is then supposed to trickle down to other farmers. Again, this approach works with the full-time farmer but the semi-commercial, part-time farmer does not have time to attend such training schools. Women farmers also tend to be omitted from such training because they do not have the time to attend and are often not full-time farmers.

Government role in national IPM policies

Agenda 21 suggested that governments, with the support of the relevant international and regional organizations, should set up national policies to ensure the safe and appropriate use of pesticides, pesticide pricing and distribution. Pesticides may also harm what they aim to protect, destroying crops through misapplication and drift. When broad-spectrum pesticides are applied, the natural balance of the ecosystem is disturbed. Both pests and their natural enemies may be destroyed allowing increased infestation by pesticide-resistant and other insects.

Pesticide labelling, providing farmers with understandable information about safe handling, application and disposal, was also advocated in Agenda 21. In some countries this becomes a problem where there are many illiterate farmers, but this is not the case in the Anglophone Caribbean. Here, the problem is following the instructions on the label under field conditions. Small quantities of pesticides may be repackaged without instructions and then sold. Inappropriate doses may be used because the proper measuring devices for mixing are not available. Sometimes farmers will mix different types of chemicals in order to spray for everything at the same time so reducing time and labour inputs. Such customized mixtures are usually less efficacious than the individual chemicals applied separately. If the mixture is too weak it can lead to pesticide resistance and, if it is too strong, pesticide residues can be left on crops when they go to market. Several women farmers in Barbados, interviewed in 2005, reported having problems working out measurements and proportions of chemicals for small scale production, especially when mixing chemicals imported from the USA where metric measures are not used (Richardson, 2005).

Farmer perceptions of the health risks of pesticide use

When asked about the danger to human health of pesticide use, most farmers did not consider it very serious. In a study in Jamaica, few farmers admitted to knowing anyone who had suffered from pesticide poisoning and there seemed to be little awareness of 'collateral damage' to family members from clothing worn during spraying being left in the house or washed with the family laundry (Schlosser, T., 1999). Empty containers left in the field or yard, or occasionally used to store water, were also not seen as dangerous. However, when the costs of hospitalization of people suffering from pesticide poisonings were taken into account, at least in Jamaica, then the problem of pesticide misuse can be seen to be quite a considerable financial burden on the national government. The new biorational options, such as the use of pheromones, are much safer for hand application and will reduce the health dangers to farmers (Clarke-Harris & Fleischer, 2003), but they are not always available and, generally, farmers do not trust their efficacy (Morgan, 2004).

In Jamaica, the Pesticide Control Authority (2004) reported that agricultural pesticides poisoned 348 persons in 2002-03. A high proportion of all cases were children of less than five years of age. Fifty-six per cent of the poisoning occurred on farms and 23 deaths were recorded. Patients suffering from chemical poisoning utilized 2,164 bed days in hospital in 2002-03 at a total cost of J$7,760,104. The World Health Organization (WHO) estimated in 1986 that one million cases of intentional pesticide poisoning, with 20,000 fatalities, occur annually. A joint study by the WHO and the United Nations Environmental Program (UNEP) in 1990 estimated three million hospitalized cases, of which 220,000 resulted in fatalities.

While sales of pesticides in developed countries have declined or stagnated, those in developing countries have increased significantly (Farah, 1994). This difference is compounded by the fact that some pesticides banned in the global North because of their danger to humans and the environment are still being sold to poor developing countries. Some 2,321,609 kg of pesticides were imported into Jamaica in 2002-03. This represented a slight decline over the previous year but, at the same time, there was a corresponding decline in traditional agriculture (bananas and sugar for example) (Pesticide Control Authority, 2004). However, pesticides are also manufactured in Jamaica and the leading manufacturer has seen a strong increase in export sales (Morgan, 2004). In Barbados there was a 2.2 per cent increase in imports of chemicals between 2002 and 2003 and a 2.5 per cent increase in domestic exports (BSS, 2004). In 2003, chemicals, pesticides, insecticides and so on made up 11 per cent of total imports into Barbados and 13 per cent of total exports (Morgan, 2004).

Farmers in the Caribbean are still resistant to using IPM, however. In a 2003 survey of 135 small farmers in Barbados, 52 per cent used chemical pesticides and 12 per cent used traditional non-chemical controls, but 21 per cent knew about IPM (Momsen, 2003). When asked to rank the problems they faced the third and fourth ranked problems were insect pests and plant diseases, after the cost of irrigation water, and theft of crops. Thieves sometimes took crops from farm fields shortly after application of pesticide, while they were still dangerous to eat. In Jamaica, some 15 per cent of farmers harvested crops less than a week after they had been sprayed with pesticides (Schlosser, G., 1999). There was clearly a need for assistance with controlling these pests and diseases. However, even those who used chemicals did not apply them to the food they ate themselves but only to the food they sold to tourists or supermarkets, where appearance mattered. In the Rio Grande Valley in Jamaica farmers apply 75.9 per cent of the pesticides they use on their orchard crops (bananas and coffee) which are mostly grown for export, while only 15.5 per cent of pesticides are used in home gardens, concentrated on the vegetable and root crops grown for sale (Spence & Thomas-Hope, 2005). This suggests that farmers know that pesticides on food are dangerous.

Farmers generally feel that pesticides are safe to use, although they feel that some are too dangerous (Table 9.1). Sommerville (2004), in a survey in Jamaica, found that 16 per cent of small farmers interviewed thought that pesticides were harmful if eaten, while eight per cent thought they could kill and were poisonous, but only 31 per cent admitted to feeling unwell after exposure to pesticides. Morgan (2004) found that half the farmers he interviewed in Jamaica did not think that the present generation of pesticides was harmful and some boasted that they had been working with pesticides for so long that they were now immune. In an earlier survey of 140 small farmers in Jamaica by Tina Schlosser (1999) 52 per cent reported symptoms of poisoning, such as difficulty breathing, dizziness and weakness, but only 8.6 per cent sought medical attention. In a meeting I attended with leaders of the women farmers of Barbados in July 2005, they reported that one of their group had just been admitted to hospital with pesticide poisoning. This heightened their awareness of the dangers of pesticide use which they had previously belittled when asked (IICA, pers comm, July 2005). This suggests a general lack of recognition of these dangers and perhaps almost a resistance to such recognition, even among well-educated women farmers, which contradicts some earlier findings of greater awareness among women than among men farmers (Momsen, 1981).

Table 9.1   Views on pesticide safety among 50 farmers in two areas of Jamaica

Pesticide View	Yes	No
Pesticides are a Community Hazard	2	39
Some pesticides are too dangerous	36	4
Some pesticides are safe	25	14
Pesticides are safe for farmers	30	5
Ever felt unwell when exposed to pesticides	15	33

Source: Adapted from Sommerville (2004)

This casual attitude to the use of chemicals is reflected in the use of safety measures by farmers. The use of protective clothing is rarely followed, although the requirements are well known. When asked, farmers say they use the required protection, but this is rarely seen in the field. Grossman (1992) reports that farmers in St Vincent sprayed barefoot as the muddy slopes were too steep and slippery to be negotiated in boots. In Barbados, it is thought to be 'macho' not to use protective clothing and that at least one visit a year to the hospital for a dose of oxygen is to be expected.

In Jamaica, Tina Schlosser (1999) found that only 14 per cent of farmers always wore protective clothing when spraying, while 63 per cent never wore protective clothing. Smith (2003), in a survey of farmers in the Rio Grande Valley in Jamaica, found that 81 per cent of farmers wore rubber boots and 26 per cent wore gloves, but few other items of protective clothing were worn. In a Barbados survey (Momsen, 2003), only 10 per cent of farmers admitted to using no protective clothing, while 49 per cent said that they used rubber gloves, 43 per cent used a mask and 29 per cent wore boots. A small number said they wore long sleeved shirts and long pants or overalls, a respirator or goggles. These answers at least suggest that farmers know they need to wear protective clothing, although observations in the field indicate that, in practice, only boots and rubber gloves were commonly used. Many farmers feel that in the tropics it is too hot to wear the full range of protective clothing, although this very heat and humidity make chemical absorption through the skin more likely. Tina Schlosser (1999) notes that several farmers displayed a 'resistance myth' whereby they claimed that one is able to get used to poisons with frequent use'. Many felt that toxicity was related to the smell of the pesticide and therefore pesticides with strong odours were often deemed the most dangerous. In fact, this does not determine toxicity in humans. Such attitudes to pesticide usage undermine national efforts to implement the objectives of Agenda 21 and also the sustainability of the farm population.

Farmers' attitudes to utilization of IPM

In Jamaica staff of the Caribbean Agricultural Research and Development Institute (CARDI) and the Rural Agricultural Development Agency (RADA) have been working for at least ten years to introduce IPM methods to farmers, while in Barbados there has been little interest in IPM *per se* and indeed the government offers subsidies to farmers to buy sprayers and it provides advice on the type and quantity of pesticides to use (BMARD, 2004). However, the Barbados government is also promoting and subsidizing organic agriculture and the use of locally made organic pesticides (BMARD, 2004). Despite these differences in official government programmes, attitudes to IPM are very similar in the two islands.

Sixty per cent of farmers interviewed in Jamaica, in areas where IPM Farmer Field training sessions had been held, thought that IPM was 'good' or 'very good' (Somerville, 2004) (Table 9.2). In Barbados only 43 per cent had even heard of IPM (Momsen, 2003) and, of this group, few seemed to think it was relevant to their farms, making remarks such as 'it's not commercial' or 'it's too slow'.

Table 9.2   Farmers' views of integrated pest management in two areas of Jamaica

Pesticide View	Number	Percent
Very good	7	14
Good	23	46
Not so good	15	30
Need to see it work	3	6
No good	1	2
Don't know	1	2
Totals	**50**	**100**

Source: Adapted from Sommerville (2004)

IPM practices such as 'scouting', or looking for infestations of pests and only spraying when they are present and threshold spraying, when infestation reaches a certain level, were rarely followed. Most farmers used prophylactic spraying, that is spraying on a regular weekly or even more frequent basis to prevent the emergence of pests. This was more expensive than the recommended practices but it took less time in checking on levels of pests. Farmers undertook this regular spraying because they felt it was more difficult to gain control once a pest attacked a field (Morgan, 2004). They were also familiar with this method and had used it for many years and 82 per cent reported that they were 'satisfied' or 'very satisfied' with pest control on their farms (Morgan, 2004). Among the twelve farmers in Jamaica who had been trained in IPM methods in the previous twelve months, three had reverted to regular prophylactic spraying (Morgan, 2004). The use of pesticides and herbicides is less laborious than hand weeding, scouting and hand picking of insect pests. Crop rotation, field sanitation and nursery management were also recommended IPM practices. However, farmers could not see the benefit of removing crop residues from fields as it involved extra work and, in the case of cabbages, new heads would grow back (Morgan, 2004). Of the 50 farmers interviewed in his study in Jamaica, Morgan (2004) found that only 26 per cent practiced IPM strategies. In areas where pheromone traps had been introduced to deal with the sweet potato weevil they were hardly being used because they were expensive, re-infestation could occur from neighbouring farms and the proper use had not been taught by extension agents. Farmers also reported that when supplies of these traps ran low, people resorted to stealing them (Sommerville, 2004). Few farmers knew any other IPM methods for control of pests. Clearly, knowledge and adoption of IPM methods have not extended far beyond the demonstration plots despite a decade of research in Jamaica and the success of IPM methods on callaloo and sweet potatoes which has allowed these crops to be exported to the USA.

Governments in the islands control the pesticides imported and sold through government outlets. Chapter 19 in Agenda 21 talks of the need for institutional frameworks for management of toxic chemicals, and the prevention of illegal traffic in toxic and dangerous products across international borders. These frameworks have been set up in most of the Caribbean, but in many places they are ineffectual because of lack of money for monitoring. Many farmers buy their chemicals from private retailers. These people have to be licensed by the government but the inspectors are scarce. One such store in Jamaica used the success of the application of its goods on the owner's fields as a marketing ploy to attract buyers, even though the owner was using banned pesticides (Morgan, 2004). In Barbados advice from agrochemical store owners was used as frequently as information from official government sources when farmers were looking for pesticides and herbicides (Momsen, 2003). Obsolete pesticide stocks are found throughout the region, including some agrochemicals no longer permitted in the USA. Even where banned chemicals are not being used, the national provision of toxic waste management centres for their disposal is inadequate and there is little pressure on farmers to comply with methods of safe disposal (Thomas-Hope, 1998).

Gender: Changing roles of women

Although Agenda 21 made it clear that gender aspects of IPM had to be considered, the nature of these is very complex and often time- and space-specific. Avoidance of chemicals and production of organic vegetables is becoming established in the Caribbean, as it has in the North, as a response to demand from both the local middle class and from tourists. However, most of the organic producers in the region tend to be men as developing such a business needs considerable capital and marketing expertise. In a 2005 study of women farmers in Barbados about one third wanted training in organic methods and one farmer said she wanted 'to improve the quality of produce, which is organic, without using chemicals' (Richardson, 2005). They usually see as their main market the visiting gourmand and the chefs at the high-end hotels where these tourists stay. There is a growing demand in the local market from the middle class but many of this group are becoming hobby farmers, growing their own foodstuffs. So the new trend seems to be, partly at least, externally driven but this has not always been so. In 1979, it was observed in Trinidadian village markets that some women farmers and market women were charging premium prices for food grown without chemicals (Harry, 1980). Thus, the interest in such things has a long history in the region, especially among women farmers.

In the past, surveys have found that women farmers tried to avoid spraying and would usually employ a man to do this task (Momsen, 1981). This was explained in terms of the health effects of the spray, especially for nursing or pregnant women. In the Caribbean there is a high proportion of women small-scale farmers and women undertake all farm tasks to some degree, but the one task that they were consistently least likely to carry out themselves was pesticide spraying (Momsen, 1981).

However, the results of recent surveys show that these gender differences are changing and disappearing (Momsen, 2003; Richardson, 2005). The results of the 2003 survey in Barbados (Momsen, 2003) revealed that only three women farmers hired men to spray their crops and these three farmers were aged 60, 65 and 79. For these three women, age-related infirmities may have forced them to depend on hired help, but it may also reflect a generational change among women farmers. Of the 42 women farmers interviewed in 2003, 20 did all farm tasks themselves, nine did not use pesticides, six had a male family member do the spraying and four did the spraying jointly with their male partner. This change has been facilitated by the increasingly widespread use of handheld sprayers on small farms.

Today, Caribbean women farmers are generally well educated and choose to farm for income, and as a way of life, rather than as subsistence producers. The Caribbean Network of Rural Women Producers (CANROP), founded in 1999, aimed in five years to become a 'vibrant, unified thriving organization with well-trained Members, capable of supporting their developing needs in the area of value-added activities on a sustainable basis' (Reid, 2005). CANROP is funded by the Inter-American Institute for Cooperation on Agriculture (IICA) which serves Latin America and the Caribbean. Starting with four Anglophone countries plus Haiti as an observer in 1999, by 2005 four more English speaking countries had joined and Suriname had become a Temporary Member. Each country has its own CANROP Chapter with local leaders. Thus, a regional non-governmental organization, funded by a supra-regional organization, has brought together rural women from across the Caribbean to work together for sustainable development. In discussions with the leadership of the CANROP group in Barbados in July 2005, ideas were suggested for a woman poultry farmer to produce smoked turkeys and for a woman herb farmer to make seasoning mixes. At the same time, training programmes were set up to assist in making the products produced by the Barbadian members of CANROP acceptable in export markets in terms of meeting labelling and packaging standards. With the stimulus of the regional organization, local women farmers are collaborating to improve their profitability and so to increase the sustainability of their enterprises. By tapping into local demand and export markets, and producing for the tourists' on-island consumption and for souvenirs, they have moved beyond the traditional women farmers selling their surplus production in the marketplace. They have established a sustainable lifestyle which is taking advantage of the new interest in the hotel industry for environmentally friendly and sustainable tourism, and by extension, through the demonstration effect, for the growing demand for a wider range of locally produced fresh products from the Caribbean middle class.

Conclusion

Agenda 21 stresses that states should adopt national strategies for sustainable development which build upon and harmonize the various economic sectors and social and environmental policies currently in force locally. For most territories of the Caribbean, tourism and agriculture are the leading sectors of the economy and projects bringing the two together in terms of sustainable practices should reinforce both sectors (Pemberton *et al.*, 2002; IICA, 2000). Governments are calling for more use of locally produced foods by the tourist industry and the major hotels are attempting to implement this (Ministry of Tourism, Barbados, 2003). Many of these hotels are also promoting their sustainable tourism credentials. Hotel management is setting up supply contracts with individual farmers for specific items, especially fresh herbs and salad crops. The main problem has been insufficient local supply to serve large hotels.

In Barbados in the 1960s about one third of food supplies used by hotels were locally produced. By the 1980s the proportion had increased to about one half as a greater variety and better quality of produce became available (Momsen, 1998). However, it now appears that despite the best efforts of hoteliers and various government agencies, the proportion of locally produced food consumed by hotels has fallen again (Ministry of Tourism, Barbados, 2003; Richardson, 2004). A few specialist farmers, many of whom are highly capitalized, well-educated expatriates or return migrants, have benefited. Yet the new interest in local produce has failed to turn back the movement out of agriculture, despite new investment and encouragement by the Barbadian Ministry of Agriculture (Momsen, 2005). Thus, overall, there may be a reduction in the use of agrochemicals to the benefit of ground water and marine resources, but the decline is more likely to be the result of falling agricultural production rather than increasing use of Integrated Pest Management (IPM) techniques. Sustainable tourism may be becoming dependent on food imported from elsewhere, predominantly the United States. Once again, the two sectors are failing to support each other (Torres & Momsen, 2004).

Yet, awareness of the need for sustainability in both sectors is at an all-time high in most islands at both government and agency level. This should augur well for the future, but it will only be achieved if the financial benefits of sustainability are clear to all involved. IPM can reduce variability of yields and costs (Goodhue & Klonsky, 2004), but such results are not seen by most small farmers. However, new regional groupings such as CANROP, and the proposals for the development of a sustainable organic agricultural industry in the Caribbean by the Commonwealth Secretariat (2005), suggest that regional initiatives may be reaching the grassroots whilst short-circuiting national policies. Thus, a new layer of policy makers at the regional level, including CAST for tourism, appears to be providing leadership for the sustainability of the agriculture/tourism nexus. If these regional NGOs can succeed in making both forward linkages to external funding agencies and backward linkages to national governments, then the region as whole may well achieve a more sustainable and healthier future for its two main industries of agriculture and tourism.

References

Barbados Ministry of Agriculture and Rural Development (BMARD) (2004) *Farmers Almanac 2004*. Agriculture Information Services, Barbados.

Barbados Statistical Service (BSS) (2004) Overseas Trade. *Barbados Statistical Service Bulletin,* 20, No. 12.

Caribbean Agriculture and Fisheries Programme (CAFP) (2004) *Regional Integrated Pest Management*. CAFP Workshop, Tobago, 5 April.

Caribbean Tourism Organisation (CTO) (1997) *Caribbean Tourism Investment Guide*. CTO, Barbados.

Caribbean Tourism Organisation (CTO) (1998) *Proceedings of the first Caribbean Hotel and Tourism Investment Conference*. CTO, Barbados.

Clarke-Harris, D. (2002) *Mission Report of the Regionalisation Workshop on Development of IPM in Leafy Vegetables that Currently Experience High Pesticide Input*. Centeno, Trinidad and Tobago.

Clarke-Harris, D. & Fleischer, S.J. (2003) Sequential sampling and biorational chemistries for management of Lepidopteran pests of vegetable Amaranth in the Caribbean. *Journal of Economic Entomology,* 96, 798-804.

Commonwealth Secretariat (2005) *Policy Proposals for the Development of a Sustainable Organic Agricultural Industry in the Caribbean*. PROINVEST, Georgetown, Guyana and the Commonwealth Secretariat, University of Guyana.

Sustainable Development

Farah, J. (1994) Pesticide Policies in Developing Countries. Do They Encourage Excessive Use? *World Bank Discussion Paper*. IBRD and World Bank, Washington DC.

Goodhue, R.E. & Klonsky, K. (2004) A General Methodology for Evaluating the Determinants of Pest Control Decisions. *Final Report to the Department of Pesticide Regulation, California*. Department of Agricultural and Resource Economics, University of California, Davis, CA.

Grossman, L.S. (1992) Pesticides, people and the environment in St Vincent. *Caribbean Geography*, 3, 175-186.

Grossman, L.S. (1998) *The Political Ecology of Bananas. Contract Farming, Peasants and Agrarian Change in the Eastern Caribbean*. University of North Carolina Press, Chapel Hill and London.

Harry, I.S. (1980) *Women in Agriculture in Trinidad*. Unpublished MSc thesis, University of Calgary, Canada.

Inter-American Institute for Cooperation on Agriculture (IICA) (2000) *Proceedings of the Regional Agro-Tourism Conference: Agro-Tourism as a Sustainable approach to Economic Growth*. IICA, Trinidad and Tobago.

Inter-American Institute for Cooperation on Agriculture (IICA) (2005) Personal communication in meeting held at IICA offices, Barbados, July.

Kleysen, B. & Campillo, F. (1996) *Rural Women Food Producers in 18 Countries of Latin America and the Caribbean*. IICA, San José, Costa Rica.

Martin, G. (2006) Conservation and tourism planning on the Caribbean coast of Costa Rica. In Pugh, J. & Momsen, J.H. (eds) *Environmental Planning in the Caribbean*. Ashgate, Aldershot.

Ministry of Tourism, Barbados (2003) *Draft Report on Inter-Sectoral Linkages Study, Tourism and Agriculture*. Ministry of Tourism, Barbados.

Momsen, J.D. (1981) Women in small scale farming in the Caribbean. In Horst, O. (ed.) *Papers in Latin American Geography in Honor of Lucia C. Harrison*. CLAG, Muncie, Indiana, pp. 44-56.

Momsen, J.H. (1998) Caribbean tourism and agriculture: new linkages in the global era? In Klak, T. (ed.) *Globalization and Neoliberalism: The Caribbean Context*. Rowman and Littlefield, Lanham MD, pp. 115-133.

Momsen, J.H. (2003) Survey of Small Farmers in Barbados. Unpublished report, University of California, Davis, CA.

Momsen, J.H. (2005) Caribbean Peasantry Revisited: Barbadian Farmers over Four Decades. *Southeastern Geographer*, 45, 42-57.

Momsen, J.H. (2006) Introduction to Pugh, J. & Momsen, J.H. (eds) *Environmental Planning in the Caribbean*. Ashgate, Aldershot.

Morgan, O.A. (2004) *Socio-Economic Factors influencing the Adoption of Integrated Pest Management by Cabbage Farmers in Douglas Castle, St Ann and Mafoota, St James, Jamaica*. Unpublished MSc thesis, Environmental Management, University of the West Indies, Jamaica.

Patterson, K.A. (1996) *The Political Ecology of Nontraditional Agricultural Exports and an IPM Project in Jamaica*. Unpublished MSc thesis, Geography Department, Virginia Polytechnic and State University.

Payson, K. (2005) *Engaging Women. Facilitating Women's Agricultural Involvement with a Pluralistic Extension Model in Trinidad.* Unpublished doctoral thesis, University of Florida, Gainesville.

Pemberton, C.A., Wilson, L.A., Garcia, G.W. & Khan, A. (2002) Sustainable development of Caribbean agriculture. In Goodbody, I. & Thomas-Hope, E. (eds) *Natural Resource Management for Sustainable Development in the Caribbean.* Canoe Press, University of the West Indies, Jamaica.

Pesticide Control Authority (2004) *Annual Report 2002-2003.* Jamaica Information Service, Kingston, Jamaica.

Planning Institute of Jamaica (PIOJ) (2002) *Agriculture.* Planning Institute of Jamaica, Kingston, Jamaica.

Pugh, J. (2001) Local Agenda 21 and the Third World. In Desai, V. & Potter, R.B. (eds) *The Arnold Companion to Development Studies.* Arnold, London, pp. 289-293.

Quarrie, J. (ed.) (1992) *Earth Summit 1992.* The Regency Press Corporation, London.

Reid, M-L. (2005) *CANROP Annual Strategic Work Plan, 2005-2006.* IICA, Trinidad.

Richardson, P.E. (2004) *Tourism and Agriculture in Barbados: Understanding Linkages.* Unpublished BSc (Hons) dissertation, Geography Department, University of Edinburgh.

Richardson, P.E. (2005) *Survey of Women Small Farmers.* Unpublished report to UNIFEM, Bridgetown, Barbados.

Saito, K.A. (1991) Extending help to women farmers in LDCs. *Finance and Development*, 28, 29-32.

Schlosser, G. (1999) *Gendered Production Roles and Integrated Pest Management in Three Jamaican Farming Communities.* Unpublished MSc thesis, Geography Department, Virginia Polytechnic and State University.

Schlosser, T. (1999) *Local Realities and Structural Constraints of Agricultural Health: Pesticide Poisoning of Jamaican Small-holders.* Unpublished MSc thesis, Geography Department, Virginia Polytechnic and State University.

Smith, H. (2003) *Economics of Agrochemical Use and Biodiversity on Small Farmers' Plots in the Rio Grande Valley, (Jamaica).* Unpublished MSc research paper, Environmental Management, University of the West Indies, Mona, Jamaica.

Sommerville, E. (2004) *Socio-economic Factors influencing the Willingness of Sweet, Potato Farmers to Adopt Participatory Integrated Pest Management in Hounslow, St Elizabeth and South Manchester (Jamaica).* Unpublished MSc research paper, Environmental Management, Department of Geography and Geology, University of the West Indies, Jamaica.

Spence, B. & Thomas-Hope, E. (2005) Agrobiodiversity and the economic cost of agrochemical use among smallholder farmers in the Rio Grande Valley, Jamaica. *PLEC News and Views*, New Series, 6, 11-15.

Thomas-Hope, E. (1998) *Solid Waste Management: Critical Issues for Developing Countries.* Canoe Press, University of the West Indies, Mona, Jamaica.

Torres, R.M. & Momsen, J.H. (2004) Challenges and potential for linking tourism and agriculture to achieve pro-poor tourism objectives. *Progress in Development Studies*, 4, 294-318.

World Health Organization (WHO) (1990) *Public Health Impact of Pesticides Used in Agriculture*. WHO, Geneva.

Chapter 10

Factors Affecting the Sustainability of Cotton Production: Changing Rural Livelihoods in the North-West Region in Zimbabwe

Nick James

Introduction

Cotton is Zimbabwe's second most important export crop after tobacco (Mariga, 1994) and, moreover, 75 per cent of the crop emanates from the smallholder sector (Larsen, 2002). The role of tobacco in the national economy is rapidly declining, however, because of falling global demand and the deepening crisis among Zimbabwe's large scale commercial farms since the early 1990s. Cotton thus remains important for export earnings, even though it is faced with increasing global competition, including the effects of controversial subsidies for cotton farmers in the USA (Watkins, 2003).

While the argument that cotton as a cash crop contributes to poverty features in this chapter, the aim is also to analyse the relative sustainability of cotton as a crop that communal (smallholder) farmers depend on for a livelihood. The chapter starts by analysing the development of environmental policies, and particularly how these have been implemented in the North-West region of Zimbabwe. Recent shifts to participatory approaches to rural development have come out of long-term conservation policies. This section also examines some of the nuances in the history of environmental policies starting in the 1930s. Since 1992, the sustainable development rhetoric has been to attempt to achieve sustainable agricultural systems. Secondly, the chapter will examine Zimbabwe's cotton industry and the extent to which it remains important for the national economy. National productivity has seen a downward trend during and since the 1990s, when privatization was implemented, and so the industry has faced uncertainty. Thirdly, the chapter will examine the case of Gokwe North District, part of the North-West region of Zimbabwe, which is especially dependent upon cotton. Throughout the twentieth century, research into cotton and its agro-economic viability was focused in the North-West (Reid, 1971; Mariga, 1994; Worby, 1995; Nyambara, 1999). Analysis at the household level gives insight into agro-ecological and socio-economic advantages in this region for growing cotton.[1] However, household food insecurity and other forms of poverty in the region can be traced back to the political economic relations between the state and the local areas since the 1960s (Worby, 1994; James, 2002a). This section examines the specific history of cotton growing in Gokwe North District, before focusing on cotton cropping among households in the Nembudziya area. The section examines the agro-ecological dynamics and complexities in Nembudziya and it assesses the changing decisions by households in their cropping strategies. Evidence strongly points to significant changes in soil fertility at the field level. Finally, the chapter explains the bio-physical and agro-economic reasons as to why cotton farming is unsustainable in the North-West region of Zimbabwe. Despite national and institutional ambitions to increase production and productivity rates, yields within the communal areas have remained low and moreover, environmental degradation and soil fertility decline has become increasingly evident.

Evidence from a sample of households in the North-West region of Zimbabwe shows that a combination of forceful introduction of cotton in communal areas, agronomic exploitation of soils and emergent social inequalities have resulted in serious underdevelopment in the region (James, 2002a). This chapter consequently demonstrates that no appropriate sustainable development policies have been implemented in a region that has consistently provided a product that comprises a significant part of the nation's export earnings. The analysis shows that people are taking the initiative to seek alternatives to avoid being impoverished by cotton.

Environmental policies in the North-West region

Zimbabwe has a long history of environmental awareness and applied conservation policy (Bowyer-Bower, 1996; Munro, 2003; Keeley & Scoones, 2003). A National Conservation Strategy has been applied since the Rio Earth Summit in 1992 (Chenje & Johnson, 1994), while environmental impact assessments are management tools to mitigate environmental degradation and some of the methods date back to the early twentieth century (Beinart, 1984). Concern for sustainable development has focused on socio-economic vulnerability, poverty and social justice and research has shown dynamic and changing 'local level interactions between how people achieve food security (and other basic needs) *and* their natural environment' (Moorehead & Wolmer, 2001: 95 emphasis added). The change in focus since the 1990s links also to a shift from state-led, top-down policy to more local, NGO-based and livelihood-focused approaches (Keeley & Scoones, 2003). Such a livelihood focus (Wolmer & Scoones, 2003) has given insight into much more complex situations, showing notable differences among households as well as significant changes over time (Scoones, 1997).

There has thus been a shift away from 'rational', purposive environmental policy, based only on science and technocratic understanding (Drinkwater, 1989),

---

1 Original PhD research by the author was undertaken between 1997 and 2000.

to a more flexible and loose policy, based more closely on local politics and social relations (Keeley & Scoones, 2003). The more linear model of agricultural or rural development, based on the European-devised model of 'mixed farming' for smallholders, has been replaced by the concept of many 'pathways' of change (Scoones & Wolmer, 2002). The conceptual framework of 'sustainable livelihoods' therefore enables local people, and associated institutions, to produce and activate relevant strategies that combine the biophysical environment with livelihoods (Forsyth, 2003).

That said - and there are several sustainable development policies in Zimbabwe on wildlife, forest resources, indigenous woodlands and resettlement (Chenje & Johnson, 1994) - soil fertility is neglected. There are several new research initiatives focusing on the issue, but they have not gained the attention that soil conservation and soil erosion had in previous decades (Keeley & Scoones, 2003). During the 1940s and 1950s, soil conservation fitted in with the ambitious policies to create contour ridges on all sloping cultivated land (Hagmann & Murwira, 1996) and soil erosion provided the dramatic pictures of gulley and sheet erosion (Stocking, 1996). During the 1980s, and particularly in the North-West, the focus changed to the rapid technical transformation of agriculture among smallholder farmers (Zinyama, 1992). The focus on technical changes in the communal areas of Zimbabwe included the application of chemical fertilizers and manure and, therefore, neglected other options for sustaining soil fertility (Campbell *et al.*, 1998). Furthermore, the technical extension services rarely acknowledged the double constraint on farmers of a restriction on livestock numbers in communal areas and the significant expense of chemical fertilizers (Scoones *et al.*, 1996).

There has been a long history of agrarian reform in Zimbabwe. Recently, challenges have been taking place to accepted norms, discourses and technical understanding (Keeley & Scoones, 2003). For example, the Land Apportionment Act of 1930 divided land leaving black Zimbabweans with less fertile soils. The 'centralization' policy that followed was in part devised by an individual called Emory Alvord and the impetus behind that led to the Native Land Husbandry Act of 1951. The dominant policy objective was to achieve a level of productive success among smallholder farmers using the 'mixed farming' model (Keeley & Scoones, 2003). 'Centralization' involved organizing homesteads into straight lines and separating grazing and cultivated land; thus it arguably 'facilitated control and surveillance of rural populations' (Keeley & Scoones, 2003: 134).

The legacy of this type of agrarian reform continued through to the 1980s when 'villagisation' was applied throughout the communal areas of Zimbabwe (Munro, 1998). Initially 'villagisation' (using the same principle as 'centralization') served to be a remedy for land disputes and also to service the land distribution issue. However, land pressure meant that the new policy was 'land reform and efficient use of lands' and therefore reminiscent of Alvord's programmes first initiated in the 1930s (Nyambara, 2001: 275). Alvord was a well-travelled agricultural technician and at the time he took it as given that European farming practices were superior and indirectly this led to 'more top-down, command-and-control response in the African farming areas' (Keeley & Scoones, 2003: 134). That approach to agricultural and environmental policy continued until the 1990s. It was in that decade that changes began and Keeley & Scoones (2003: 149) asked 'Are there, then, possibilities for new more diverse, inclusionary and participatory forms of policy process?' Following the Rio Earth Summit (1992) new norms and changing institutions emerged, but this was simultaneous with several contradictory political and economic developments in Zimbabwe.

Post-Independence policy on the environment centred around conservation and in efforts to 'help arrest continued land degradation in the country' (Bowyer-Bower, 1996: 9). While this continued in principle along the same lines as the previous decades of environmental policy, several difficulties emerged as rural economic growth began to conflict with established policies from the colonial era (Bowyer-Bower, 1996). In particular, as Zinyama (1995: 219) writes: 'The communal areas are characterized by widespread soil erosion and river siltation, [and] loss of genetic diversity due to vegetation clearance for human settlement ...'

The earlier soil conservation policy projects did not reach the North-West region; after 1960 the focus was on resettlement and then in the 1970s it was on cotton extension efforts. During the 1980s 'villagisation' and growth in the cotton industry became the main priority. The region became a major recipient of population (Zinyama & Whitlow, 1986). The focus on cotton led to neglect of policies linked to sustainable development including CAMPFIRE[2] and some of the forestry policies (Moyo *et al.*, 1991). Thus, while soil fertility research was vigorously pursued through the University of Zimbabwe (Waddington *et al.*, 1998), it rarely filtered through to the cotton growing areas (see, for example, Campbell *et al.*, 1998). Cotton is known as a crop that contributes to land degradation through cultivation practice, as well as in intense consumption of soil nutrients (see section below; Stocking, 1972; James 2002a).

The North-West is predominantly made up of communal lands and thus the District Councils are in control of over cropping, conservation and organisation of the land for grazing and cultivation. This is carried out through the Ministry of Lands Agriculture and Rural Resettlement and it is operated via the Department of Agricultural and Technical Extension Services (generally referred to as AGRITEX) (Bowyer-Bower, 1996). Besides the focus on growth in the communal areas, another important facet in the neglect of sustainable development policy in the North-West is the political focus on resettlement and 'land acquisition'. Moyo *et al.* (1991: 136) emphasize 'that sustainable development in Zimbabwe is hinged upon the need to redress the mistakes of the past'. The country profile by the Johannesburg Summit on Zimbabwe points to a national vision in Zimbabwe to achieve commercial agriculture throughout the smallholder sector by 2020, with sustainable farming systems and a reversal of environmental degradation (United Nations, 2002).

---

2   For a critical review of CAMPFIRE (Communal Areas Management Programme for Indigenous Resources) in the North-West see Alexander & McGregor (2000).

Cotton farming: Agrarian transformations

Cotton farming is an important part of the development process in North-West Zimbabwe (GNRDC, 2000). Moreover, the majority of households are dependent upon the crop for their livelihoods. The analysis below shows that while several agro-ecological advantages exist in the North-West for cotton, there are, nevertheless, some serious concerns about its long-term viability (see also Castro, 1998).

Cotton is a cash-crop grown in several parts of the world, with significant mid-latitude advantages in terms of photosynthetic potential and, therefore, greater yields compared to African cotton growing areas (Porter, 1995). Cotton is unique in that, as a modern commodity, it requires both technical and agronomic expertise as well as labour intensity for economic success. While in areas of the USA and Asia cotton is extensively cultivated and harvested using machinery, in Zimbabwe it has been hand-picked, making for better quality of lint. Nevertheless, particular political, institutional and agro-ecological settings need to be right for cotton cropping to be successful (Keeley & Scoones, 2003). McCann (1999) points out that cotton is a crop formerly native to Africa that has been agronomically developed in the North and reintroduced to Africa in the twentieth century (see also Ruwitah, 1997).

As emphasized in Isaacman and Roberts (1995), cotton was introduced into Africa commercially in the early twentieth century by the different colonial regimes in Europe. The aim was to exploit abundant and cheap labour and therefore to compete more effectively with the United States and other mid-latitude producers. However, 'Colonial officials had to confront the fact that their cotton programmes were not yielding the volume and quality of cotton they sought and that obligatory cotton production contributed to persistent rural challenges to the colonial order' (Isaacman & Roberts, 1995: 11). The legacy of an institutional system of technical, regimented and formalized cotton cropping has thus continued through to more recent decades (Mariga, 1994).[3] The post-Independence system of cotton cropping in Zimbabwe combined state-led technical structures inherited from colonial times (Nyambara, 1999) and smallholder cropping strategies to create the so-called 'second agricultural revolution' in Zimbabwe during the 1980s (Rukuni & Eicher, 1994).

The history of cotton farming in Zimbabwe is well documented, showing both temporal and spatial unevenness in its relative success (Mariga, 1994; Worby, 1995; Nyambara, 1999; James, 2002a). Implementation of the Native Land Husbandry Act (1951) saw a new technical focus for increasing production throughout the smallholder agricultural sector (Scoones *et al.* 1996). After consolidating agronomic research, the momentum to grow cotton in Zimbabwe began in the 1960s, partly influenced by the urgency of the Unilateral Declaration of Independence (UDI) in 1965 (Rukuni, 1994a; Worby, 1998a) and, since then, it has spread from the North-West to several other relatively remote parts of the country (Hasler, 1996; Alexander & McGregor, 2000; Chimhowu, 2003). Once actively promoted by the

---

3 See detailed historical analysis of cotton cropping in Kenya in Castro (1998).

state agricultural extension services, the adoption of cotton by communal farmers gained momentum (James, 2002a).

Before returning to closer analysis of agrarian and agro-ecological realities under cotton, it is important to examine the macro-economic conditions that drive cotton cropping in Zimbabwe. The most important trajectory has been for greater total production, bigger yields and more streamlined market competition (Mariga, 1994), all with the singular objective of sustaining an increase in export earnings (Takavarasha, 1994; Larsen, 2002). Policy focus among Zimbabwe's agricultural institutions has been to achieve 'a dynamic production-revolution in Communal Lands through the development of new technologies and the commercialization of new crops' (Rukuni, 1994b: 33). Since legislation over land resources in Zimbabwe does not particularly promote sustainable development, and policy documents like the National Conservation Strategy lack clarity (Moyo *et al.*, 1993), it is hardly surprising that protection for the environment has hardly featured in the cotton growing areas. While policies for sustainable development are directly implemented in other sectors (Clarke, 1994; Alexander & McGregor, 2000; Munro, 2003), policy considerations in the cotton regions remain severely neglected.

During the 1990s some thirty years of state-control of the cotton industry came to an end when competition was introduced to the market (Larsen, 2002). The break-up of the parastatals led to a serious undermining of the quality control system. Initial restructuring centred on greater commercialization, but in 1994 the World Bank put pressure on Zimbabwe to deregulate and liberalize the cotton trade (Larsen, 2002). Ginning and marketing companies Cargill (a transnational corporation) and Cotpro (an arm of the Commercial Cotton Growers Association) entered into competition with the newly named Cottco (formerly CMB – Cotton Marketing Board). While the cotton industry in Zimbabwe relied on relatively good prices internationally during the 1980s, lint prices fell sharply in the 1990s. The three companies competed mainly by offering different packages to growers, but the state-controlled Cottco led the pricing system (Worby, 1998b). Communal farmers began to face mounting constraints. Inflation increased and economic stagnation made it difficult to secure input credit. That said, Zimbabwe produced 350,000 tonnes of seed cotton in 2000, which compares to a record year when communal farmers produced 323,000 tonnes in 1987-88 (Larsen, 2002).

Zimbabwe's cotton has two particular advantages: one is the higher quality of hand-picked, compared to machine-harvested lint. The second is cheap labour. Europe buys half of Zimbabwe's cotton and it is willing to pay a premium because it is better for dying and blending with other synthetic fibres (Larsen, 2002). Both Cottco and Cargill are able to bypass traders and supply directly to spinners in Europe, Asia and South Africa. With greater liberalization through the International Monetary Fund Structural Adjustment Programmes, the 'reform' of Zimbabwe's economy has led to a greater inflow of textile goods (including second-hand clothing), especially since the 1990s. This resulted in severe damage to the national textile industry and, as a result, more than 80 per cent of the total production is exported compared to 50 per cent in the 1980s (Larsen, 2002).

Larsen (2002) concludes that there was a lack of impetus to succeed nationally following privatization. The systems of primary purchase, ginning and marketing of cotton in Zimbabwe consequently remained the same as before liberalization. More pointedly, and recognized elsewhere, there is no direct attention to sustainable development within the cotton industry (Castro, 1998; Gibbon, 1999).

With this assessment of relative stability in the cotton system, two points need further clarification. It is unclear as to whether the economic crisis in Zimbabwe and the downward spiral of international cotton prices (Takavarasha, 1994) can be withstood in coming years. The cotton cropping area in Zimbabwe in 2004-05 was severely affected by declining international prices and the problem was further exacerbated by a severe drought (Admos Chimhowu, pers comm). With little direct policy attention on either 'sustainable livelihoods' or sustainable development from a biophysical perspective, it is necessary to raise serious questions about future prospects for millions of Zimbabweans living in relatively marginal cotton-dependent areas such as the North-West.

Local perspectives: Cotton farming among households in Gokwe North District

The previous section provided some insight into the ambivalent situation of Zimbabwe's cotton industry, combining a robustness based on long-term structures including marketing, agronomy, extension and training, with recent problems within a flagging global market. The focus now shifts to cotton farming households in the District of Gokwe North (Figure 10.1).

First, it is important to provide some explanation of the reasons why cotton became so predominant in such a relatively remote and agro-ecologically harsh region of Zimbabwe (Worby, 1992). Second, drawing on the author's research in the late 1990s, analysis is provided of household conditions among those growing cotton. The research shows that a select few households make a good living from cotton, while several wealthy households deliberately choose not to grow cotton (see also Nyambara, 1999). The majority of households struggle to make a living out of cotton, while their poorer counterparts cannot afford to grow cotton, and therefore struggle to make an income from other crops like maize. Furthermore, the general modernization of agro-ecological dynamics and the exploitation and destruction of natural vegetation result in a combination of loss of wild sources of food (James, 2002b) *and* a transformation away from indigenous and traditional forms of cropping, including the growing of 'minor crops', such as bambarra nut, sweet potato, small grains (millet and sorghum), melons and cow peas (FAO, 1985). Each of these factors, including the greater dependence on growing cotton, places pressure on household food security in the area.

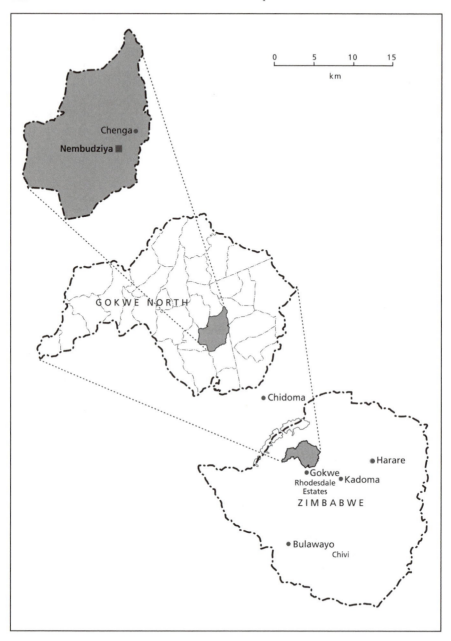

**Figure 10.1   Locating Nembudziya Ward One within Gokwe North District in
Zimbabwe (Source: James, 2002a)**

Historical context of cotton growing in Gokwe North District

In order to evaluate whether cotton is a viable crop for Gokwe North District in the North-West region, it is important to look back over developments in the twentieth century. Mariga (1994) makes the point that the introduction of cotton took place after several decades of tests and agronomic research (see also Taylor, 1919; Cameron, 1937; Gledhill, 1979). Although this suggests that the region is relatively suitable for cotton, several difficulties, including pest problems, small yields and crop failure, need to be overcome. However, prior to the 1930s the North-West (known as Sebungwe) was famed for its tobacco (Kosmin, 1977) and this provided strong social relations between the Shona (*Shangwe*) and the Ndebele people in the South-West of the country. Going further back in history, the region had been a trade route to the Zambezi and to the ocean through Mozambique, and David Livingstone once prospected coal in 1856, as did the British South Africa Company in 1894 (Chorley, 1945).

Before the 1950s, some successful cotton crops had been recorded in the region close to Kadoma (a base for the Cotton Research Institute), but transport and infrastructure into the region remained undeveloped. The North-West was tsetse fly country, with dense Miombo woodland, and ideal habitat for malaria-carrying mosquitoes, making the region unattractive for white non-indigenous farmers.

Soon after the Second World War, however, some two thousand families were expelled from 'high veldt' areas (which became major landholdings including the Rhodesdale Estates owned by the British multinational company Lonrho) (Ranger, 1985; Worby, 1994, 2000) and they were resettled in Gokwe. In the following ten years, one hundred thousand Africans, then described as 'squatters' by the colonial authorities, were moved to 'unassigned' land in Sebungwe (later known as Gokwe) (Nyambara, 1999).[4] At the same time, there was a second phase after the Land Apportionment Act and 'Centralization' in Alvord's (see above) vision for modernising African farming in the form of the Native Land Husbandry Act (James, 2002a). This concerted effort to make the early resettlement work depended on controlling tsetse fly (Taylor, 1982; Child & Riney, 1987). Chorley (1945: 5) points out that the outbreaks of 'sleeping sickness' in the 1920s and 1930s led to 'the area [being] *terra incognita* except to a few game poachers'. Furthermore, it became necessary to provide sufficient infrastructure, including provision of surface water, schools and roads, and to enable livelihood opportunities for thousands of new arrivals to the area (James, 2002a; see also Chinodya, 1982). Initially, these in-migrants settled on the southern fringes of the region including Sanyati, Kana (Matame) and, later in the 1960s, in Chidoma (Nyambara, 1999; Worby, 2000). The in-migrants were resettled by the then Native Commissioners into villages under their own headmen, but only after formal permission from the indigenous

---

4   The Sebungwe District comprised '17,793,300 acres, in remote and tsetse-ridden area [to] be left unassigned' (Palmer, 1977: 160). Unassigned land was not decided upon and essentially not suitable for white farmers.

chiefs (Worby, 1994). The technical allocation of land for households was based on 'carrying capacity', then concluded as 150 acres with seven head per family (Worby, 2000). This included the homestead, a garden, a field and access to grazing for ten cattle. Initially, the settlers produced maize, sorghum and millet as the main crops (James, 2002a). Specifically, Gokwe agricultural staff abandoned the Land Husbandry Act and, in unison with the 'community development' approach of the 1960s, they worked using more sensitive and persuasive extension methods (Worby, 2000). Among the resettled farmers there was initial resistance to growing cotton, but after Reid's (1971) efforts 'the cropped area and the cash value of the cotton crop increased exceptionally' (Worby, 2000: 120).

The 1960s were also especially politically volatile in the North-West (Nyambara, 1999). People hated forced resettlement as the new area meant harsh living conditions and increased contraction of diseases, including malaria and sleeping sickness (*Trypanosomiasis*). Additionally, different factions of 'freedom' fighters operated in the region and many people were suspicious of the extension services because of their links with, and legacy of, the despised Land Husbandry Act. The authorities made greater efforts to move people further into the region, despite mounting resistance to increasingly rudimentary resettlement conditions (Collett, 1963-1965). The war for Independence escalated later in the 1960s but, against this, infrastructural development took place in the 1970s and Nembudziya became a destination for road vehicles, including buses. One road came from Gokwe and another from Kadoma via Sanyati. Nembudziya thus began to welcome increasing numbers of in-migrants (especially from the Chidoma group). Headman Nembudziya provided an open welcome, and the land was flat and the soils soft, thus making it easier to till without cattle.[5] 'Starting in 1963, a cotton advisory officer was stationed at the Cotton Research Institute [in Kadoma] to facilitate liaison between researchers and extension workers' (Mariga, 1994: 227). Although cotton was introduced, the people moving into Nembudziya resisted it, and sometimes refused to grow it, until the 1970s. As the war for Independence had begun, these became politically very unstable times, making it difficult for cotton growers as well as the agricultural extension services (Reid, 1971; Ranger, 1998; Nyambara, 1999). Despite this, however, 'the 'dark interior' that Gokwe once evoked in the colonial mind was now shown to be amenable to illumination of rational planning' (Worby, 1998a: 56).

After Independence in 1980, the 'second agricultural revolution' saw active state promotion of cotton (Nyambara, 1999; James, 2002a). During the 1980s in Gokwe the number of registered farmers with the Cotton Marketing Board (CMB) grew five-fold to nearly a quarter of a million. The organisation of the cotton industry was robust and impressive (Reid, 1971; Worby, 1998a). The agricultural extension work required discipline among the farmers. Reid enthuses about households that 'preferred to curtail food production for their families and rather grow cash crops and buy food' (Reid, 1971: 60). The training, discipline and entrepreneurial skills required for cotton cropping needed considerable investment by households

---

5   The area for Nembudziya's three wards is approximately 35 square kilometres.

and state institutions alike (James, 2002a). '[Reid] simply accorded his clients the dignity of being viewed as 'economic men' in the mould proposed by neo-classical theory' (Worby, 2000: 120). Reid therefore saw good coordination of the different administrative departments (training officers, loan managers and transporters), as well as the focus on relative success of the cash crop producers (Worby, 2000). The advantage fell to the in-migrants who had brought with them experience of working with ploughs and other more technical knowledge, while the indigenous inhabitants became disadvantaged. The process of 'commoditization'[6], integrated with different forms of labour organisation, led to greater differentiation both socially and in land holdings (Worby, 1995; Nyambara, 2001).

Cotton soon became the main industry in Gokwe, and new regional dynamics emerged in the 1970s. After initial resistance, cotton farming rapidly expanded into several communal areas many of which had not been previously cultivated.[7] Cattle were eventually permitted into the region and the extension services, particularly after Independence, were emphatically focused on training communal farmers. Gokwe nevertheless fitted into the characterization of a 'food insecurity paradox', where economic growth, agrarian expansion and the creation of wealth were taking place, while simultaneously a significant number of households were becoming considerably poorer (Jayne *et al.,* 1994). Worby (1992) concludes that the overall regional process of commoditization, new social relations and cultural mixes led to the undermining of traditional and indigenous agricultural practices among the Shangwe people.

Cotton cropping among households in Nembudziya, Gokwe North District

Nembudziya is an area in Gokwe North District (Figure 10.1), including three wards, and it is a headmanship formerly with people (including the Gondes) under Chief Chireya. Nembudziya is also the name adopted for the emerging 'town', technically termed a District Service Centre (DSC), and then a 'Growth Point' in 2001.[8] Nembudziya Ward One has 21,579 hectares split into 16 per cent woodland, 4 per cent bush and 80 per cent cultivated area. Nembudziya Ward One is located in Natural Region III with 500 mm to 700 mm mean annual rainfall, relatively high temperatures, infrequent rains and it is subject to inter- and intra-seasonal droughts (James, 2002a). Nembudziya Ward One has the highest total population in Gokwe North District (and one of the highest densities, with nearly 70 people per square kilometre). Gokwe has an overall density of 22 people per square kilometre.[9]

---

6   See theoretical analysis in Watts (1999).

7   The tobacco that featured in this area before the 1930s was grown on small pockets of land and mainly close to rivers and streams (Kosmin, 1977).

8   A 'growth point' is a term devised during the late 1970s as part of an 'Integrated Plan for Rural Development'. Such an urban setting has been granted new privileges and opportunities including planning permission for infrastructural expansion, state investment and business tax incentives (Gasper, 1988).

9   Noting that this is before the split into two Districts in 1992.

Primary research data were drawn from 25 households in five selected villages in Nembudziya Ward One.[10] An 'interview-administered questionnaire' was the main method used to compile information from households.[11] Questions followed a logical sequence, building up a range of information from each household and, therefore, gaining the confidence of interviewees. The questionnaire began with household descriptions, then field observations, agricultural practice, resources, and ended with a broad discussion on food security. Approximately 10 visits (one hour each) were made to each household over three separate field trips to Zimbabwe.

After the initial visits to each selected household, research began in the fields with the collection of two soil samples from each household property. In total, 50 soil samples were analysed by the Soil Science Department in the Faculty of Agriculture at the University of Zimbabwe. Levels of the main indicators of soil fertility were measured, including calcium, magnesium, sodium, nitrogen, phosphorus, potassium, organic carbon and pH. The household participants chose two contrasting sites for collecting the soil samples. The 'a' samples came from areas of the field considered as having relatively 'good' soil fertility. The 'b' samples came from areas with lower fertility. The Shona phrase '*ivhu aina chikafu*' (the soil that has no food) was used to discuss the concerns that households had with declining soil fertility (James, 2002a).

Results showed that 18 of the 25 surveyed households in Nembudziya in late 1998 to 1999 grew cotton annually (Table 10.1).

Discussions with householders showed a mixture of reasons for their not growing cotton during the 1998 to 1999 season but, in general, the crop was becoming less popular and, in some cases, agriculturally impossible to grow successfully.

Total field acreage ranged from four to 25, with a median of 10 acres. Space devoted to cotton, among those that grew it, ranged from 20 per cent to 60 per cent. Reasons for the differences within and between villages varied, including preferring other crops, expense of the seed and concern about soil fertility. Yield rates gave the clearest indication of the contrasts in productivity. The average among those households choosing to grow cotton that season was 216 kg per acre. Official statistics point to yields among communal farmers of 700 kg per ha (283 kg per acre) or above, then the average for the remainder is closer to 100 kg per acre. In Table 10.1 the data for the number of weedings and sprayings gives an indication of the level of attention required to successfully achieve sellable cotton. For example, household 3M in Baro planted five acres (40 per cent) with cotton. They weeded four times during the season and applied pesticides on five different occasions. After all this effort, their yield was 140 kg per acre.

---

10 For full and critical explanation of the methodology see James (2002a).

11 The structure and detail of the questionnaire is adapted from Elliott (1989: Appendix 3). Moore and Vaughan (1994) provided an influence to follow a mixture of methods including a flexible questionnaire approach: 'We collected data using participant observation, oral history, survey, and semi-structured interview methods' (p. xv).

Table 10.1   **Cotton cropping among households in five villages during the 1997 to 1998 season**

Village	House-hold[1]	Total field acreage	Acres of cotton (per cent of total)	Bales of cotton (yield kg/acre)	Number of weedings	Number of chemical sprayings
Gonde	1P	16	4 (25)	2 (100)	8	4
	2M	5	2 (40)	2 (200)	8	3
	3P	8	0 (0)	0 (-)	0	0
	4W	5	0 (0)	0 (-)	0	0
	5W	20	6 (30)	4 (133)	8	3
			Total	> 4		
Baro	1P	11	7 (60)	2 (57)	5	3
	2W	10	2 (20)	1.5 (150)	5	2
	3M	12	5 (40)	3.5 (140)	4	5
	4P	8	0 (0)	0 (-)	0	0
	5W	6	0 (0)	0 (-)	0	0
			Total	< 6		
Gazimbi	1M	5	3 (65)	6 (400)	4	4
	2P	15	6 (40)	4 (133)	3	4
	3W	7	3 (40)	2.5 (167)	4	5
	4P	13	3 (20)	6 (400)	3	4
	5W	25	10 (40)	5 (100)	4	3
			Total	23.5		
Chenga	1W	10	5 (50)	21 (840)	5	4
	2W	11	7 (60)	21 (600)	4	5
	3M	20	12 (60)	9 (150)	4	4
	4P	7	3.5 (50)	2.5 (143)	3	3
	5P	-	-	-	-	-
			Total	53.5		
Chigova	1P	15	7.5 (50)	1 (27)	3	3
	2W	6.5	0 (0)	0 (-)	0	0
	3M	4	1 (20)	0 (-)	2	4
	4P	12	2.5 (20)	2 (80)	4	3
	5W	10	3 (30)	1 (67)	5	3
			Total	4		

Source: Household survey (James, 2002a: 268)

Significant differences occurred in the yields achieved among the households *within* the villages and notably *between* villages. Interviews with the householders show that the yields had fallen significantly since the 1970s and 1980s, when cotton was at its peak in the area. Several householders noted that the soils in their fields were too 'sandy' (infertile) to grow cotton. Mariga (1994) and Agritex officers in Nembudziya argue that low yields are a direct result of poor husbandry, including deficient tillage skills, a lack of consistent pest control and insufficient fertilizer application. They suggest that with improved management in these areas it is estimated that four bales of cotton can be harvested from one hectare (800 kg per acre). This is only achieved by one household in the sample surveyed. Nevertheless, Mariga (1994) finds that the yields in communal areas fell from six bales per hectare in the 1980s to less than three and a half (0.7 tonnes per ha. = 283 kg per acre) during the 1990s. The official position is therefore extremely ambitious and Mariga's (1994) evidence shows that, while yields fell during the 1980s, the total national production increased. This suggests an increase in the number of cotton farmers.

Research observation and results from household interviews showed that extension service officers and agricultural business operators functioned over increasingly expanded areas and thus neglected areas that began farming cotton in the 1970s (James, 2002a). Part of this is to work with new areas and new farmers, but it also reflects the relative decline in economic relevance of the farmers getting smaller yields from their fields (see discussion below).

Table 10.1 shows that only five households out of 25 were at ease with growing cotton. Of six that did not grow cotton, three reasons were given. One household confessed to being time-constrained because of engagement in off-farm income earning activities; three had fields with severely infertile soil and two argued that they were too poor to afford cotton seed and inputs, including fertilizer and pesticides. Therefore, the majority of households in Nembudziya grew cotton because they were duty-bound, but also because, apart from maize, there was not an obvious alternative cash-crop (James, 2002a).[12]

Reasons for households not achieving the expected or optimal yield rates were complex. For example, Nyambara (1999: 9) finds that 'high levels of marketed cotton were achieved by a minority of producers'. Table 10.1 shows how the farmers in one village (Chenga) produced significantly more cotton than farmers in the other four villages. Skill and luck varied with sufficient soil fertility and other husbandry skills, including weeding, spraying, fertilizer application and picking. However, the most cited reason for the decline in yields was a fall in soil fertility during the 1990s.

Agro-ecological analysis of Nembudziya

Climatically, and using Zimbabwean categorisations, Nembudziya sits on a zone between Natural Region III and IV (Vincent & Thomas, 1960). The official rainfall for Nembudziya is 700 mm mean annual rainfall (MAR), which fits in the middle of Scholes's (1997) classification of savanna woodland. Acacia dry woodland (<400 mm MAR) contrasts with broad-leafed Miombo woodland (≥ 900 mm MAR). When the natural vegetation with trees is transformed into an agrarian landscape, this involves a degree of deforestation and, arguably, other forms of land degradation

---

12 Wider analysis for these external pressures to farm cotton can be found in Worby (1998a) and Nyambara (1999).

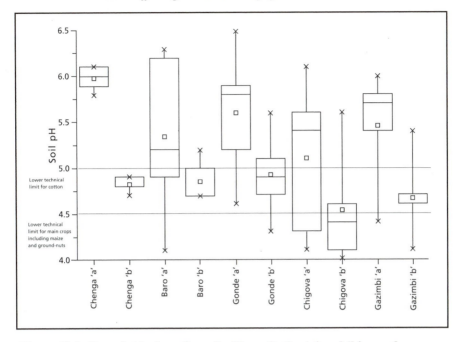

Figure 10.2 Box plot to describe soil pH results for 'a' and 'b' samples among five villages in Nembudziya (Source: Field research and household survey James, 2002a)

(Whitlow, 1988; see also Beinart, 1996). While the 'natural vegetation' is Miombo woodland (James, 2002a), it has been all but removed to make way for cultivation (Whitlow, 1988). The high demand for mopane wood (*Colophospermum mopane*[13]) has seen this tree replaced by *Combretum.*[14] Miombo woodland exists in some 'sacred woodlands' (Clarke, 1994) and the presence of baobab (*Adansonia digitata*), mungongo nut (*Schinziophyton (Ricinodendron) rautanenii*) and thorny acacia suggest the presence of more arid conditions.

The landscape in Nembudziya is relatively flat and, although the soils contrast sharply over small distances, the general description is of soft silty soils and sodic mopane clays (see Table 10.2). Vincent & Thomas (1960) conclude that the agricultural potential of soils in Sebungwe (Gokwe) is very limited. Analysis of the soils in fields belonging to the surveyed households in Nembudziya showed significant differences *within* the fields, as well as *between* them. Full soil fertility analysis of all samples showed that 'a' samples were significantly more fertile

---

13 Host for 'mopane worm' (*Gonimbrasia belina*); valuable browse and fodder for cattle; very strong and durable building wood; excellent fuel (James, 2002a: Appendix 7.1).

14 *Combretum celastroides* and *C. elaeagnoides*. Relatively impenetrable thick wooded areas; often noted as reinvading disturbed areas (James, 2002a: Appendix 7.1).

using soil acidity (pH) indicators than 'b' samples. Soil acidity at pH 5 is the lower technical limit for cotton and pH 4.5 for maize. Figure 10.2 shows that many 'a' and 'b' samples are below pH 5, while one village recorded severe infertility with several samples below pH 4.5. The household survey revealed that this was because of continuous cotton and maize cropping, in some cases since the early 1970s.

Other evidence, including the general decline in cotton production in Nembudziya during the 1990s, pointed to deterioration in local soil fertility. Since the soils were different *within* the fields (see also Scoones, 1998), it is difficult to distinguish the impacts of cultivation and cropping strategies from those occurring through natural erosion and leaching. For the households surveyed, the problems of productivity of cotton were relatively new (emerging in the 1990s), suggesting that a number of factors combined to cause a yield decline. These included greater input prices (for example, fertilizer and pesticides), severe droughts in the 1990s, questionable seed quality, soil erosion and continuous cotton cultivation over three decades.

Soil fertility decline seems to be the main factor behind the decline in cotton productivity, although other agrarian factors were important, including less extension attention and input quality. Prices also worsened the livelihood situation for households. As discussed in earlier sections, there is no direct policy in place to sustain soil fertility, which is so important to households. Waddington *et al.* (1998) compiled some research in Zimbabwe on soil fertility. However, these projects had not reached Nembudziya and the North-West.

Does the drive to grow cotton leave exhausted soils in its wake as it spreads to newly accessible areas (see, for example, Hasler, 1996)? Reij *et al.* (1996) conclude that there is not an easy relationship between agrarian transformation and sustainable soil fertility. Middleton (1997: 78) asks: 'What enables, encourages or compels people to mismanage their physical environment?' It seems important, therefore, to combine research into anthropogenic and biophysical factors acting as 'proximate determinants of fertility' (McGregor, 1994: 319). So, how might cotton as a crop be primarily responsible for declining soil fertility in Nembudziya? This question will now be examined.

Diverse dynamics in cotton cash cropping in Nembudziya

As discussed in earlier sections, the cotton industry is oriented primarily for export income (Rau, 1991). Within the householders' fields, cotton competes for land space as well as soil nutrients (Nyawata, 1988; James, 2002a). Cotton also takes up a high proportion of labour for activities, including careful tillage, continuous weeding and the frequent spraying of pesticides. The continuous weeding throughout the rains undoubtedly exposes the soil, thus exacerbating its erodibility. Cotton also takes a great deal of time to hand-pick (Worby, 1992). Although Zimbabwe's cotton fits into a niche market in Europe, this hand-picked quality comes at a cost with up to 10 weeks of intense and continuous picking by householders and paid labourers. On occasions, school children have been drafted in to assist with this work (Worby, 1992).

The household survey confirmed that agriculture is at the heart of Nembudziya's economy (GNRDC, 2000; James, 2002a). The two main crops were cotton and maize and most of the residents were people that had settled since the 1960s. The agricultural system in operation, therefore, was neither subsistence nor particularly indigenous or traditional. This is more in line with the argument by Scoones and Wolmer (2002) that there are different 'pathways' of change based on particular circumstances in different rural areas. The drive and incentive for all households to grow cotton occurs at all levels, from the state agricultural institutions to local politicians, and via a discourse that this is what you do with your field. While the drive to grow cotton remains, the combination of economic difficulties and new policy structures (including participatory approaches) have afforded possibilities for other options in the North-West. Some wealthy farmers have chosen to grow tomatoes (Nyambara, 1999), while many poorer households have recently given up growing cotton (see Table 10.1). That evidence points to important changes, including the lessening expectation for households to grow cotton and also that it has become rejected as *the* crop to provide livelihood security. The thrust of this chapter has been to examine whether the pressure and requirement to grow cotton has been helpful in achieving either environmental sustainability or household food security.

This section explains how householders increasingly grapple with a crop that takes so much of their labour and evidently exploits their given environment in various ways. Despite the North-West being relatively remote and socio-economically marginal (James, 2002a), most known indigenous and traditional farming methods have been vilified, forgotten or banned by state institutions and the general discourse of modernity. This modernity, presented as modernization and development, started with the in-migrants and then cotton during the 1960s, and has continued through the 'second agricultural revolution' in the 1980s and with more recent privatization of the cotton industry in the 1990s (see earlier sections). The only counter-discourse has emerged out of the 'participatory' movement, seeking to find alternatives to cotton and maize dominance. Early farming in Sebungwe was based on riverine cultivation and commercial tobacco cropping. Farming along the riverine areas required no fallow period, no deliberate rotation and it was not necessary to apply manure. It was possible to grow two crops annually, one coinciding with the rains and one winter crop, including green leaf vegetables (Kosmin, 1977; Worby, 1992).

The cotton companies (for example, Cottco and Cargill), Zimbabwe Farmers' Union (ZFU), Agritex and the Natural Resources Board (NRB) all provide ongoing technical help for cotton farmers. These institutions seek to increase overall production as well as yield levels. The predominant advice given by Agritex was to clear the land: to cut down all the trees on the field area, maintain continuous weeding, stick to mono-crop (for example, cotton or maize) and apply chemical fertilizers. This technical advice is however being questioned more and more (Murwira *et al.*, 2000). The householders in Nembudziya appeared to avoid or had little to do with Agritex (see above). This adds to the argument that households already involved in cotton cropping over two or three decades were neglected by policies that might have encouraged more sustainable practice in terms of soil fertility maintenance.

Analysis of soil fertility management in Nembudziya

While there is evidence of simultaneous rejection of cotton and the easing off of pressures to grow it, the detailed evidence of practice within the fields suggests a wide range of efforts to protect and sustain soil fertility. This points to evidence of a mixture of methods, the awareness of soil fertility decline and a willingness to experiment. Fallowing (resting the soil) is constrained and experimentation is relatively limited. The evidence suggests, however, that some households hold on to older and more traditional cropping strategies. Table 10.2 shows in some detail the different methods that households applied to look after their soils.

Only three households of the 25 surveyed made no particular effort to actively sustain their soils (James, 2002a). Less than a third of the households used chemical fertilizers. As with research in other parts of Zimbabwe (Scoones, *et al.* 1996), there are several practical concerns with inorganic fertilizers. The cost of fertilizer has risen to levels beyond what most households can afford. It is also argued that chemical fertilizers do little to enhance the soil structure and organic content (Scoones *et al.*, 1996). Interestingly, only four households claimed to apply fertilizer each year according to extension advice from Agritex.

Eighty per cent of the surveyed households applied manure. Ash, compost, and leaf litter (*murakwani*) application is varied among a small number of households.

Table 10.2 Fertility management on 25 fields in Nembudziya, 1998

Soil texture[2]	Fertilisation method	Fallow per cent and reasons	Rotation and intercropping	Observed soil erosion or degradation[3]	New crops and/or different methods[4]
Gonde (Nembudziya)					
Medium sandy loam	Some manure from relative's kraal	25 per cent: shortage of labour and erosion	Cotton–maize; each crop has a patch	Rill erosion; declining fertility	Sorghum (Rukweza; mapfunde); millet (mhunga)
Fine sand; patchy (gawa[5])	None	5 per cent: close to gawa	Cotton–maize; pumpkin in maize	No erosion; patchy fertility	Occasionally mhunga
Clay loam (gawa)	Good natural fertility	23 per cent: reason not given	Cotton–maize; intercropping with beans	A little surface erosion	A few lines of legumes; another garden close to homestead
Sandy loam (gawa)	Fertilizer every two years; manure (mupfudzi); green manure (murakwani); ashes (dota); spread anthill (churu)	No fallow: use of all space including gawa for sweet-potatoes and rice	Cotton–maize rotation	Two rills noted; fertility constant	Experiment with runinga (Sesamum indicum)

continued

Baro (Maselukwe)

Medium loam	Fertilizer with good rains; manure (mupfudzi); green manure (murakwani); ashes (dota); spread anthill (churu)	20 per cent: some years for rest or due to soil exhaustion	Cotton-sunflower-maize; maize-groundnuts rotation; intercropping: watermelon, pumpkin, cucumbers, ipwa, beans	One bad rill; declining fertility	
Fine sandy loam (gawa)	'Naturally fertile'	20 per cent: close to gawa, also when short of cash for seed	Cotton-maize; intercropping: roundnuts (nyimo), groundnuts (nzungu), pumpkin	Some rills; fertility patchy but consistent	mhunga
Medium fine sand (gawa)	Ashes; green manure	2 per cent: gombo (edge) area	Cotton-maize-nyimo and nzungu; intercropping: magaka, mubooro, ipwa, mavisi, nyemba	Some rills; fertility declining	Sunflower; mhunga
Fine sandy loam	Fertilizer occasionally; mupfudzi; murakwani	20 per cent: in patches and close to edges	No rotation; inter-crop maize with nyimo	No erosion evident and fertility deemed to be consistent	Sunflower

continued

Fine sandy loam	Manuring planned; some fertilizer; anthill spreading	No fallow: use of two fields, 'very busy'	Cotton-maize	No erosion; fertility declining	Access to garden
Sandy; patchy	Manuring carried out before ploughing	2 per cent: small field	Cotton-maize or rukweza; inter-crop pumpkins, water melon (mavise), melons, beans	Some rill erosion on one corner; fertility declining	Aims to graze cattle, which leave manure; tried fertilizer (uncertain results)
Sandy loam	Manure every three years; anthill	2 per cent: farthest corner	Cotton-maize	No erosion; patchy fertility	Trying 'Pannar' maize; tried R501, R201 and sunflower
Sandy loam	Winter plough; manure; green manure; anthill spreading	1 per cent: (although not included in original assessment a new area adjacent to field was being cleared in 1999)	Cotton-maize and groundnuts-sunflower; intercropping pumpkin in maize	Small rills appearing; fertility declining and patchy in one area	Plan to put manure along lines of crops
Clay and sandy areas	Manure annually	2 per cent: edges	Cotton-maize; groundnuts-rukweza or mapfunde	No erosion; some evidence of smaller crops	Crops of beans to support the soil; different maize

Clay loam	Fertilizer on small patch 1998; manure (mupfudzi); green manure (murakwani); spread anthill (churu)	5 per cent: edges and infertile areas	Move the patch of groundnuts each year	Minimal or no surface erosion; fertility consistent	Paprika for two seasons; chillies; rice (1996-1997); aims to rotate more
Loamy with patches of sand	Fertilizer; manure (mupfudzi); green manure (murakwani); spread anthill (churu)	2 per cent: area close to gawa	Cotton-maize-groundnuts; inter-crop one line of ipwa (for weeders to eat)	Sandy areas declining in fertility; grass strips to prevent erosion	Sunflower (nine bags); red and pink beans

continued

Clay and sandy areas	Manure sometimes	2 per cent; gawa and sandy area	Cotton-maize-rukweza; intercropping magaka, pumpkin, ipwa	No erosion; patchy fertility	Aim to fallow sandy area
Sandy loam	na	na	na		na
Chigova (Sando)					
Fine sandy loam	Manure sometimes	No fallow	Cotton-maize-groundnuts; inter-crop ipwa, muboora, mbambaira	No erosion; fertility patchy	Dry-planting with cotton
Fine sand	Fertilizer; compost; manure; ashes	2 per cent: minimal	Maize-sorghum-sunflowers; inter-crop pumpkin	No erosion; 'soil is becoming exhausted'	Have previously taken soil to laboratory to check what is needed
Sandy loam	Fertilizer; anthill; manure	3 per cent: not recognized	Maize-cotton-groundnuts or roundnuts (bambarra)	No erosion	Beans; R201 (in drought years); 'Pannar' maize
Sandy	Mulching and ploughing in weeds	18 per cent: left for two years	Cotton-maize; groundnuts, roundnuts and ipwa in maize	No erosion; fertility the same	Mapfunde; sunflower
Fine light sand	Murakwani; manure (every five years)	20 per cent: awaiting seed	Maize-cotton-groundnuts and beans; inter-crop pumpkin, magaka, makavu	Some sheet erosion; patchy fertility	Sunflower; mhunga (all eaten by birds)

Source: Field research and household survey (James, 2002a)

1   P = 'poor'; M = 'medium' and W = 'wealthy'
2   Other variations are described in chapter on soils.
3   This refers to erosion observed on the surface of the field or evidence provided by the farmer/householder.
4   Referred to in the questionnaire as 'experimentation'.

The practise of leaf litter application has been brought in from southern regions of Zimbabwe (Wilson, 1990). Some households spread termitaria to enhance the nutrients in the top-soil (such as calcium, magnesium, nitrogen and potassium) and the cation exchange capacity (CEC)[15] in the clays (Nyamaphene, 1986). Fallow (*gura*) is controversial and contradictory in Nembudziya. Some fields were left to 'rest' because of severe infertility. Scoones *et al.* (1996: 122 emphasis in original) point out that 'fallowing is rarely *intentionally* used as a fertility management method'. In Nembudziya 'fallow' was a consequence of soils becoming exhausted and other social reasons including labour and time constraints and the lack of seed. It is therefore rarely used explicitly as a method for enhancing the soil fertility. Rotation in Nembudziya appeared to be primarily cotton-maize-cotton. This is despite the fact that both crops are heavy consumers of the important soil nutrients.[16] Isaacman (1996) sees the speed of nutrient depletion under cotton as contributing to high rates of erosion (see also Stocking, 1972). Such rotation between the two crops consequently has questionable advantages beyond the avoidance of diseases specific to each crop spreading from one year to the next.

Intercropping was observed among 16 households, but this varied from lines of roundnuts (*Voandzeia (Vigna) subterranea*) and groundnuts (*Arachis hypogaea*), both legumes and therefore nitrogen fixers[17], to the use of cucurbits to keep moisture in the soil, suppress weeds and to provide extra food. Experimentation (*kuedza*) featured in all households ranging from trials with sunflower and sesame to patches of small grain cereals like sorghum and millet. Most experimentation was small-scale and often in the gardens or in fields closer to the homestead.

Another area of interest in management of fields includes leaving trees within fields. This has important cultural as well as agro-ecological importance (Wilson, 1989). However, most people followed advice from Agritex to remove all trees (a campaign called *kugochamopane* – to burn all the mopane trees). The aim was threefold: to control tsetse fly and wildlife, to clear land for cultivation and, since the 1970s, to maximize sunlight for cotton, as well as minimizing the harbouring of pests.[18] All of these factors coincided with a relative decrease in knowledge of, and cultural engagement with, trees. The removal of trees bears direct relation to an increase in run-off erosion during the rains. Despite this declining attachment, however, trees left in fields ranged from 0.3 to 4.45 per hectare (compared to Wilson's 1989 findings in Chivi of two to four trees per hectare) (James, 2002a).

---

15 The varying levels of clay and organic matter in soil correlate to a degree with its ability to exchange and supply ions of calcium, magnesium, sodium and potassium (Thomas & Goudie, 2000).

16 Maize consumes 23.9 N and 4.3 P kg/ha^{-1}yr (Kellman & Tackerbury, 1997).

17 Nitrogen, like phosphorus and potassium, is extremely important for plant growth. Anything that enhances its availability within the soil is advantageous.

18 *Azanza garckeana* is a fruit tree known to harbour the pink boll-worm.

Concluding comments: questioning national and local action on sustainable development in the case of cotton

Households in Nembudziya began to adjust to changing conditions in the 1990s by becoming more discerning in their decisions about whether or not to grow cotton. In households surveyed there was a realization that cotton was not fulfilling livelihood needs because of falling yields and low buying prices, set against steeply rising input prices. The decline in yields occurred concurrently with soil fertility decline and real increases in the costs of inputs. The overall trend in the cotton industry is to continue exploiting new soils further afield, in areas not previously cultivated. However, soil fertility is becoming a scarce 'national treasure' in Zimbabwe, and one worth preserving (Waddington *et al.,* 1998). Such views on soil fertility have influenced some policy, but so far there is little or no evidence of any focused effort to retain and re-establish soil fertility in areas like Nembudziya. The positive programmes exemplified in Murwira *et al.* (2000) and Keeley & Scoones (2003) need also to feature in the cotton growing areas, especially as these are home to many of the rural Zimbabweans. Agritex officials have gained insight to new participatory approaches and therefore their adherence to exact technocratic methods has loosened (Agritex, 1998). The combination of 'political pressure and budgetary constraints; delivery problems across the extension service ... and the actions of a few key 'policy entrepreneurs' ... created some 'room for manoeuvre' in one of the largest government departments in the country' (Keeley & Scoones, 2003: 159).

This chapter has shown that cotton became the predominant industry in the North-West of Zimbabwe for many reasons: economic, agro-ecological and political. During the 1960s, it was introduced because the region had comparative advantages including sunshine, drought tolerance in cotton and available labour. For international reasons the Rhodesian (pre-Zimbabwean) regime was forced to try to be self-sufficient and cotton was an important product for the textile industry. Cotton thus fitted in with the projects of fulfilling the Land Husbandry Act, 'community development' in newly resettled areas, national production and, to some extent, quelling some rebellion among Africans in the then described Tribal Trust Lands. Cotton production gained momentum in the 1970s and by the 1980s became the second export crop for Zimbabwe. The hand-picked lint attracts a premium on the export markets and that, in addition to the limited practical alternatives and relatively cheap labour, sustained the industry.

As part of Zimbabwe's 'second agricultural revolution' (in the 1980s) cotton became the focus of state and private institutions. The aim was for greater total production, as well as productivity in yield terms. This momentum and dynamic profoundly transformed the agrarian setting of the North-West. Only a few farmers have been successful over the decades. The majority increasingly struggle to make a living from cotton.

This research has shown the neglect in efforts to sustain the livelihood prospects for households within cotton growing areas. Equally important has been the comprehensive neglect in attention to the depletion in soil fertility after several years of cotton and maize cultivation. The conservation and thus sustainable development focus has instead been in other areas and in other sectors including wildlife, forests and mechanical soil conservation.

References

Agritex (1998) *Learning Together through Participatory Extension. A Guide to an Approach Developed in Zimbabwe*. Department of Agricultural, Technical and Extension Services, Harare.

Alexander, J. & McGregor, J. (2000) Wildlife and politics: CAMPFIRE in Zimbabwe. *Development and Change*, 31, 605-627.

Beinart, W. (1984) Soil erosion, Conservation and ideas about development: a southern African exploration, 1900–1960. *Journal of Southern African Studies*, 11, 52-83.

Beinart, W. (1996) Soil erosion, animals and pasture over the longer term. Environmental destruction in Southern Africa. In Leach, M. & Mearns, R. (eds) *The Lie of the Land. Challenging Received Wisdom on the African Environment*. James Currey, London, pp. 54-72.

Bowyer-Bower, T.A.S. (1996) Criticisms of environmental policy for land management in Zimbabwe. *Global Ecology and Biogeography Letters*, 5, 7-17.

Cameron, G.S. (1937) Some aspects of the promotion of cotton growing in Southern Rhodesia. *Empire Cotton Growing Review*, 14, 24-30.

Campbell, B., Frost, P., Kirchman, H. & Swift, M. (1998) Nitrogen cycling and management of soil fertility in small scale farming systems in Northwestern Zimbabwe. *Journal of Sustainable Agriculture*, 11, 19-39.

Castro, A.P. (1998) Sustainable agriculture or sustained error? The case of cotton in Kirinyanga, Kenya. *World Development*, 26, 1719-1731.

Chenje, M. & Johnson, P. (eds) (1994) *State of the Environment in Southern Africa*. Report by the Southern African Research and Documentation Centre in collaboration with IUCN (The World Conservation Union) and Southern African Development Community (SADC), Harare.

Child, G.F.T. & Riney, T. (1987) Tsetse control hunting in Zimbabwe, 1919-1958. *Zambezia*, XIV, 11-71.

Chimhowu, A.O. (2003) *Land Resettlement and Livelihoods in Rural Zimbabwe: A Comparative Study of State Sponsored and Spontaneously Resettled Households in Hurungwe District*. Unpublished PhD thesis, Institute for Development Policy and Management, University of Manchester.

Chinodya, S. (1982) *Dew in the morning*. Mambo Press, Gwelo.

Chorley, J.K. (1945) The Sebungwe District. *Proceedings of the Rhodesia Scientific Association*, 40, 5-16 (NAZ S/RH352 V.40).

Clarke, J. (1994) *Building on Indigenous Natural Resources Management: Forestry Practices in Zimbabwe's Communal Lands*. Forestry Commission, Harare.

Collett, C.W. (1963-1965) Delineation of communities. *Part two of the Report on Gokwe Tribal Trust Lands: Gokwe District*. (NAZ s2929/7/3).

Drinkwater, M. (1989) Technical development and peasant impoverishment: land use policy in Zimbabwe's Midlands Province. *Journal of Southern African Studies*, 15, 287-305.

Elliott, J.A. (1989) *Soil Erosion and Conservation in Zimbabwe: Political Economy and the Environment.* Unpublished PhD thesis, Loughborough University, UK.

FAO (1985) *The role of minor crops in nutrition and food security.* Food and Agricultural Organisation Committee on Agriculture, Session 8, Rome.

Forsyth, T. (2003) *Critical political ecology. The politics of environmental science.* Routledge, London.

Gasper, D. (1988) Rural Growth Points and rural industries in Zimbabwe: Ideologies and policies. *Development and Change*, 19, 425-466.

Gibbon, P. (1999) Free competition without sustainable development? Tanzania cotton sector liberalization, 1994/95 to 1997/98. *Journal of Development Studies*, 36, 128-150.

GNRDC (Gokwe North Rural District Council) (2000) *District Strategic Plan, 2000-2004.* Draft GNRDC, Midlands Province.

Hagmann, J. & Murwira, K. (1996) Indigenous SWC in Southern Zimbabwe: a study of techniques, historical changes and recent developments under participatory research and extension. In Reij, C., Scoones, I. & Toulmin, C. (eds) *Sustaining the Soil. Indigenous soil and Water Conservation in Africa.* Earthscan Publications Limited, London, pp. 97-106.

Hasler, R. (1996) *Agriculture, Foraging and Wildlife Resource Use in Africa. Cultural and Political Dynamics in the Zambezi Valley.* Keegan Paul International, London.

Gledhill, J.E. (1979) The Cotton Research Institute, Gatooma. *Rhodesia Agricultural Journal*, 76, 103-118.

Isaacman, A. (1996) *Cotton is the Mother of Poverty. Peasants, Work, and Rural Struggle in Colonial Mozambique, 1938-1961.* James Currey and Heinemann, London and Portsmouth.

Isaacman, A. & Roberts, R. (eds) (1995) *Cotton, Colonialism, and Social History in sub-Saharan Africa.* James Currey and Heinemann, London and Portsmouth.

James, N. (2002a) *A Geographical study of Nembudziya, Gokwe North, Zimbabwe. The Relationship between Agrarian Environmental Change and Household Food Security in a Cotton Growing Area.* Unpublished PhD thesis, Edge Hill College, Lancaster University.

James, N. (2002b) *Behind food security: Good meals, new delicacies, and crying for the old foods. Learning from food culture in Nembudziya, Gokwe North, Zimbabwe.* Unpublished paper originally presented to 'Livelihoods' panel at African Studies Association (ASAUK) Conference 'What can we learn from Africa?' The Manor House, University of Birmingham, 9-11 September.

Jayne, T., Chisvo, M. & Rukuni, M. (1994) Zimbabwe's food insecurity paradox: Hunger amid abundance. In Rukuni, M. & Eicher, C. (eds) (1994) *Zimbabwe's Agricultural Revolution.* University of Zimbabwe Publications, Harare, pp. 289-303.

Keeley, J. & Scoones, I. (2003) *Understanding Environmental Policy Processes: Cases from Africa*. IDS, Sussex University.

Kellman, M. & Tackaberry, R. (1997) *Tropical Environments. The Functioning and Management of Tropical Ecosystems*. Routledge, London.

Kosmin, B. (1977) The Inyoka Tobacco Industry of the Shangwe People: The Displacement of a Pre-Colonial Economy in Southern Rhodesia, 1898 – 1938. In Palmer, R. & Parsons, N. (eds) *The Roots of Rural Poverty in Central and Southern Africa*. HEB, London, pp.268-288.

Larsen, M.N. (2002) Is oligopoly a condition of successful privatization? The case of cotton in Zimbabwe. *Journal of Agrarian Change*, 2, 185-205.

Mariga, I.K. (1994) Cotton research and development. In Rukuni, M. & Eicher, C. (eds) *Zimbabwe's Agricultural Revolution*. University of Zimbabwe Publications, Harare, pp. 219-233.

McCann, J.C. (1999) *Green Land, Brown Land, Black Land. An Environmental History of Africa, 1800-1990*. James Currey, Oxford.

McGregor, J. (1994) Review article. Environmental knowledge under scrutiny. *Journal of Southern African Studies*, 20, 317-324.

Middleton, N. (1997) Classics in human geography revisited: Blaikie, P.M. (1985) *The political economy of soil erosion in developing countries*. Longman, London. *Progress in Human Geography*, 21, 77-79.

Moore, H.L. & Vaughan, M. (1994) *Cutting Down Trees: Gender, Nutrition and Agricultural Change in the Northern Province of Zambia*. James Currey, London.

Moorehead, S. & Wolmer, W. (2001) Food security and the environment. In Devereaux, S. & Maxwell, S. (eds) *Food security in sub-Saharan Africa*. ITDG, London, pp. 93-116.

Moyo, S., Robinson, P., Katerere, Y., Stevenson, S. & Gumbo, D. (1991) *Zimbabwe's Environmental Dilemma. Balancing Resource Inequities*. ZERO, Harare.

Moyo, S., O'Keefe, P. & Sill, M. (1993) *The Southern African Environment. Profiles of the SADC Countries*. Earthscan Publications Limited, London.

Munro, W.A. (1998) *The Moral Economy of the State. Conservation, Community Development and State Making in Zimbabwe*. Ohio University, Centre for International Studies.

Munro, W.A. (2003) Ecological 'crisis' and resource management policy in Zimbabwe's communal lands. In Bassett, T.J. & Crumney, D.E. (eds) *African Savannas. Global Narratives and Local Knowledge of Environmental Change*. James Currey, Oxford, pp. 178-204.

Murwira, K., Wedgwood, H., Watson, C. & Win, E.J. with Tawney, C. (2000) *Beating Hunger. The Chivi Experience. A Community-Based Approach to Food Security in Zimbabwe*. Intermediate Technology Publications, London.

Nyamapfene, K.W. (1986) The use of termite mounds in Zimbabwe peasant agriculture. *Tropical Agriculture*, 63, 191-192.

Nyambara, P.S. (1999) *A history of Land Acquisition in Gokwe, Northwestern Zimbabwe, 1945-1997*. Unpublished PhD thesis, Northwestern University, Evanston, Illinois.

Nyambara, P.S. (2001) The politics of land acquisition and struggles over land in the 'communal' areas of Zimbabwe: the Gokwe region in the 1980s and 1990s. *Africa*, 71, 253-285.

Nyawata, O.I. (1988) Macroeconomic management, adjustment and stabilisation. In Stoneman, C. (ed.) *Zimbabwe's Prospects: Issues of Race, Class, State and Capital in Southern Africa*. Macmillan, London, pp. 90-117.

Palmer, R. (1977) *Land and Racial Domination in Rhodesia*. Heinemann, London.

Porter, P.W. (1995) Note on cotton and climate: A colonial conundrum. In Isaacman, A. & Roberts, R. (eds) *Cotton, Colonialism, and Social History in sub-Saharan Africa*. James Currey and Heinemann, London and Portsmouth, pp. 43-49.

Ranger, T. (1985) *Peasant Consciousness and Guerrilla War in Zimbabwe*. James Currey, Oxford.

Ranger, T. (1998) Zimbabwe and the long search for independence. In Birmingham, D. & Martin, P.M. (eds) *History of Central Africa. The Contemporary Years since 1960*. Addison Wesley Longman Limited, Harlow, pp. 202-229.

Rau, B. (1991) *From Feast to Famine: Official Cures and Grassroots Remedies to Africa's Food Crisis*. Zed Press, London.

Reid, M. (1971) An agricultural programme at Gokwe. *Rhodesia Agricultural Journal*, 68, 2-8.

Reij, C., Scoones, I. & Toulmin, C. (1996) *Sustaining the Soil. Indigenous Soil and Water Conservation in Africa*. Earthscan Publications Limited, London.

Rukuni, M. (1994a) The prime movers of Zimbabwe's agricultural revolution. In Rukuni, M. & Eicher, C. (eds) *Zimbabwe's Agricultural Revolution*. University of Zimbabwe Publications, pp. 1-14.

Rukuni, M. (1994b) The evolution of agricultural policy: 1890-1990. In Rukuni, M. & Eicher, C. (eds) *Zimbabwe's Agricultural Revolution*. University of Zimbabwe Publications, pp. 15-39.

Rukuni, M. & Eicher, C. (eds) (1994) *Zimbabwe's Agricultural Revolution*. University of Zimbabwe Publications.

Ruwitah, A. (1997) The mystery of cotton. *The Zimbabwean Review*, 3, 3-5.

Scholes, R.J. (1997) Savanna. In Cowling, R.M., Richardson, D.M. & Pierce, S.M. (eds) *Vegetation of Southern Africa*. Cambridge University Press, Cambridge, pp. 258-277.

Scoones, I., Chibudu, C., Chikura, S., Jeranyama, P., Machaka, D., Machanja, W., Mavadzenge, B., Mudhara, M., Mudziwo, C., Murimbarimba, F. & Zirereza, B. (1996) *Hazards and Opportunities. Farming Livelihoods in Dryland Africa. Lessons from Africa*. Zed Press, London.

Scoones, I. (1997) The dynamics of soil fertility change: historical perspectives on environmental transformation from Zimbabwe. *Geographical Journal*, 163, 161-199.

Scoones, I (1998) Investigating soil fertility in Africa: Some reflections from research in Ethiopia and Zimbabwe. In Bergstrom, L. & Kirchmann, H. (eds) *Carbon and Nutrient Dynamics in Natural and Agricultural Tropical Ecosystems*. CAB International, Oxford, pp. 245-259.

Scoones, I. & Wolmer, W. (eds) (2002) *Pathways of Change in Africa. Crops, Livestock and Livelihoods in Mali, Ethiopia and Zimbabwe.* James Currey, Oxford.

Stocking, M.A. (1972) Planting pattern and erosion on a cotton crop. *The Rhodesia Science News*, 6, 231-236.

Stocking, M. (1996) Soil erosion. Breaking new ground. In Leach, M. & Mearns, R. (eds) *The Lie of the Land. Challenging Received Wisdom on the African Environment.* James Currey, London, pp. 140-154.

Takavarasha, T. (1994) Agricultural pricing policy. In Rukuni, M. & Eicher, C. (eds) *Zimbabwe's Agricultural Revolution.* University of Zimbabwe Publications, pp. 153-174.

Taylor, H.W. (1919) Cotton culture. *Rhodesia Agricultural Journal*, 16, 197-201.

Taylor, R.D. (1982) Buffer zones: resolving conflicts between humans and wildlife interests in the Sebungwe, Zimbabwe. *Zimbabwe Agricultural Journal*, 79, 179-184.

Thomas, S.G. & Goudie, A. (eds) (2000) *The Dictionary of Physical Geography.* Blackwell Publishers, Oxford, 3rd Edition.

United Nations (2002) *Zimbabwe, Country Profile.* Johannesburg Summit in 2002.

Vincent, V. & Thomas, R.G. (1960) *An Agricultural Survey of Southern Rhodesia: Part 1 – Agroecological.* Government Printer, Salisbury.

Waddington, S.R., Murwira, H.K., Kumwenda, J.D.T., Hikwa, D. & Tagwira, F. (eds) (1998) *Soil Fertility Research for Maize-Based Farming Systems in Malawi and Zimbabwe.* Proceedings of the soil fertility Net Results and Planning Workshop held 7-11 July at Africa University, Mutare, Zimbabwe. Soil Fertility Net and CIMMYT - Zimbabwe, Harare, Zimbabwe, 312 pp.

Watkins, K. (2003) The phoney war over subsidies. *The Guardian Society*, March.

Watts, M. (1999) Commodities. In Cloke, P., Crang, P. & Goodwin, M. (eds) *Introducing Human Geographies.* Arnold, London, pp. 305-314.

Whitlow, J.R. (1988) *Land Degradation in Zimbabwe: A Geographical Study.* Department of National Resources, Harare, Zimbabwe.

Wilson, K.B. (1989) Trees and fields in southern Zimbabwe. *Journal of Southern African Studies*, 15, 1-15.

Wilson, K. (1990) *Ecological Dynamics and Human Welfare: A Case Study of Population, Health and Nutrition in Zimbabwe.* Unpublished PhD thesis, University of London.

Wolmer, W. & Scoones, I. (eds) (2003) *Livelihoods in Crisis? New Perspectives on Governance and Rural development in Southern Africa.* Institute of Development Studies Bulletin, Volume 34, Number 3.

Worby, E. (1992) *Remaking Labour, Reshaping Identity: Cotton, Commoditization and the Culture of Modernity in Northwestern Zimbabwe.* Unpublished PhD thesis, McGill University, Canada.

Worby, E. (1994) Maps, names and Ethnic Games: The Epistemology and Iconography of Colonial Power in North western Zimbabwe. *Journal of Southern African Studies*, 20, 371-392.

Worby, E. (1995) What does agrarian wage labour signify? Cotton, commoditization and social form in Gokwe, Zimbabwe. *Journal of Peasant Studies*, 23, 1-29.

Worby, E. (1998a) Inscribing the State at the 'edge of beyond': danger and development in north-western Zimbabwe. *Political and Legal Anthropology Review*, 21, 55-70.

Worby, E. (1998b) Tyranny, parody, and ethnic polarity: Ritual engagements with the state in Northwestern Zimbabwe. *Journal of Southern African Studies*, 24, 561-578.

Worby, E. (2000) 'Discipline without oppression': sequence, timing and marginality in Southern Rhodesia's post-war development regime. *Journal of African History*, 41, 101-125.

Zinyama, L. (1992) Technology adoption and post-independence transformation of the small-scale farming sector in Zimbabwe. In Drakakis-Smith, D. (ed.) *Urban and Regional Change in Southern Africa*. Routledge, London, pp. 180-202.

Zinyama, L.M. (1995) Sustainability of small-holder food production systems in Southern Africa: the case of Zimbabwe. In Binns, T. (ed.) *People and Environment in Africa*. John Wiley and Sons, Chichester, pp. 215-224.

Zinyama, L. & Whitlow, R. (1986) Changing Patterns of Population Distribution in Zimbabwe. *GeoJournal*, 13, 365-384.

Chapter 11

How Compatible is Customary Tenure with the Aims of the Swaziland Environmental Action Plan?

Erik Van Waveren

Introduction

In Swaziland, as elsewhere in the world, there has been growing concern about the sustainability of the use of the natural resource base. Swaziland is a small, but relatively densely populated, kingdom in Southern Africa bordered by South Africa and Mozambique. The economy is based on agriculture and agro-industry. The urbanization rate is low, and 80 per cent of the population live in rural areas, most of which are, at least to some extent, dependent upon agriculture for their livelihood (Government of Swaziland (GOS), 1998a). Unsustainable use of the natural resource base is thus directly and indirectly affecting a large part of the population. Subsequent to the United Nations Conference on Environment and Development (UNCED) in 1992, Swaziland set up the Swaziland Environment Authority whose brief was to promote sustainable development within the Kingdom. In 1997, the Cabinet approved the Swaziland Environment Action Plan (SEAP), according to which 'Rapid population growth (3.4% [per annum]), industrialisation, urbanization, increasing agricultural demands, and a declining economy are among factors which are fast degrading the natural resource base and this, in turn, is posing a threat to sustainable development'(GOS, 1997: 1). The Action Plan identifies improved natural resource management for increased production as one of five major programme areas for action. Land shortage and land tenure are seen as major constraints, with increasing population pressure as the underlying cause. An improved use of the land, based on agro-ecological zoning, is seen as one of the specific strategies to attain the sustainable increase in production envisaged.

Swaziland covers a wide range in elevation and associated agro-ecological conditions due to its location on the eastern slope of the Southern African Plateau. From the high-lying, cool and humid, steeply dissected Highveld in the west, it extends down to the low-lying, warm and semi-arid undulating plains of the Lowveld in the east.

Two fundamentally different types of land tenure co-exist in Swaziland: one based on customary law, and one based on western property law introduced by the colonial administration. This has resulted in a division of rural land into two major types: Swazi Nation Land (SNL) and Title Deed Land. The latter is held under freehold title, and covers about one quarter of the country. SNL is held in trust by the King for the Swazi Nation and comprises nearly all of the remainder of the rural land (Remmelzwaal & Vilakati, 1994). SNL is largely (but not entirely) under customary tenure. This customary tenured land (CTL) is under direct control of the traditional authorities and the power to allocate land rests with the Chief of the area. Swaziland differs from other Southern African states in that the customary tenure system has remained relatively unaffected by external interventions. The intended purpose of CTL is to provide a means of living for Swazi families, and all married men are entitled to acquire land by professing allegiance to a Chief (although land is also increasingly allocated to female heads of households). They receive utilitarian rights to land whilst the property rights remain with the King (Armstrong, 1986). The customary tenure system has thus been providing access to land for Swazi households, and the vast majority of these have made use of this for purposes of housing, agriculture, grazing, and the collection of raw materials.

This social security function of CTL (as a resource to provide Swazi families with a basic level of sustenance) is likely to remain important in the foreseeable future. Economic growth has remained slow following the adoption of the SEAP and job opportunities are poor, with a high and rising unemployment rate (estimated at 34 per cent in 2000) (CIA, 2004). The capacity of CTL to reconcile this social security function with the agricultural development objectives envisaged in policy documents has been questioned since Independence by Maina (1977), Funnell (1991) and others. Serious food deficits encountered by many rural households on CTL over the past years (FAO/WFP, 2004) illustrate that these households are far from food-secure and that this question is still pertinent. The most recent production shortages have been largely caused by a late onset of the rainy season in combination with below average rainfall. This, however, hides the underlying problem. Climatic drought (two or more consecutive years with rainfall well below average) is a recurrent phenomenon in Southern Africa (Gommes, 1996). The current land use is thus ill-adapted to the variability in rainfall that typifies the regional climate. The SEAP marked the customary tenure system as one of the main causes for the inefficient use of the land. It sees clearly defined, enforceable and transferable property rights as fundamental to efficient market activity and, therefore, also as a precondition for sustainable agricultural development on CTL. The Swazi (traditional) elite, however, has remained largely opposed to changes in the tenure system because a reduced level of control over land will erode its power base (Sallinger-McBride & Picard, 1986; Levin, 1997). In line with the objectives of SEAP, Government has recently adopted the Rural Resettlement Policy (GOS, 2002) to improve land use on CTL. It is important to note that this policy focuses on rationalization of land use patterns through resettlement, that is a re-arrangement of land *within* rural communities, and that its implementation is foreseen *within* the existing customary tenure arrangements. A land policy, addressing more explicitly the reform of land rights on CTL as called for by the SEAP (Mhlanga *et al.*, 1998), has not (yet) been approved.

To date, control over land resources on CTL has thus remained firmly in the hands of the traditional authorities. For reasons explained in the following section, land use and land allocation are closely linked on CTL. The compatibility of this customary system of land allocation with the call for sustainable agricultural development as set out in the SEAP remains, therefore, a critical issue and it will be examined in this chapter.[1] Specific attention will be paid to implications of this allocation system for the distribution of land for agricultural purposes. To what extent do chiefs take into account the production potential of land when allocating it for small-scale farms and to what extent does their power to do so strengthen or undermine the aims of the SEAP regarding the development of sustainable agriculture?

Land allocation and land use under customary tenure

CTL covers nearly 55 per cent of Swaziland and it is found in all agro-ecological zones (Van Waveren, 2003). By the turn of the last century, CTL supported about 80,000 homesteads, or approximately 600,000 people. This equates to a homestead density of 8.4 homesteads per square kilometre. The population on CTL has grown significantly in past decades and population density has doubled since Independence in 1968, despite the enlargement of the area under customary tenure by 15 per cent over the same period through the purchase and incorporation of former privately owned farms (Jones, 1968; GOS, 1998b).

The Swazi Administration Act of 1950 (with amendments in 1979) has provided guidance to the traditional authorities in the (re-) allocation of land. This act specifies, *inter alia*, that land allocations are intended for the establishment of homesteads and fields for crop production. Subsequent governmental development policies have been in line with this and have continued to see agriculture as the basis for development (see, for example, GOS, 2002). According to the Land Use Map of Swaziland (Remmelzwaal & Dlamini, 1994), nearly 12 per cent of CTL is covered by cropland, the remaining (non-allocated) land is used for multiple purposes, including extensive grazing, the collection of natural materials and products (grass, wood, wild foods), and hunting. The farming systems are small-scale, subsistence-oriented and often mixed, comprising both crop and livestock production. Agricultural statistics show that nearly all homesteads (92 per cent) have land allocated for cropping purposes (GOS, 1993). Most of these rely entirely on rainfed cultivation. Maize is the dominant crop on CTL, including the semi-arid parts[2], and it has accounted for over 80 per cent of the total production in the past decade. Cotton is the major

---

1   This chapter is based on PhD research carried out by the author from 1997-2003.

2   This follows the FAO classification of moisture zones based on the length of growing period. A growing period begins when the rainfall is equal to, or greater than, half the potential evapotranspiration. It ends when rainfall is less than half the potential evapotranspiration and the available soil storage water has been evapotranspired. A semi-arid moisture regime has a

rainfed cash crop. Yields are generally low, particularly under semi-arid conditions (GOS, 1993; FAO/WFP, 2004). Irrigation takes place on a communal basis on small-scale and micro schemes, as well as on individual micro schemes. The total area under these types of irrigation is not known precisely, but it is certainly less than five per cent of the total cultivated area (Van Waveren, 2003). Reference is made to Funnell (1991) for a detailed discussion on agricultural production systems on CTL and Swaziland in general.

Over time, the land allocation system has resulted in patterns of dispersed homesteads surrounded by croplands on most of the CTL. Because of the specific uses of individual land allocations (crop production, housing), the traditional authorities have thus, in effect, controlled the pattern of land use. In places, however, it has also been affected by government interventions. This has been the case on former private farmland, which was purchased by government and converted to CTL, and on areas resettled under the various rural development programmes, which the government embarked on in the 1970s and 1980s. Resettlement refers here to rearrangements of land use and settlement patterns within individual communities, and its main purpose was to rationalize land use patterns. This was done through a separation of land for cropping, residential and grazing purposes, through consolidation of fields into larger and rectangular units and, in some areas, by establishment of a minimum holding size (generally five hectares).

The Central Rural Development Board (CRDB) is mandated to regulate and administer land use on behalf of the traditional authorities. In drawing up development plans, the CRDB is advised by local committees, as well as by the Ministry of Agriculture and Co-operatives (MoAC). The CRDB is thus, at least on paper, a platform for participatory development. However, it should be emphasized that the allocation of land has remained the prerogative of the chiefs. The CRDB and MoAC have thus essentially advisory positions as far as land distribution is concerned. The CRDB is not well equipped to effectively deal with the current situation. It lacks the institutional capacity and relies heavily on the MoAC for technical advice (GOS, 2002). For administrative purposes, CTL has been subdivided into Rural Development Areas (RDAs). The extension service and other interventions have been organized accordingly. Significant revisions in this institutional set-up are foreseen in the aforementioned Rural Resettlement Policy (GOS, 2002) that has been adopted recently by Government to improve the use of land under customary tenure. In this policy, it is proposed that the MoAC will take overall responsibility for resettlement (as noted earlier, this refers mainly to the rationalisation of land use patterns *within* communities). In addition, a co-ordinating and advisory body, which represents other relevant Departments and involves traditional structures, shall be set up. At a local level, committees shall be established. These will be responsible for all aspects of community land use planning and management, subject to approval from the MoAC or the proposed resettlement coordinating body. The Chiefs will get

---

total length of growing period (LGP) from 90 to 180 days, including short dry periods (FAO, 1978).

executive responsibilities in order to implement the approved plans. The proposed institutional changes are intended to strengthen the planning and land management capacities at local levels. This is fully in line with the objectives of the SEAP. But, as discussed in the previous section, this policy does not address the more fundamental changes in user rights called for by the SEAP.

Land Allocation Efficiency

The aim of the research was to evaluate the extent to which traditional authorities have considered the availability and quality of land in the allocation of cropland. This was assessed by comparing cropland distributions, and the changes therein since Independence, with soil and climatic patterns.

Land allocation efficiency (LAE) is introduced here as a measure of the degree to which land allocation takes into account the availability and quality of land for a specific purpose. It is determined by two factors: (a) the distribution of allocations relative to physical suitability (quality) of the land in terms of soil and climatic conditions for the purpose intended (in this case crop production) and (b) the number of allocations. The former is referred to as the spatial efficiency (SE). It is measurable by comparing land use and land quality patterns using spatial correlation analysis (see Box 11.1). This can be done because land use and land allocation patterns are closely linked on CTL (see previous section). The LAE is important to farmers as it determines the quality and size of their cropland allocations.

Box 11.1   Spatial correlation analysis

Spatial correlation analysis is used to determine the level of similarity of spatial distribution patterns of two variables (in this case land use and land quality).

This type of geographic analysis requires the preparation of a raster-based map for each of the two variables. The maps should have the same resolution and cover identical areas. Raster cells in corresponding positions on the two maps thus represent the same geographic position. Each cell can thus be assigned two values (in our case a value for the type of land use and a value for the quality of the land). Hence, each individual cell can be considered as an element (case) of the total statistical population (all cells in the map). This allows commonly used bivariate correlation analysis techniques to be employed. Spatial efficiency can thus be quantitatively expressed by means of a correlation coefficient. The level of significance is difficult to interpret in this type of analysis, as it is strongly affected by the number of cases, which is usually very high on raster maps.

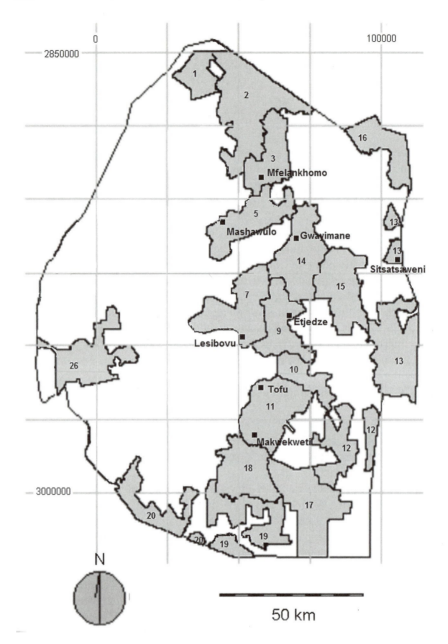

**Figure 11.1   Semi-arid Rural Development Areas and sample communities in
the Swaziland study**

The analysis focuses on semiarid CTL. It was carried out at two scales: at a local level in selected communities, in order to provide an indication of how local traditional authorities have been allocating their available land resources, and to establish the resulting changes in the quality and size of the cropland allocations; and at a regional level to assess the effects of local level land allocation practices on the regional distribution of land. In order to assess the effect of population increase on land distribution, the LAE in the late 1990s was compared with that around Independence.

The main findings are discussed briefly below. For further details on results and methodology, see Van Waveren (2003).

Local-level Land Allocation Efficiency

The local-level LAE was assessed in eight communities (Figure 11.1). These communities represented a range of natural and economic conditions, and they were different in terms of accessibility and settlement history. Three of the communities were resettled, while no significant external intervention in land distribution had taken place in the others. In all, the vast majority of the homesteads had access to cropland (Table 11.1). Farmers relied mostly on rainfed agriculture, as access to water for irrigation was very limited in all communities (in terms of volume and extraction points) during most of the period following Independence. The communities together covered about one per cent of both the total area and the total number of homesteads on semi-arid CTL[3].

Recent and detailed socio-economic data were available for these communities (EDRCP, 1997, 1998). The changes in local land use patterns were established from aerial photography and field surveys. The local soil patterns were mapped and subsequently reclassified on the basis of depth, drainage, and slope gradient, into three land quality classes: (I) land without serious limitations; (II) land with serious limitations; and (III) land with severe limitations for small-scale crop production. Land classes I and II are both considered arable, or suitable for crop production, but conditions on the latter are marginal, which makes crop production on such land more risk-prone in terms of production, and more susceptible to degradation.

---

3   The selected communities do not form a statistically representative sample. This is primarily because the independent variables (soil and terrain conditions, homestead density) are not normally distributed in space, but occur in patterns. This problem of spatial autocorrelation is common in geographic analyses and it cannot be resolved by random selection or enlargement of the sample size.

Table 11.1　Physical characteristics of the communities sampled in the study

Community	Area (km²)	Allocations (1999)		Annual Rainfall (mm)	Land quality (%)			Accessibility Ranking[1]
		Total Homesteads (no.)	With cropland (%)		Class I	Class II	Class III	
Resettled								
Sitsatsaweni	9.0	123	80	800	43	27	36	6
Mfelankhomo	3.9	47	93	700	22	55	23	1
Mashawulo	7.5	81	100	850	24	47	29	3
Non-resettled								
Tofu	3.2	53	93	650	22	34	44	2
Lesibovu	6.6	35	91	650	30	26	44	7
Makwekweti	11.5	46	89	750	22	31	47	5
Gwayimane	15.1	96	92	650	9	66	25	4
Etjedze	2.0	30	100	700	21	48	31	8

[1] Based on the total distance to the nearest town/market; and length and quality of the feeder road from the community to the main road (1 is highly accessible; 8 is poorly accessible)

The results of the analysis showed considerable differences in LAE between the communities. Two important observations can be made in this respect:

1. The settlement rate within the communities was not related to the availability of land suitable for crop production. Land availability and quality thus appear not to have been major considerations in the decision to allocate land to newcomers. Because of this, considerable differences in land resource availability per homestead developed between the communities. There is no indication that this is currently balanced by other sources of income.

2. Land allocations since Independence generally resulted in more efficient land use patterns within the individual communities. These patterns, however, have not necessarily developed more efficiently in communities with a relatively high pressure on the land resource base: no significant relationship was found between the variation in SE between the communities and the pressure on arable land, *i.e.* the mean area of class I and II land available per homestead.

The relationship between land allocation and land availability is discussed in more detail below.

Land availability, settlement rate and holding size

The annual settlement rate, availability of arable land and gross field (cropland) area within the communities are given in Table 11.2. The continued allocation of land since Independence has resulted in a substantial increase in the total number of homesteads within all the communities. The average annual settlement rate was 3 per cent, which was comparable to the overall rate on semi-arid CTL. Considerable differences were, however, found between the communities with rates ranging from 1.5 per cent to 4.6 per cent. The increase in the number of homesteads resulted, of course, in a corresponding reduction in the availability of arable land (land suitable for crop production) on a per homestead basis. The findings, however, show that it did not result in a substantial expansion of the total area under cultivation. This implies that in order to accommodate newcomers, the existing cropland allocations were reduced in size by the traditional authorities. This reduction in holding size followed the general trend on CTL (see agricultural sample surveys). Note that the gross field area given in the table is larger than the actual cropland allocation as it includes the homestead area, access roads and field boundaries, which were too small to map separately.

Table 11.2   Settlement, availability of arable land and mean gross field area in 1999 and in the 1970s by community

Community	Average annual Settlement Rate	Availability of arable land (ha/hstd)			Gross fields area (ha/hstd)		
	(%)	99	70s	Δ%	99	70s	Δ %
Resettled							
Sitsatsaweni	2.1	4.7	7.8	-40	2.6	4.4	-39
Mfelankhomo	2.0	6.4	10.1	-36	4.7	7.0	-33
Mashawulo	2.1	6.6	11.6	-43	3.5	10.3	-66
Not resettled							
Tofu	4.1	3.4	10.5	-68	2.8	8.5	-67
Lesibovu	1.4	10.6	15.5	-32	4.6	5.8	-21
Makwekweti	1.5	13.3	20.4	-35	8.3	8.6	-9
Gwayimane	4.6	11.7	28.8	-59	5.4	11.9	-55
Etjedze	3.5	4.6	9.2	-50	3.0	6.0	-50

No significant correlations were found between the rate of settlement and the availability of arable land (the average areas of class I and II land available per homestead in the 1970s), rainfall, and accessibility. This has resulted in considerable differences between the communities in land resource potential for crop production per homestead. This is illustrated by the situations at Tofu, Etjedze, Makwekweti, and Lesibovu. In the former two communities high settlement rates were coupled with a relatively low availability of arable land, while in the latter two the rate of settlement was very low, despite the availability of comparatively large areas of arable land.

Spatial efficiency

The relationship between land availability and land allocation discussed above does not provide information on what types of land have been actually allocated for crop production. This is given by the spatial efficiency, or the degree of similarity between the cropland pattern and the land quality distribution. The results from spatial efficiency analysis are given in Table 11.3.

Table 11.3   Spatial efficiency, percentage of land class used as cropland and quality of the cropland area by sample area

Community	Spatial efficiency (Cramer's *V*)		Percentage of land class used for crop production						Land class distribution within fields area in 1999 (ha/homestead)		
			1999			Change (absolute)					
	99	70s	I	II	III	I	II	III	I	II	III
Resettled											
Sitsatsaweni	0.81	0.81	83	18	3	0	0	0	2.2	0.4	0.1
Mfelankhomo	0.24	0.22	60	64	36	-2	7	-3	1.1	3.0	0.7
Mashawulo	0.52	0.59	54	50	7	-30	-28	-18	1.2	2.1	0.2
Not resettled											
Tofu	0.45	0.29	78	44	31	10	3	-6	1.1	0.9	0.8
Lesibovu	0.53	0.31	46	35	3	10	12	-7	2.6	1.7	0.3
Makwekweti	0.67	0.36	68	51	5	34	11	-1	3.8	3.9	0.6
Gwayimane	0.46	0.32	59	39	14	20	2	3	0.8	4.1	0.5
Etjedze	0.71	0.71	88	46	16	0	1	0	1.2	1.4	0.3

The findings can be summarized as follows. First, the communities show a large variation in the level of spatial efficiency as indicated by the variation in Cramer's correlation coefficient. This coefficient is 0, if the land use is distributed randomly, and 1 if the land use pattern perfectly matches the land quality pattern. The land distribution resulted in a relatively high level of SE in three communities: Sitsatsaweni (with a correlation coefficient of 0.81), Makwekweti (0.67), and Etjedze (0.71)[4]. The cropland distribution by land class shows that in these communities, most class I land was allocated for crop production in the late 1990s, while most class III land was unallocated. At Sitsatsaweni, the cropland distribution and class I land distributions matched particularly closely: nearly all class I land was allocated for crop production

---

4   The level of significance is very high in all cases ($\alpha < 0.005$), This is, however, difficult to interpret (see Box 11.1).

and very few cropland allocations were positioned on class II or III land. The other communities showed lower levels of spatial efficiency. This was caused by:

1. A significant over-allocation of cropland in terms of the availability of class I land, in combination with an inefficient use of class II land. This has resulted in a large proportion of the fields being located on class II and III land. Mfelankhomo provides a clear example of where such allocation practices resulted in very low SE.
2. A highly inefficient use of the available Class I land. At Lesibovu, for instance, nearly half of the fields were located on class II and III land, despite the fact that there was sufficient class I land available to accommodate all cropland allocations.

Second, the SE has improved *with* increasing homestead density since Independence in most of the communities. This resulted from an increased use of class I land, in most cases combined with a decreased use of class III land for crop production. The former is a consequence of land allocation. The latter could also have been caused by individual farmers abandoning their poorest land and intensifying crop production on their better land. The use of class II land increased slightly in the majority of the communities. The SE remained constant at a high level in two communities (Sitsatsaweni and Etjedze) and it decreased in one community only (Mashawulo). It is important to observe that this increase in SE occurred exclusively in non-resettled areas. The resettlement of Mfelankhomo and Mashawulo did not result in an improvement of the SE, despite the objective to rationalize the agricultural use of the land in these communities.

The third observation is that both the quality and size of the allocations were closely associated with the availability of arable land. This is illustrated in Figure 11.2, which shows the average area of arable land allocated in the late 1990s in relation to the availability of such land. Because the area of non-arable land allocated was proportionally small in most communities, a similar relationship existed between the size of the allocation (including all types of land) and the area of arable land potentially available. This relationship has become more pronounced over time. This suggests that the holding size is no longer determined primarily by economic conditions, particularly labour availability, as has been suggested in the literature (Low, 1986), but increasingly also by the differences between communities in the physical resource base.

Regional-Level Land Allocation Efficiency

The regional land allocation efficiency was determined by comparing land use patterns with soil and landform patterns and rainfall zones on semiarid CTL. Homestead distributions provided a proxy for the changes in land distribution since Independence, and they were obtained from census surveys of 1966 and 1997 (Jones,

1968; GOS, 1998b). The soil and landform patterns were derived from the available physiographic map of Swaziland (Remmelzwaal, 1993) and the rainfall zones were constructed from rainfall data provided by the Meteorological Office.

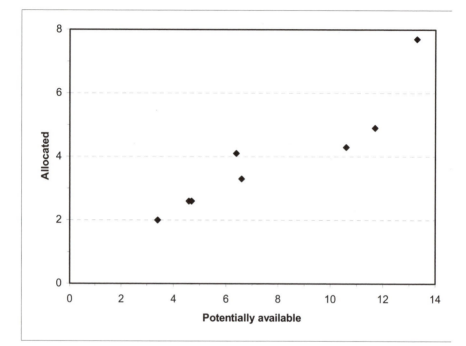

Figure 11.2   Arable land that is potentially available and actually allocated (in ha/homestead)

The regional LAE was found to be low on semi-arid CTL. At this scale, the association between cropland distribution and occurrence of arable land was weak[5]. This was not improved by taking differences in rainfall into account. The level of spatial efficiency has changed only marginally since Independence. This has resulted in a large regional variation in quality and potential availability of cropland per homestead, and it is in line with the large differences in land resource availability observed between communities at a local level. This spatial variation in land availability is illustrated in Figure 11.3, which depicts the average area of arable land (class I and II land) potentially available per homestead. The unit of analysis is

---

5   The spatial efficiency shows a weak positive association between the homestead density and the occurrence of arable land (Cramer's $V = 0.22$). This association is even lower when only Class I land is considered ($V = 0.06$).

the land quality unit. This is an area of land with similar landforms, soils and agro-climatic conditions within an RDA. The results are aggregated by RDA.

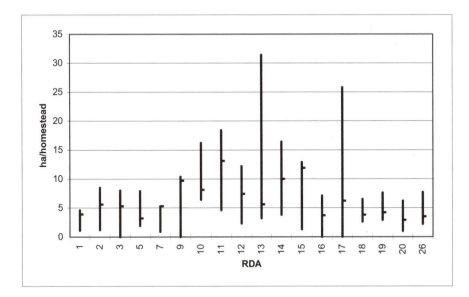

Figure 11.3 **Distribution of total area of Class I and II land per homestead by RDA, median (dot) and $P_5 - P_{95}$ range (line)**

The spatial median value and the 5th to 95th percentile range by RDA given in the graph reflect the considerable variation in land resource availability that occurred between and within the RDAs. The median, for instance, varied from 13 hectares per homestead in RDA-11 to 2.9 in RDA-20. Most RDAs also had a large internal variation. This was most pronounced in RDAs 13 and 17. Relatively favourable conditions for crop production occurred widely in RDAs 9, 11, 14, and 15. All had median values of 10 hectares or more. Such conditions also occurred in RDAs 13 and 17, but to a much more limited extent, as indicated by the very high P_{95} in combination with a low median value.

Land distribution and off-farm income

Rural households on CTL do not generally depend exclusively on crop production for their livelihood. Off-farm labour, remittances and livestock, for instance, have been important alternative sources of income (Low, 1986; Funnell, 1991). These may well have affected the actual need for cropland, and thus help to explain the land distribution patterns that have developed over time. This can no longer be verified due to a lack of historical information on sources of household income in the communities. Household economic data available for the years 1997 and 1998 (EDRCP, 1997, 1998) provide an indication of the relationship between the land distribution and the current need for land. The main sources of income reported for 1997 and 1998 are summarized by community in Table 11.4. Note that many homesteads had multiple sources of income. The totals per community therefore exceed 100 per cent.

As discussed earlier, the large majority of homesteads in the communities had cropland allocations in the late 1990s (Table 11.1). Household surveys showed that these holdings (homesteads with cropland allocation) used this land for rainfed crop production. Nearly all holdings reported to have planted maize. Cotton was grown by some farmers as a cash crop in addition to maize, if sufficient land was available to do both. Farmers also sold maize, but only in communities with comparatively favourable rainfall conditions (Sitsatsaweni and Mashawulo). Households thus produced primarily for home consumption, and secondarily for marketing purposes. The proportion of homesteads involved in the latter varied considerably between the communities. Livestock ownership also varied. In most communities, the majority of homesteads owned livestock (goats, cattle, donkeys), but less than half reported to have cattle. The major part of the homesteads also received off-farm sources of income but, again, with a considerable variation between the communities. These rainfed production systems, relying on multiple sources of income, are the norm on semi-arid CTL (GOS, 1993, 1998a).

Table 11.4   Sources of income by community (in percentage of homesteads)

Community	Sale of crops	Livestock	Cattle	Wages, Remittances
Lesibovu	55	65	44	52
Tofu	38	52	46	63
Makwekweti	52	83	64	71
Mashawulo	52	52	45	85
Mfelankhomo	21	45	34	68
Sitsatsaweni	38	31	12	59
Gwayimane	50	73	67	50
Etjedze	62	74	68	62

The differences between the communities in terms of access to the various sources of income described above do not support the notion that the cropland distribution in the late 1990s reflected the actual requirements for such land. This is for the following reasons. Firstly, communities with a relatively constrained physical resource base did not have an above-average access to off-farm income. In Tofu and Etjedze, for instance, the gross field areas are relatively small (< 3 ha per homestead), and of relative poor quality with, on average, just over one hectare of

Class I land allocated per homestead. Both areas also receive below average rainfall. Despite this comparatively constrained physical environment, just over 60 per cent of the homesteads received off-farm income from remittances and wage labour; this is about average for all communities. Makwekweti, on the other hand, combined a relatively favourable physical potential for crop production (relatively high rainfall, large average holding size of good quality), with a relatively high percentage of homesteads receiving off-farm income (71 per cent). Secondly, in communities with a constrained availability of suitable cropland, households were not holding livestock more frequently; that is they were more reliant upon non-allocated (grazing) land as a source of income. Thirdly, landlessness was not coupled with above average access to other sources of income, or use of non-allocated (grazing) land. Among the landless homesteads, small homesteads, homesteads without livestock, homesteads with less than two employed members, and homesteads without any form of income are over-represented. In other words, landless homesteads are also more likely to be economically weaker in other respects.

The survey data show that within communities a similar picture emerges. Individual homesteads with more off-farm activities were also more likely to produce cash crops and to hold more livestock. This observation is important as it suggests that lack of off-farm income is not compensated by on-farm income and vice versa. Thus, homesteads relying less on land for sustenance tend to utilize more land, both allocated cropland and unallocated grazing land. This supports earlier findings on social and economic stratification on CTL as described by, for instance, Terry (2001) and Barendrecht & Brouwer (1988).

Opportunities for sustainable production improvement

Improvement of crop production levels, as called for in the SEAP, can be achieved by intensification (resulting in improved yields), by expansion of the area under crop production, or by a combination of both. An expansion of the area under cultivation requires the availability of land with soils suitable for this purpose. Intensification does not, of course, require expansion of the cultivated area, but becomes attractive to farmers only if the benefits exceed the costs, and if it is more profitable than expanding the area under low-input farming. The profitability depends on the attainable yield under the specific biophysical and management conditions, the costs of inputs and labour, and the prices of outputs. Opportunities for intensification thus depend on biophysical, as well as economic conditions. In general, semi-arid conditions are not conducive for intensification of rainfed cropping systems, as the limited moisture availability depresses the dependable yield level in most years. This is also the case on semiarid CTL. Opportunities for intensification under the economic conditions of the late 1990s were limited to land with a somewhat higher rainfall, in combination with favourable soil conditions, such as a good infiltration rate, a high water holding capacity and a high inherent fertility. Such conditions occur, for instance, on Class I land in Sitsatsaweni and Mashawulo (Van Waveren, 2003). That intensification is not an attractive option for many farmers under the current agro-economic environment, particularly on the more marginal lands, is illustrated by the structural decline in the use of agricultural inputs in the last decade. Current estimates indicate that fertilizer sales to small farmers have reduced by approximately 50 per cent, and that of hybrid maize seed by 85 per cent over that period (FAO/WFP, 2004).

LAE analyses showed that land allocation practices resulted in a wide variation in the land resources farmers (potentially) have access to, both at a regional scale, and between communities. This, in turn, has resulted in a high spatial variation in conditions suitable for the expansion of cropland, as well as for intensification of rainfed cropping systems on semi-arid CTL. The continuation of the current land allocation practices will thus affect the opportunities for sustainable production improvements differently in different communities (see also Box 11.2).

Some communities have become critically short of the physical resources needed to maintain or enhance productivity under increasing homestead densities. Typically, such communities are located in the drier parts of semi-arid CTL and have a high SE, and thus the largest part of their arable soils allocated. Marginal soils are widely used for crop production as well, increasingly so where the arable soils-homestead ratio has become very small. Access to water is insufficient to substantially improve crop production by means of irrigation. Etjedze provides an example of such communities. In these physical environments, the opportunities for further expansion of the cultivated area on soils suitable for crop production are extremely limited, and the attainable yields and gross-margins are not sufficiently high to stimulate further intensification under the current agricultural marketing conditions. If the lack of physical resources is not compensated by relatively high off-farm labour opportunities, and the analyses show that this is not necessarily the case, such communities are likely to move away from sustainable land management under the socio-economic conditions projected for the foreseeable future. This is because of the decreasing availability of the land resources required to keep up the level of productivity on a per homestead basis and the increasing risk of erosion associated with the expansion of cultivated land on non-arable and marginal soils (De Wit, 1994). The land allocation efficiency is thus expected to fall with continued land allocation under such conditions. This, in turn, is expected to lead to increasing levels of food insecurity. This scenario is supported by studies elsewhere (see, for instance, Conelly & Chaiken, 2000).

Other communities still have sufficient physical resources to absorb new homesteads. Such communities have a low or moderate level of SE in combination with a relatively large area of land and arable soils per homestead. Lesibovu and Makwekweti provide examples of this situation. An enhancement of the spatial efficiency will be required eventually to improve the quality of the existing cropping land and make more arable soils available for crop production. The findings suggest this may develop gradually as a result of the continuing allocation of land and the need to improve the returns per hectare, particularly under traditional settlement patterns. In resettled communities, this process may be obstructed by the rigid subdivision in land for cropping and grazing purposes, which may need to be reconsidered to allow the LAE to improve. There are no indications that in these communities the physical resource base will be a major constraining factor negatively affecting the sustainability of land management for the foreseeable future under the socio-economic conditions projected.

Box 11.2   Land allocation and opportunities for sustainable rainfed agricultural development

The availability of suitable land to allocate to new homesteads for crop production depends on the spatial efficiency and the availability and quality of arable land.

The graph shows the availability of arable land per homestead and the level of spatial efficiency for each community in 1997. Arable land is all land suitable for crop production, whether it has already been allocated or not. Square markers are used where the area of arable land contains more than two ha per homestead of Class I land.

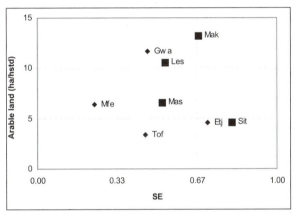

Communities with a high spatial efficiency (> 0.67) already utilize most of their arable land for crop production, and have avoided non-arable land for this purpose. Allocation of land suitable for crop production to newcomers can only be done by reducing the size of the existing holdings. To what extent this can be realized without significantly affecting the livelihood security depends on the area of arable land available per holding. Makwekweti can thus absorb considerably more new settlers than Etjedze. It also depends on the production potential of the land. Sitsatsaweni has better soils (a relatively high proportion of the arable land comprises of Class I land), which would allow for smaller holdings for a similar production level.

Communities with an intermediate or low SE (< 06.7) utilize their land less efficiently. A rearrangement of the land use pattern could improve the quality of the existing holdings and the sustainability of the land use. To what extent newcomers can be accommodated depends again on the area of arable land available per homestead. For instance, the absorption capacity at Lesibovu is relatively high (also because of the comparatively high area of class I land per homestead), while the capacity at Tofu is very low due to a comparatively small area of arable land, which is also mostly Class II land.

The above situations describe both ends of the range of conditions that occur on semi-arid CTL. In other communities there is some scope for development, but to a more limited extent. This is the case, for instance, in communities with a high SE and a constrained access to arable soils, but where a relatively favourable rainfall regime allows for further intensification on the existing fields area (for example, Sitsatsaweni). This situation also occurs where a constrained access to arable soils is caused by the combination of a poor soil resource base and a low SE. Under such conditions, the cultivated area can be expanded and the soil quality of the land under cultivation can be improved to some extent by a redistribution of land. Gwayimane and Mfelankhomo are examples of such communities.

No specific conclusions can be drawn regarding the opportunities for sustainable land management on semi-arid CTL from statistical inference of the findings of the communities studied. However, the trends established in the sub-regional land distribution, and the effects of the land distribution on opportunities for development defined at local level, suggest that, at this point in time, a minority of the homesteads are located in physical production environments conducive to maintaining or improving the level of sustainable land management under conditions of increasing pressure on land. With a continuation of the current land allocation practices, the over-all proportion of homesteads in physical environments with opportunities for intensification or expansion will further decrease. In addition, the decreasing farm sizes will force farmers to use their remaining lands more intensively. This will make traditional (low cost) management practices, such as fallowing, increasingly more difficult to implement. If this forced intensification is not balanced by the appropriate management measures, such as an increased use of fertilizers, it may result in (further) depletion in soil fertility and thus an overall decrease in productivity on CTL.

Implications for sustainable agricultural development

This study provides evidence of inefficient land distribution on CTL, particularly at a regional level. This has been caused by insufficient consideration of the agricultural resource base in the issuance of new land allocations and it has resulted in large differences in land resource availability between communities. This shortcoming has not prevented the development of efficient land allocation patterns within individual communities under increasing land pressure. This is in line with findings in other parts of sub-Saharan Africa to the effect that local indigenous management systems are capable of developing efficient forms of land use (Tiffen *et al.*, 1994; Field-Juma, 1996; Ogolla & Mugabe, 1996; Philips-Howard & Oche, 1996; Watson *et al.*, 1998). The findings, however, indicate that this high level of efficiency is not generally applicable. Communities (including the local traditional authorities) on CTL clearly differ in their capacity to efficiently manage and utilize land resources. The need for uniformity in the application of customary law and regulations in land allocation has been raised before by Brown (1988), but with specific reference to land security issues and not as much to land distribution.

The customary system has also proved to be sufficiently flexible to continue to provide land to an increasing number of rural households. This, however, has come at a cost: a decrease in holding size (30 per cent to 60 per cent within most of the communities studied). In the past, this may not have been a serious problem, as the holdings on semi-arid land were comparatively large, and with the reduction in size, the quality of the fields has increased due to the better spatial efficiency levels employed. Moreover, off-farm wage labour opportunities were readily available at that time (Low, 1986). The findings show that some part of the communities have now reached the point where average holding sizes are already small (net allocations of two hectares or less)[6], and further improvements in quality by improving the spatial efficiency are no longer possible. Other communities still have sufficient arable land to accommodate new holdings but, in case the allocation of new croplands is not carefully controlled, such communities are likely to end up in the same situation. The analysis suggests that less than half of the communities still find themselves in this comparatively favourable position, and that their number will continue to diminish rapidly if the current trends are not reversed.

Communities are thus finding themselves in an increasingly difficult situation. They can, and often do, make the best of the situation they are in, by using available space more efficiently. They do not, however, appear to be able to control the most critical factor: the rate of settlement. This is a complex issue in which social aspects and vested interests of the traditional leaders play a significant role. Firstly, it touches upon a fundamental function of CTL, which is to provide Swazi households with a means of sustenance (often supplementing other sources of income). Secondly, the allocation of land is often economically and politically beneficial to traditional leaders, which may well override environmental concerns (Sallinger-McBride & Picard, 1986; Levin, 1997).

The demand for land for subsistence purposes is expected to continue to rise, as there are no indications that off-farm job opportunities will considerably improve in the foreseeable future (CIA, 2004; GOS, 1997). The findings of this study suggest that, with the established allocation practices, this will result in a further decline of the average holding size and, eventually, to a decrease in the quality of cropland (by bringing more marginal land under cultivation). This will affect the livelihood of the poorest households most, as these have less land and less off-farm sources of income. It will also reduce the opportunities for market-oriented production, as most farmers would require additional land for this. These factors combined will constrain a sustainable rise in productivity envisaged in the SEAP and other policy documents. The continuation of the current land allocation practices will also make

---

6   Over two hectares would be required to produce the average maize consumption per homestead in a below average rainfall year. This is based on an average homestead size of 7.3, a per capita consumption of 135 kg (including post harvest losses) and a yield of 0.45 tonnes/ha (FAO/WFP, 2004).

it increasingly difficult to reconcile these very different economic functions of CTL. The findings also confirm the reservations of Funnell (1991) concerning the capacity of the current land allocation system to enable the agricultural transformation.

Conclusions

To honour its commitment to the implementation of Agenda 21, Swaziland has adopted the Swaziland Environmental Action Plan (SEAP). This action plan outlines implementation strategies and plans for improved environmental management, as well as recommendations for the development of a supporting policy framework. Improved natural resource management for increased (agricultural) production was identified as one of the major programmes of action. A mismatch between land use and land suitability, and land shortage, were seen as major factors limiting sustainable agricultural production.

In Swaziland, the larger part of the land is still managed under customary tenure arrangements. On this customary tenured land (CTL), land use is mainly determined by local-level land allocation practices. From this study, it can be concluded that, in general, this customary system of land allocation is not compatible with the sustainable agricultural development objectives of SEAP and other national agricultural development strategies and policies. This is because these agricultural development objectives do not fit in well with the social security function and the political value of CTL. The continued allocation of land for social and political reasons is threatening opportunities for sustainable agricultural development, as well as the basic capacity to sustain rural livelihoods, over time, on an increasingly larger part of CTL.

The Rural Resettlement Policy that was adopted in 2002 (GOS, 2002), potentially provides important tools to improve the land allocation efficiency within communities, as it proposes mechanisms to build up institutional and technical capacities to ensure that chiefs will give due consideration to the availability of land of adequate quality before allocating it. Its implementation, however, would not stop the erosion of the social security function of CTL, because, with time, land would become unavailable for newly established families in a growing number of communities once all the good quality arable land had been allocated. With its emphasis on community level land distribution, it would also not address the issue of over-allocation of land that already exists in some of the communities (for example, Tofu and Etjedze). This would require a regional redistribution of land, between communities and between chieftancies.

The above underscores the need to develop a long-term development strategy of CTL that is realistic, location-specific and addresses the specific requirements of the different land use systems envisaged. Any prolongation of the current *status quo* will reduce the opportunities for sustainable crop production on an increasingly larger part of CTL. This will firstly affect the opportunities for market-oriented production because of the higher requirement for land, and then subsistence-oriented production. Also, without intervention, fundamental changes in the role of CTL in the Swazi society seem unavoidable.

References

Armstrong, A.K. (1986) *Legal Aspects of Land Tenure in Swaziland*. University of Swaziland/Ministry of Agriculture and Co-operatives/University of Wisconsin-Madison, Mbabane, Swaziland.

Barendrecht, J. & Brouwer, M.A. (1988) Family cycle or social stratum: an analysis of spending behaviour of Swazi urban workers. In Tieleman, H.J. (ed.) *Scenes of Change: Visions on Developments in Swaziland*. African Studies Centre, Leiden, pp. 104-120.

Brown, C.K. (ed.) (1988) *Report on the National Workshop on Land Tenure in Swaziland*. Uniswa, Kwaluseni.

CIA (2004) The World Fact Book. http/www/cia.gov/cia/publications/factbook. Accessed 4/1/04.

Conelly, W.T. & Chaiken, M.S. (2000) Intensive farming, agro-diversity, and food security under conditions of extreme population pressure in Western Kenya. *Human Ecology*, 28, 19-51.

De Wit, C.T. (1994) Resource use analysis in agriculture: A struggle for interdisciplinarity. In Fresco, L.O., Stroosnijder, L., Bouma, J. & Van Keulen, H. (eds) *The Future of the Land. Mobilising and Integrating Knowledge for Land Use Options*. John Wiley & Sons, Chichester, pp. 41-56.

EDRCP (1997) *Socio-Economic Study for the Selection and Baseline Survey for Dams to be Rehabilitated/Constructed*. Earth Dam Rehabilitation and Construction Programme (II), Ministry of Agriculture and Co-operatives, Mbabane.

EDRCP (1998) *Socio-Economic Study for the Selection and Baseline Survey for Dams to be Rehabilitated/Constructed*. Earth Dam Rehabilitation and Construction Programme (II), Ministry of Agriculture and Co-operatives, Mbabane.

FAO (1978) *Report on the Agro-Ecological Zones Project. Volume 1: Methodology and Results for Africa*. World Soil Resources Report 48, Food and Agriculture Organisation of the United Nations, Rome.

FAO/WFP (2004) *Special Report: FAO/WFP Crop and Food Supply Assessment Mission to Swaziland*. FAO and WFP, Rome.

Field-Juma, A. (1996) Governance and sustainable development. In Juma, C. & Ojwang, J.B. (eds) *In Land we Trust: Environment, Private Property and Constitutional Change*. Initiatives Printers, Nairobi and Zed books, London, pp. 9-38.

Funnell, D.C. (1991) *Under the Shadow of Apartheid. Agrarian Transformation in Swaziland*. Avebury, Aldershot.

Gommes, R. (1996) *Rainfall Variability and Drought in Sub-Saharan Africa since 1960*. Food and Agriculture Organisation of the United Nations, Rome.

GOS (1993) *Swaziland Census of Agriculture 1992-1993*. Central Statistical Office, Government of Swaziland, Mbabane.

GOS (1997) *Swaziland Environmental Action Plan (Volumes I and II)*. Swaziland Environment Authority, Ministry of Tourism, Environment and Communications, Government of Swaziland, Mbabane.

GOS (1998a) *Swaziland Annual Agriculture Survey 1997-1998*. Central Statistical Office, Government of Swaziland, Mbabane.

GOS (1998b) *Report on the 1997 Population Census*. Central Statistical Office, Government of Swaziland, Mbabane.

GOS (2002) *Rural Resettlement Policy*. Ministry of Agriculture and Cooperatives, Government of Swaziland, Mbabane.

Jones, H.M. (1968) *Report on the 1966 Swaziland Population Census*. Swaziland Government, Mbabane.

Levin, R. (1997), *When the sleeping grass awakens*, Witwatersrand University Press, Johannesburg.

Low, A.R.C. (1986) *Agricultural development in Southern Africa. Farm-Household Economics and the Food Crisis*. James Currey, London.

Mhlanga, A.B.N., McDermott, M. & Johnson, S. (1998) The Kingdom of Swaziland and the issue of land tenure reform. In *Proceedings of the International Conference on Land Tenure in the Developing World, with a focus on Southern Africa*. University of Cape Town, 27-29 August: 457-466.

Maina, M.N. (1977) *Handing Over Report*. Ministry of Agriculture, Mbabane.

Ogolla, B.D. & Mugabe, J. (1996) Land tenure systems and natural resource management. In Juma, C. & Ojwang, J.B. (eds) *In Land we Trust: Environment, Private Property and Constitutional Change*. Initiatives Printers, Nairobi and Zed books, London, pp. 85-116.

Philips-Howard, K. & Oche, C. (1996) Local farming in the former Transkei, South Africa. In Rey, C., Scoones, I. & Toulmin, C. (eds) *Sustaining the Soil: Indigenous Soil and Water Practices in Africa*. Earthscan, London, pp.181-190.

Remmelzwaal, A. (1993) *Physiographic Map of Swaziland*. Project: FAO SWA 89/001, Ministry of Agriculture and Co-operatives, Mbabane.

Remmelzwaal, A. & Dlamini, W.S. (1994) *Present Land Use map of Swaziland*. Project: FAO SWA 89/001, Ministry of Agriculture and Co-operatives, Mbabane.

Remmelzwaal, A. & Vilakati, J.D. (1994) *Land Tenure Map of Swaziland*. Project: FAO SWA 89/001, Ministry of Agriculture and Co-operatives, Mbabane.

Sallinger-McBride, J. & Picard, L.A. (1986) Patrons versus Planners: The political contradictions of integrated rural development in Swaziland. *Journal of Contemporary African Studies*, 5, 119-144.

Terry, A.K (2001) Who benefits from rural development projects? A case study of the Komati Pilot Project, Swaziland. *South African Geographical Journal*, 83, 18-27.

Tiffen, M., Mortimore, M. & Gichuki, F. (1994) *More People, Less Erosion. Environmental Recovery in Kenya*. Wiley, Chichester.

Van Waveren, E.J. (2003) *Land Resource Distribution under Customary Tenure in Swaziland: A Geographic Analysis with Special Attention to Semiarid Land.* Unpublished PhD thesis, University of the West of England, Bristol, UK.

Watson, E.E., Adams, W.M. & Mutiso, S.K. (1998) Indigenous irrigation, agriculture and development, Marakwet, Kenya. *The Geographic Journal*, 164, 67-84.

Chapter 12

Water Management for Agriculture in Tunisia: Towards Environmentally Sustainable Development

Wendy Woodland and Jennifer Hill

Introduction

Environmental protection has become a theoretical foundation of Tunisia's long-term development strategy. The roots can be traced to 1987 and the aspirations for social and economic reform that were held by Tunisia's first democratically elected government. More recent inspiration has come from the goals and recommendations for action of the United Nations' Agenda 21, which arose from the Earth Summit of the United Nations Commission for Environment and Development (UNCED) in Rio de Janeiro in 1992. Responding to the Rio summit, Tunisia established a National Sustainable Development Commission (CNDD) in 1993 to ensure the integration of environmental protection into development and to promote sustainable development in all national development plans. Operating in this way, it acted as a conduit for the drafting of a national Agenda 21 programme in 1995. This programme developed strategies for three environmental sectors: water management (the focus of this chapter); biological diversity and a national anti-desertification plan (Ministry of Environment and Land Use Planning, 2001).

Tunisia's national Agenda 21 programme defined the following objectives for the sustainable management and utilization of the country's water resources (Ministry of Environment and Land Use Planning, 2001: 55):

1. development and integrated management of water resources
2. evaluation of water resources
3. protection of water resources, water quality and aquatic ecosystems
4. provision of potable water and sanitation
5. ensuring quality and availability for sustainable production to meet human consumption
6. adaptation to extreme situations; droughts, floods and climate changes.

The strategy for the integrated management of water resources involves mobilizing all possible groundwater reserves and 90 per cent of surface waters, along with diversifying into non-conventional sources and promoting soil and water conservation (Ministry of Environment and Land Use Planning, 2001: 55). The objectives arise from two challenges for the long-term conservation of water resources in Tunisia: an inherent disparity in the distribution of resources across the country (Table 12.1); and an unsustainable increase in the consumption of water by a number of sectors in recent decades.

Tunisia contains three different climate zones: Mediterranean, semi-arid and arid, which experience differing water availability. The northern Mediterranean area experiences an annual water surplus, where precipitation exceeds evapotranspiration. This surplus supports Tunisia's only perennial river: the Medjerda. In the semi-arid central part of the country, both the annual rainfall and the number of days with rain decrease progressively in a southerly direction. The southernmost arid zone, which begins around the latitude of the Chott el Djerid and the Matmata Plateau, experiences an annual water deficit due to low rainfall and high rates of evapotranspiration. This zone is, however, underlain by part of the North-West Sahara Aquifer System and it consequently contains the largest reserves of artesian water in Tunisia (Table 12.1).

Table 12.1   Distribution of potential water resources in Tunisia

	Mediterranean		Semi-arid		Arid		Total	
Potential resources	Million m³	%	Million m³	%	Million m³	%	Million m³	%
Surface water	2190	78	320	38	190	19	2700	58
Phreatic ground water	395	14	222	26	102	10	719	15
Deep ground water	216	8	306	36	728	71	1250	27
Total	2801	100	848	100	1020	100	4669	100
% of total	60		18		22		100	

Source: Ministère de l'Agriculture (1998)

Due largely to these differences in potential water resources, there exists a number of distinctive methods of water management for agriculture across Tunisia. The northern Mediterranean region is dominated by modern reservoir-fed irrigation. In the semi-arid central part of the country modern dams have been constructed in the north of the zone, but rainwater harvesting and terraced wadi systems predominate towards the south. In the arid south, surface storage of water is unfeasible so communities practice traditional rainwater harvesting within small hillside catchments or oasis irrigation using artesian water.

Tunisia is acutely aware of the finite nature of its water resources and the need to distribute water equitably. The Shari'a water law is one of the fundamental tenets of Islam under which just enough water is consumed to meet community needs without wastage. It can be viewed as an exemplar of sustainability because it requires that water is used equitably over space and time, replenishing current reserves and safeguarding future supplies. It therefore incorporates certain key ideals of sustainability, particularly the integration of decision-making across social, environmental and economic spheres in order to promote social justice within and across generations, and to enhance quality of life, local participation and environmental protection (Connelly & Smith, 1999).

Twice during recent history, however, the country has moved away from the Shari'a water code as community management of water has been replaced by centralized government control, with independent regional offices administering irrigated areas. This began with nationalization of water during French colonial rule in the late nineteenth century and was consolidated after Independence as the Tunisian Water Code (1975). During the next 25 years Tunisia prioritized the mobilization and artificial pricing (known as 'valorization') of water resources via master plans for the north, centre and south of the country; investment in the water sector consumed between 40 per cent and 65 per cent of the budget of the Ministry of Agriculture during this period (Bahri, undated). This activity supported the country's strategy of integrating its economy, including the agrarian sector, into world markets (Egger, 1990; Martín Castellanos, 1996; World Bank, 1996; Dillman, 2001). It greatly extended irrigated farmland, diversifying production from cereals and livestock to include fruit farming (olives, citrus fruits, apricots, almonds) and vegetable farming (potatoes, tomatoes, peppers, artichokes, cucumbers). Investment also helped to increase the use of technology, to develop credit and to modify the land tenure regime (Kassab, 1981). The resulting demand for water supply prompted the construction of dams to replace local water harvesting techniques and to provide more reliable reserves of surface water for agricultural land. The sustainability of many of these dams has been called into question for a number of reasons that will be outlined in this chapter. Increased agricultural consumption of artesian water in the south of the country over the past 50 years has placed a similar burden on subterranean aquifers (UNESCO, 2005) exposing both surface and ground water to the risk of depletion from over-consumption.

Increased water consumption by the agricultural sector has been mirrored by the industrial and service sectors (particularly via international tourism). This reflects the growing contribution of these sectors to the country's gross domestic product (GDP). In 2000, the percentage of Tunisia's GDP contributed by agriculture, industry and services was 59 per cent, 29 per cent and 12 per cent respectively (World Resources Institute, 2003).

These activities have placed unsustainable demands on Tunisia's water reserves and the country's government has recognized that 'due to the lack of an adequate protection of such resources, a major risk could affect the sustainability of development and lead the country to face major constraints in terms of water quantities and quality in the medium, but mostly in the long term' (Ministry of Environment and Land Use Planning, 2001: 55). This awareness, together with Tunisia's obligations to the Rio Convention and Agenda 21, was reflected in the commissioning of two surveys of water resources and demand in 1995 and 2000 (*Eau 2000* and *Eau XXI*). These studies culminated in a comprehensive Water Sector Review (*Etude sur le Secteur de l'Eau*) upon which the government's current sustainable water programme (*Strategie de Gestion de l'Eau*) is based. It plans for the mobilization, exploitation and improved quality of water resources by 2030 and builds upon Tunisia's expertise in the fields of water resource mobilization and integrated management in a context of aridity, water scarcity and social and economic restraints (Vidal, 2001). An increasingly significant outcome of the programme is the re-introduction of local water management using indigenous techniques. In its national report to the Rio +10 conference in Johannesburg in 2002, Tunisia outlined its progress in sustainable water management (Ministry of Environment and Land Use Planning, 2001) and emphasized its integrated approach which takes into account economic, social, institutional and ecological considerations. Local management 'which is governed by consultations and negotiation' together with 'active participation of responsible partners in decision-making' was encouraged 'to ensure water sustainability through rational utilization' (Ministry of Environment and Land Use Planning, 2001: 58).

Whether this is rhetoric or reality may be appraised by a study of water management techniques across Tunisia, and it forms the subject of this chapter. Two case studies are used to describe contrasting water management techniques: traditional small-scale rainwater harvesting and modern large-scale dam irrigation[1]. Sustainability is examined using a human ecological approach, which addresses the interlocking nature of society and environment using ideas and methods of geography, ecology and anthropology (Simmons, 1997; Marten, 2001). The research focuses on links between the physical environment, socio-cultural viability and economic viability to evaluate the contribution that both local indigenous techniques and centralized water management techniques for agriculture have made to realising Tunisia's national aspirations for water resource sustainability.

Contrasting water management techniques and issues of sustainability

The geographical position of Tunisia and the locations of the case study areas within the country are highlighted in Figure 12.1. The Matmata Plateau, in the south of the country, exemplifies small-scale rainwater harvesting and the Zeroud Basin in the central steppe highlights modern, large-scale dam irrigation. The Matmata Plateau is composed of Cretaceous limestone and it stands between 200 m and 700 m high (Coudé-Gaussen & Rognon, 1988; Golany, 1988). It separates the alluvial Jeffāra Plain and the Mediterranean Sea from the sand dunes of the Sahara Desert (Figure 12.1).

---

    1   Traditional management is defined as techniques dating back to ancient times relying mainly on human labour. Modern systems, by contrast, rely on machinery and advanced technology.

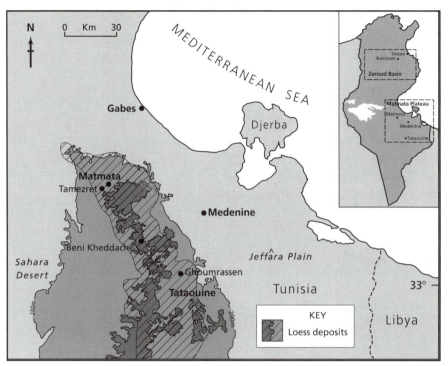

Figure 12.1   **The Matmata Plateau, southern Tunisia. This area includes, from
north to south, the delegations of Matmata, Beni Kheddache,
Ghoumrassen and Tataouine. The inset shows the geographical
locations of the case study areas**

The plateau falls within the arid zone, with average annual rainfall varying between
100 mm to 250 mm depending on location. Actual evapotranspirative losses vary
between 400 mm to 500 mm per annum resulting in a negative annual water budget
of 200 mm to 300 mm (Frankenberg, 1980). Summer temperatures frequently exceed
40°C, moderating to a seasonal average of 20°C during winter (Golany, 1988). Valleys
to the west of the Plateau are covered by loess deposits transported from the Grand
Eastern Erg of the Sahara Desert during the Upper Pleistocene and middle Holocene
(Coudé-Gaussen & Rognon, 1988; Dearing *et al.*, 1996). Loess soils are composed
of aeolian sand and silt which easily form a surface crust, facilitating overland flow
in catchment areas, but necessitating tillage of cropped areas (Boers *et al.*, 1986a,
b). Loess also has a low cation exchange capacity and it is highly susceptible to
leaching (Tabor, 1995). The natural vegetation of alfa grass, with an average ground
cover of 20 per cent, affords little protection to the soils during high intensity rains
(Chahbani, 1984).

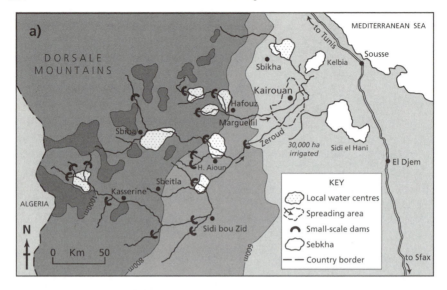

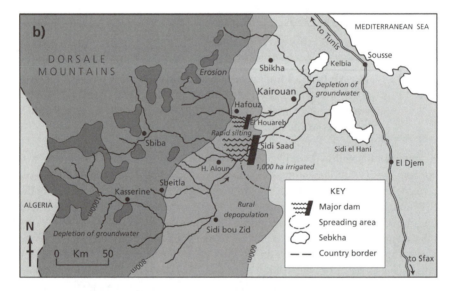

Figure 12.2 The Zeroud Basin, central Tunisia: (a) decentralized and (b) centralized water management

Central Tunisia can be divided into two geographical regions (Figure 12.2). To the west, the mountains of the Dorsale give way to the Plain of Kairouan in the east.

The plain stands at an altitude of between 200 m and 400 m and it is covered in alluvial Miocene and Pliocene (clay-sand) deposits. Rainfall across the region varies between 200 mm to 350 mm per annum, but temperatures attain 35oC in summer and actual evapotranspirative losses reach 600 mm to 700 mm per annum resulting in a negative annual water balance of between 300 mm and 400 mm (Frankenberg, 1980; Guillaud & Trabelsi, 1991). The climate supports semi-arid steppe vegetation, characterized by herbs and dwarf shrubs. With lack of plant cover and steep gradients in the highlands, runoff is collected rapidly by wadis that descend from the Dorsale (Brierley, 1981). The largest of these is the Zeroud, with a drainage basin of 8,950 km2 and an average annual water supply of more than 100 million cubic metres, despite flowing on average for just 30 days per year (Guillaud & Trabelsi, 1991). The wadis are high energy, erosive systems that respond rapidly to high magnitude events in the form of single peak floods (sensu Graf, 1988).

Traditional rainwater harvesting

In southern Tunisia, crops are at risk from physiological drought and so rainwater must be collected, concentrated and transferred to cropped areas quickly to minimize losses via evaporation and runoff. Such macrocatchment rainwater harvesting (Bruins *et al.,* 1986; Pacey & Cullis, 1986; Barrow, 1999) has a long history in the Matmata Plateau, dating back many hundreds of years to the original Berber inhabitants. Here, climate, topography and soils together make rainwater harvesting very effective. The majority of rain falls as high intensity-low frequency downpours which can exceed average annual rainfall by a factor of between two and twelve (Bahri, undated). Overland flow is generated rapidly and it travels quickly over the steep slopes, supplying water and soil to valley bottoms. Earthen check dams (tabias) are sited progressively downslope to trap eroded material from the valley sides and this material is levelled to form agricultural fields (jessour) (Figure 12.3).

Water that is trapped behind tabias after rain events infiltrates into the soil and it can create a temporary, phreatic water supply. Valley sides are sometimes manipulated to enhance overland flow: vegetation cover is reduced and low walls are constructed to divert water quickly to jessour. This reduces evapotranspiration in the catchment area and increases water supply to the cropped area. The rainfall multiplier effect of rainwater harvesting depends primarily on the ratio of catchment area to cropped area. On the western outskirts of Matmata, a ratio of 6:1 translates into field sizes approximating 0.6 ha and catchment sizes of around 4 ha, varying slightly with site, topography and capability of the builders (Hill & Woodland, 2003) (Figure 12.4). Water yields are lacking for this region, but according to the National Academy of Sciences, if infiltration and evaporation losses are prevented, 10mm of rain falling on a 1 ha semi-arid catchment can yield around 100,000 litres of water (Barrow, 1987).

Farmers practice agroforestry on the jessour: the mutually supportive growth of annual crops and trees (Barrow, 1999). They are able to grow relatively demanding trees such as olives, almonds, figs, pomegranates and date palms. Annual crops

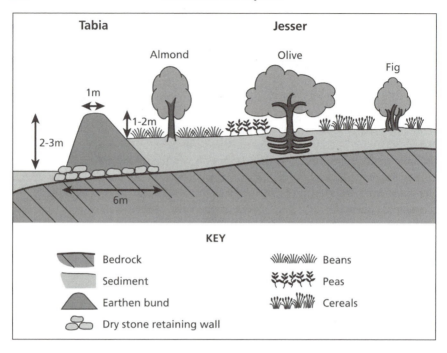

Figure 12.3   Cross-section of a typical jessour system in southern Tunisia

include barley, peas, lentils, beans and watermelons, and fodder crops are also grown. Cultivation is largely subsistence, but a limited surplus is sold at local markets. Small parcels of land, totalling 2 ha to 3 ha in size, are under extended family or tribal ownership (Zaibet & Dunn, 1998). These are often scattered across the landscape so fragmentation of holdings is a concern (World Bank, 1996; Gharbi, 1998).

Vernacular knowledge and craftsmanship, derived from centuries of interaction with the local environment, has been used to equip tabias with different types of overflow. These promote effective water distribution and allow some flexibility against climatic extremes. Lateral overflows are employed in 60 per cent of the tabias in the Matmata Hills (Bonvallot, 1979). These are purpose-made breaches in the earthen bunds at valley sides which permit excess water to flow by gravity onto the terrace below, ensuring irrigation water with minimal erosive capability. Erosion of the overflows themselves is often reduced by strengthening their floors and sides with stones.

The engineering of tabias, particularly the height of the overflow threshold, ensures that fields downslope are not deprived of water by higher fields, leading to crop failure. Equally, the height of the threshold prevents the build up of too much water after storms such that the root zone remains waterlogged for long periods. This enhances the agricultural potential by increasing root aeration, and reducing soil salinization because water infiltrates efficiently and is used rapidly by crops (Rapp & Hasteen-Dahlin, 1990).

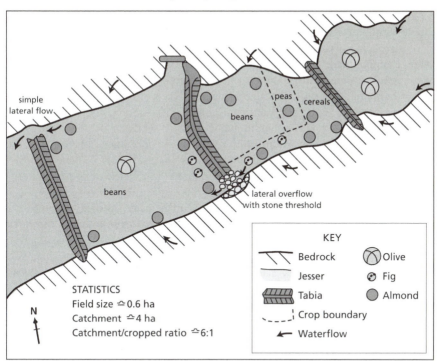

Figure 12.4 Plan view of a rainwater harvesting catchment on the western outskirts of Matmata

Central overflows, which are present in 38 per cent of tabias in the Matmata Hills (Bonvallot, 1979), require greater manpower and more materials to construct when compared with lateral overflows. Dry stone or cement walls retain the earth of the tabia and the overflow floor is stepped downslope to dissipate the energy of escaping water. Once financed by the state, their use has declined in many remote areas because they are unsustainable, both structurally and environmentally. Unable to respond to high magnitude events, because their dimensions are literally set in stone, they are unable to evacuate the volume of floodwater and, consequently, they rupture. This is in contrast to the simple lateral overflow, which is eroded at its edges until its hydraulic radius is sufficient to release water ahead of bund rupture. Additionally, the low floors and great widths of the central overflows mean that little water is actually trapped behind the tabias for use by crops and to replenish groundwater. Natural regulation within the system, as it responds to the vagaries of an unpredictable climate, is thereby reduced due to the influence of central control. Furthermore adaptability, acquired from years of experience, had been replaced by physical rigidity. Local autonomy was also diminished, as farmers invested more money in construction and maintenance, and this finance often came from state loans or remittances from emigrants (Barrow, 1987).

Small-scale hydraulic works prove sustainable in the face of extreme events. An example is their response to exceptional rains in March 1979. Between the 3rd and the 6th of March, many parts of the Matmata Plateau received rainfall approaching their average annual total. The average annual rainfall of Matmata, for example, is 222 mm, yet the area received 120 mm in one day (Fersi, 1978; Bonvallot, 1979). These high intensity rains fell on soils with considerable levels of antecedent moisture. Their saturation, together with steep slopes, engendered catastrophic floods. Discharge in the Oueds Zmertene and Krecheb in the Matmata Hills reached 1,000 cumecs and 2,000 cumecs respectively (Bonvallot, 1979). In the delegations of Tataouine and Beni Kheddache 1,400 km of agricultural tracks were seriously damaged by flood waters (Bonvallot, 1986). These two areas suffered the collapse of 70 per cent to 80 per cent of their agricultural bunds, whereas Matmata suffered damage of less than 10 per cent (Bonvallot, 1979). The proportion of damage suffered by tabias was equal whether they were equipped with lateral or central overflows, but the extent of damage differed. Central overflows suffered a greater degree of damage requiring more manpower and materials to repair. Around Tataouine, heavy investments of manpower were needed to reconstruct overflows, rebuild tabias and reshape jessour. Around Matmata, however, substantially less manpower and investment were required to repair small breaches in tabias, to replace stones in overflows, and to arrest rill erosion into jessour (Bonvallot, 1979). Significantly, community work using local materials allowed a rapid response to the altered environment. These landscapes can be reworked effectively and they are thereby sustainable environmentally over long time frames and across climatic extremes.

In terms of economic sustainability, rainwater harvesting permits precise local control of water for the common good and it offers the possibility of rural livelihoods that can be grasped by smallholders without the necessity for large amounts of credit, expensive inputs or costly infrastructure (Barrow, 1999). It does not lead to dependency, with its concomitant rigidity in a changeable environment, and it tends to avoid the local imbalances between more wealthy and poorer people (King, 1999).

Rainwater harvesting is labour-intensive, however, and the total number of inhabitants across the region is declining, especially in terms of the younger generation who have been attracted to national urban centres or cities abroad (Shah, 1994). This has led to abandoned terraces, increased runoff, and gulley erosion in concentrated pockets. If the population declines any further, dryland agriculture will become unsustainable demographically.

Modern dam irrigation

Development of modern large-scale dams has taken place in central Tunisia, immediately south of the Dorsale. The Kairouan Programme, initiated in 1975, centred on the construction of two large dams in the neighbouring Zeroud and Marguellil Basins. Financially and technically supported by foreign investment (via the Canadian Government), the aims were to reduce flooding in the Kairouan Plain, to develop irrigated areas downstream of the dams and to supply the city of Kairouan with an improved water supply (Guillaud & Trabelsi, 1991). The Sidi Saad Dam, in the Zeroud Basin, came into service in 1982. By 1986, the dam was supplying water, via a system of gravity flow pipes, to irrigated perimeters up to 15 km away (Guillaud & Trabelsi, 1991). This led to a substantial rise in the acreage of olive and almond trees in the low steppe, and to an extension of market gardening using poly-tunnels for early winter fruit and vegetables. Land is either collectively managed or under nuclear family or joint sibling ownership (Zaibet & Dunn, 1998).

Water flow in the Zeroud and Marguellil Basins had been regulated for centuries by means of a network of small barrages and 30 local dams. Such decentralized management maintained a number of spreading areas, which irrigated 30,000 ha and replenished local water tables (Figure 12.2a). The cost of these small-scale works has been estimated at only TD 6 million, as they utilized local equipment and 40,000 local labourers (El Amami, 1986). This heritage could have been used to sustain decentralized water systems, but following the severe floods of 1969, which caused 150 deaths on the Kairouan Plain (Guillaud & Trabelsi, 1991), the decision was made to construct a single large dam at Sidi Saad (Figure 12.2b). Costing TD 60 million, the dam initially supplied an irrigated area of 4,000 ha which has subsequently decreased to 1,000 ha[2] (El Amami, 1986). Although proving itself in terms of flood control during the heavy rains of 1990 (Guillaud & Trabelsi, 1991), it has produced an irrigated area just one thirtieth of the size of the original, at ten times the cost.

With an obvious economic disadvantage compared to small-scale hydraulic works, how do such large-scale developments compare in terms of long-term sustainability? High intensity downpours falling on exposed friable soils in the centre of the country mean that the large-scale developments are liable to rapid, but spatially and temporally unpredictable, sediment input. Based on reservoir siltation rates measured between 1982 and 1993, the probable service duration of the Sidi Saad Dam has been calculated as 87 years (Zahar, 2001), though it must be stated that with such a short time series, statistical uncertainty is high. This figure falls notably short of the generational history recorded by the dryland jessour systems. Additionally, the Sidi Saad Dam would face a drastic reduction of its predicted service duration if it were to experience rains of similar magnitude to those of autumn 1969. These rains generated 2,500 million cubic metres of water at Sidi Saad measuring station in just two months, more than the annual average for all Tunisian watercourses. The discharge reached 17,050 cumecs on 27th September, an immense figure when compared with the annual average of just three cumecs. An estimated 275 million cubic metres of solids were mobilized, which is equivalent to 14 years' sediment supply (Cruette *et al.*, 1971). These figures must be compared with a flood spillway capable of evacuating 7000 cumecs and a storage capacity of 209 million cubic

---

2   El Haoureb Dam in the neighbouring Marguellil Basin was completed in 1990 and has irrigated an additional 2,250 ha since 1991. The development followed the abandonment of an already initiated plan to construct 40 hillside lakes, to reinforce macrocatchment management and to promote afforestation (data from Guillaud & Trabelsi 1991 and El Amami 1986).

metres (Zahar, 2001). If the dam had been constructed prior to the rains, it would have been unable to contain the flood peak and would have been filled completely with sediment. In Tunisia, large-scale water storage schemes provide some 66 per cent of the available water resources and demand for agriculture is increasing continuously (Baban *et al.*, 1999). The storage loss to sedimentation is a problem that could well represent a serious threat to future agricultural development.

The Sidi Saad reservoir is losing its live storage capacity whilst its surface area for evaporation remains the same (Ben Mammou, 1997). It will most likely have to be abandoned less than 100 years after construction (Zahar, 2001); compare this with the continued use of depressions for rainwater harvesting in the south of the country which have been farmed for generations. Indeed, all dams south of the Dorsale exist in an area of negative water balance and are therefore outside the limits of climatic viability. Essentially, with increasing surface to volume ratios, the reservoirs become less efficient over time (Baban *et al.*, 1999). Dam walls are difficult and costly to raise to prolong life, unlike tabias when their jesser suffer rapid sedimentation. The scale of the hydraulic works renders adaptive response to extreme events difficult. The structures must be sufficient to withstand high magnitude events from the outset, but predicting the vagaries of this marginal environment, where inter-annual variability of precipitation ranges between 30 per cent and 40 per cent (Frankenberg, 1980), is notoriously difficult.

With a reliable supply of water over the short term, the problem has arisen of over-watering crops. Irrigation water infiltrates into the soil and the excess not used by plants is drawn back to the surface by evaporation. This process brings salts to the surface that reduce soil fertility and decrease yields. Salinization is aided by capillary rise from groundwater, which records a salt content of 1.5g/l by the dam, increasing to 5g/l near Kairouan (Besbès, 1978). Construction of the Sidi Saad Dam has led to a rise in the piezometric level in the local area and this further enhances susceptibility to salinization (Baba Sy & Besbès, 2001). Additionally, the increased pumping of groundwater in the coastal zone to feed market gardens means that salt is drawn in from coastal waters (Paniconi *et al.*, 2001). The high salinity limits the utility of groundwater to crops as most give restricted yields between 1.5g/l-3.5g/l (Barrow, 1987). To combat salinization at the field level, farmers have moved away from basin flooding and furrow irrigation towards trickle irrigation. Today, perforated plastic pipes can be observed in many fields following crop lines and administering a low rate of water application directly to plant roots. This minimizes losses via surface runoff, evaporation and deep percolation and maximizes delivery to the root zone (Overman, 1976). For these reasons, the application efficiency of trickle irrigation is between 70 per cent and 95 per cent, compared with that of basin or furrow irrigation, which stand between 50 per cent to 90 per cent and 50 per cent to 70 per cent respectively (Withers & Vipond, 1988). Thus, indigenous practical knowledge is used at the scale of individual holdings, but it is presently unable to penetrate to the higher administrative levels of water planning.

In the upper levels of the catchment, reduced irrigation has led to decreased recharge of local water tables, declining crop yields and rural depopulation (El Amami, 1983).

Thus, even though the annual increase in agricultural activity between 1975 and 1985 was 5.5 per cent in the Kairouan Plain, compared to 3.6 per cent for Tunisia as a whole (Ministère de l'Économie, 1986), the spatial distribution of the development was very uneven and so too was the social distribution. Modern developments and state structural adjustment policies have favoured large landowners and produced a notable land distribution problem: the bottom 46 per cent of landholders possess only 8 per cent of land, whilst the top 3 per cent own 35 per cent (King, 1999).

Modern large-scale hydraulic works are symbols of prestige and development acquired since Independence (Oosterbaun, 1985; Barrow, 1987). With such gigantism comes planning and management that are dominated by politicians and engineers, minimizing decision-making by agricultural producers. In part, there is evidence of the hydraulic society proposed by Wittfogel (1957), as there is certainly an imposition of organization and decisions, but these frameworks are far from despotic. Local knowledge concerning water management and conservation is utilized by central policy, but only at the field level (through tillage, irrigation, fertilizing and crop rotation), not across the wider hydrological landscape. Surface water and groundwater are no longer used conjunctively across land units, yet this level of integration is crucial to long-term viability of water resources as it helps redress the disequilibria of regional water imbalances.

Reviewing sustainability

The efficiency of minor hydraulic works in southern Tunisia is currently being maintained, but a crucial development has reduced sustainability in the north: the abandonment of community based indigenous knowledge, which demonstrated physical and social adaptability to a dynamic and often extreme environment. Adaptability is the precursor to reliability and it is under threat in large-scale developments. Such developments possess rigid physical and social structures that are not easily adapted to the vagaries of climate. Modern large-scale developments have provided no more reliability over space and time than earlier small-scale works and they often result in less irrigated land per unit of water stored. Over long time frames modern developments are more susceptible to extreme events than community works. The only difference is that modern dam developments can provide short-term yield maximization but this requires greater volumes of water leading to insidious environmental degradation.

These findings imply that water is not just a physical resource; it also impinges upon socio-cultural and economic arenas (Table 12.2) and all of these must be considered to some extent within sustainability debates.

Table 12.2   Reviewing sustainability of the contrasting water management techniques

Technique	Review	
	Advantages	Disadvantages
Rainwater harvesting Ecological	Reciprocal link between surface water and groundwater Integration of hydrology across land units Water use to meet community needs Reduction of slope instability, soil erosion and flash flooding Reduction of soil waterlogging and salinization Long-term security of water and harvests Tempers extreme events Carrying capacity defined by nature	
Socio-cultural	Promotes equitable water distribution Irrigates large areas collectively Maintains indigenous knowledge Provides local employment Decentralized, allowing community autonomy Allows flexibility in a dynamic, often extreme, environment	Fragmented landholdings due to tenure and landscape Effort in construction and maintenance Threat of rural depopulation due to forces of modernization
Economic	Cheap, using local materials and labour Economic benefits remain in the community	Little contribution to national economy. To do so would require development of infrastructure and markets
Dam irrigation Ecological	Careful irrigation can raise productivity in localized areas	Water use surplus to community needs Depletes aquifers Soil erosion in upper catchment and salinization in lower catchment Poor long term security of water and harvests Succumbs to extreme events Carrying capacity defined by society

Socio-cultural	Reduces devastating single peak floods Produces highly productive yields in the short term	Central decision-making fosters dependence on exogenous forces Relatively small areas irrigated Uneven spatial and social distribution of water Inflexible within a dynamic, often extreme, environment Threat of depopulation in upper catchments
Economic	Integration into global markets Collective/nuclear ownership means plot rationalisation	Expensive to construct and maintain engineering and agricultural infrastructure

The future: Combining traditional and modern approaches for sustainability

The aim of the contrasting water management techniques described in this chapter is to equilibrate spatio-temporal inequalities in water resources. Rainwater harvesting stores water in the root zone below the catchment during wet seasons to cover water requirements throughout growing seasons, whilst large dams store water above ground within the catchment to overcome annual and inter-annual deficiencies. There is a precarious equilibrium, however, dividing hydrological hazards and resources in Tunisia. Traditional management was able to physically partition the continuum between hazards and resources in favour of the latter through construction of jessour systems. Thus, a potentially hazardous environment of slope instability, flash flooding (*sensu* Graf, 1988), soil erosion and drought was transformed into a secure environment by resourceful management. It was achieved by subtle manipulation of the landscape at micro and local scales using trial and error practical experience and drawing upon a community memory that allowed prediction of future success or failure. Collective community action and cumulative knowledge allowed high reliability farming akin to that noted within pastoralist communities (Roe *et al.*, 1998). The environments are not perceived as risk-laden and therefore 'critical' but as reliable (Kasperson *et al.*, 1996, 1999; van Steenbergen, 1997). The communities demonstrate a history of sustained production in difficult environments and it is likely that such adaptability and flexibility will continue to sustain agriculture into the future, if it can survive the threats of modernization via new settlements and the lure of employment in the service sector of major cities.

Future socio-economic development in Tunisia will require the mobilization of water resources to meet demands from several sectors. Forecasts (Table 12.3) indicate that agriculture will remain the largest consumer of water followed by the domestic, industrial, and tourism sectors. The agricultural sector demand is expected to peak in 2010, and to decrease thereafter as water-conservation measures are consolidated.

An anticipated doubling of water consumption by the tourist industry by the year 2030 is linked to tourism development in coastal urban areas, especially around the resorts of Hammamet and Djerba. Industrial consumption is also expected to double over the same period, concentrated in the industrial centres of Sfax, Gafsa and Tunis (Bahri, undated). Improved socio-economic conditions of low-income groups and rural communities' access to drinking water will lead to a growth in demand for drinking water and sewage services. The forecast of water requirements are inexact, however, because they depend upon future economic and demographic trends.

Table 12.3   Projected future annual water demand by sector from a 1996 base-line (mm^3 yr^{-1})

Year	1996	2010	2020	2030
Agriculture	2115	2141	2082	2035
Domestic (urban & rural)	290	381	438	491
Industry	104	136	164	203
Tourism	19	31	36	41
Total	2528	2689	2720	2770

Source: Ministère de l'Agriculture (1998)

Tunisia's 10th Economic and Development Plan (which runs from 2002 until 2006) continues to promulgate the mobilization of water resources via a comprehensive system of large and small dams, and improved connectivity between surface and groundwater reservoirs within and between basins to supply inland areas with water from the north of the country (Ministry of Development and International Cooperation, 2002). However, as highlighted here, Tunisia's management of water resources cannot be based simply on the impoundment and mobilization of water from the north to the arid south. Demands for water will continue to increase and, without sustainable use, it is estimated that the country's water resources will be exhausted by 2020 (Geissner, 1998). The time for action is running out, and clear prerogatives are needed, followed by their application.

Across Tunisia, therefore, new waves of proactive water conservation measures are being implemented. Tunisia's submission to the Rio +10 conference (Ministry of Environment and Land Use Planning, 2001: 56), for example, cites the implementation of 'works aimed at water and soil conservation (treatment of slopes with water-retention systems, structures for spreading and mobilizing flood waters, 'jessours', etc.)'. One such example is a soil and water conservation programme, centred in the Governorats of Kairouan, Siliana and Zaghouan, which began in 2000. The project exemplifies the balance that can be achieved between large-scale centralized development and small-scale decentralized management based on modernized indigenous technology and undertaken with local participation. The programme is managed jointly by the Directorate for Water and Soil Conservation of the Tunisian Ministry of Agriculture, the United Nations' Food and Agriculture Organization and the Italian Government. The programme's specific objectives are to ensure the sustainable management of natural resources over the long term, to strengthen the active participation of local people and to develop partnerships between the local population, technical services, the local administration and non-governmental organizations (FAO, undated). The programme has encouraged an increased uptake of field-scale water harvesting methods and it has helped local farmers to create a network of small hillside dams to collect surface runoff, a technique which began to be introduced at a national scale during the 1990s. The programme makes local people proactive and autonomous in the pursuit of local sustainable development and it engenders in them a sense of ownership within natural resource management. Dependency is replaced by empowerment, as local people have the ability to make decisions and to take some actions to secure their future. Clearly, the future viability of modern dam developments depends largely on such diffuse management of the surrounding hillside catchments.

By 2001, as part of this programme, 586 small reservoirs and 224 small hilltop dams had been completed throughout Tunisia (Ministry of Environment and Land Use Planning, 2001). These second generation works have reduced siltation rates in the large dams and, through basal seepage into sand, replenished local aquifers (Grünberger *et al.*, 1999; Montoroi *et al.*, 2001). This encourages rural populations to remain settled as the groundwater reserves help reduce the risks of crop cultivation in an unpredictable environment. The process of water development in the centre of the country appears to be coming full circle with a return to small-scale management to complement and sustain the large-scale hydraulic works. Such a dovetailing of different scales and technologies, integrated under a national planning structure, promotes a controlled but flexible approach to water management. This is crucial to long-term viability as it does not simply absorb indigenous expertise, but allows local voices to be heard in terms of hydrological and financial requirements (Richards, 1985; Frost, 1987; Agnew & Anderson, 1992). The benefits of water and soil conservation measures were clearly demonstrated during a period of drought between 1998 and 2002. Despite a downturn in agricultural productivity, the impact of the drought might have been worse had it not been for the water and soil conservation measures implemented in the preceding period (OECD, 2004).

Overwatering of arable crops by irrigation has been tackled assertively by sectoral reforms which include adjustments to water tariffs and the implementation of financial incentives to encourage farmers to adopt new irrigation technologies. Tunisia has embraced a new irrigation policy which gradually shifts water management responsibilities and costs to local water user associations (WUAs). Via public water-saving programmes and incentives, farmers are encouraged to adopt low-pressure drip or sprinkler irrigation or to modernize their irrigation equipment. Depending on farm size, farmers receive a subsidy for between 40 per cent and 60 per cent of the cost of new equipment (Vidal, 2001). Water savings of 25 per cent have been reported (Vidal, 2001), but the capacity of farmers to finance new irrigation technologies and their willingness to participate in WUAs is a key constraint to water conservation (Vidal, 2001). Stronger financial incentives through water pricing and the allocation of use rights to WUAs are expected to enhance the future uptake of water-saving irrigation technologies.

In southern Tunisia, it is important to support production from rainwater harvesting as competition for water increases across the country between industrial, domestic and agricultural uses (World Bank, 1996). Emphasis must be removed from the use of the central overflow and lateral overflows must be restored. These are well known to local families and are more easily managed by them. This would safeguard sustainable use of the highlands, promoting soil and water conservation *in situ* (Missaoui, 1996), and it would protect the piedmont against floods and erosion.

The sustainable management of artesian water is particularly pertinent given its increased consumption from the North-Western Sahara Aquifer System (NWSAS) by Algeria and Tunisia over the past 50 years. The NWSAS covers 1,000,000 km^2 of which 700,000 km^2 are in Algeria, 80,000 km^2 are in Tunisia and 250,000 km^2 lie in Libya. Present estimates of annual water extraction amount to 540 hm^3 in Tunisia, 1,100 hm^3 in Algeria and 250 hm^3 in Libya; 90 per cent of this water is used for agriculture (UNESCO, 2005). The aquifer is therefore a trans-border resource whose sustainable management requires an internationally co-operative approach. A programme to achieve this began in 1999 as a response to chapter 12 of Agenda 21 and article 16 of the United Nations Convention to Combat Desertification, which required improved environmental monitoring in Africa that would better inform decision-makers and stakeholders. The programme is managed by the *Observatoire du Sahara et du Sahel* (OSS), an independent international organization composed of African and European countries and which is based in Tunis. Its aims are to combat desertification and attenuate the effects of drought via two axes: environmental monitoring and shared management of water resources. Although the OSS NWSAS programme is directed principally at combating desertification, it is highly pertinent to sustainable water use for agriculture. The primary objective of the programme is to strengthen information sharing between the three countries so that the state of the aquifer is comprehensively understood. Based on this information, models containing scenarios based on socio-economic data for 2050 may be used as a basis for tripartite consultations for sustainable exploitation of the water reserves within the NWSAS. The programme aims to promote 'basin awareness' that favours rational joint management of shared water resources and it aims to encourage countries to implement community management tools and strategies to optimize water utilization and guarantee conditions required for food security.

Tunisia has also created associations of underground water users to conserve irrigation water drawn from shallow aquifers (Vidal, 2001). A water sector investment programme (*PISEAU*), which is financed with the assistance of international and bilateral agencies, has made the development of new underground water contingent on the setting up of such organizations. This is a recent development and it is too early to assess whether local water user associations are managing aquifers in a sustainable manner.

Reforms within the water sector are only one of several measures required to safeguard the sustainable management of water resources. To allocate water more equally, land distribution and ownership need addressing via a structural change policy that can redistribute land and push private ownership beyond the 90 per cent figure at which it presently stands (World Bank, 1996; Zaibet & Dunn, 1998). The Ministry of Agriculture is currently defining a land consolidation programme and a plan for land exchange that would result in larger parcels. Price support for agriculture also needs reviewing. Irrigated agriculture receives a water price subsidy of 20 per cent to 30 per cent of its real exploitation cost, a figure that amounted to TD 52 million in 1996 (World Bank, 1996). Water prices should be reviewed to cover not only the direct operating and maintenance costs of supply, distribution and management, but also to cover the capital costs of investment. Such price realignment should encourage more rational use and reduce individual wastage in the intensively cultivated northern areas, but politically they are difficult to implement (Vidal, 2001). In the south of the country, care must be exercised when promoting rain-fed cash cropping as there is a risk that years of good rainfall may coincide with high market prices for crops, tempting farmers to overstress the land (Barrow, 1988).

Programmes must be developed that disseminate information concerning water supplies, increase public awareness and encourage training and research. Such information must filter from senior management, through regional staff, to the general agricultural public. There are reported incidences where water saving programmes have not focused sufficiently on training farmers in the optimum use of equipment. This means that the introduction of new techniques, such as drip irrigation, do not result in significant water savings. Furthermore, the use of brackish or salty water has often clogged irrigation equipment (Vidal, 2001).

Economic and social development in Tunisia has, in the past, compromised the country's water supplies. A key policy objective of the Tunisian government remains to promote integrated development that will reduce rural depopulation and encourage rural development. This will require not only improvement in the supply of domestic water, which is less than 70 per cent in rural areas (Vidal, 2001), but also the sustainable exploitation of water resources. The signs are that nationally the value of small-scale traditional water management is again being accepted. This must be supported in the south, to maintain rural populations, and it must be redeveloped in the north to complement the modern dam developments. Across the country, the environmental, economic and socio-cultural sustainability of traditional methods can help to reduce the negative impacts caused by inappropriate modern programmes and augment their positive impacts. Indeed, a mix of modern and traditional methods, integrating international negotiation across territories and local participatory community management, seems to have been acknowledged as the practical foundation to sustainable water supply in the new millennium.

248 *Sustainable Development*

References

Agnew, C. & Anderson, E. (1992) *Water Resources in the Arid Realm*. Routledge, London.

Baba Sy, M.O. & Besbès, M. (2001) Dam-aquifer multisystem modelling for the Wadi Merguellil basin, Tunisia. *IAHS-AISH Publication*, 269, 135-138.

Baban, S.M.J., Foster, I.D.L. & Tarmiz, B. (1999) Environmental Protection and Sustainable Development in Tunisia: an overview. *Sustainable Development*, 7, 191-203.

Bahri, A. (undated) *Water Resources Development and Management In Tunisia.* National Research Institute for Agricultural Engineering, Waters and Forestry, Ariana, Tunisia.

Barrow, C.J. (1987) *Water Resources and Agricultural Development in the Tropics*. Longman, Harlow.

Barrow, C.J. (1988) The present position and future development of rain-fed agriculture in the tropics. *Outlook on Agriculture*, 17, 112-119.

Barrow, C.J. (1999) *Alternative Irrigation. The Promise of Runoff Agriculture*. Earthscan Publications Limited, London.

Ben Mammou, A. (1997) Identification et caracterisation geotechnique des sediments de retenues des barrages de Tunisie. *Bulletin – International Association of Engineering Geology*, 55, 65-76.

Besbès, M. (1978) *L'inventaire des ressources en eaux souterraines de la Tunisie centrale.* Unpublished PhD thesis, Université Pierre et Marie Curie, Paris.

Boers, Th. M., De Graaf, M., Feddes, R.A. & Ben-Asher, J. (1986a) A linear regression model combined with a soil water balance model to design micro-catchments for water harvesting in arid zones. *Agricultural Water Management*, 11, 187-206.

Boers, Th. M., Zondervan, K. & Ben-Asher, J. (1986b) *Micro-Catchment-Water-Harvesting (MCWH) for arid zone development*. Agricultural Water Management, 12, 21-39.

Bonvallot, J. (1979) Comportement des ouvrages de petite hydraulique dans la région de Médenine (Tunisie du sud) au cours des pluies exceptionelles de mars 1979. *Cahiers ORSTOM Série Sciences Humaines*, 16, 233-249.

Bonvallot, J. (1986) Tabias et jessour du sud Tunisien: agriculture dans les zones marginales et parade à l'érosion. *Cahiers ORSTOM Série Pédologie*, 22, 163-171.

Brierley, G.J. (1981) The wadis of the Sousse region, central Tunisia. In Harris, R. & Lawless, R.I. (eds) *Field Studies in Tunisia*. University of Durham, pp. 4-16.

Bruins, H.J., Evenari, M. & Nessler, U. (1986) Rainwater harvesting agriculture for food production in arid zones: the challenges of African famine. *Applied Geography*, 6, 13-32.

Chahbani, B. (1984) *Contribution à l'étude de l'érosion hydrique des loess des Matmatas et de la destruction des jessour.* Bassin versant de l'Oued Demmer, Beni Kheddache, Sud Tunisien. Unpublished PhD thesis, University of Paris (Panthéon-Sorbonne).

Connelly, J. & Smith, G. (1999) *Politics and the Environment*; from Theory to Practice. Routledge, London.

Coudé-Gaussen, G. & Rognon, P. (1988) The Upper Pleistocene loess of southern Tunisia: a statement. *Earth Surface Processes and Landforms*, 13, 137-151.

Cruette, J., Rodier, J.A., Dubée, G. & Gaulde, R. (1971) Mesures de débits de l'Oued Zeroud pendant les crues exceptionnelles de l'automne 1969. *Cahier ORSTOM Série Hydrologie*, 13, 33-64.

Dearing, J., Livingstone, I. & Zhou, L.P. (1996) A late Quaternary magnetic record of Tunisian loess and its climatic significance. *Geophysical Research Letters*, 23,189-192.

Dillman, B. (2001) Facing the market in North Africa. *Middle East Journal*, 55, 198-215.

Egger, U. (1990) The performance of the agrarian sector in Tunisia: an indicator system to measure the performance of agrarian strategies. *Quarterly Journal of International Agriculture*, 29, 132-145.

El Amami, S. (1983) Changing concepts of water management in Tunisia. *Impact of Science on Society*, 1, 57-64.

El Amami, S. (1986) Traditional versus modern irrigation methods in Tunisia. In Goldsmith, E. & Hildyard, N. (eds) *The Social and Environmental Effects of Large Dams*. Volume 2. Wadebridge Ecological Centre, Cornwall, pp. 184-188.

FAO (undated) *Soil and water conservation programme in the Gouvernorats of Kairouan, Siliana and Zaghouan 200-2005*. Http://www.fao.org/tc/tcdm/italy/op_tun028_en.asp?lang=en. Accessed 24/1/06.

Fersi, M. (1978) *Dossier pluviométrique de Matmata*. DRES, Tunis.

Frankenberg, P. (1980) Evapotranspiration, bilan de l'eau et variabilité des précipitations en Tunisie en relation avec l'agriculture. *Méditerranée*, 40, 49-55.

Frost, D.H. (1987) *Developing water resources in low rainfall areas*. Conference on Developing World Water. Grosvenor International, London.

Geissner, K. (1998) Wasserhaushalt in Tunesien. *Geographische Rundschau*, 50, 414-421.

Gharbi, M. (1998) Terres privees, collectives et domaniales en Tunisie. *Land Reform Land Settlement and Cooperatives*, 1, 82-92.

Golany, G.S. (1988) *Earth Sheltered dwellings in Tunisia. Ancient Lessons for Modern Design*. University of Delaware Press, Newark.

Graf, W.L. (1988) *Fluvial Processes in Dryland Rivers*. Springer-Verlag, London.

Grünberger, O., Montoroi, J-P. & Albergel, J. (1999) *Evaluation par bilan isotopique de la recharge d'un aquifère induite par le fonctionnement d'une retenue collinaire. Premiers résultats sur le site d'El Gouazine (Tunisie centrale)*. Volume des abstracts, Colloque International sur l'apport de la Géochimie Isotopique dans le Cycle de l'Eau. ENIS, Hammamet, Tunisie, 6-8 avril, pp. 52-53.

Guillaud, C. & Trabelsi, M. (1991) Gestion des resources hydriques en Tunisie centrale: les projets Sidi Saad et El Haoureb. *Hydrology for the Water Management of Large River Basins*. Proceedings of the Vienna Symposium, August 1991. IAHS Publication, 201, 129-138.

Hill, J.L. & Woodland, W.A. (2003) Contrasting water management techniques in Tunisia: towards sustainable agricultural use. *Geographical Journal*, 169, 342-357.

Kasperson, J.X., Kasperson, R.E. & Turner II, B.L. (1996) Regions at risk: exploring environmental criticality. *Environment*, 38, 4-15.

Kasperson, R.E., Kasperson, J.X.. & Turner II, B.L. (1999) Risk and criticality: Trajectories of regional environmental degradation. *Ambio*, 28, 562-568.

Kassab, A. (1981) L'agriculture Tunisienne sur la voie de l'intensification. A*nnales de Geographie*, 497, 55-86.

King, S.J. (1999) Structural adjustment and rural poverty in Tunisia. *Middle East Report*, 210, 41-43.

Marten, G.G. (2001) *Human Ecology: Basic concepts for Sustainable Development*. Earthscan, London.

Martín Castellanos, A.J. (1996) Las políticas de regadíos en los países del Magreb dentro de la estrategia de desarrollo agrario. *Noticiario de Historia Agraria*, 11, 111-130.

Ministère de l'Agriculture (1998) Stratégie du secteur de l'eau en Tunisie à long terme (2030). *Eau XXI*. Ministère de l'Agriculture, Tunis.

Ministry of Environment and Land Use Planning (2001) *National Report on Tunisia's achievements in the area of sustainable development and in implementing Agenda 21*. Ministry of Environment and Land Use Planning, Tunis.

Ministry of Development and International Cooperation (2002) *The Tenth Plan in Brief* 2002-2006. Ministry of Development and International Cooperation, Tunis.

Ministère de l' Économie (1986) *Activités Économiques – Gouvernorat de Kairouan*. Ministère de l' Économie, Tunis.

Montoroi, J-P., Grünberger, O. & Nasri, S. (2001) *Hydrochemical behaviour of waters in a Tunisian hill reservoir watershed and reservoir impact on alluvial aquifer*. Recueil des résumés, Séminaire International 'Les petits barrages dans le monde méditerranéen'. Tunis, Tunisia, 28-31 May.

OECD (2004) *African Economic Outlook: Tunisia*. OECD, France.

Oosterbaun, R.J. (1985) Modern water control systems for agriculture in developing countries. In Mock, J.F. (ed.) *Symposium on Man and Technology in Irrigated Agriculture*.

Overman, M. (1976) *Water: Solutions to a Problem of Supply and Demand*. Open University Press, Milton Keynes.

Pacey, A. & Cullis, A. (1986) *Rainwater Harvesting: the collection of rainfall and runoff in rural areas*. Intermediate Technology Publications, London.

Paniconi, C., Khlaifi, I., Lecca, G., Giacomelli, A., & Tarhouni, J. (2001) Modelling and analysis of seawater intrusion in the coastal aquifer of eastern Cap Bon, Tunisia. *Transport in Porous Media*, 43, 3-28.

Missaoui, H. (1996) Soil and Water conservation in Tunisia. In Pereira, L.S., Feddes, R.A., Gilley, J.R. & Lesaffre, B. (eds) *Sustainability of Irrigated Agriculture*. Proceedings of the NATO Advanced Research Workshop, Vimeiro, Portugal, 21-

26 March, 1994. Kluwer Academic Publishers, Dordrecht, Netherlands, pp. 121-135.

Rapp, A. & Hasteen-Dahlin, A. (1990) Improved management of drylands by water harvesting in Third World countries. In Boardman, J., Foster, I.D.L. & Dearing, J.A. (eds) *Soil Erosion on Agricultural Land.* Wiley, New York, pp. 495-511.

Richards, P. (1985) *Indigenous Agricultural Revolution: Ecology and Food Production in West Africa.* Hutchinson, London.

Roe, E., Huntsinger, L. & Labnow, K. (1998) High reliability pastoralism. *Journal of Arid Environments*, 39, 39-55.

Shah, N. (1994) Arab labour migration: a review of trends and issues. *International Migration*, 32, 3-28.

Simmons, I.G. (1997) *Humanity and Environment: A Cultural Ecology.* Longman, Essex.

Van Steenbergen, F. (1997) Understanding the sociology of spate irrigation: cases from Balochistan. *Journal of Arid Environments*, 35, 349-365.

Tabor, J.A. (1995) Improving crop yields in the Sahel by means of water-harvesting. *Journal of Arid Environments*, 30, 83-106.

UNESCO (2005) *Presentation du SASS (aquifer programme).* UNESCO Publishing.

Vidal, A. (2001) *Case studies on water conservation in the Mediterranean region.* International Programme for Technology and Research in Irrigation and Drainage. Food and Agriculture Organization of the United Nations, Rome.

Withers, B. & Vipond, S. (1988) *Irrigation Design and Practice.* Batsford, London.

Wittfogel, K.A. (1957) *Oriental Despotism – A Comparative Study of Total Power.* Yale University Press, New Haven.

World Bank (1996) *Tunisia's Global Integration and sustainable Development: Strategic Choices for the 21st Century.* Middle East and North Africa Economic Studies, World Bank, Washington.

World Resources Institute (2003) *Country Profile – Tunisia. Http://earthtrends.wri. org/pdf_library/country-profile/ene_con_788.pdf.* Accessed 24/1/06.

Zahar, Y. (2001) L'estimation probabiliste des durées de service futures des barrages en Tunisie. Essai de caractérisation et proposition d'une formule régionale. *Revue Internationalle de l'Eau*, 1, 71-80.

Zaibet, L.T. & Dunn, E.G. (1998) Land tenure, farm size and rural market participation in developing countries: the case of the Tunisian olive sector. *Economic Development and Cultural Change*, 46, 831-848.

Chapter 13

Managing Indonesia's Marine Resources: the Role of Indigenous Communities

Alan Terry and Samantha Shepherd

Introduction

Between 1970 and 1995 the number of people engaged in the worldwide fishing industry increased from 13 million to an estimated 30 million, more than 95 per cent living in the developing world (FAO, 1997). Total world marine fish production rose from 20 million tonnes in 1950 to between 85 and 90 million tonnes per annum in the 1990s, since when it appears to have levelled out. It is estimated that 70 per cent of marine species that are commercially exploited have reached or exceeded sustainable annual catch levels (FAO, 1997). In some fisheries, such as the Newfoundland Grand Banks cod fishery, over-fishing had made stocks commercially extinct (Kurlansky, 1997). These pressures have been interpreted by many as the consequences of the 'tragedy of the commons' (Hardin, 1968). Hardin concludes that in the absence of limits to an open access resource such as a fishery, individual fishing units have no incentive to limit their catches because by so doing, they will forego individual gain. Further, individual restraint will be futile because it will enable others to take what they have tried to conserve. This logic encourages competition, which leads to the inevitable decline in stocks. To prevent this, Hardin's supporters emphasize the need for limits on fishing administered by independent agencies. Hardin's neo-Malthusianism approach '… was widely taken in policy and academic circles to be an argument against local customary management of resources and in favour of privatization and outside intervention' (Neumann, 2005: 27).

The universal validity of Hardin's model has been challenged by empirical research from a wide range of cultures, environments and production systems. These suggest that many of the assumptions underlying it are over-simplistic and fail to take into account the institutional arrangements that have arisen where many users share a single resource (Blaikie, 1985; Hecht, 1985; Cordell, 1987; Berkes, 1989; Jentoft & McCay, 1996; Ruddle, 1998; Burke, 2001). Where such arrangements exist, they are based on customary law and are characterized as being grounded in complex social relationships within communities. Thus, fishers may be responsible for controlling access to the resource and in these circumstances fish should not be viewed as an open access resource, the crux of Hardin's theory. In such systems, regulations tend to be unwritten and require mutual respect for the rules by all those who depend upon the resource (Ostrom, 1990; Cleaver, 2000). However, the seabed has commonly been viewed as an open access resource throughout much of Indonesia (UNEP, 2004) and in these circumstances, Malthusian pressures may give rise to the 'tragedy' (Pet-Soede & Erdmann, 1999; Jackson *et al.*, 2001).

This chapter presents a case study of the fishing practices and management of marine resources by the Bajau community of the Tukangbesi Archipelago off the south-east corner of Sulawesi, Indonesia. The aim of the chapter is to analyse the evolution of Indonesia's environmental policy with respect to marine resources since the 1992 United Nations (UN) Conference on Environment and Development. The chapter highlights the increased role that 'the community' is supposed to play, as set out in Agenda 21, in improving management of these resources and it analyses the moves towards a more inclusive model in the context of the Wakatobi Marine National Park. To what extent have the ideals, as set out by Indonesia in a variety of environmental plans since the 1992 UN Conference on Environment and Development, been achieved by the Park's managers and what, if any, are the factors that undermine the objectives of a more sustainable use of the resources which are found within the Park? In other words, has the attempt to hand back some control to indigenous resource users from the central control exercised by government agencies helped to improve the sustainability of the marine resources that the Marine National Park was set up to protect?

The Indonesian marine environment

The archipelago of Indonesia is the largest in the world, extending over a distance of approximately 5,000 km by 2,000 km, containing approximately 20,000 islands and with 100,000 km of coastline (Indonesian Draft National Action Plan: Working Group for the Coral Reef Sub-Component, 2004). National sovereignty extends to 5.8 million km^2, three times that of the land surface. Indonesia contains five distinct marine ecosystems, from coral reefs to sea grass beds and mangrove swamps, and it includes the highest marine biodiversity in the world (BAPPENAS, 1993; Warren-Rhodes *et al.*, 2003) resulting in its designation as a zone of mega-biodiversity by Conservation International (2005). For example, Indonesia has 37 per cent of the world's fish species (National Environmental Action Plan (1998-2001), 1997). The coral reefs contain over 90 per cent of the world's coral species, with 82 genera and 590 species of scleractinian corals being found in the region (Veron, 2000; Warren-Rhodes *et al.*, 2003).

This environment is vital to the livelihoods of a large proportion of Indonesia's 215 million people as 93 per cent live within the coastal zone, defined as within 100 km of the coastline (Shi & Singh, 2003). Of these, 41 million live on the coast and about half of them live in coastal villages and are dependent upon their local coastal resources for their livelihoods. The FAO (2000) stated that 2.5 million people were engaged in capture fisheries and 2.2 million in aquaculture in 1996. Ninety per cent of the industry was classified as small-scale (FAO, 2000). It is estimated that population will rise to 276 million by 2020, with coastal populations growing at twice the national average (UNEP, 2004). Pressures upon the marine and coastal resources also arise from the wider region. Warren-Rhodes *et al.* (2003: 482) estimate that 'In SE Asia, total seafood demand is about four times the sustainable total production theoretically available from coral reefs in the region'. This over-exploitation arises mainly from China and illustrates how external market forces are impacting upon marine biodiversity and undermining Indonesian commercial and semi-subsistence fisheries. Concerns exist over destructive fishing methods, such as the use of cyanide in the live reef fish trade which is non-selective and is believed to kill coral (Warren-Rhodes *et al.*, 2003); the widespread use of explosives, which increases as competition for dwindling fish stocks increases; and muro-ami (reef breakage to drive fish into nets) (DeVantier *et al.*, 2004). It is estimated that up to 50 per cent of Indonesia's reefs have been degraded and 85 per cent are threatened by human activities such as coastal development, over-fishing and marine based pollution (Burke *et al.*, 2002). They estimate that the reefs of Indonesia provide annual economic benefits of $US 1.6 billion but that over the next twenty years, over-fishing, destructive fishing and sedimentation could cost $US 2.6 billion. However, DeVantier *et al.* (2004: 92) state that 'At present neither status nor future viability of the fisheries are well understood ... and ... For many fisheries their status may be summarized as being: Illegal, Unreported and Unregulated'. Not only is the scale of fishing likely to change, but it is expected that a shift will occur from subsistence towards commercial fishing. 'The rapidly increasing population, level of poverty, greater commercialization, decline in resources, lack of effective regulation and poor to non-existent enforcement is expected to cause significant future deterioration' (DeVantier *et al.*, 2004: 93). This increase is, in part, related to government policy. Since the economic crash of 1997, the Directorate General of Fisheries (DGF) has launched PROTEKAN 2003 (Boosting the Export of Fisheries Commodities) which was designed to increase fisheries production and aqua-culture and to deregulate some fisheries policies (Directorate General of Fisheries, undated). The DGF estimated that the rate of exploitation of fishing in Indonesian waters was only 57 per cent of its potential and it envisaged a further 26,600 fishing vessels added to the fleet between 1997 and 2003, employing an additional 828,000 people. The marine environment was therefore considered as an economic safety valve to compensate for the fall in employment and incomes that accompanied the 1997 crash. Between 1994 and 2000, landings of all types of fish from Indonesian boats rose by 4.16 per cent per annum to 4.36 million tons (Ministry of Maritime and Fishery, undated). Although the Ministry of Maritime and Fishery's second policy objective is for 'constraint-based development which means every development activity in the coastal area needs to fulfil sustainable development criteria' (Ministry of Maritime and Fishery, undated: 2), economic necessity seems to be pushing government policy into increasing substantially the pressure on maritime resources. Thus, the scale and complexity of the problems facing Indonesia's environmental regulatory bodies provides a huge challenge for those who must ensure that its marine resources continue to maintain their biodiversity and livelihood functions. This pressure varies with the highest rates of exploitation in the west, the eastern areas having more potential to increase output.

The management of fisheries resources is based upon fish quotas. The total allowable catch (TAC) is set at 80 per cent of the estimated potential yield which is 6.2 million tons per year. Thus, in theory, the total catch in 2000 (4.36 million tons) was 88 per cent of this 'sustainable' TAC level (4.96 million tons), although this contradicts other findings which show that the pelagic fish catch is above the TAC (United Nations, 1997). Further, the FAO predict that if fish consumption per capita is to be maintained, given Indonesia's predicted doubling of population within 25 years, the demand for fish would rise to over 8 million tons per annum, which is 'far beyond the potential yield of marine fish resources' (FAO, 2000: 4). If population rose to a more conservative 276 million by 2020, this 31 per cent rise would, if per capita fish consumption remained the same, still lead to a rise in demand to 5.63 million tons per annum, well above the TAC.

Although some of this expected increase in fish consumption can be made up by the development of aquaculture, this is not without problems. For example, shrimp cultivation has led to the destruction of large areas of mangrove, whilst intensive fisheries create further demand for capture fish. They also create pollution problems that adversely affect coral reefs and other marine resources. However, as we shall see in the case study, some methods are more benign and they may be able to address some of the problems caused by over-exploitation.

Indonesian marine environmental planning

Marine conservation began with the formation of the Directorate of Marine Conservation within the Department of Forestry in 1981. The system of marine protected areas began in 1982; their aim is to contribute towards marine sustainability (Alder et al., 1994). The first national conservation plan was compiled in 1982, but it did not include marine protected areas until revision between 1993 and 1995. Coincidentally, two other strategies were developed. In 1989, the Office of the State Minister for Population and Environment compiled the National Strategy for Management of Biological Diversity, with a follow up Country Study on Biodiversity in 1992, prepared for the 1992 UN Conference on Environment and Development. In 1993, the National Development Planning Agency (BAPPENAS) published the National Biological Diversity Action Plan (NBAP). In 1995-96 The State Ministry of Environment and KONPHALINDO, an environment and development NGO published *An Atlas of Biodiversity in Indonesia* summarizing the status of Indonesia's biodiversity, its significance, measures taken to conserve it and the constraints faced. Indonesia also ratified major environmental conventions of which 'by far the most strategic international treaty ratified by Indonesia is the UN Convention on the Law of the Sea (UNCLOS), which ... contains provisions ... to protect and conserve fragile marine ecosystems and threatened marine life' (National Environmental Action Plan (1998-2001), 1997: 477).

Since the United Nations Rio Convention in 1992, Indonesia has developed Agenda 21-Indonesia. This is a 'comprehensive national strategy for sustainable development' (National Environmental Action Plan (NEAP) (1998-2001), 1997: 3) and is used 'as a reference for planning and programme implementation' (NEAP, 1997: 4). This has four sections; Human Services; Waste Management; Land Resource Management and finally Natural Resource Management. The final section deals with the biodiversity convention and marine and coastal zone management, the focus of this chapter. The intention was to produce 'an important reference for developing and implementing the Seventh Five-Year Development Plan...the Second Long-Term (25 Year) Development Plan, as well as other sectoral and regional planning documents' (NEAP, 1997: 4). In theory therefore, since 1997 sustainable development has become a central element in all aspects of central and local government planning.

Because of this multiple track approach, no specific agency has overall responsibility to manage biodiversity, although the State Ministry of Environment coordinates policies. With respect to marine resources, the responsible national authorities include the Directorate General of Forest Protection and Nature Conservation (PHPA) who manage protected areas, including Marine National Parks, and the National Development Planning Agency (BAPPENAS) who supervise particular programmes such as COREMAP which seeks to protect and improve the management of coral reefs. The other authority that deals with Marine Protected Areas is the Ministry of Marine Affairs. However, despite the fact that by 1997 Indonesia was one of the few countries in the world to have completed a national study, management strategy and national action plan as required by the UN Convention on Biological Diversity (1992), both terrestrial and marine resources have continued to be degraded.

A further complication arises from the fact that fisheries administration is under the control of the Directorate General of Fisheries (DGF) and Provincial and Regional Fisheries services. Local fisheries are the responsibility of the local Governor at provincial level and the Head of District or Mayor at the district or municipal level. These regional authorities are under the control of the Department of Home Affairs who receive technical guidance from the DGF (FAO, 2000).

The objective of sustainable biodiversity management is based upon resource carrying capacity, community participation, equitable sharing of benefits and a holistic knowledge system. These broad principles are developed within the National Biological Diversity Action Plan (NPAP) as *in situ* conservation in protected areas, *in situ* conservation in non-protected areas, conservation of marine and coastal ecosystems and *ex situ* conservation. This has been modified into five Programme Areas in the Agenda 21-Indonesia document:

1. Programme 1: (in situ conservation in protected areas): the prevention of degradation
2. Programme 2: (in situ conservation in non protected areas): biodiversity in agro-ecosystems
3. Programme 3: (ex situ conservation): breeding of species and preservation of gene pools.

The first three programmes '...cannot be conducted without knowledge of conservation and the sustainable utilization of biodiversity. Such knowledge is often linked to traditional systems which are currently being eroded' (National Environmental Action Plan (1998-2001), 1997: 478). This explains the remaining Programmes:

4. Programme 4: The protection of traditional knowledge systems
5. Programme 5: The development of a sustainable utilization system where the sharing of benefits is one of the most important components.

The outcome was supposed to be that 'by the twenty-first century, a national movement in sustainable management of biodiversity can be developed in which broad community participation is assured' (National Environmental Action Plan (1998-2001), 1997: 478).

   Since 2000, ten countries within Southeast Asia have attempted to co-ordinate their development of Marine Protected Areas through the World Commission on Protected Areas Southeast Asia Marine Working Group. Of five themes identified as the pillars of a Regional Action Plan, one is 'Community awareness, involvement, empowerment and development' (IUCN, undated).

   This initiative has been one factor in providing the impetus for pre-existing Indonesian Marine National Parks to adopt a more inclusive approach to their management strategies. Another factor was the replacement of President Suharto's dictatorship in 1998, which resulted in a less centralized system of government. Although central government retains control of marine resources between 12 and 200 miles offshore, Law 22 (1999) 'devolves control to provinces and regency between 4 and 12 miles and within 4 nautical miles respectively ... This law repeals many of the complex and vague regulations governing coastal regions involving a wide arrange of sectoral interests which had resulted in inconsistent and politically influenced decisions regarding uses of coastal resources in the past' (Clifton, 2003: 393).

The Wakatobi Marine National Park

The Wakatobi Marine National Park (WMNP) was designated in 1996 and extends over 13,000 km^2 (Stanzel *et al.*, 1997) (Figure 13.1). It is one of the highest priorities for conservation due to the diversity of marine life and the scale and condition of its coral reefs (Halim *et al.,* 2004). Eighty thousand people live within the park (Operation Wallacea, 2003a, b) in approximately 64 villages. Ninety-two per cent are the Wakatobi ethnic group, whilst the Bajau or sea gypsies are the largest ethnic minority. The WMNP consists of four main inhabited islands, Wangi-Wangi, Kaledupa, Tomia and Binongko. It was created to protect coral reefs and fish stocks from destruction from over-fishing and inappropriate fishing methods which have damaged much of the reef systems. Despite being in existence for nearly a decade, the threats of over-fishing, destructive reef fishing practices and outside fishers remain. The latter threat is both direct in terms of additional fishing pressure, but also indirect as this 'reduces the sense of ownership and responsibility among local communities' (Halim *et al.,* 2004: 3), thus making it more difficult to involve them meaningfully in WMNP management.

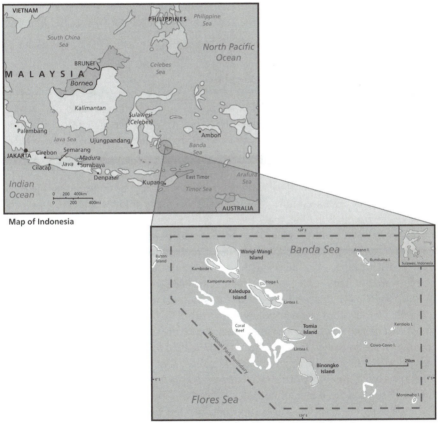

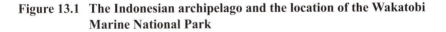

Figure 13.1 The Indonesian archipelago and the location of the Wakatobi Marine National Park

Research methodology

The research described here was carried out under the auspices of Operation Wallacea, in the Bajau village of Sampela that lies off the island of Kaledupa (Figure 13.1). The Bajau are a minority in the park, but their almost total reliance upon marine resources and lack of access to terrestrial resources makes them a key stakeholder in the WMNP's more inclusive strategy. The sampled village has a population of approximately 1,400 people in approximately 200 families. Operation Wallacea is a series of biological and social science expedition projects designed to underpin the achievement of specific wildlife conservation aims. It has carried out extensive research into the state of the marine resources and has also been involved with research into the socioeconomic aspects of the region. One of the authors lived in the village and carried out a variety of participative research methods, focus groups and discussions with key informants within the village and with other stakeholders. Since then research has involved discussions with key stakeholders related to Operation Wallacea.

The evolution of the management regime

For the first four years the WMNP attempted a centralized command and control regime in which the role of communities living within it was generally viewed as a problem to be managed (Majors *et al.*, 1995a, b). The power of the WMNP is compromised because the Fisheries Ministry has the authority to grant fishing licences within the park. Unofficially, the Fisheries Ministry retains control over the pelagic fishing areas, whilst the WMNP authority tries to exert tighter control over the coral reefs (Tim Coles, pers comm). The main management policies undertaken by the WMNP are zoning, the objective of which is to 'promote conservation of biological resources and at the same time provide for a variety of uses while minimising conflict between user groups' (Francis *et al.*, 2002); registration, in which local fishers are provided with licenses to permit fishing in certain areas; and enforcement, carried out by wardens. This strategy seems to have been a failure. Clifton (2003) noted that WMNP wardens tended to see their priority as rule enforcement rather than education, a classic fortress conservation policy (Neumann, 2005). In addition, Clifton (2003) noted that of a total of 80 interviewees on two of the four major islands none stated that they were consulted at any stage of the Wakatobi MNP establishment from initial survey work through to designation and subsequent planning of resource usage. Unsurprisingly, this study observed that only 30 per cent were able to refer to any of the MNP rules. Thus a lack of consultation early in the life of the MNP has resulted in a lowering in its effectiveness to conserve the marine environment. Funding problems have meant that it is difficult to impose the licensing system throughout the MNP, whilst the warden department experiences rapid turnover of staff and low morale. All of these problems illustrate the practical problems of implementing more sustainable management systems within the developing world. Therefore, the original strategy faced significant hurdles. The national and international moves to a more inclusive management strategy after the fall of Suharto and the adoption of the IUCN Regional Action Plan for Marine Areas has provided the impetus for the MNP to try to devolve management down to a more local level within it. This process has yet to be completed, but a number of small areas have been handed over to their local communities, of which a pioneer was the Hoga No Fishing Zone. A complicating factor that has slowed up the new WMNP strategy is that since it was formed, new local districts have been established, one of which, Wakatobi District, lies entirely within the WMNP. This level of government is responsible for local economic development, which includes fishing, but its members lack the capacity at present to carry out their responsibilities effectively. The WMNP also needs to liaise with the South East Sulawesi regional government, local communities, NGOs and the private sector. Thus by early 2005, a fully inclusive community-led management strategy had yet to be implemented. Because of the presence of Operation Wallacea, a proactive stakeholder in the WMNP, the Kaledupa area, which includes Hoga has advanced more quickly than other parts of the park in implementing the inclusive strategy.

The WMNP's new approach reflects the view of the 1992 United Nations Conference on Environment and Development, which emphasized that successful implementation of sustainable policies would only be achieved by encouraging grass-roots involvement in resource management. In theory, local indigenous institutions that are involved in managing communal resources should be at the heart of initiatives that encourage sustainable use. Pomeroy (1994) and Rivera (1995) state that due to a lack of funding and expertise, state control over marine resources in the developing world is inadequate, a factor that exists in Wakatobi MNP. Consequently, empowering existing indigenous groups is vital in attempts to alleviate over-exploitation of such resources. Rivera (1995) believes that they are likely to be most appropriate because their members have most to lose if the resources are degraded. In contrast Berkes (1993) and Campbell *et al.* (2001) suggest that they tend to over-exploit resources and believe the state needs to exert more control over them to prevent degradation. Majors (1995a), Djohani (1996) and Mehta *et al.* (1999) argue that the key to successful management of marine reserves is the inclusion and involvement of local communities in their management, acting to empower the groups concerned. A division therefore exists between those who see the role of local communities as central to the success of communally managed resources and others, such as Berkes (1993) and Campbell *et al.* (2001), who are more sceptical.

Community based management: The Bajau

The remainder of this chapter will examine the Bajau, to assess their attitude to managing the communal marine resources, and whether they have the capacity and willingness to become a positive influence within the WMNP if they are given more opportunity to engage in co-managing the local marine environment with the park authority. Until approximately 40 years ago, the Bajau were nomadic. Since then, they have settled into small coastal villages such as Sampela. They are almost entirely dependent upon the exploitation of marine resources and the majority are still engaged in small-scale, semi-subsistence fishing. Clifton (2003: 394) argues that the Bajau 'demonstrate a high level of concern over fish stocks ... a relatively homogeneous fishery in terms of equipment, a history of collective action and strong vested interests in resource management' which makes them good candidates for delegating responsibility for managing the communal marine environment in their immediate localities.

The Bajau have experienced a number of important changes as they have come into more constant contact with outside modern influences. These have begun to alter their belief and value systems, their fishing methods and for a minority, their reliance upon a subsistence existence.

Changing Bajau fishing techniques in response to a decline in stock

All fishing traditionally involved the use of gill nets and spears. Since the 1970s nylon nets and lines began to be introduced from Sulawesi. These were up to four times more effective at catching fish than traditional methods, but their introduction was slow because of the high costs involved. However, all fishers have gradually adopted them. Coinciding with this change was the abandonment of many traditional beliefs by the Bajau (Bottignolo, 1995). These identify sea gods that must be respected through the conservation of natural resources. The undermining of these beliefs, especially amongst the young, has resulted in different attitudes to the conservation of fish, especially a willingness to exploit them to accumulate wealth. In recent years, a larger number of Bajau men have migrated to Singapore and Malaysia. This has accelerated the decline in traditional beliefs among the young and has also, through remittances, given some households access to more cash income. Within the Bajau community, this has resulted in greater differential in income and a minority of Bajau have begun to develop more commercial capital-intensive fishing methods with larger boats for which they obtain fishing licences.

For the majority, traditional subsistence fishing was largely abandoned after the introduction of nylon nets allowed a temporary increase in catches. The loss of these beliefs and practices can also be linked to the abandonment of the nomadic lifestyle. These changes in attitude, together with population growth and a concentration of fishing effort into a smaller area resulted in over-exploitation. The perception of a decline in fish catches in recent years is widespread (Clifton, 2003). The Bajau have responded in ways that are to a certain extent contradictory. Confounding those expecting a 'tragedy of the commons' scenario to unfold as stocks dwindle, some fishers have responded by constructing offshore fish aggregation devices called rompongs. These are semi-submerged structures that act like small-scale reefs. Despite initial scepticism amongst the Bajau, as fish stocks declined the method became more attractive for some households. In 1999 the first rompong co-operative was set up in Sampela. Each rompong supports 3 fishers, limited to one per household. Money was needed to construct the rompongs and to purchase the motorized boats needed to reach them. Table 13.1 demonstrates the positive impact that rompongs can have both in terms of reducing the percentage of immature fish caught and the increased economic returns as a consequence of the larger average catch size.

Table 13.1   A comparison of reef versus romping fishing

Comparison	Reef	Rompong
Average size of fish caught (cms)	15	22
Percentage immature fish caught	27	16
Average market price per fish (Rp)	5,000	10,000

The co-operative members receive one third of the revenue from the catch; the remainder is invested in new rompongs, maintaining the existing ones and maintaining boats. The headman of the village runs the co-operative. By 2000, the Bajau had constructed 10 rompongs, but four of these have recently been destroyed in a storm. The adoption of rompongs demonstrated that the Bajau are aware of a decline in fish stocks and it indicates that they are able to react to such adversity in an innovative manner. However, the technique is currently not sufficiently economic to warrant its widespread adoption, as the recent loss of nearly half the capital stock indicates. This is despite the fact that the average price of fish caught at rompongs is twice that from reefs. It has been suggested that the loss of rompongs during the short stormy season could be avoided if rompongs were individually owned as, at present, it is difficult to get full co-operation of each co-operative when the rompongs need to be brought ashore.

Although the previous developments suggest that local fishers have reacted positively to the evidence of over-fishing by seeking alternative methods of conserving fish, since 2000 many small-scale fishers have responded in a different way by introducing large fish fences. In Kaledupa, the number grew from 10 in 2003 to 110 in 2004, although not all are owned by the Bajau. These extend up to 400 m into the sea and fish are funnelled by them into traps. This has developed as a result of the collapse in the reef fisheries catches by more conventional means and it is having a huge impact on the remaining stocks (Tim Cole, pers comm). Such behaviour, which sees an increasing pressure on the resource as it becomes scarcer, is more characteristic of those heading towards Hardin's 'tragedy of the commons'. It casts doubts on the ability of local communities to manage their communal resources sustainably as pressure increases on them and, therefore, on the strategy of the MNP.

Official responses to over fishing: The Hoga No Fishing Zone

In 2000 the Bajau of Sampela requested that Operation Wallacea help them establish a No Fishing Zone. The objective for this area was to protect breeding stocks of reef fish and commercially exploited invertebrates such that, over the years as the stocks built up in the protected area, the overspill would benefit the adjacent fished areas. In September 2000 the Park authorities agreed to the implementation of this plan and handed management of the 500 m stretch of reef on Hoga Island to the Sampela community. Community policing has been very effective; transgressors have had to explain and apologize for cheating in front of the whole village. In addition, those reporting confirmed transgressions are rewarded with Rp50,000 and the transgressors are fined Rp200,000. These have proved to be a major disincentive to cheating by Sampela fishermen and the Park rangers have enforced sanctions against any attempted exploitation of the No Fishing Zone by people from other communities. Important factors in explaining the success of the scheme include its small size, the simplicity of the rules, the location near the community and the fact that it was initiated by and enforced by them (Clifton, 2003). Smith (paper in preparation) shows that in the zone some grouper species have witnessed a growth in population by 250 per cent to 300 per cent since it was implemented.

Despite the introduction of the Hoga No Fishing Zone, it has been unable to prevent the decline of the fish stocks in the reef areas beyond the No Fishing Zone which, in some cases, are now close to collapse (Tim Cole, pers comm). This is because it is too small an area to offset the devastation caused by the widespread use of fish fences in adjacent areas. Similarly, rompongs are unable to reverse the decline that is taking place on the wider reef areas.

In response, the WMNP is, with the co-operation of Operation Wallacea, introducing a buy-out scheme for many fishing licences. To succeed, this has to coincide with the introduction of alternative livelihoods. At present, the most promising include the extension of agar farming, based on the sustainable exploitation of seaweed (Kinch *et al*, 2003), and the development of coral farming, where individuals are assigned corals that are grown in special containers on the sea bed and which are then harvested sustainably. Both these developments point to some form of 'privatization' of a previously communal resource. This is, therefore, a Hardinian solution to over-exploitation of a communal resource, rather than reliance upon improving the indigenous institutional arrangements whilst continuing to use it in a communal manner.

However, the new WMNP strategy is also trying to address the problem through extensive consultation with communities and educational initiatives with the view to handing over more power to local communities for the fish stocks closest to their community. Thus, two emerging strategies can be discerned since the shift to a more inclusive management approach in the WMNP. The first, as witnessed by agar farming and coral farming, indicates a conversion from communal to privately owned resources as the key. The second, as witnessed by the Hoga No Fishing Zone and likely extensions into other areas, demonstrates a more institutional response to the problem. Linked to this is the development of ecotourism, with visitors paying communities for access to their marine environments.

Conclusion

The Bajau have reacted positively to the Hoga No Fishing Zone. With its greater emphasis upon community-based monitoring and enforcement, there appears to be sufficient flexibility in the traditional and WMNP management systems to accommodate an evolving, but mutually beneficial system. The Hoga No Fishing Zone has addressed some of the weaknesses in the original MNP strategy, and giving increased prominence and control to the Bajau has helped to reduce their sense of alienation from the MNP. The Stakeholder Area has clearly defined boundaries, involves the community in the monitoring and enforcement of the resource and generally supports traditional authority, which had been eroded by external factors. Sanctions are clearer and understood by potential transgressors and enforcers. Through a long period of consultation between the community and external organizations, traditional authority has been strengthened and not weakened, contradicting the forecast of Fox (1993).

However, Agrawal & Gibson (1999) argue that current attempts to redress the failure of top-down conservation initiatives by placing greater emphasis on community based management is an inherently flawed approach, because the concept of community lacks clarity. This results in the ignoring or oversimplification of the internal complexities that compromise a community's ability to manage a resource coherently. Rather than emphasising a community in terms of a small spatial unit, a homogeneous social structure and shared norms, they argue that if communities are to be placed closer to the centre of natural resource management, then a more overtly political approach should be taken which focuses on the 'Multiple interests and actors within communities, on how these actors influence decision making and on the internal and external institutions that shape the decision making process' (Agrawal & Gibson, 1999: 629).

At present, the Bajau tend to be treated as a single community with an understanding that all share similar aims with respect to management of the marine resources (Clifton, 2003). However, this is unlikely and the development of a small group of commercial fishers illustrates the differences that exist within the Bajau. Although the majority still use subsistence or semi-subsistence methods, a significant minority have access to larger vessels and undertake commercial activities. Wealthier families are less reliant upon fishing than poorer families. A key factor in accumulating more wealth is the ability to obtain paid employment in Malaysia or Singapore. Alternative sources of wealth occur if individuals can become traders. Capital is needed to become a trader but bank loans are difficult to obtain because the Bajau are suspicious of outsiders and most do not fully understand how banks work. Paradoxically, those least reliant upon marine resources may place the greatest pressure on them. They have access to capital for bigger boats and a greater incentive to over-fish because they control larger markets via their trading networks. They are the most 'modernized' and have least respect for the rules administered mainly by traditional leaders. While present concerns may prove groundless, they suggest that in a modernizing world a major threat to community-based management regimes is the threat to the internal cohesion of the communities themselves, which appear to have been downplayed in the adoption of community based conservation policies at the national and regional level. However, in the past year, the MNP Authority appears to be accepting the need to develop a more sophisticated understanding of the internal complexities of its community stakeholders, although these have yet to be resolved (Halim *et al.*, 2004) and this may yet prove that Clifton's (2003) optimism for the potential of the Bajau to provide a positive input to managing the marine resources may be justified.

References

Alder, J., Sloan, N.A. & Uktolseya, H. (1994) A comparison of management planning and implementation in three Indonesian marine protected areas. *Ocean and Coastal Management*, 24, 179-198.

Agrawal, A. & Gibson, C. (1999) Enchantment and disenchantment: the role of community in natural resource conservation. *World Development*, 27, 629-649.

Berkes, F. (1989) Co-management and the James Bay Agreement. In Pinkerton, E. (ed.) *Co-Operative Management of Local Fisheries: New Directions for Improved Management and Community Development*. University of British Columbia Press, Vancouver, pp. 189-208.

Berkes, F. (1993) Success and failure in marine coastal fisheries of Turkey. In Bromley, D.W. (ed.) *Making The Commons Work. Theory, Practice and Policy*. ICS Press, Institute for Contemporary Studies, San Francisco, California.

Blaikie, P. (1985) *The Political Economy of Soil Erosion in Developing Countries*. Wiley, New York.

Bottignolo, B. (1995) *Celebrations with the Sun: An Overview of Religious Phenomena among the Bajou*. Ateno de Manila, University Press, Manila.

Burke, B. (2001) Hardin revisited: a critical look at the logic of the commons. *Human Ecology*, 29, 449-476.

Burke, L., Selig, E. & Spalding, M. (2002) Reefs at Risk in Southeast Asia. World Resources Institute. Cited in DeVantier, L., Alcala, A. & Wilkinson, C. (2004) The Sulu-Sulawesi Sea: Environmental and Socioeconomic Status, Future Prognosis and Ameliorative Policy Options. *Ambio,* 33, 88-97.

Campbell, B., De Jong, W., Luckert, M., Mandondo, A., Matose, F., Nontokozo, N., & Sithole, B. (2001) Challenges to Proponents of Common Property Resource Systems: Despairing Voices from the Social Forests of Zimbabwe. *World Development,* 29, 589-600.

Cleaver, F. (2000) Moral ecological rationality, institutions and the management of common property resources. *Development and Change*, 31, 361-383.

Clifton, J. (2003) Prospects for co-management in Indonesia's marine protected areas. *Marine Policy*, 27, 389-395.

Conservation International (2005) http://www.biodiversityhotspots.org/xp/Hotspots/ cape_floristic/conservation.xml. Accessed 14/12/05.

Cordell, J. (1987) Social marginality and sea tenure in Bahia. In Cordell, J. (ed.) *A Sea of Small Boats* (Cultural Survival Report No. 26). Cultural Survival Inc., Cambridge, MA, pp.125-151.

DeVantier, L., Alcala, A. & Wilkinson, C. (2004) The Sulu-Sulawesi Sea: Environmental and Socioeconomic Status, Future Prognosis and Ameliorative Policy Options. *Ambio*, 33, 88-97.

Directorate General of Fisheries, Government of Indonesia (undated) http://www. indoocean.com/fishery/fisheries_development_policy.htm. Accessed 12/04/05.

Djohani, R. (1996) *The Marine Conservation Development Programme in Indonesia*. World Wildlife Fund, Jakarta.

Food and Agricultural Organization (FAO) (1997) *Review of the State of the World Fishery Resources; Marine Resources* (Fisheries Circular No. 920). FAO Fisheries Department, Rome.

Food and Agricultural Organization (FAO) (2000) http://www.fao.org/fi/fcp/en/ IDN/body.htm. Accessed 12/04/05.

Fox, J. (1993) The tragedy of open access. In Brookfield, H. & Byron, Y (eds) *Southeast Asia's Environmental Future The search for sustainability*. United Nations University, Kuala Lumpur, pp. 302-315.

Francis, J., Nilsson, A. & Waruinge, D. (2002) Marine Protected Areas in the Eastern African Region: How Successful Are They? *Ambio*, 31, 503-511.

Halim, A., Ridwan, W., Mirza, P., Santiaji, V., Subijanto, J., Mous, P., Soekirman, T. & Satriani, D. (2004) *Support for the establishment of effectively managed MPA platform sites as foundations for resilient networks of functionally connected marine protected areas*. Wakatobi National Park, Progress Report, September 2004.

Hardin, G. (1968) The tragedy of the commons. *Science, 162,* 1243-1248.

Hecht, S. (1985) Environment, development and politics: capital accumulation and the livestock sector in eastern Amazonia. *World Development*, 6, 663-684.

IUCN (undated) http://wepa.iucn.org/biome/marine/seasia/workshop.html. Accessed 13/04/05.

Jackson, J., Kirby, M., Berger, W., Bjorndal, K., Botsford, L., Bourque, B., Bradbury, R. & Cooke, R. (2001) Historical overfishing and the recent collapse of coastal ecosystems. *Science, 293,* 629-638.

Jentoft, S. & McCay, B. (1996) From the bottom up: participatory issues in fisheries management. *Society and Natural Resources*, 9, 237-250.

Kinch, J., Bagita, J. & Bate, M. (2003) Exploring the potential for seaweed farming in Milne Bay, Papua New Guinea. *SPC Fisheries Newsletter*, 104, 25-31.

Kurlansky, M. (1997) *Cod*. Vintage, London.

Majors, C. (1995a) *Notes for Operation Wallacea: Report on Wakatobi Marine Park, contributed to Operation Wallacea Summary Results of the 1995 Marine Survey of the Wakatobi Islands, South-East Sulawesi and Proposed Survey Program for 1996*. For LIPI/PHPA/WDI Steering Committee Meeting.

Majors, C. (1995b) *Operation Wallacea: Summary of the 1995 Marine Survey of the Wakatobi islands*. Internal Report.

Mehta, L., Leach, M., Newell, P., Scoones, I., Sivaramakrishnan, K. & Way, S. (1999) *The Role of Uncertainty and Institutions in Natural Resources Management*. IDS Discussion Paper 372. University of Sussex, Brighton.

Ministry of Maritime and Fishery, Government of Indonesia (undated) http://www.indonesia.nl/articles.php?rank=12&art_cat_id=33. Accessed 12/04/05.

Neumann, R.P. (2005) *Making Political Ecology*. Hodder Arnold, London.

National Environmental Action Plan (1998-2001) (1997) Jakarta, Ministry of Environment.

Operation Wallacea (2003a) Formation and proposed management for the Kaledupa Stakeholder Zone. http://www.opv@,aU.coni/stakeholder%20zone.htm. Accessed 21/6/04.

Operation Wallacea (2003b) Proposed enforcement programme. http://www.opwall.conv'2004%20proposed%20wakatobi%20enforcement%20programme.htm Accessed 21/6/04.

Ostrom, E. (1990) *Governing the Commons: The Evolution of Institutions for Collective Action*. Cambridge University Press, Cambridge.

Pet-Soede, L. & Erdmann, M. (1999) An Overview and Comparison of Destructive Fishing Practices in Indonesia. *SPC Live Reef Fish Bulletin*, 4, 28-36.

Pomeroy, R.S. (ed.) (1994) *Community Management and Common Property of Coastal Fisheries in Asia and the Pacific Concepts, methods and experience*. International Centre for living Aquatic Resources Management, Manila.

Rivera, R.A. (1995) *Approaching Coastal Resource Management through Community Property Rights Arrangements*. Tambuyog Development Centre, Philippines.

Ruddle, K. (1998) The context of policy design for existing community-based fisheries management systems in the Pacific islands. *Ocean and Coastal Management*, 40, 105-126.

Shi, H. & Singh, A. (2003) Status and Interconnections of Selected Environmental Issues in the Global Coastal Zones. *Ambio*, 32, 145-152.

Smith, D. (paper in preparation, June 2005), Centre for Environment and Society, Department of Biological Sciences, The University of Essex.

Stanzel K.B., Newman H., Sugiyanta, E. & Majors, C. (1997) *Progress Report on the 1996 Marine Survey of the Tukangbesi (Wakatobi) Archipelago, South East Sulawesi, Indonesia*. Wallacea Development Institute, Jakarta.

United Nations Environment Programme (UNEP) (2004) Action for Mangrove Management in Indonesia. Presented at the Fifth Meeting of the Regional Working Group for the Mangrove Sub-component of the UNEP/GEF Project: *Reversing Environmental Degradation Trends in the South China Sea and Gulf of Thailand*. Trat Province, Thailand, 20 September.

United Nations (1997) http://www.un.org/dpcsd/earthsummit. Accessed 14/04/05.

Veron, J.E.N. (2000) *Corals of the World*. 3 Vols. Australian Institute of Marine Science.

Warren-Rhodes, K., Sadovy, Y. & Cesar, H. (2003) Marine Ecosystem Appropriation in the Indo Pacific: A Case Study of the Live Reef Fish Food Trade. *Ambio,* 32, 481-488.

Chapter 14

Environmental Policies for Modern Agriculture?

Christian Brannstrom and Anthony M. Filippi

Introduction

The Brazilian Cerrado, a savanna ecoregion of tree and grass species covering approximately two million square kilometres south and east of the Amazon rainforest, is threatened by the expansion of agriculture and pasture. Since 1979 in the north-eastern region of Brazil, soyabean, cotton and maize cultivation on modern farms have rapidly expanded at the expense of Cerrado vegetation. The rise of soya is especially dramatic. In 1979, soya was hardly planted in the north-east, but in 2004, approximately 1.3 million hectares were cultivated with soya, with nearly two-thirds just in the western region of Bahia state (USDA, 2005a: 23). Meanwhile, environmental activists and state officials often complain that recently created farms lack the required 20 per cent of farm area as Legal Reserve (LR), which, according to federal forest and environmental crimes legislation (Brannstrom, 2001: 1348), must remain in native vegetation. The ensuing environmental debate on modern farming is led not by state agencies, but, surprisingly, by a private association of farmers.

The western region of Bahia is useful to examine as an example of a much broader phenomenon in developing countries. Modern agricultural systems produce high yields, but depend on fossil fuels and generate many negative environmental and human health effects. For many critics, 'sustainable modern agriculture' is a tragic oxymoron; to reduce or eliminate the many petroleum inputs into modern farming is to abandon the idea of modern agriculture (Kimbrell, 2002). Yet critics of modern agriculture come in numerous varieties (Thompson, 1995). Some scholars urge that agricultural subsidies should be directed to 'sustainable' farming practices (Pretty *et al.*, 2001; Tilman *et al.*, 2002: 675). Others favour strategies that specifically enhance habitat for wildlife on farmland (Green *et al.*, 2005: 552). Amongst OECD countries more than 350 subsidy schemes promote improved environmental conservation on farmland (Herzog, 2005). With global cereal production estimated to double by 2050 (Tilman *et al.*, 2002), the policy challenges of reducing or eliminating the harmful environmental effects of agriculture will only increase in number and complexity. These challenges will be especially difficult to resolve in the developing countries where agricultural area has increased, more than offsetting the decline in agricultural land in developed countries (Green *et al.*, 2005: 550-551). Agricultural expansion is projected to be especially strong in South America and sub-Saharan Africa (Alexandratos, 1999: 5912; Dros, 2004).

The dilemma of modern agriculture and environmental conservation was addressed only tangentially by the 1992 United Nations Conference on Environment and Development (UNCED), or the Rio Conference. Agenda 21 included a chapter on 'promoting sustainable agriculture', but the main emphasis of this chapter was to promote food security amongst the rural poor, recognizing that agriculture must increase production in existing cultivated land whilst avoiding expansion on marginal land. FAO-sponsored World Food Summits, held in 1996 and 2002, continued the Agenda 21 emphasis on food security by pledging to reduce the number of undernourished people by 50 per cent by 2015. The Convention on Biological Diversity (CBD), signed at the Rio Conference, was intended to conserve biodiversity, encourage sustainable use of biota and promote the equitable distribution of biodiversity benefits (Adams, 2001: 90-92). However, critics have argued that the CBD has an 'anti-agricultural' bias by assuming that agriculture in developing countries destroys wild biodiversity (Wood & Lanné, 2005: 77, 81-84).

Against this global perspective, the case of Brazil's soya farming sector, with the specific example of the leading-edge frontier of western Bahia state, is relevant to evaluate the local implications of national-scale 'sustainability' policy making. In this chapter we argue that the national level 'sustainability' debate has had few tangible implications, with one exception, amongst western Bahia's modern farms. A regional-scale private farmers' association has taken the lead from ineffectual state agencies in crafting policy initiatives for the environment. It is not yet clear whether these policies amount to 'greening' or 'greenwashing'. However, the case makes clear that local private interests have captured the national 'sustainability' discourse, which has created a dilemma for 'public' agencies. Should state agencies follow the lead of a powerful private group, or should they develop their own initiatives that may inspire resistance amongst land managers? As we argue here, the private sector is an unexpected actor, omitted from Agenda 21 concerns in Brazil, but it is also both a powerful ally and formidable opponent in sustainability policymaking.

We begin with a review of the sustainability policy debate in Brazil, with special attention to agriculture and the Cerrado ecoregion. Most scholarly writing has been devoted to activities other than modern agriculture, and overall the Cerrado has attracted relatively little analysis. We then outline the broad characteristics of Brazil's soya development, focusing on the Cerrado and discussing the case study region of western Bahia state in north-eastern Brazil. To sharpen the discussion, we use high-resolution satellite remote sensing data to classify land covers. This analysis indicates that critics of modern agriculture in western Bahia are generally correct in alleging excessive Cerrado removal, but significant areas of Cerrado still remain. Next, we discuss the recent environmental policy initiatives and the main actors in western Bahia; our analysis targets a private farmer organization that outpaces state agencies. The discussion focuses on implications of our remote-sensing classification, the apparent divergence between national level sustainability discourses and regional policymaking, and whether the 'private' policies amount to 'greening' or 'greenwashing'.

Sustainable development policy-making in Brazil

Formal sustainable development policy in Brazil is institutionalized in three political-geographical scales. At the federal level, the Ministry of the Environment (MMA) oversees the Commission for Sustainable Development Policies (CPDS; Comissão de Políticas de Desenvolvimento Sustentável), which was charged in 1997 with developing Brazil's Agenda 21. CPDS members, representatives of federal ministries and civil society organizations, completed a report in June 2000 that outlined six areas (sustainable agriculture; sustainable cities; infrastructure and regional integration; natural resources management; reduction of social inequalities; and science and technology for sustainable development) for sustainability policies. After publishing this report, the CPDS organized public consultations throughout Brazil. In 2002 the CPDS published a document listing numerous sustainable development priorities toward Brazil's Agenda 21 commitments (CPDS, 2002).

How did modern agriculture fare in the Agenda 21 document? First, agriculture was viewed as a sector that could contribute to reducing Brazil's vast socio-economic inequalities. Redistribution of farmland could be combined with new land uses to reduce Brazil's 'social debt' (*dívida social*). Second, agriculture should become sustainable, although the authors admitted that this would be difficult. Suggestions included developing sustainability indicators specific to agriculture, but these tasks remained even more opaque than the proposal for redistributing farmland to reduce poverty.

Far more radical was the discussion of modern agriculture in a third area, regarding forests and biodiversity. Unsurprisingly, the authors of Agenda 21 favoured increasing the number and territory of conservation units, establishing biodiversity corridors linking protected areas, and enforcing landowners' compliance with the federal Legal Reserve requirements. But nothing less than the soya economy was called into question with proposals for the Cerrado ecoregion, as the authors argued for the end of soybean cultivation, which they characterized as 'an exported product of low value added' and prey to falling international prices (MMA, 2002: 70).

Brazil's Agenda 21 priorities are supposed to be inserted into its multi-year planning exercise, known as the multi-year plan or Plano Plurianual (PPA). The most recent PPA, covering 2004-07, included funds for implementing the Agenda 21 priorities (as published in MMA, 2002), establishing local sustainable development fora and encouraging local Agenda 21 schemes. In fact, Agenda 21 is self-contained within its own section, at odds with the other objectives of the 2004-07 PPA. For example, the goal of the 2007 agricultural harvest is 150 million tonnes (mainly soybeans and maize), nearly double the output during the mid 1990s. The goal for Brazil's trade balance, for which agriculture is essential, is an increase from US$17 billion to US$21 billion (MPOG, 2003). Thus, Brazil's Agenda 21 priorities and its

PPA targets are contradictory toward modern agriculture. Should modern farming help reduce poverty or should it maintain Brazil's monetary stability?

How has the modern agricultural sector fared overall in sustainability policymaking outside federal governance? Several developments outside the formal Agenda 21 policymaking process merit discussion. Brazil's individual states have considerable policy-making powers for environmental governance (Ames & Keck, 1997). In water management, for example, one may observe different policy models for including civil society leaders in watershed governance throughout Brazil (Brannstrom, 2004; Lemos & Oliveira, 2004). Mato Grosso state, Brazil's leading soybean producer, has developed an innovative fire-prevention policy (Fearnside, 2003b). Bahia state has reformed its management system for conservation units (Oliveira, 2002).

But sustainability concerns in the commercial farming sector have received far less attention by scholars. Main concerns have been reporting implications of federal requirements that 80 per cent of private farmland in the Amazon rainforest region be devoted to a 'legal reserve' of native vegetation; in the Cerrado, the requirement ranges from 20 per cent to 35 per cent (Brannstrom, 2001; Nepstad *et al.,* 2002; Fearnside, 2003b). Scholarly analysis has also been devoted to chemical pollution (Laabs *et al.,* 2002) and the rapid adoption of zero-tillage cultivation (Ekboir, 2003; Landers *et al.,* 2003).

Brazil's more than 5,000 municipalities are also important political spaces for formal sustainable development policymaking, but the implications for modern agriculture are unknown. Since 2002, municipalities in Bahia state, for example, may petition the state environmental agency to receive powers of environmental impact review over some agricultural land uses. Municipalities receiving this power must have an environmental council with members including councilors and representatives from business, non-governmental organizations and state agencies. Other municipal governments in Brazil have decentralized powers, yet very little scholarly research has been done on synthesizing myriad policymaking experiences at the municipal level.

Sustainability issues often cut across federal, state and municipal political geographies. The environmental licensing process includes state actors, private interests and non-governmental organizations (NGOs) (Eve *et al.,* 2000; Rothman, 2001; Fearnside, 2002). Policies for the co-management of common-pool resources involve several bureaucratic actors at municipal, state and federal levels (McGrath, 2000; Brown & Rosendo, 2000; Cardoso, 2002; Glaser & Oliveira, 2004). In the Amazon region, resource governance includes many state and non-state actors (Hall, 1997, 2000; Nepstad *et al.,* 2002; Fearnside, 2003a), with extractive reserves, 'sustainable' logging and environmental services having received special attention (Fearnside, 1997, 2000; Abakerli, 2001; Scholz, 2001; Holmes *et al.,* 2002). In addition, NGO advocacy networks have had considerable successes in attempts to 'leverage' environmental concessions from governments (Keck, 1998; Kolk, 1998; Hochstetler, 2002; Rodrigues, 2004). NGOs in Paraná state initiated lawsuits against farmers who lacked the 20 per cent Legal Reserve on their properties (Bacha, 1996: 167).

The Brazilian soybean revolution and the Cerrado ecoregion

Brazil, the world's second largest soya producer after the USA, accounts for nearly 28 per cent of world production (FAO, 2005; USDA, 2005b). Soya is highly significant to Brazil's farming sector, which generates nearly half of the country's export revenues. The soybean sector has grown dramatically since the early 1970s, a result of favourable public policies, global demand, agronomic innovations and suitable land (Warnken, 1999; Fearnside, 2001). Production increases since 1970 pushed output over 15 million tonnes in the 1980s, over 20 million tonnes in the 1990s, to 50 million tonnes in 2003 and to a predicted 62 million tonnes in 2005 (USDA, 2004, 2005a and b). The distribution of soya farming has grown from a relatively small area in southern Brazil to a wide swathe in central Brazil, especially Mato Grosso state, the country's leading producer (Figure 14.1). US analysts view the north-eastern states of Brazil, mainly Bahia, Maranhão and Piauí as the country's 'new frontier' for soybean cultivation, arguing that only ten per cent of arable land has been cleared for crops. The southern regions of Maranhão and Piauí states have approximately one and five million hectares, respectively, of Cerrado considered 'suitable' for soya cultivation (USDA, 2004: 30-31).

Brazil's soya expansion in the past two decades occurred largely in the Cerrado (savanna) ecoregion. The Cerrado, extending over approximately two million square kilometres, is comprised of several vegetation physiognomies from grassland to woodland. Cerrado grassland is known as *Campo* or *Campina* and is dominated by herbaceous species; by contrast, Cerrado woodland or *Cerradão* has trees between eight and 15 metres. Trees in the Cerrado *sensu stricto* physiognomy reach five to eight metres in height with canopies covering 20 per cent to 70 per cent of land surface (Coutinho, 1978; Ribeiro & Walter, 1998). Calls for urgent conservation measures, mainly increased area and number of conservation units, to protect the Cerrado's biodiversity (Ratter *et al.*, 1997; Furley, 1999; Oliveira & Marquis, 2002) are based on the idea that the Cerrado is being rapidly crushed by an agricultural juggernaut (Klink *et al.*, 1993; Alho & Martins, 1995; Klink & Moreira, 2002).

Estimates of Cerrado conversion to agriculture or pasture within the past three decades range from 40 per cent to 80 per cent, because of ambiguous land-cover categories and unspecified accuracy assessment procedures. Yet most claims of Cerrado destruction (Alho & Martins, 1995; Myers *et al.*, 2000) have been based on Mantovani & Pereira's (1998) non-refereed paper that, according to Jepson's (2005) critique, applied ambiguous land cover categories (for example, Cerrado 'not anthropogenically altered' or 'human-influenced areas without native vegetation cover') to scenes of Landsat 30-metre resolution satellite data, without using either *in situ* reference data or accuracy assessment. Similar problems appear in a Conservation International study, analysing one-kilometre satellite data, which concluded that 55 per cent of the Cerrado had been converted to 'human-influenced areas without native vegetation cover' by August 2002. The study's authors predicted that if the estimated 1.1 per cent annual rate of clearance continues, the Cerrado would be 'completely destroyed' by 2030 (Machado *et al.*, 2004: 4-5, 8). However, the study did not use *in situ* reference data, nor did the authors perform an accuracy assessment, so that the land-conversion estimates for the Cerrado remain confused. In fact, the only refereed publication on Cerrado land conversion concluded that, in a 3,900 square kilometre region of eastern Mato Grosso state, Cerrado loss between 1986 and 1999 was 70.1 per cent, but net loss was 20.2 per cent because large areas of Cerrado regenerated (Jepson, 2005).

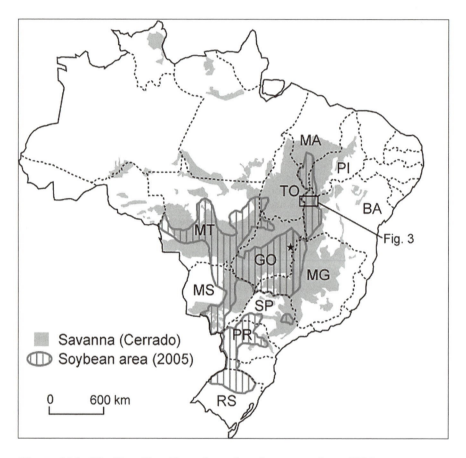

Figure 14.1   The Brazilian Cerrado and main soya regions, 2005

Sources: Fearnside 2001; Théry 2000; USDA 2005a. Abbreviations indicate states of Bahia (BA), Goiás (GO), Maranhão (MA), Mato Grosso (MT), Minas Gerais (MG), Paraná (PR), Piauí (PI), Rio Grande do Sul (RS), São Paulo (SP), and Tocantins (TO),

The western region of Bahia state is the epicentre of north-eastern Brazil's soybean boom. Modern agriculture has caused Cerrado vegetation in western Bahia state to decline dramatically in the past 25 years. Government policies, appropriate technologies and suitable agronomic conditions for soya cultivars attracted farmers from southern Brazil (Smith et al., 1998; Warnken, 1999; Kaimowitz & Smith, 2001). Today this leading-edge agricultural district of western Bahia state has 1.5 million hectares under cultivation, where only scattered cattle grazed in 1979. Presently most cultivated area is devoted to soybeans (870,000 hectares), maize (180,000 hectares), cotton (200,000 hectares) and irrigated coffee (13,000 hectares).

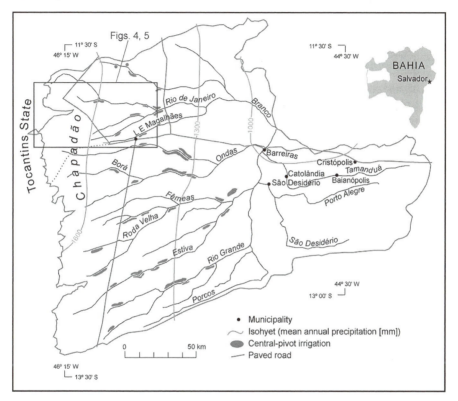

Figure 14.2   Western Bahia, with inset showing area covered by satellite remote sensing data

Large farms dominate western Bahia's agricultural landscape. Farms larger than 500 hectares claim three-quarters of owner-occupied farmland, but they account for less than five per cent of the region's total number of farms (IBGE, 2003). Preferred agricultural land is in the flat areas between streams, in what is known as the 'Chapadão' (Figure 14.2). Anecdotal accounts suggest that US farmers, taking advantage of the low cost of land, are purchasing soybean farms in western Bahia (Romero, 2002). Western Bahia's main city, Barreiras (population 115,000), attracts farmers from southern Brazil, suppliers of agricultural inputs and poor migrants from rural north-eastern Brazil (Haesbaert, 1997); Luis Eduardo Magalhães, also known as Mimoso d'Oeste, has grown rapidly from petrol station to city of more than 20,000 inhabitants.

A key policymaking organization in western Bahia is AIBA (Associação de Agricultores e Irrigantes da Bahia), a private group of approximately 1,200 large farmers who comprise the vast majority of the region's commercial farms. Its farmer-members are technologically sophisticated entrepreneurs who typically farm at least 1,000 hectares. Commonly, they live in Barreiras or Luis Eduardo Magalhães, preferring to hire full-time administrators who reside on their sprawling farms. Many farmers sold small properties in the south of Brazil during the early 1980s and migrated to western Bahia in search of cheap farmland. Since its inception in the early 1990s, AIBA lobbied state and federal governments for improved infrastructure and favourable subsidies. AIBA's directors maintain close relations with federal, state and municipal officials and proclaim the overall economic importance of its farmer-members: four million tonnes of agricultural output required approximately US$500 million in investment per annum (Santa Cruz Filho, 2002). In 1999 AIBA established an environmental desk, staffed by an agronomist who was charged with lobbying state officials on environmental matters, developing in-house policies and encouraging farmer-members to comply with state and federal environmental regulations (Brannstrom, 2005).

What are the main environmental issues regarding modern agriculture? The magnitude of land-cover change since 1979 is enormous, but actual data are sparse. An analysis of land-cover change between 1985 and 2000, covering a region of 108,000 square kilometres at the 1:250,000 map scale, found that 'intensive agriculture' expanded from 631,175 hectares to 1.6 million hectares in western Bahia. By contrast, Cerrado and Cerrado grassland decreased from 4.2 million to 3.3 million hectares and 2.0 million to 1.8 million hectares, respectively (EMBRAPA ca., 2003).

To map land covers at a larger cartographic scale, we focused our analysis on approximately 3,000 square kilometres, covering farmland and Cerrado vegetation near Luis Eduardo Magalhães. We obtained a high-resolution Landsat 7 Enhanced Thematic Mapper Plus (ETM+) scene (WRS 220/68; acquired 2 September 2002). The near-infrared (NIR) band (band 4, 0.75-0.90 micrometres) is shown in Figure 14.3. In this region, farms plant soyabeans, cotton and maize during the November-March wet season; in the dry season (when the Landsat scene was acquired) land covers include bare soil, agricultural weeds, millet and sorghum. According to our Gaussian maximum likelihood classification analysis (overall accuracy is 76.6 per cent) (Figure 14.4), Cerrado land covers (including Cerrado *sensu stricto* and *Campina*) occupied 28 per cent of the study area, whilst non-irrigated agriculture extended over 50 per cent. Unclassified pixels, which were mainly masked areas not of interest to our analysis, totaled 12.5 per cent, while burned areas covered 6 per cent and other land covers were 3 per cent.[1]

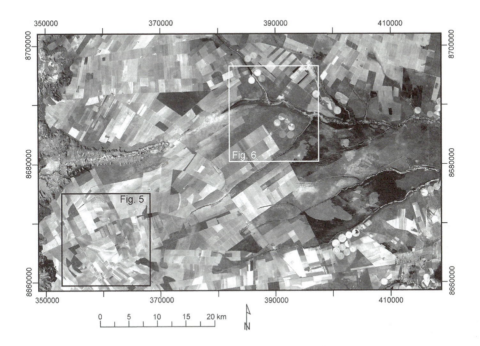

Figure 14.3   Study region within Landsat 7 ETM+ scene, band 4 (near-infrared) (220/68, acquired 2 September 2002). Boxes indicate areas shown in detail in Figures 14.5 and 14.6.

This overall finding, however, obscures spatial variability within the study region. Agricultural clearing has been extensive in the far western portion of the study region, where Cerrado has been reduced to small fragments (Figure 14.5). But in other sub-regions (Figure 14.6), considerable areas of Cerrado remain intact. These areas include riparian forest, the narrow humid grassland between Cerrado *sensu stricto* and riparian forest, in addition to *Cerradão* (savanna woodland). Here, central-pivot irrigation fields are located near streams, where water is obtained for growing soya and cotton, in addition to coffee and papaya. Nearby, an extensive Cerrado region is still intact, because a violent land dispute has discouraged investment in modern agriculture. Fire, perhaps set by hunters illegally, often intrudes on this Cerrado

---

1   Full discussion of methods and results is in our unpublished paper, 'Remote classification of savanna (*Cerrado*) land covers on northeastern Brazil's agricultural frontier'.

fragment. However, nearly all areas of existing Cerrado are subject to continued clearing for increased farmland.

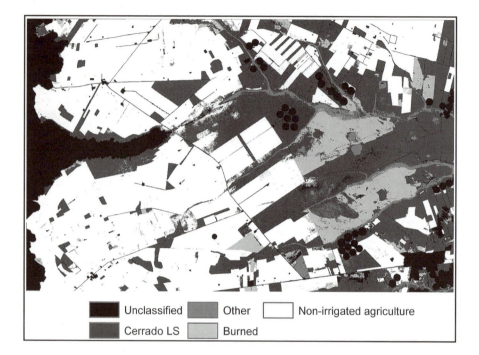

Figure 14.4 **Land cover in study region resulting from the maximum likelihood classification algorithm. Non-irrigated agriculture (50.2 per cent), Cerrado (28.2 per cent), Unclassified (12.5 per cent), and Burned (6.4 per cent) were the main classes. Remaining classes ('Other', including** *Cerradão*, **Water, Riparian Forest and Eucalyptus) total 2.7 per cent of total area. They are combined here for improved visualization.**

Modern agriculture: A disaster for Western Bahia?

Rapid land-cover change in western Bahia has inspired three main critiques against modern agriculture, *contra* the optimistic assessment of Maia Gomes (2001). First, modern farms have cleared excessive areas of Cerrado. Critics allege that one-fourth of all farms in the productive uplands lack the 20 per cent Legal Reserve area, the federal requirement for maintaining part of private farmland in native vegetation (Brannstrom, 2005). Our remote sensing analysis cannot confirm this charge, as we lack a map of properties that could be overlain on our classified Landsat imagery.

Critics further sustain that savanna clearing has caused higher peak stream flows in the wet season and lower flows during the dry season.

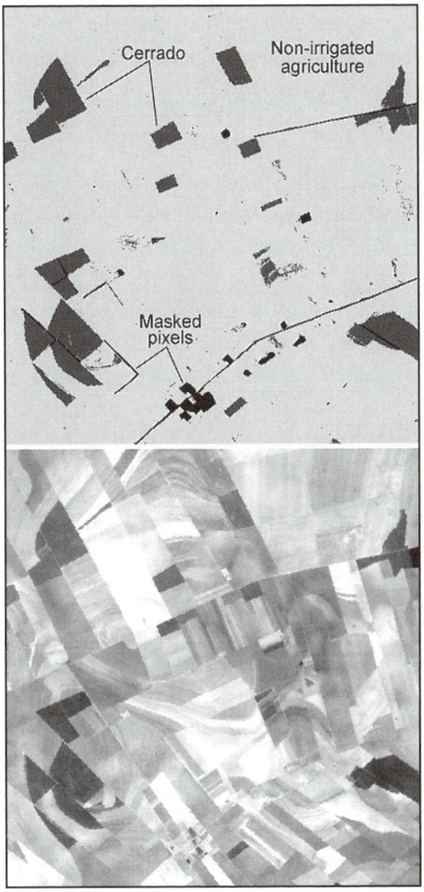

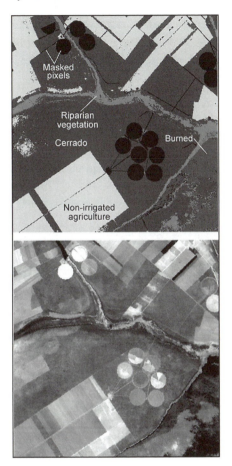

Figure 14.5
Detail of land covers in study region. Modern Agriculture has largely replaced Cerrado vegetation, which is limited to small and isolated fragments. Classified Landsat data (top) shows Cerrado fragments surrounded by agriculture. Bottom image is Landsat band 4 (near-infrared) of the same area; white areas probably represent bare soil

Figure 14.6
Detail of land covers in study region. Classified Landsat data (top) indicates large tracts of Cerrado vegetation near irrigated and non-irrigated agricultural fields. Riparian vegetation is largely intact, except sites of stream water pumping for irrigation. Bottom image is Landsat band 4 (near infrared) of the same area.

Second, critics argue that central-pivot irrigation in western Bahia uses surface water excessively and has caused reduced stream flow. Approximately 600 central-pivots are in operation, but only 35 were in operation in 1989. Indeed, the state water agency closed several rivers to irrigation licenses, and admits that it may have over-licensed some rivers. In response, farmers drill for groundwater, which allows them to locate irrigated fields away from streams and on flatter land.

Third, modern agriculture may degrade the region's soils. Western Bahia's highly weathered oxisols naturally have very low presence of clay-sized particles. Conventional soil preparation leaves soil exposed during much of the May-October dry season. The Brazilian government's agricultural research agency warned of 'desertification' risk because organic matter and clay content rapidly decline under mechanized cultivation (Spera *et al.*, 1999: 22-24). Loss of organic matter is a key factor in the decline of agricultural productivity and encourages soil erosion by wind and water (Silva *et al.*, 1994). However, the region's farmers are adopting the zero-tillage technologies that followed the south-to-north spread of soya cultivation in Brazil.

These specific criticisms inform two contradictory narratives explaining the state of modern agriculture in western Bahia. One idea is that modern agriculture is an environmental disaster for the region's 'fragile' environment. These critics, who include government employees and environmental activists, usually blame state agencies that encouraged agricultural settlement. They often specifically blame southern Brazilian farmers who migrated to the region as somehow culturally predisposed to degrade natural resources. A second idea, espoused by leaders in the farming sector, accepts the accuracy of some criticisms, such as the claim that the region suffered from an initially degrading phase of agriculture. According to AIBA, a new 'sustainable' agriculture is developing. Although the state encouraged 'disorganized land occupation' (AIBA, 2002: 2), exploitative 'adventurer' farmers have since moved on to clear land elsewhere, such as in neighbouring Piauí state to the north. According to this argument, farmers who stayed in western Bahia display a growing environmental concern and respond well to AIBA's environmental initiatives. It is this second narrative that supports AIBA's environmental policymaking, which 'constitutionally, should have been developed by the public sector' according to its spokesman (Raisa, 2004). Thus, AIBA situates itself with this second idea, criticising the state for poor regulation, and depicting its environmental agenda as filling a policy vacuum that the state created.

Sustainability policymaking in Western Bahia: Greening or greenwash?

Amongst the several actors pursuing sustainable development for modern agriculture in western Bahia, AIBA has established itself as the leader. In response to criticisms of modern agriculture, the federal government's 'Green Protocol' and possible backlash from European export markets, AIBA has developed three main environmental initiatives.

First, AIBA has elaborated a Cerrado conservation policy comprised of several initiatives, such as a proposal for an ecological corridor, conservation-oriented land occupation strategy, establishment of a nursery for reforestation of Legal Reserve areas, a reconnaissance study of soil erosion and support for research on the Cerrado. But perhaps the most important of these is bringing farmer-members into compliance with federal and state environmental legislation. This policy is more tangible than initiatives of state or federal forest agencies, which provide few resources for the staff in western Bahia to enforce command-control policies (Brannstrom, 2005). AIBA's actions are a response to both federal and state mandates. Federal legislation, effective in February 1998, defined as 'environmental crimes' acts that include operating a farm without license or authorization from competent state agencies. AIBA cited this provision of the 1998 Environmental Crimes Law to warn farmers that they must license their farms with Bahia's environmental agency, or face fines and even prosecution (AIBA, 2004e). Toward this end, AIBA negotiated a one-year licensing extension with the state environmental agency, and throughout 2004 AIBA encouraged members to download required forms from its web site. These forms allow farmers time to seek the three required licenses, from the same state agency, to legalize their farms environmentally. By signing these forms, farmers pledge to either register existing Legal Reserve areas with state authorities, or to create the 20 per cent Legal Reserve area on their farms (AIBA 2004a, b). Use of the forest code as legal instrument to force landowners to create Legal Reserves has generated considerable hostility elsewhere in Brazil (Brannstrom, 2001: 1354).

An important factor in AIBA's Cerrado policy is the federal government's 'Green Protocol'. Established in 1995, the 'Green Protocol' commits five federal banks to include environmental variables, such as compliance with environmental legislation, as criteria in approving credit (Young & Roncisvalle, 2002: 22-3). Thus, banks supplying agricultural credit, such as the Banco do Brasil, would block funds to farmers who lacked environmental licenses or failed to comply with the 20 per cent Legal Reserve requirement. Whether banks possess the technical staff to determine compliance is unknown; however, AIBA has taken this environmental review seriously enough to warn members in early 2004 that 'official [state-owned] banks have informed us that environmental licensing will be an essential criterion' in processing loans for farm production and investment (AIBA, 2004c, d). Nevertheless, the numerous farmers who receive credit from 'green soya' contracts signed with multinational corporations, such as Bunge and Cargill, are not held to the same environmental standards.

But AIBA also recognized the limits of its Cerrado policy. During 2004, AIBA was involved in multi-party discussions with Bahia's environmental agency toward a new statewide forest code. This 'modernization' of state laws is widely thought to be a key priority of Bahia's state administration. AIBA reported to its members that it managed to change a clause that would have increased the Legal Reserve obligations to 50 per cent of farm area, up from the federal 20 per cent minimum. AIBA also reported that NGOs were pressuring state officials to include a clause that would prohibit the cutting of plant species defined as 'rare', 'in danger of or threatened with extinction' or necessary for subsistence extraction. According to AIBA, this clause would have made mechanized farming in the Cerrado 'practically impossible' (AIBA, 2004f).

A second environmental policy AIBA has implemented is construction of a recycling centre for agrochemical containers, which began operation in July 2001. Federal law, passed in 2000, required recycling of used agrochemical containers that had been discarded, buried or burnt. With state and non-state partners, AIBA led an alliance to obtain funding but kept day-to-day management responsibility for the facility. AIBA's officials often use the recycling centre to indicate its good faith in environmental compliance; farmers in the region pay for hauling empty containers to the centre.

AIBA's third policy intervention is in water-resources management, where it has pursued two separate activities. First, AIBA helped fund a study of the aquifer beneath western Bahia's modern farms. Joining forces with the state's water agency, AIBA's funding and logistical support were essential for necessary field work that would monitor the aquifer's characteristics. The study, released in 2004, provided basic data that the state water agency will use to develop a protocol for licensing well irrigation. Second, AIBA participates in committees and councils as a representative of the irrigated agriculture sector. AIBA sits on a national level committee for developing a tariff system for bulk water usage; but it also has been influential in state-level policy debates. In 2002 AIBA forced the state water agency to back away from a policy that would have excluded non-state actors from the state water council that would develop water tariff protocols. AIBA questioned the constitutional basis of its exclusion, arguing that it was contradictory to federal water law. AIBA also demanded the formation of a stakeholder committee in the Grande River Valley at a time when the state water agency's director was opposed to the idea.

AIBA often uses the idea of 'sustainability' to justify its environmental policies, both to its members and to its own sceptical officials. AIBA's narrative of its adoption of environmental issues emphasizes how, in the late 1990s, its directors were worried that the organization was overly concerned with commodity marketing whilst ignoring environmental issues. In its newsletters, AIBA warned farmers that they would soon confront 'marketing difficulties' if they failed to comply with Brazil's environmental laws (AIBA, 2001b). Environmental policies were needed to 'correct the distortions' of past land uses that were 'obviously incompatible with environmental equilibrium' (AIBA, 2001b, unpaginated).

Nevertheless, evidence that AIBA's environmental policies are still subordinated to the imperative to increase agricultural production is not difficult to obtain. Whilst supporting 'sustainability' AIBA touts the fact that some three million hectares of Cerrado in western Bahia have yet to be cleared (Santa Cruz Filho, 2002). The present 1.5 million hectares are just the beginning; AIBA predicts expansion to 2.05 million hectares by 2008 (AIBA, 2003: 5). In addition, AIBA's own documents offer the congratulatory self-praise because it 'participated directly in the extraordinary transformation of the then-infertile lands of Bahia's savannas into infinitely productive agricultural fields' (AIBA, 2001a, unpaginated). These statements raise the possibility that environmental policies are intended to soften environmental opposition to further expansion of agriculture.

Ambiguity toward environmental initiatives is also apparent in a recent editorial published in AIBA's newsletter. A top official stated what many modern farmers in Brazil believe, but few have actually put into print: that developed countries, forming an 'international lobby', created a 'web of lies' about Brazil's modern farming sector. According to this argument, the success of Brazil's agro-export sector has come at the expense of the environment (Pitt, 2004). Furthermore, environmental NGOs and the Brazilian media are the dupes of the subsidized farming sectors of developed countries who accept the 'lies' about Brazilian agriculture's environmental performance.

Discussion

It is outside the scope of this chapter to determine whether modern agriculture in western Bahia, with its reliance on fossil fuels for energy, control of weeds and pest control, and imported nutrients, can ever be 'sustainable'. Such a discussion is purely theoretical because, at present, modern soybean agriculture is a major source of foreign exchange and occupies enormous areas in Brazil. We focus instead on three substantive points, stressing compliance with Brazil's existing environmental laws rather than 'sustainability'.

First, classification of existing land covers revealed that the critics of modern agriculture are half right. Cerrado vegetation has been largely removed in the far west of the study area; but in other areas, especially along stream valleys unsuited to modern farming, significant tracts of Cerrado remain. We do not yet know the ecological integrity of remaining Cerrado, but intact Cerrado gives credibility to one of AIBA's initiatives. For example, AIBA has floated the idea of creating an ecological corridor that would link the large area of intact Cerrado to smaller remnants. Under this plan, farmers without Cerrado, and thus in violation of the Legal Reserve provision, could establish their 20 per cent Legal Reserve on another farmer's land, a manoeuvre permitted by existing forestry legislation. Our remote-sensing analysis may prove useful in modelling AIBA's ecological corridor plan against other options, such as attempts to regenerate Cerrado around existing fragments. In any event, areas of remaining Cerrado vegetation are destined to become the focus of a policy debate: will the Legal Reserve problem be regional, in the form of a region-wide conservation programme led by AIBA, or will establishment of the Legal Reserve remain the sole individual responsibility of farmers, regulated by an inadequate number of state officials operating with meagre budgets?

Second, national or state-level sustainability policymaking, but for one exception, provide only a partial framework for understanding the policy debates occurring in western Bahia state. With regard to modern agriculture, Brazil's Agenda 21 process seems more suited to satisfy concerns of environmental activists than to encourage improved environmental performance from soya farmers. Yet, as the case of AIBA indicates, some large farmers, organized in associations, have seized the 'sustainability' idea and deployed it to no small effect. AIBA is the lead institution in crafting environmental policies; it also represents the farmers who are portrayed by environmental activists (often employed in state agencies) as villains bent on destroying every last remnant of Cerrado.

The exception to this generalization is the 'Green Protocol' federal mandate that requires state-owned banks to employ environmental criteria in disbursing credit. For modern farmers, the most pressing criterion is compliance with existing legislation, thus raising the issue of the (often missing) Legal Reserve on private farmland. Instead of launching a legal battle against this provision, AIBA preferred to act as an information source for farmers who want to comply, perhaps grudgingly, with bank demands. A full understanding of how the 'Green Protocol' affects other resource uses awaits further analysis; indeed, this important instrument is notable by its absence in studies of Brazilian environmental policy.

Third, it is not yet clear whether AIBA's policies amount to 'greening' or 'greenwashing' (Brannstrom, 2005). AIBA is not alone as a private organization that deploys the national 'sustainability' discourse for the interests of its members. In places such as western Bahia, where state agencies are relatively weak, the emerging contradiction in policymaking is that a private organization creates 'public' policies. Thus, state agencies, the institutions charged with developing and implementing 'public' policies, face a dilemma: should they support the private organization's policies, or should they develop their own initiatives? If they follow the latter course, state agencies face the risk of widespread hostility amongst farmers. For example, adopting an aggressive policy to fine farmers not in compliance with Legal Reform obligations would not only be expensive, as it would rely on high-resolution satellite remote sensing data, but it would also be perceived as a disincentive to agricultural production and thus antagonize the regional elites. Supporting AIBA's policies, however, may mean that state agencies are adding a 'public' veneer to a policy intended for private interests.

Conclusion

Sustainable development policymaking in Brazil occurs within and across municipal, state and federal political-geographical scales. Brazil's modern agriculture is extremely important to the country's overall economic health, but as a sector it is largely absent from national level sustainability policymaking, and the scholarly analysis of policy debates. In addition, the motivations, actions and performance of private organizations in the sustainability debate, with regard to any resource-using sector, are not yet well described. These questions are especially pressing in the Brazilian Cerrado, a large savanna ecoregion south and east of the Amazon rainforest, that has rapidly become Brazil's grain belt.

AIBA's environmental initiatives include Cerrado conservation, agrochemical container recycling and participation in region-wide water management groups.

Cerrado conservation is important in the region; as our remote-sensing analysis indicated, modern agriculture in the study region left significant areas of Cerrado intact, as it created vast areas devoid of natural vegetation. Overall, AIBA's initiatives have taken the lead from rather ineffectual state agencies in crafting policy initiatives for the environment. It is not yet clear whether these policies amount to 'greening' or 'greenwash'. But we can affirm that the modern farming sector was unexpected in that it was omitted from Agenda 21 concerns in Brazil. As this case indicates, the organizations that represent the modern farm sector may prove to become both powerful allies and formidable opponents in sustainability policymaking.

References

Abakerli, S. (2001) A critique of development and conservation policies in environmentally sensitive regions in Brazil. *Geoforum*, 32, 551-565.

Adams, W. M. (2001) *Green Development: Environment and Sustainability in the Third World.* Routledge, London.

AIBA (2001a) *Caderno Especial AIBA.* Barreiras: [AIBA], Associação de Irrigantes do Oeste da Bahia.

AIBA (2001b) *Um novo modelo de ocupação dos cerrados do Oeste da Bahia.* Unpublished document, Associação de Irrigantes do Oeste da Bahia [AIBA].

AIBA (2002) *Caderno Especial Meio Ambiente.* Barreiras: [AIBA], Associação de Irrigantes do Oeste da Bahia.

AIBA (2003) [no title]. *InformAIBA* 9, 106.

AIBA (2004a) AIBA promove reuniões de conscientizaçãosobre a quest ãoam biental *InformAIBA* 11, 108.

AIBA (2004b) Termo de Responsabilidade Ambiental. *InformAIBA* 11, 108, 5.

AIBA (2004c) [no title]. *InformAIBA* 11, 109, 14.

AIBA (2004c) Política ambiental na região Oeste da Bahia. *InformAIBA* 11,117,12.

AIBA (2004d) [no title]. *InformAIBA* 11, 110, 2.

AIBA (2004e) Licenças Ambientais. *InformAIBA* 11, 113, 13.

AIBA (2004f) Meio Ambiente. *InformAIBA*, September, 14.

Alexandratos, N. (1999) World food and agriculture: Outlook for the medium and longer term. *Proceedings of the National Academy of Sciences,* 96, 11, 5908-5914.

Alho, C.J.R. & Martins, E.S. (1995) *De Grão em Grão, o Cerrado Perde Espaço: Cerrado--Impactos do Processo de Ocupação.* Fundo Mundial para a Natureza/ PROCER, Brasília, DF.

Ames, B. & Keck, M.E. (1997) The politics of sustainable development: Environmental policy making in four Brazilian states. *Journal of Interamerican Studies and World Affairs,* 39, 4, 1-40.

Bacha, C.J.C. (1996) Gestão florestal no Paraná. In Lopes, I.V., Bastos Filho, G.S., Biller, D. & Bale, M. (eds) *Gestão Ambiental no Brasil: Experiências e Sucesso.*

Fundação Getulio Vargas Editora, Rio de Janeiro, pp. 155-182.

Brannstrom, C. (2001) Conservation-with-development models in Brazil's agro-pastoral landscapes. *World Development*, 29, 1345-1359.

Brannstrom, C. (2004) Decentralising Brazilian water-resources management. *European Journal of Development Research*, 16, 1, 214-234.

Brannstrom, C. (2005) Environmental policy reform on north-eastern Brazil's agricultural frontier. *Geoforum*, 36, 257-271.

Brown, K. & Rosendo, S. (2000) Environmentalists, rubber tappers and empowerment: The politics and economics of extractive reserves. *Development and Change*, 31, 201-227.

Cardoso, C.A.S. (2002) *Extractive Reserves in Brazilian Amazonia: Local Resource Management and the Global Political Economy*. Ashgate, Aldershot.

CPDS (Comissão de Políticas de Desenvolvimento Sustentável e da Agenda 21 Nacional) (2002) *Agenda 21 Brasileira-Ações Prioritárias*. Ministério do Meio Ambiente, Brasília, DF.

Coutinho, L.M. (1978) O conceito do cerrado. *Revista Brasileira de Botânica*, 1, 17-23.

Dros, J.M. (2004) *Managing the soy boom: Two scenarios of soy production expansion in South America*. AIDEnvironment; World Wide Fund for Nature, Amsterdam.

Ekboir, J.M. (2003) Research and technology policies in innovation systems: zero tillage in Brazil. *Research Policy*, 32, 4, 573-586.

EMBRAPA. ca. (2003) *Monitoramento da Expansão das Áreas Irrigadas na Região Oeste da Bahia*. EMBRAPA-Monitoramento Por Satélite, Campinas.

Eve, E., Arguelles, F.A. & Fearnside, P.M. (2000) How well does Brazil's environmental law work in practice? Environmental impact assessment and the case of the Itapiranga private sustainable logging plan. *Environmental Management*, 26, 251-267.

FAO (2005) FAOSTAT database. Accessed 18 August at faostat.fao.org.

Fearnside, P.M. (1997) Environmental services as a strategy for sustainable development in rural Amazonia. *Ecological Economics*, 20, 53-70.

Fearnside, P.M. (2000) Deforestation impacts, environmental services and the international community. In Hall, A. (ed.) *Amazonia at the Crossroads: The Challenge of Sustainable Development*. Institute of Latin American Studies, London.

Fearnside, P.M. (2001) Soybean cultivation as a threat to the environment in Brazil. *Environmental Conservation*, 28, 23-38.

Fearnside, P.M. (2002) Avança Brasil: Environmental and social consequences of Brazil's planned infrastructure in Amazonia. *Environmental Management*, 30, 735-747.

Fearnside, P.M. (2003a) Conservation policy in Brazilian Amazonia: Understanding the dilemmas. *World Development*, 31, 757-779.

Fearnside, P.M. (2003b) Deforestation control in Mato Grosso: A new model for slowing the loss of Brazil's Amazon forest. *Ambio*, 32, 343-345.

Furley, P.A. (1999) The nature and diversity of neotropical savanna vegetation with particular reference to the Brazilian cerrados. *Global Ecology and Biogeography,* 8, 223-241.

Glaser, M., & Oliveira, R.D. (2004) Prospects for the co-management of mangrove ecosystems on the North Brazilian coast: Whose rights, whose duties and whose priorities? *Natural Resources Forum,* 28, 224-233.

Green, R.E., Cornell, S.J., Scharlemann, J.P.W. & Balmford, A. (2005) Farming and the fate of wild nature. *Science,* 307, 550-555.

Haesbaert, R. (1997) *Des-territorialização e identidade: A rede 'gaúcha' no nordeste.* Editora da Universidade Federal Fluminense, Niterói, RJ.

Hall, A. (1997) *Sustaining Amazonia: Grassroots Action for Productive Conservation.* Manchester University Press, Manchester.

Hall, A. (2000) Environment and development in Brazilian Amazonia: From protectionism to productive conservation. In Hall, A. (ed.) *Amazonia at the Crossroads: The Challenge of Sustainable Development.* Institute of Latin American Studies, London, pp. 99-114.

Herzog, F. (2005) Agri-environmental schemes as landscape experiments. *Agriculture, Ecosystems and Environment,* 108, 175-177.

Hochstetler, K. (2002) After the boomerang: Environmental movements and politics in the La Plata River Basin. *Global Environmental Politics,* 2, 35-57.

Holmes, T.P., Blate, G.M., Zweede, Jr. J.C., Pereira, R., Barreto, P., Boltz, F. & Bauch, R. (2002) Financial and ecological indicators of reduced impact logging performance in the eastern Amazon. *Forest Ecology and Management,* 163, 93-110.

IBGE (2003) *Censo Agropecuário; Sistema de Recuperação Automática.* Accessed 16 July 2003 at www.sidra.ibge.gov.

Jepson, W. (2005) A Disappearing Biome? Reconsidering Land-Cover Change in the Brazilian Savanna. *The Geographical Journal,* 171, 99-111.

Kaimowitz, D. & Smith, J. (2001) Soybean technology and the loss of natural vegetation in Brazil and Bolivia. In Angelsen, A. & Kaimowitz, D. (eds) *Agricultural Technologies and Tropical Deforestation.* CABI Publishing, Oxford, pp. 195-211.

Keck, M.A. (1998) Planafloro in Rondônia: The limits of leverage. In Fox, J.A. & Brown. L.D. (eds) *The Struggle for Accountability: The World Bank, NGOs, and Grassroots Movements.* The MIT Press, Cambridge, MA, pp.181-218.

Kimbrell, A. (ed.) (2002) *Fatal Harvest: The Tragedy of Industrialized Agriculture.* Island Press, Washington, DC.

Klink, C.A., Moreira, A.G. & Solbrig, O.T. (1993) Ecological impact of agricultural development in the Brazilian cerrados. In Young, M.D. & Solbrig, O.T. (eds) *The World's Savannas: Economic Driving Forces, Economic Constraints and Policy Options for Sustainable Land Use.* UNESCO, Paris, pp. 259-282.

Klink, C.A., & Moreira, A.G. (2002) Past and current human occupation, and land use. In Oliveira, P.S. & Marquis, R.J. (eds) *The Cerrados of Brazil: Ecology and Natural History of a Neotropical Savanna.* Columbia University Press, New York, pp. 69-88.

Kolk, A. (1998) From conflict to cooperation: International policies to protect the Brazilian Amazon. *World Development*, 26, 1481-1493.

Laabs, V., Amelung, W., Pinto, A.A., Wantzen, M., da Silva, C.J. & Zech, W. (2002) Pesticides in surface water, sediment, and rainfall of the northeastern Pantanal basin, Brazil. *Journal of Environmental Quality*, 31, 1636-1648.

Landers, J.N., Barros, G.S.D., Rocha, M.T., Manfrinato, W.A. & Weiss, J. (2003) Environmental impacts of zero tillage in Brazil - a first approximation. In García-Torres, L., Benites, J., Martínez-Vilela, A. & Holgado-Cabrera, A. (eds) *Conservation Agriculture: Environment, Farmers Experiences, Innovations, Socio-Economy, Policy*. Kluwer Academic Publishers, Dordrecht, pp. 341-350.

Lemos, M.C. & de Oliveira, J.L.F. (2004) Can water reform survive politics? Institutional change and river basin management in Ceará, northeast Brazil. *World Development*, 32, 2121-2137.

Machado, R.B., Ramos Neto, M.B., Pereira, P.G.P., Caldas, E.F., Gonçalves, D.A., Santos, N.S., Tabor, K. & Steininger, M. (2004) *Estimativas de perda da área do Cerrado brasileiro*. Conservação Internacional, Brasília, DF.

Maia Gomes, G. (2001) *Velhas Secas em Novos Sertões*. IPEA, Brasília, DF.

McGrath, D.G. (2000) Avoiding a tragedy of the commons: Recent developments in the manangement of Amazonian fisheries. In Hall, A. (ed.) *Amazonia at the Crossroads: The Challenge of Sustainable Development*. Institute of Latin American Studies, London, pp. 171-187.

Mantovani, J.E. & Pereira, A. (1998) *Estimativa da integradidade da cobertura vegetal do cerrado/pantanal através de dados TM/Landsat*. Paper presented at the Simpósio Brasileiro de Sensoriamento Remoto, São José dos Campos. MMA (Ministério do Meio Ambiente, Brazil) (2002) *Agenda 21 Brasileira: Ações Prioritárias*. Publisher unknown, Brasília, DF.

MPOG (Ministério do Planejamento, Orçamento e Gestão, Brazil) (2003) *Plano Plurianual 2004-2007. Projeto de Lei*. Publisher unknown, Brasília, DF.

Myers, N., Mittermeier, R.A., Mittermeier, C.G., da Fonseca, G.A.B. & Kent, J. (2000) Biodiversity hotspots for conservation priorities. *Nature*, 403, 853-858.

Nepstad, D., McGrath, D., Alencar, A., Barros, A.C., Carvalho, G., Santilli, M. & del Vera Diaz, M. (2002) Frontier governance in Amazonia. *Science*, 295, 629-630.

Oliveira, J.A.P. de. (2002) Implementing environmental policies in developing countries through decentralization: The case of protected areas in Bahia, Brazil. *World Development*, 30, 1713-1736.

Oliveira, P.S. & Marquis, R.J. (eds) (2002) *The Cerrados of Brazil: Ecology and Natural History of a Neotropical Savanna*. Columbia University Press, New York.

Pitt, S. (2004) Paradox nacional: Produtor é penalizado por produzir. *InformAIBA* 11, 117, 2.

Pretty, J., Brett, C., Gee, D., Hine, R., Mason, C., Morison, J., Rayment, M., van der Bilj, G. & Dobbs, T. (2001) Policy challenges and priorities for internalizing the externalities of modern agriculture. *Journal of Environmental Planning and Management*, 44, 263-283.

Raisa, A. (2004) Editorial. *InformAIBA* 11, 109, 2.

Ratter, J.A., Ribeiro, J.F. & Bridgewater, S. (1997) The Brazilian Cerrado vegetation and threats to its biodiversity. *Annals of Botany*, 80, 223-230.

Ribeiro, J.F. & Walter, B.M.T. (1998) Fitofissionomias do bioma Cerrado. In Sano S.M. & Almeida, S.P. (eds) *Cerrado: Ambiente e Flora*. EMBRAPA, Planaltina, DF, pp. 89-166.

Rodrigues, M.G.M. (2004) *Global Environmentalism and Local Politics: Transnational Advocacy Networks in Brazil, Ecuador, and India*. State University of New York Press, Albany.

Romero, S. (2002) U.S. farmers put down roots in Brazilian soil. *New York Times*, 1 December.

Rothman, F.D. (2001) A comparative study of dam-resistance campaigns and environmental policy in Brazil. *Journal of Environment and Development*, 10, 317-344.

Santa Cruz Filho, H. (2002) Editorial. *InformAIBA*, August, 2.

Scholz, I. (2001) *Overexploitation or Sustainable Management: Action Patterns of the Tropical Timber Industry: The Case of Pará (Brazil) 1960-1997*. Frank Cass Publishers, London.

Silva, J.E., Lemainski, J. & Resck, D.V.S. (1994) Perdas de matéria orgânica e suas relações com a capacidade de troca de catiônica em solos da região de cerrados no oeste baiano. *Revista Brasileira de Ciência do Solo*, 18, 541-547.

Smith, J., Winograd, M., Gallopin, G. & Pachico, D. (1998) Dynamics of the agricultural frontier in the Amazon and savannas of Brazil: analysing the impact of policy and technology. *Environmental Modeling and Assessment*, 3, 31-46.

Spera, S.T., Reatto, A., Martins, E.S., Correia, J.R. & Cunha, T.J.F. (1999) *Solos areno-quartzosos no Cerrado: problemas, características e limitações ao uso*. EMBRAPA Cerrados, Planaltina, DF.

Théry, H. (2000) *Le Brésil*. Armand Colin, Paris.

Thompson, P.B. (1995) *The Spirit of the Soil: Agriculture and Environmental Ethics*. Routledge, New York.

Tilman, D., Cassman, K.G., Matson, P.A., Naylor, R. & Polasky, S. (2002) Agricultural sustainability and intensive production practices. *Nature*, 418, 671-677.

USDA (2004) *Brazil: Oilseeds and Products Annual 2004*. GAIN Report #BR4611. Foreign Agricultural Service, Brasília, DF.

USDA (2005a) *Brazil: Oilseeds and Products Annual 2005*. GAIN Report #BR5613. Foreign Agricultural Service, Brasília, DF.

USDA (2005b) *Oilseeds: World Markets and Trade (August)*. Foreign Agricultural Service, Washington, DC.

Warnken, P.F. (1999) *The Development and Growth of the Soybean Industry in Brazil*. Iowa State University Press, Ames, IA.

Wood, D. & Lanné, J.M. (2005) 'Received wisdom' in agricultural land use policy: 10 years on from Rio. *Land Use Policy*, 22, 75-93.

Young, C.E.F. & Roncisvalle, C.A. (2002) *Expenditures, Investment and Financing for Sustainable Development in Brazil*. United Nations (CEPAL/ECLAC), Santiago, Chile.

Chapter 15

Uniting National Aspirations and Local Implementation in Sustainable Development: Lessons Learnt and Ways Forward

Alan Terry, Jennifer Hill and Wendy Woodland

Introduction

The myriad debates concerning sustainable development in the developing world preclude any attempt to formulate a definitive set of conclusions and recommendations from a relatively small range of case studies, despite their diversity within varying socio-economic, cultural and environmental contexts. Nevertheless, for the sake of simplicity in structuring the book, the chapters were organized according to three themes which concerned the challenges, opportunities and progress made in uniting national aspirations and local implementation in sustainable development. These were the measurement of sustainable development, the role of education in sustainable development and the significance of diverse voices in the practice of sustainable development.

The themes reveal a tension in implementing the post-Rio idea of sustainability. This is because there was simultaneously an expectation that national governments (via National Environmental Action Plans) would identify overarching environmental goals, whilst encouraging local actors (via Agenda 21) to exercise their understanding of the environmental challenges facing them. The consequences have been a plurality of perceptions and actions that have often failed to meet national aspirations. Key factors that have prevented this appear to be the problem of translating from one scale to another, whether upwards or downwards; the unwillingness of the powerful to redistribute their power in a way that would enable diverse local actors to manage their environment more rationally; the failure of the education system to successfully challenge conventional values and practices; an inability to agree on the current state of the environment and the direction in which it is moving; insufficient resources to translate useful ideas into improvements on the ground and an inability to move from sectoral planning so that economic and environmental policy goals are often incompatible with one another.

Measuring sustainable development

Any debate concerning environmental response to human impact, whether it follows a more or less sustainable path, requires some ability to measure and understand past, present and future states of that environment. This can be seen in the resettlement of former white commercial farms in Zimbabwe (Elliott *et al.,* Chapter 2). The need for such debate is crucial at a time when communal systems are being reconsidered in a more positive light, coinciding with growing emphasis on the potential of a more decentralized approach to natural resource management (Shackleton *et al.,* 2002). In Zimbabwe, the absence of systematic monitoring and evaluation of the social and environmental outcomes of resettlement led to a privileging of powerful neo-Malthusian narratives (Neumann, 2005). These narratives argued that the future of fertile commercial farming areas would most likely mirror degraded communal areas. Evidence gained from short-term evaluations, however, did not reflect the highly variable nature of both the physical and socio-economic environments in which resettlement was taking place. Such evidence tends to miss long-term trends (Swift, 1996). Lacking baseline evidence, and with little appreciation of spatio-temporal variations in the physical resource base, the resettlement scheme was ripe for over-generalized assessments. Into this veritable 'fog of war', Elliot and her co-authors provide evidence that a conventional linear degradation narrative cannot explain the complex, multi-directional spatial and temporal land cover changes that have occurred within individual scheme areas. This partly reflects the significant variability in the agro-ecological potential of different schemes, but it also demonstrates the utility of longer term analyses. Of particular importance here is the realization that scale does matter to sustainability assessment (Marston *et al.,* 2005).

   Elliot *et al.* use sequential air photo and GIS analysis to provide objective evidence of patterns of land cover change as a result of resettlement. The use of a scientific method to highlight environmental outcomes illustrates that a simplistic debate over whether modern or indigenous derived knowledge is better able to uncover the multiple realities in 'traditional' systems is less important than understanding the potential and limitations of any chosen method. The authors hope that the collection of scientific data in Zimbabwe can be used to make environmental issues more visible in future resettlement planning and to integrate issues of sustainable development into mainstream policy making in a way that they have not been to date.

   An examination of community-based rangeland degradation indicators in Botswana highlights the need to look through alternative optics (Blaikie, 1995) when environmental parameters are measured with the aim of improving management systems (Dougill and Reed, Chapter 3). A move to bottom-up measurement has been promulgated as an important element in enabling participatory projects to reach their full potential (Lingayah, *et al.,* 1999). In Botswana, however, indicators that reflected local community knowledge about their proximate environments were validated by scientific methods. Such a process can reveal the relative strengths and weaknesses of conventional expert-led, top-down sustainability indicators compared to bottom-up, community-led indicators. In this case, conventional expert-led indicators of degradation over-simplified degradation assessment by leading to polarized views of either 'good or bad' rangeland, rather than focusing on management adaptations to ecological changes that retained overall pastoral system productivity. The process of knowledge production provided a practical benefit for environmental managers which reliance upon conventional indicators was unable to achieve. The research did uncover some similarities in the two types of indicators, however, suggesting a need to unite different knowledge systems (Agrawal, 1995).

Although Dougill and Reed admit that it is too early to evaluate the impact of rangeland assessment guides on either management systems or the state of rangeland vegetation, they appear confident that the process by which the guides were created is robust and therefore the indicators will prove useful to land managers, whether they be pastoralists or outside scientists. They do, however, identify two problems based on wider application of their community developed indicators. A methodological problem involved the issue of scaling up from local to regional and national scales such that improved national monitoring of degradation could be initiated based on community-led approaches. The authors acknowledged that their ability to collapse locally derived scales into fewer, more widely applicable ones was not a process that could be undertaken easily because, even when the transformations were transparent, local detail would be subsumed in the process. They did believe, however, that as long as the method remained hybrid (in that the process was validated scientifically), it may be possible to derive modified community-developed indicators that could apply to large uniform agro-ecological zones. More conventional environmental degradation monitoring approaches (such as ecological survey and satellite remote sensing) would retain a role in evaluating the relevance of such community-based assessments of land degradation problems. A second, and more invidious problem, existed outside the control of hybrid researchers. Once again, it involved the need to break down the neo-Malthusian discourses espoused by policy makers, trainers of extension workers and many involved in the formal management of natural resources. At present, national policy interventions in Botswana fail to address land degradation issues that matter to rural people. Despite research providing information on both local and scientific indicators of degradation, policies remain focused on traditionally powerful degradation narratives. The result is that the broader structures within which land users operate remain unchanged as the root causes of the problem are ignored. If participatory methodologies are to be incorporated into policy, greater attention must be paid to these broader systems of policy-making and governance.

A green national accounting system is proposed by Atkinson (Chapter 4), which relies on experts to estimate a market value for tropical forest resources in Peru and India such that national accounts reflect the impact of forest conversion to other land uses. This is a complex procedure as it requires calculation of multiple natural and social values for forests. These include values for timber, which vary by type and age, carbon sequestration, watershed services, soil and biodiversity conservation and a range of non-timber forest products including fuel, food and medicine (Haripriya, 2001; Gavin, 2004). Such a system promotes the conservation of forest biodiversity through the use of neo-liberal market forces (Brown, 2002). Key issues for policy makers, with respect to national accounting for sustainable development, are the identification of critical natural capital (CNC), threshold levels and indications regarding how serious for human well-being a breach of any relevant threshold is likely to be (Muradian, 2001; Ekins *et al.,* 2003; Huggett, 2005; Lindenmayer & Luck, 2005). Integration of ecology, economics and sociology is essential to operationalize the concept of CNC as a tool for moving towards more balanced environmental planning (Rennings & Wiggering, 1997; Chiesura & De Groot, 2003).

One problem of applying such a national accounting system is that different groups may attribute different values to the same resource. Powerful actors outside of the immediate vicinity can influence the values assigned to a resource, whilst local actors can, as Dougill and Reed demonstrate, use their knowledge of the resource to manage it sustainably over time. Thus, although the concept of green national accounts is a huge step forward when attempting to assess the current state of sustainability in a country, the scale at which the accounts are derived is likely to miss, or even misinterpret, the impact of a particular management regime. This situation has been well documented for West African forest resources by Leach & Mearns (1996), Fairhead & Leach (1996) and Oates (1999). It is also partly acknowledged by Atkinson and, given the complexities of trying to understand what is happening across a large area, the methods outlined in his chapter should perhaps be blended with those adopted by Dougill and Reed to further hybridize the methodology relating to the measurement and management of the environment. The methodology of identifying indicators to green national accounts therefore needs dovetailing with attempts to create community-developed indicators. As some of the main gaps in the former reflect problems in assigning a value to non-marketable aspects of resources, whilst the latter attempt to identify what people actually know and value about their environment, opportunities would seem to exist to refine green accounts so that they are the subject of significant stakeholder participation during their formulation. Refinement of these indicators is necessary to account fully for environmental costs and benefits during the development process. Despite these reservations, many governments around the world are currently implementing green accounting frameworks as one response to the need to monitor progress towards or away from sustainable development.

Quinn and Marriott (Chapter 5) evaluate a decade of national water management policy in South Africa. They adopt the premise that, within the context of water resource management, sustainability can be assessed and they combine the criteria of Gleick (1998) and Dowdeswell (1998) to form a framework for evaluating progress towards sustainability. This framework covers eight aspects from basic human water rights, through ecosystem water rights and water quality management, to participative decision making and long term renewability. Their conclusion is that the water laws have already had a major positive impact on the lives of many of South Africa's citizens. Commitments to equity and ecological rights are well developed and the concept of ecological reserves helps to identify specific geographical locations that have a minimum right to water that takes precedence over all other users. How this might be assessed under the circumstances of, for example, extreme drought are not explored, but this element of the law does place the environment in a privileged position compared to most countries.

The need for non-extractive land uses such as forestry to possess extractive licenses is a noteworthy attempt to ensure that their hidden demand for large quantities of water, an external cost to other users in the same catchment area, is reflected in the pricing system. In attempting to identify the actual amounts of water used by forests of various types and in various stages of growth and then assigning the true value of that water in the form of a license, it might be possible to begin to use this process to create more transparent green accounts in the form outlined by Atkinson. However, in order to achieve a true net value, the license fee should also reflect the social benefits of forest resources such as soil conservation and carbon sequestration, a step which does not appear to have been contemplated in the Act. A crucially important step in enabling the Act to function has been the strengthening of a national monitoring system which enables changes in water quality and quantity over time and space to be assessed, a crucial omission in the Zimbabwean resettlement scheme outlined by Elliot *et al.*

Issues remain in South Africa with the identification of what constitutes good water quality, mainly due to a lack of trained manpower within the relevant departments and an inability to enable effective participatory management in the Catchment Management Associations. Implicit in the analysis is the problem of scaling up from local to regional and national scales such that no discontinuity exists between decisions taken at one location that, although logical in that context, will have detrimental impacts further afield. These issues are likely to place considerable strain on the implementation of the Act and an area that seems to require further research is the extent to which different local or regional pressures, whether physical or social, create specific problems in applying the new laws. The criterion that human action will not impair long-term renewability of freshwater stocks and flows is possibly the most difficult to evaluate, particularly since the success of this endeavour will only be known in years to come. Incremental improvement is perhaps the best indicator of a long-term trajectory, but this implies the need to evaluate improvements against goals and targets set out in plans. As Elliot *et al.* note, such baseline data are often absent. Finally, although not stated explicitly, the concept of an ecological reserve suggests that those responsible for drafting the law were influenced by concepts that see environmental systems as achieving some sort of equilibrium over time. Given the prevalence of non-equilibrium ecological systems in many semi-arid environments of South Africa, it would be interesting to see the extent to which, in practice, those charged with identifying critical limits to water resources accept the fact that systems may be able to cope with what might have been considered as fatal shocks by those with a traditional equilibrium trained background.

The role of education in sustainable development

Given that the concept of sustainable development is rooted in the idea of inter-generational equity, it is unsurprising that the international community has emphasized the role of children in relation to achieving sustainability. Indeed, environmental education is recognized globally as critical for the successful pursuit of sustainable development (WCED, 1987; UNESCO, 1997, 2002). Ferguson and Thomas-Hope (Chapter 6) argue that Jamaica's environmental education discourse is a direct outgrowth from the global hegemonic sustainability discourse. The role of environmental education in Jamaica is to promote sustainable development, thereby changing attitudes and behaviour towards the environment so that its degradation does not harm economic growth, especially in the tourism sector.

The formal education system in Jamaica has not been very effective in educating students about sustainable development. This undermines the ability of the system to change student attitudes and behaviour towards the environment. In general, there is little appreciation of the mutual inter-relationship between humans, nature and the environment. The authors argue that environmental education tends to reproduce the *status quo*, a situation which fails to develop students' critical awareness of ideas and knowledge transmitted to them which, in turn, means that little effective challenge is made to the hegemonic discourses that have created extant environmental problems. Thus, there is little appreciation by the educators or the educated that locally derived knowledge is legitimate in the face of ideas transmitted through the formal classroom system.

Ferguson and Thomas-Hope see a possible development in pedagogic practice by creating a curriculum that allows a critique of the current dominant Jamaican discourse and which allows study of alternative environmental discourses in order to align more closely with national and local needs. It would be useful, for example, to engage with a range of indigenous alternatives that are located in Jamaica or elsewhere in the region. Local and individual knowledges need to be acknowledged and pedagogic practices need to be changed such that students become active thinkers and not passive recipients of other people's knowledge. This relates partially to the quality of the teachers. Finally, schools need to practice what they preach and, through the actions of the staff and the values imparted, they should demonstrate how the environment could be treated with more respect by those who are members of the school community. These innovations are more difficult in an education system which itself is inadequately resourced, but as the authors acknowledge, this is not an insurmountable or valid reason for failing to act.

From the perspective of Ferguson and Thomas-Hope, environmental education needs to be the subject of change before it can become the agent of change with respect to attitudes and behaviours that encourage sustainable development. To be an effective vehicle for sustainable development, environmental education might very well need to undergo a critical shift in order to move beyond its lingering role as a reproducer of hegemonic environmental values. However, this conclusion could probably be made for all education systems as in practice there is little evidence that any but a minority of students voluntarily incorporate such changes into their post-school life choices.

The changes suggested for the Jamaican education system relate entirely to changes *within* the system. This omits an important element outlined by Ansell (Chapter 7) that Agenda 21 calls for young people to be given the opportunity to engage more directly in decision-making in the world outside of the education system and it certainly considers them well equipped to contribute to sustainable development. In fact, when given the opportunity, children are able to act as commentators on the environment, especially with respect to the ways that they use it and are affected by it. Ansell's analysis of education and sustainable development in Lesotho in the post-Rio period differs from that of Ferguson and Thomas-Hope. Rather than seeing the outcome of The Earth Summit as the promotion of a hegemonic discourse that promotes a particular type of knowledge, she argues that it actually promotes diverse knowledge claims which now need to be integrated into the curriculum. Rather than focusing exclusively on cognitive knowledge, environmental education should promote affective knowledge (involving emotion and sensation), gained partly from immersion in the environment. Environmental education should give credence to diverse knowledge systems, including science, cultural and social sensitivities. However, as Ansell points out, even by the time of the second Earth Summit in Johannesburg in 2002, the UN were unable to find many successful models of environmental education in any country. Since 1992, environmental education has become one of three emerging issues identified by the Education Strategy Plan which specifically mentions both indigenous and non-indigenous skills as part of the programme of learning.

Supported by 'northern' educationalists, the Lesotho Environmental Education Support Project (LEESP) seeks to change curriculum, teacher training, monitoring and the setting up of Model Schools, the last point being similar to the approach adopted in Jamaica. A key challenge in the implementation of environmental education in Lesotho schools is the fact that environmental education, as conceived in Agenda 21, does not fit the education paradigm that currently exists in the country. A paradigm shift is required in the way in which teachers think about their role. Environmental education requires teachers to work together to construct complex ideas that transcend disciplinary boundaries. However, changing the basic structure of a highly centralized exam-driven system, in which subject specialists see any attempt at inter-disciplinarity as a potential threat to the integrity of their part of the curriculum, is a major challenge. Another fundamental barrier relates to the fact that Lesotho's education system has historically focused on the transfer of Western knowledges, with teachers serving as conduits and students as passive recipients. As in Jamaica, the structural problems linked to a lack of adequate resources within the education sector will also have inhibited LEESP in its attempt to make environmental education more fit for purpose. The initiative does, however, look at the long-term and it may be possible to overcome some of the barriers, especially as a new generation of teachers enters the system that may have benefited from the attempt at paradigm change within the training colleges.

In contrast to examining the role of the formal education sector, Newton's analysis (Chapter 8) of the attempt to make Namibia's agricultural extension service more gender-aware highlights the role of a less formal education system in promoting more sustainable skills and attitudes. By embedding gender-aware programmes into its National Agricultural Policy, the post-colonial government has attempted to redress the neglect of former 'native reserves'. This is an attempt to address sustainable development through projects that, by addressing the interests of women, begin to tackle rural poverty. In theory, this should create government institutions in which a bottom-up, participatory and gender-aware staff exist.

The structure established to facilitate transmission of new ideas in Namibia has the potential to be empowering as the spread of new technology and the ability to take women out of traditional engendered spaces has, in some circumstances, been able to reduce the specific roles acceptable to men and women. It provides opportunities for women to gain confidence and ideas that can be converted into new livelihood strategies. However, by failing to pre-examine the social differences that existed within communities, even within the female population, the preferred structures by which new knowledge may be transmitted to farmers has been undermined. Women are still not seen as having the status to be carriers of new knowledge and, in a patriarchal society, most do not have the confidence to overcome these setbacks. The research argues, therefore, that for the policy to reach its objectives, a much better understanding of the relationships within communities and between communities and key outsiders needs to occur (Cooke & Kothari, 2001). Additionally, there needs to be an awareness of the historical and political context in which such interventions are being implemented if they are to have a hope of reaching their full potential of poverty reduction and improvements to the sustainability of the agricultural system. Newton suggests, however, that deep-seated attitudes may not be challenged by agricultural extension workers whose main realm is in technical matters and this points to the need for a deeper engagement with experts who have a greater insight into the workings of indigenous social systems.

The significance of diverse voices in the practice of sustainable development

There has been increasing criticism of a simplistic understanding of communities in sustainable development projects. Communities are not small homogeneous entities, existing without internal conflict and therefore able to act as democratic units (Leach *et al.*, 1997; Agrawal & Gibson, 1999). In fact, the actors who influence their local environment are socially differentiated in a number of ways, including gender, ethnicity, religion, economic status and political persuasion. Participation of relevant stakeholders is crucial to sustainable development, not as a top-down management process that co-opts people passively, but as active, empowered agents (Craig & Mayo, 1995). Participatory development therefore needs careful definition and application, especially in terms of differential empowerment (Cooke & Kothari, 2001).

Dougill and Reed (Chapter 3) highlight that, crucial to the establishment of a successful community-based natural resource management project in Botswana, is the inclusion of many stakeholders (communal and commercial pastoralists, rich and poor, extension workers and policy-makers) in identifying range degradation indicators. This empowers community members and strengthens social capital, as predicted by Macgillivray *et al.* (1998). Similar results have been witnessed as a consequence of engagement with the community indicator development process in the slums of India and South Africa (Terry, 2001).

Dougill and Reed adopted an iterative expert-community dialogue, combining scientific and local knowledges, to establish a more diversified understanding. Such hybrid or fusion knowledge (Batterbury *et al.*, 1997; Nygren, 1999; Brown, 2002; Thomas & Twyman, 2004) could prove to be a useful tool in improving rangeland sustainability. The authors stress that community-led methods of rangeland degradation monitoring in Botswana should be more directly and quickly fed back into the formal planning process and that new community-based institutions should have formal Government support, especially through reform of Extension Services from being top-down dissemination, to being bottom-up and facilitative of implementing community-led monitoring and management planning. Though necessary, institutional change in Botswana is not easy to accomplish, especially as the implications of successful community-based indicators, and the management schemes based upon them, may marginalize those professionals who view their role as one of policing irrational users of natural resources (Blaikie, 2000). The blindness of outside 'experts' to the potential benefits of community involvement in more strategic management decisions is an ongoing theme in many of the chapters in this book and it represents a major obstacle to unlocking the untapped knowledge within communities. Local knowledge can be more powerful in influencing national decision-making compared to the expert opinion provided by international academic debate, but it must be viewed objectively and used in national policy decision-making.

Newton (Chapter 8) highlights the importance of marginalized community groups such as women to the goal of sustainable development (see also Momsen, 1991; Braidotti *et al.,* 1994; Visvanathan, 1997; Kothari, 2001; Williams, 2004). This issue came to the forefront of the international development agenda through forums such as the Earth Summit in 1992 and the Millennium Summit in 2000, with specific millennium development goals targeted at gender equality and sustainable development. Newton examines attempts within the Ministry of Agriculture, Water and Rural Development in Namibia to integrate gender within its agricultural extension services. She shows that the creation of committee structures responsible for disseminating agricultural knowledge across communities gives limited recognition to existing networks of social interaction, many of which are gendered. Newton concludes that, although the adoption of the extension approach provides considerable benefits for women in terms of meeting practical gender interests and improving access to a range of livelihood strategies, the majority of them remain excluded from more 'empowering' benefits that challenge the existing gender division of labour. These findings suggest that policy makers should focus more on how development intervention is internalized at the development interface to allow more local and relevant strategies against vulnerability to evolve. These are likely to be inclusive of more community members, making them more sustainable in the long term. Women's relationships with the environment are differentiated, however, so their varied interests and responses need segregating (Middleton *et al.,* 1993).

Momsen's examination of recent changes in relation to gender, agriculture and tourism in the Caribbean (Chapter 9) indicates that the move to both sustainable tourism and sustainable food production has been strongly encouraged by the action of hegemonic powers, traditionally seen as dominating the Caribbean region. Such top-down planning has led to slower uptake at the grassroots level because of poor implementation and lack of local understanding of the benefits of farming practices such as integrated pest management (IPM). Farming using IPM techniques requires active management on the part of farmers as they must constantly gather and evaluate information about pests, crops and weather conditions. This level of management is especially difficult for smallholder, part-time farmers who rarely keep records. In addition, the use of IPM practices frequently requires a greater reliance on contact with agricultural advisors and researchers. Such contact is least available to small-scale, semi-commercial farmers, especially women, as the few available advisors tend to concentrate on working with large-scale export producers. Consequently, many small-scale farmers have heard of IPM but few are applying it. Many local women farmers, however, have established a sustainable lifestyle which is taking advantage of the new interest in the hotel industry for environmentally friendly and sustainable tourism. Women appear to be more responsive than men to the possibilities of new demands within the regional tourist sector. This suggests that new actors in the sustainability debate may be coming to the fore in the absence of a clear, consistent and appropriate lead from government.

Despite the fact that Agenda 21 emphasizes the need for participation by the wider community, there is little evidence of this having been achieved in Zimbabwe's National Conservation strategy. James (Chapter 10) shows that, despite a long history of commitment to conservation of farmland by central government, there has been little attempt to conserve soil fertility in cotton-growing regions, particularly in communal areas. This situation appears to have persisted since the adoption of more participatory, livelihood-focused approaches, a period that also coincided with a liberalization of the Zimbabwean cotton industry. Prior to the 1990s state agricultural institutions and local politicians drove households to grow cotton. Most indigenous farming methods were vilified by state institutions and marginalized by the general discourse of modernity. The 'participatory' counter-discourse focused on finding alternatives to cotton and maize dominance. While there is evidence of rejection of cotton growing by some households since the 1990s, empirical evidence of practice within fields in Nembudziya suggests a range of efforts by householders to protect and sustain soil fertility under cotton. There is support, therefore, for different 'pathways' of change based on particular stakeholders and their circumstances in different rural areas (Scoones & Wolmer, 2002). Overall, despite national and institutional ambitions to increase cotton productivity, yields within the communal areas have remained low and environmental degradation has increased. The government has failed to recognize the attempts by farmers in long-established cotton producing areas to improve soil fertility through experimentation on their farms, which could provide valuable lessons, if scaled up, to other cotton producing regions. In reality, little emphasis has been placed on community participation, but this is hardly surprising given the apparent disengagement with the local physical environment by the key supporting agency.

A similar pessimistic tale, though with reference to the compatibility of land allocation and sustainable agricultural development, can be seen in Van Waveren's study of customary tenured land in Swaziland (Chapter 11). Here, an indigenous system of managing land appears to be incompatible with the aims of the Swaziland Environmental Action Plan (SEAP) that seeks to increase the productivity and sustainability of farms on customary tenured land. Traditional powers are reluctant to change the system of land allocation because it is the basis of significant economic and political leverage, as well as being the essential means by which the King retains political power. Consequently, land is often allocated irrationally, resulting in a mismatch between the best soils and arable fields. As in Zimbabwe, farmers appear to make the most of a poor situation by acting rationally within an often irrational system and concentrating their efforts onto the best land that has been allocated to them. This is in line with findings in other parts of Sub-Saharan Africa to the effect that local indigenous management systems are capable of developing efficient forms of land use (Tiffen *et al.*, 1994; Juma & Ojwang, 1996; Reij *et al.*, 1996; Watson *et al.*, 1998).

Given the regional imbalance between the distribution of population and good quality arable land in Swaziland, for sustainable rural development to have a more realistic chance of succeeding requires a radical reform of the means by which land is allocated at this scale. The political sensitivity of this, however, together with the innate conservatism of the majority of the rural Swazi population, makes this a remote possibility at present. Given the widespread nature of this type of land tenure and allocation throughout Sub-Saharan Africa, it is unlikely that this situation is unique to Swaziland. The above underscores the need to develop a long-term development strategy of customary tenured land that is realistic, location-specific and addresses the specific requirements of the different land use systems. Any prolongation of the current *status quo* will reduce the opportunities for sustainable crop production on an increasingly larger part of the customary tenured land.

Woodland and Hill (Chapter 12) demonstrate how, after a long period of marginalization dating from the French colonial period and carried into post-independent Tunisia, indigenous skills and knowledge are being re-integrated with modern methods in the sustainable management of water resources. The subtleties of traditional rainwater harvesting systems, which allowed community-responsive adjustments between rainfall events, were largely unrecognized by water engineers trained under a Western education system. Instead, construction of large concrete dams in marginal rainfall zones favoured structures that were too rigid physically and socially to respond to extreme rainfall events. Recognition, however, of the failure of large-scale modern dams and reservoirs to provide cost-effective water supplies over an extended time period has probably been a major factor in the reintroduction of small-scale indigenous water harvesting methods in the upper catchments of these developments in an attempt to extend their lives by reducing sedimentation rates. Such projects render communities proactive and autonomous in the pursuit of local sustainable development and it engenders in them a sense of ownership within natural resource management. Local people are empowered to make decisions and to take action to secure their future. Such a dovetailing of different scales and technologies, integrated under a national planning structure, promotes a controlled but flexible approach to water management. This is crucial to long-term viability as it does not simply absorb indigenous expertise, but allows local voices to be heard in terms of hydrological and financial requirements (Agnew & Anderson, 1992).

Rediscovery of the value of indigenous knowledge is only part of the strategy to achieve sustainable use of the country's water resources. Thus, reliance upon market mechanisms via the raising of water tariffs to agriculture, currently and perversely subsidized, together with subsidies on more efficient modern drip irrigation systems, are also being employed to try to cut wastage and inappropriate use of water. These efforts have been undermined by inadequate training and application of such technologies, which points to the need for better liaison between modern water managers and indigenous managers, with a two-way communication of appropriate skills and knowledge.

Whilst such developments seem encouraging, structural imbalances in the national and wider economy suggest that the long-term viability of the strategies is questionable. Out-migration to urban centres within Tunisia and international migration to the European Union is reducing the essential supply of labour on which indigenous and modern water saving technologies depend. Whether such technologies can provide livelihoods that can compete with the lure of higher off-farm incomes, plus the perception of greater social and economic returns in urban centres remains a key question. A further consideration relates to the current mining of internationally shared 'fossil' artesian water in the south of Tunisia. At present, it is unclear whether institutional arrangements for its management will be able to prevent a tragedy of the commons. A similar situation exists with the exploitation of shallow water aquifers and it will be interesting to see whether local or international institutions are more successful in creating a sustainable use of their respective resources. This could provide a useful contrast between these newly established local and supra-national institutions and it will be important in the future that lessons are transmitted from one scale to another.

The problem of managing communal resources from a national to a highly localized level is identified in Terry and Shepherd's research into marine resource management by the Bajau community of the Tukangbesi Archipelago in Indonesia (Chapter 13). Despite a comprehensive engagement with the sustainability discourse in the post-Rio period, translated into a series of comprehensive plans that place sustainability at the heart of decision making, major obstacles can be identified that have prevented the vision from becoming reality. Since 1997, as a result of economic stagnation, fish resources have been viewed as a potential alternative source of wealth with plans for major expansion in fishing effort. This has been possible because of an inability to identify sustainable limits to fishing and a poor understanding of the current state of fish stocks. However, because of institutional complexity in managing marine resources, with multiple and often contradictory aims within competing bodies, the attempt to impose sustainability at the heart of the dominant narrative is undermined. These fuzzy boundaries between institutional responsibilities create uncertainties that Ostrom (1990) has identified as being detrimental to the sustainable management of communal resources. As pressures on fish stocks increase, from increasing population and increasing incomes within Indonesia and the wider region, the challenges facing all institutions are intensifying.

Challenges even extend to within protected marine national parks. The fortress policy (Neumann, 2005) that was initially adopted in the Wakatobi Marine National Park (WMNP) has, since 1997, been partly modified to accommodate a more inclusive approach with local communities. However, increasing differentiation within communities is making it more difficult to devise all-inclusive strategies. This is due to a decline in traditional values, especially amongst younger and/or wealthier members, and a greater engagement with the outside world, especially through the influence of market forces. In addition, the reaction to a decline in fish stocks seems to be contradictory by individual groups of fishers within communities. Whilst some have reacted by investing in 'conservation' methods, others seem to be adopting a more short-term unsustainable attitude by using fish traps. Attempts by the independent conservation organization, Operation Wallacea, to diversify livelihoods into alternative sustainable sources of income are in their early stages and it is therefore difficult to judge their effectiveness in reducing pressure on the remaining fish stocks. Similarly, the small-scale Hoga No-Fishing-Zone has achieved some success within its boundaries, involving the community in monitoring and enforcement of the resource, and re-emphasizing traditional authority. The concept of the local community in this area lacks clarity (Agrawal & Gibson, 1999) and this suggests that a major threat to community-based management is the lack of internal cohesion in the communities themselves. This appears to have been downplayed in the adoption of community based conservation policies at the national and regional level. However, in the past year, the WMNP Authority appears to be accepting the need to develop a more sophisticated understanding of the internal complexities of its community stakeholders, and this may yet facilitate the Bajau in managing their marine resources more sustainably.

Although increasing the number of no-fishing-zones would probably be beneficial, it is difficult to envisage a situation where, even if there was complete coverage, reliance upon community-based management would be sufficient to overcome major external pressures. This means that central or local modern institutions need to retain overall control of communal fish stocks to enable them to meet the challenges of over-fishing at the national and regional level. The message of Indonesia's attempt to manage its marine resources therefore appears to be ambivalent about the ability of national aspirations to be translated into local action. To rely upon local management systems appears to be naïve, but conflicting power bases within national and regional organizations make it difficult to create rational sustainable planning from the top down. Newman and LeDrew's (2005) analysis, however, of the post-1997 performance of Indonesia's Bunaken National Park does provide a more optimistic scenario.

Brannstrom and Filippi (Chapter 14) provide an example of how, in the absence of strong leadership from the public sector, national level 'sustainability' debate has had few tangible implications in Brazil's new soybean frontier of Bahia state. A regional-scale private association of farmers has taken the lead from ineffectual state agencies in crafting policy initiatives for the environment. These developments have occurred since 1999 when the *Associação de Agricultores e Irrigantes da Bahia* (AIBA), a policy-making body of approximately 1,200 large-scale farmers, opened an environmental desk which has lobbied state officials on environmental matters and encouraged farmers to comply with environmental laws. The state environmental body is poorly funded and this makes it difficult for it to ensure such compliance. By encouraging all farmers to comply with the law, AIBA projects itself as a champion of the environment. In so doing, it champions a discourse that acknowledges the past negative impacts of commercial farming on the Cerrado environment, but also emphasizes that past mistakes have been recognized and reversed.

The alternative discourse promoted by state employees and environmental activists is that commercial agriculture has been an environmental disaster. This interpretation suffers from three disadvantages: a lack of reliable environmental data, an associated unwillingness to acknowledge that Cerrado may be more resilient than generally acknowledged and a lack of political power compared to AIBA. Given the huge area of Cerrado that remains to be converted, itself championed as a necessary policy by AIBA, the suspicion of the environmental lobby is that AIBA is willing to promote relatively small-scale conservation for the prize of accessing huge areas of virgin Cerrado.

It is not yet clear whether the policies of AIBA amount to 'greening' or 'greenwashing', but the case study makes clear that local private interests have captured the national 'sustainability' discourse and this has created a dilemma for 'public' agencies. The private sector is an unexpected actor, omitted from Agenda 21 concerns in Brazil, but it is also both a powerful ally and formidable opponent in sustainability policymaking. This case study is unlikely to be unique and, wherever state-led environmental agencies are faced with resource constraints, they are likely to face a similar dilemma.

Achieving sustainable development: Ways forward

The case studies presented within this book do not provide a uniform message with respect to the achievability of sustainable development in the developing world, rather they range from optimistic to pessimistic. However, even where the conclusions of chapters are not positive, the insights they reveal should prove beneficial in identifying ways around the policy impasse.

A major challenge facing those charged with promoting sustainability remains the question of what we know about environmental changes and how they should be measured. This is influenced by strongly-held received wisdoms that are difficult to challenge in the absence of new knowledge. This can be created by modern technology in the form of remotely sensed data, or by a more careful integration of modern and indigenous ways of seeing the world. The possibilities and limitations of these approaches are set out clearly in the first three case study chapters and it would appear that further attempts at integrating the different approaches are still required. Comprehending and ensuring environmental resilience is paramount, which requires understanding of the dynamics and inherent disequilibria of ecosystems (Sullivan, 1996; Stott, 1997; Sullivan & Rohde, 2002) and the solution may lie in resilience management (Walker *et al.,* 2002).

A second challenge involves the role of environmental education. In the formal sector, this will become more important in an urbanized world where the majority of children will learn about the concept of sustainability in school. There has been, and will continue to be, a replacement of traditional learning of indigenous skills and knowledge by children as their homes and livelihoods become more and more isolated from the 'natural' world. From the examples provided, it is worrying that even in the presence of significant outside support, as in the case of Lesotho, fundamental weaknesses within the education system can still act as major barriers to improving the delivery of education for sustainability. However, as Ferguson and Thomas-Hope state, the question still exists as to which sustainability discourse makes most sense for the developing world.

The role of indigenous knowledge tends to be marginalized or even ignored by those charged with managing the environment at a national level. Whilst there are incidences where systems based on such knowledge have proved to be more effective than their modern counterparts, for example water management in Tunisia and community developed indicators in Botswana, it is also apparent that they can be a barrier to the concept of sustainable development as seen in Swaziland and Namibia. The rather pessimistic view about the future of sustainable rural development expressed by Sinha (2000: 201), which doubts the ability of governments to 'reach environmental enlightenment … and … act consistently in the interests of the poor', is partly refuted by South Africa's significant advances on both fronts and this provides a good model for other developing countries to follow. It must be recognized, however, that most lack the sophisticated and relatively well-funded institutions and relatively strong economic base that enables the modern state to enforce its will. The role of the private sector is less clear in the one study where it appears to play a significant role in the environmental debate. The example of a private association of farmers in Brazil suggests that it has become aware of the need to green its image in the post-Rio political climate. In its attitude towards the environment, however, it remains committed to expansion of commercial farming at the expense of Cerrado as long as this remains profitable.

The main conclusion that may be drawn from the chapters assembled here is that whilst the agency of the state can act as a positive element in the move towards sustainability, for example through the promotion of more participatory methods that may help to unlock new ideas and bring new insights into the sustainability debate, in many cases it still lacks the institutional ability to identify and thereby successfully prosecute the sustainability campaign. Significant challenges remain in reconciling the state's short- and long-term policy objectives, especially where central power is based upon maintaining the *status quo* which may, through either design or benign neglect, act against the interest of a greener future. This represents a significant challenge for the role of education for sustainability which, in most cases, functions within a system that is dependent upon state finances and therefore promotes the interests and values of its paymasters. However, the case studies also provide the hope that hybrid or fusion knowledge can provide new insights into the state of the environment, which will provide a way forward where supported by the state and key private and community institutions. The case studies contained within this book highlight that there remain a host of complex and contested challenges to unite the scales of the global and the local in order to encourage progress towards sustainable development.

References

Agnew, C. & Anderson, E. (1992) *Water Resources in the Arid Realm*. Routledge, London.

Agrawal, A. (1995) Dismantling the Divide between Indigenous and Scientific Knowledge. *Development and Change*, 26, 413-419.

Agrawal, A. & Gibson, C.C. (1999) Enchantment and disenchantment: the role of community in natural resource conservation. *World Development,* 27, 629-649.

Batterbury, S., Forsyth, T. & Thomson, K. (1997) Environmental transformations in developing countries: hybrid research and democratic policy. *The Geographical Journal*, 163,126-132.

Blaikie, P. (1995) Changing environments or changing views? *Geography*, 80, 203-214.

Blaikie, P. (2000) Development, post-, anti-, and populist: a critical review. *Environment and Planning A*, 32, 1033-1050.

Braidotti, R., Charkiewicz, E., Hausler, S. & Wieringa, S. (1994) *Women, the Environment and Sustainable Development: Towards a Theoretical Synthesis*. Zed Books, London.

Brown, K. (2002) Innovations for conservation and development. *The Geographical Journal*, 168, 6-17.

Chiesura, A. & De Groot, R. (2003) Critical natural capital: A socio-cultural perspective. *Ecological Economics*, 44, 219-231.

Cooke, B. & Kothari, U. (eds) (2001) *Participation: The new Tyranny?* Zed Books, London.

Craig, G. & Mayo, M (eds) (1995) *Community Empowerment: A Reader in Participation and Development*. Zed Books, London.

Dowdeswell, E. (1998) Where peaceful waters flow. *Water International*, 23, 13-16.

Ekins, P., De Groot, R., Simon, S., Deutsch, L. & Folke, C. (2003) A framework for the practical application of the concepts of critical natural capital and strong sustainability. *Ecological Economics*, 44, 165-185.

Fairhead, J. & Leach, M. (1996) *Misreading the African Landscape: Society and Ecology in a Forest-Savanna Mosaic*. Cambridge University Press, Cambridge.

Gavin, M.C. (2004) Changes in forest use value through ecological succession and their implications for land management in the Peruvian Amazon. *Conservation Biology*, 18, 1562-1570.

Gleick, P.H. (1998) Water in crisis: Paths to sustainable water use. *Ecological Applications*, 8, 571-579.

Haripriya, G.S. (2001) Integrated environmental and economic accounting: An application to the forest resources in India. *Environmental and Resource and Economics*, 19, 73-95.

Huggett, A.J. (2005) The concept and utility of 'ecological thresholds' in biodiversity conservation. *Biological Conservation*, 124, 301-310.

Juma, C. & Ojwang, J.B. (eds) (1996) *In Land we Trust*: *Environment, Private Property and Constitutional Change*. Initiatives Printers, Nairobi and Zed books, London.

Kothari, U. (2001) Power, knowledge and social control in participatory development. In Cooke, B. & Kothari, U. (eds) *Participation: The New Tyranny?* Zed Books, London, pp. 139-152.

Leach, M. & Mearns, R. (eds) (1996) *The Lie of the Land: Challenging Received Wisdom on the African Environment*. The International African Institute, James Currey, Oxford.

Leach, M., Mearns, R. & Scoones, I. (1997) Challenges to community-based sustainable development. *IDS Bulletin*, 28, 4-14.

Lindenmayer, D.B. & Luck, G. (2005) Synthesis: thresholds in conservation and management. *Biological Conservation*, 124, 351-354.

Lingayah, S. MacGillivray, A. & Hellqvist, M. (1999) *Working from Below: Techniques to Strengthen Local Governance in India*. New Economics Foundation, London.

MacGillivray, A., Weston, C. & Unsworth, C. (1998) *Communities Count! A Step by Step Guide to Community Sustainability Indicators*. New Economics Foundation, London.

Marston, S.A., Jones III, J.P. & Woodward, K. (2005) Human geography without scale. *Transactions of the Institute of British Geographers*, 30, 416-432.

Middleton, N., O'Keefe, P. & Moyo, S. (1993) *Tears of a Crocodile: From Rio to Reality in the Developing World*. Pluto Press, London.

Momsen, J.H. (1991) *Women and Development in the Third World*. Routledge, London.

Muradian, R. (2001) Ecological thresholds: A survey. *Ecological Economics*, 38, 7-24.

Neumann, R. (2005) *Making Political Ecology*. Hodder Arnold, London.

Newman, C.A. & LeDrew, E. (2005) Towards community and scientific-based information integration in marine resource management in Indonesia: Bunaken National Park Case Study. *Environments Journal*, 33, 5-23.

Nygren, A. (1999) Local knowledge in environment-development - Discourse from dichotomies to situated knowledges. *Critique of Anthropology*, 19, 267-288.

Oates, J.F. (1999) *Myth and Reality in the Rain Forest: How Conservation Strategies are failing in West Africa*. University of California Press, Berkely, CA.

Ostrom, E. (1990) *Governing the Commons: The Evolution of Institutions for Collective Action*. Cambridge University Press, Cambridge.

Rennings, K. & Wiggering, H. (1997) Steps towards indicators of sustainable development: Linking economic and ecological concepts. *Ecological Economics*, 20, 25-36.

Reij, C., Scoones, I. & Toulmin, C. (eds) (1996) *Sustaining the Soil: Indigenous Soil and Water Practices in Africa*. Earthscan, London.

Scoones, I. & Wolmer, W. (eds) (2002) *Pathways of Change in Africa. Crops,Livestock and Livelihoods in Mali, Ethiopia and Zimbabwe*. James Currey, Oxford.

Shackleton, S., Campbell, B., Wollenberg, E. & Edmunds, D. (2002) Devolution and Community-Based Natural Resource Management: Creating Space for Local People to Participate. *Natural Resource Perspectives*, Number 76. Overseas Development Institute, London.

Sinha, S. (2000) The 'other' agrarian transition? Structure, institutions and agency in sustainable rural development. *The Journal of Peasant Studies*, 27, 169-204.

Stott, P. (1997) Dynamic forestry in an unstable world. *Commonwealth Forestry Review*, 76, 207-209.

Sullivan, S. (1996) Towards a non-equilibrium ecology: perspectives from an arid land. *Journal of Biogeography*, 23, 1-5.

Sullivan, S. & Rohde, R. (2002) On non-equilibrium in arid and semi-arid grazing systems: A critical comment on A. Illius & T.G. O'Connor (1999) On the relevance of nonequilibrium concepts to arid and semiarid grazing systems. Ecological Applications, 9, 798-813. *Journal of Biogeography*, 29, 1595-1618.

Swift, J. (1996) Desertification: Narratives, winners and losers. In Leach, M. & Mearns, R. (eds) *The Lie of the Land: Challenging Received Wisdom on the African Environment*. James Currey, London, pp. 73-90.

Terry, A.K. (2001) *Community Sustainable Development Indicators, Evaluation Report to DfID*. Faculty of the Built Environment, University of the West of England, Bristol.

Thomas, D.S.G., & Twyman, C. (2004) Good or bad rangeland? Hybrid knowledge, science and local understandings of vegetation dynamics in the Kalahari. *Land Degradation & Development*, 15, 215-231.

Tiffen, M., Mortimore, M. & Gichuki, F. (1994) *More People, Less Erosion. Environmental Recovery in Kenya*. Wiley, Chichester.

United Nations Educational, Scientific and Cultural Organization (UNESCO) (1997) *Educating for a Sustainable Future: A Transdisciplinary Vision for Concerted Action*. UNESCO, Paris.

United Nations Educational, Scientific and Cultural Organization (UNESCO) (2002) *Education for Sustainability: From Rio to Johannesburg* – Lessons From a Decade of Commitment. UNESCO, Paris.

Visvanathan, N. (ed.) (1997) *The Women, Gender and Development Reader*. Earthscan, London.

Walker, B., Carpenter, S. & Anderies, J. (2002) Resilience management in socio-ecological systems: a working hypothesis for a participatory approach. *Conservation Ecology*, 6, 14.

Watson, E.E., Adams, W.M. & Mutiso, S.K. (1998) Indigenous irrigation, agriculture and development, Marakwet, Kenya. *The Geographic Journal*, 164, 67-84.

Williams, G. (2004) Evaluating participatory development: tyranny, power and (re)politicisation. *Third World Quarterly*, 25, 557-578.

World Commission on Environment and Development (WCED) (1987) *Our Common Future*. Oxford University Press, Oxford.

Index

Locators shown in *italics* refer to tables, illustrations and boxes

Date Due

NOV 15 2011			

IF YOUR BOOK IS RECALLED YOUR DUE
DATE WILL BE SHORTENED. YOU WILL BE
NOTIFIED BY MAIL.